D1642994

THEFT OF A NATION

LEEDS BECKETT UNIVERSITY

DIS

Leeds Metropolitan University

17 0473509 4

LEEDS BECKETT UN
THE
DIS

TOM GALLAGHER

Theft of a Nation
Romania since Communism

HURST & COMPANY, LONDON

First published in the United Kingdom by
C. Hurst & Co. (Publishers) Ltd,
41 Great Russell Street, London WC1B 3PL
© 2005 by Tom Gallagher
Second impression, with added Epilogue, September 2005
All rights reserved.
Printed in India

The right of Tom Gallagher to be identified as
the author of this publication is asserted by him
in accordance with the Copyright, Designs and
Patents Act 1988.

A Cataloguing-in-Publication data record for this
book is available from the British Library.

ISBNs
1–85065–717–3 *casebound*
1–85065–716–5 *paperback*

LEEDS METROPOLITAN
UNIVERSITY
LIBRARY
1704735094
EDC-B
CC-78007/2006
6.9.06 $/9/06
EDC GAL

CONTENTS

Contents

ix

ACKNOWLEDGEMENTS

Responsibility for the contents of this book, and for any mistakes to be found in it, lies with me. But I acknowledge help and backing from the following quarters. I thank the counter staff at Bradford University Library for their professionalism, and especially John Horton, the social science librarian who has built up one of the most extensive collections on South-East-Europe to be found in any British university library.

The Department of Peace Studies provided a congenial environment for preparing the book. I am grateful in particular to Professor Oliver Ramsbotham and Dr Shaun Gregory, my Heads of Department from 1998 onwards for helping to ensure that it remained an institution where research counted in what was a period of decline and 'dumbing down' in the British university world.

Professor Dennis Deletant of University College London stimulated research on the subject-matter of the book and I benefited, in particular, from his own work on the bloated intelligence world in Romania. I am grateful to Daniel Necşa for making helpful comments on several chapters. It was stimulating to discuss Romanian topics of common interest with Constantin Roman as this project slowly evolved. Both he and Mark Percival provided me with texts that appeared as the finishing touches were being put to it. Andreea Busa deserves thanks for providing me with newspaper materials and arranging an interview with Şerban Radulescu-Zoner whose patience with my questioning I appreciated. Finally, during the last year of research and writing I was delighted to discover the 'brains trust' of Romanians, as well as several non-Romanians resident in the country, brought together by Matei Paun through his Yahoo group, Romania-Economics; 'chat group' is far too casual a term to use for a consortium of people who, with Matei Paun to the fore, are dedicated to creating the right intellectual climate for the intruduction of changes designed to make Romania a country where renewing a car licence or starting a business is no more onerous than it would be in Switzerland or Finland.

Jim Brooker's encouragement and backing proved invaluable at key moments. For friendship, hospitality, stimulating conversations, and invitations to worthwhile events not all strictly academic, I would like to thank the following Romanian friends and acquaintances: Elena and Iosif Ilieş, Viorel Andrievici, Smaranda Enache, and Elek Szokoly, Simona Ceauşu and Constantin Vlad, Alin Giurgiu, Anton Niculescu, Valentin Stan, Aurelian Crăiuţu, Carolyn and Ed Litchfield, Adrian Coman, and Liviu Andreescu.

Ion Iacoş, Valerian Stan, Gabriel Andreescu, Renate Weber, and Manuela Stefanescu, past and present members of the Romanian Helsinki Committee, were among the ones who educated me out of the stereotypical attitudes I must once have had of Romania and its region. Their work in challenging societal prejudice and institutional injustice has helped to revive the prospects of Romania becoming a normal and free society.

Thanks are also due to those Romanians whom I interviewed in 1999 and 2002. Finally, I would like to acknowledge the helpful assistance of the British Academy's Elisabeth Barker fund which provided me with a travel grant that enabled me to carry out interviews and gather materials as the book was nearing completion.

Bradford, July 2004   TOM GALLAGHER

BIOGRAPHIES

Antonescu, Ion (1882–1946). Military dictator (1940–4), who replaced Carol II in September 1940 and became unchallenged ruler after crushing an Iron Guard rebellion in January 1941. He allied militarily with the Nazis after their invasion of the Soviet Union in June 1941. Antonescu was Hitler's favourite external ally, and controversy still surrounds the extent of his responsibility for the mass killing of Jews. He was overthrown on 23 August 1944 and executed in Bucharest in June 1946.

Băsescu, Traian (1951–). Leader of the Democratic Party (PD) from 2001. His sharp defence of PD interests weakened the 1996–2000 multi-party government. In June 2000 he was elected mayor of Bucharest, but the PSD government prevented him from carrying out his plans to improve the city. Head of State since 2004.

Blandiana, Ana. Poet who defied the Ceauşescu regime and formed the Civic Alliance in 1991 to promote a non-party democratic alternative to the Iliescu regime. She strongly backed Emil Constantinescu's presidential bid but in the late 1990s became increasingly critical of his performance in power.

Brătianu, Ion C. (1821–91). Founder of the National Liberal Party and frequently Prime Minister between 1876 and 1888. A capable administrator who promoted economic nationalism.

Brătianu, Ion I. C. (1864–1927). Son of Ion C., he imposed the administrative system and laws of pre-1918 Romania on Transylvania after its acquisition in 1919, thereby weakening political cohesion.

Carol I (1839–1914). A member of the Catholic wing of the German Hohenzollern dynasty, he became Prince of Romania in 1866 and the country's King in 1881 when it was recognised as an independent state by the European powers. During his reign Romania enjoyed internal stability and avoided foreign entanglements.

Carol II (1893–1953). Reigned 1930–40, subverting the democratic process and establishing a royal dictatorship (1938–40). He fled abroad after the loss of Bessarabia to the Soviet union and northwest Transylvania to Hungary in 1940.

Ceauşescu, Nicolae (1918–1989). From a poor peasant background and with little formal education, he became a communist activist in his youth and was imprisoned for much of his twenties. He advanced rapidly after the communist seizure of power in 1945–7 because of the need to promote militants from an ethnic Romanian background. He was general secretary of the party from 1965 to 1989 and also Head of State after 1974. He stepped up his predecessor's policy of pursuing an independent foreign policy, and Romania's role as a communist maverick prepared to defy Moscow boosted its influence in the West. But from 1971 he pursued increasingly dogmatic policies at home. Catastrophic economic blunders led to severe food rationing in the 1980s. A flagrant cult of personality, in which his wife Elena (1916–89) featured as co-ruler, produced rumbles of discontent in the party. But his strident promotion of nationalism enabled him to overcome policy failures until the end of the Cold War fatally weakened his position. He was overthrown and, with his wife, hastily executed by former underlings on 25 December 1989 after popular uprisings in Bucharest and other cities.

Ciorbea, Victor (1954–). Lawyer and trade union leader, elected mayor of Bucharest for the centre-right in 1996. He was nominated as Prime Minister in December 1996 but failed to establish his authority over the ruling coalition parties and carry out meaningful reform. He resigned in March 1998.

Codreanu, Corneliu Z. (1899–1938). Founder of the Legion of the Archangel Michael, an anti-Semitic movement which grew in the 1930s against a background of corrupt monarchical rule and economic hardship. Its political wing was committed to installing a dictatorship based on peasantist and Orthodox values. Codreanu was killed on the orders of Carol II when his movement began to threaten the monarchy.

Constantinescu, Emil (1939–). A professor of geology at Bucharest University, he was the presidential candidate of the Romanian Democratic Convention in 1992 and 1996, the year of his victory. Except for normalising relations with Hungary and the Hungarian minority and boosting Romania's chances of joining the EU by supporting the NATO operation in Kosovo, his tenure was devoid of substantial achievement. He failed to unite fractious coalition parties and his last-minute decision not to contest the 2000 election proved disastrous for the forces backing him. He went back on a decision to quit politics by setting up the Popular Alliance in 2002.

Coposu, Corneliu (1916–95). The leading opponent of Iliescu and the ex-communists from 1990 to 1995. He had been in the leadership of the Peasant Party until he was imprisoned from 1947 to 1964. He relaunched his party in 1990 and formed the alliance with other opposition movements which led to Iliescu's defeat in 1996. He was respected for his moral stature, but some of his decisions led later to the downfall of his party.

Cuza, Alexandru Ioan (1820–73). When the principalities of Moldavia and Wallachia were united in 1859 he became the new state's first ruler, but was overthrown in 1866 by fellow nobles. The 1864 agrarian reform was the highlight of his rule.

Ferdinand (1865–1927). Nephew and heir of King Carol I. The unification of the Romanian lands (1918–19) occurred during his reign (1914–27). He was overshadowed by his popular English wife Queen Marie (1875–1938) who rallied Romanians after Germany and its allies invaded in 1916.

Funar, Gheorghe (1949–). Collective farming expert who became mayor of the Transylvanian city of Cluj by exploiting anti-Hungarian sentiment. Twice re-elected, he has successfully defied central government by exploiting nationalism.

Geoana, Mircea (1958–). Foreign Minister from the end of 2000, during a period in which Romania has joined NATO and intensified negotiations for entry into the EU.

Gheorghiu-Dej, Gheorghe (1901–65). A railway worker, imprisoned from 1933 to 1944 after leading a major strike. He was appointed head of the Romanian Communist Party after ordering the murder of his predecessor, and with Stalin's backing became the undisputed ruler of the country in 1952. He later asserted partial independence from the Soviet Union while maintaining a hardline communist system.

Iliescu, Ion (1930–). President of Romania (1990–6, 2000–4). The son of a member of the underground communist party, he completed a degree at Moscow University in the early 1950s before rapidly rising in the communist hierarchy. But from 1971 to 1989 he was relegated to minor posts because he disagreed with Ceauşescu's hardline positions. In December 1989 he played a prominent role in the inner-party putsch which resulted in Ceauşescu's overthrow. In May 1990 he was elected President after he had improved social conditions and rallied the party and state bureaucracy to his side. He was re-elected in 1992 and again in 2000 after being defeated in the 1996 contest. He rejected bold reform in order to keep the loyalty of still influential interest groups from the communist era. He was prepared to manipulate nationalism and mobilise coal-miners in order to thwart rivals from within his own party as well as the opposition. After 2000 he was packaged as a pro-Western figure ready to endorse rapid reform so as to enable Romania to enter NATO and the European Union. But he continued to indulge in populist rhetoric and protect the new oligarchy which acquired its wealth through acquiring state assets, often by irregular means. He is undoubtedly the chief architect of post-communist Romania.

Isărescu, Mugur (1949–). Governor of the Romanian National Bank from 1990 to 1999 after which he held the Premiership for the year 2000. He increased the tempo of reform but his presidential bid in 2000 failed, and with strong Western backing he returned to the bank governorship.

Măgureanu, Virgil (1941–). Head of the domestic intelligence service from 1990 to 1997, he moved from close alliance with Iliescu to being a critic of his governing record. He prevented the intelligence sector from being an unduly disruptive force in politics, but he himself was linked with some of the controversial actions in 1989–90 which enabled Iliescu and his allies to supplant Ceauşescu and defeat the non-communists.

Maniu, Iuliu (1873–1953). Leading champion of democracy before 1945 who died in a communist prison. This Transylvanian lawyer played a key role in the creation of 'Greater Romania' in 1918, but he was less successful as an administrator.

Märko, Bela (1951–). Leader since 1992 of the Democratic Union of Hungarians in Romania (RMDZ/UDMR), the main voice of the Hungarian minority, which has gone in an increasingly pragmatic direction under him, culminating in a pact with the ruling Social Democrats in 2001.

Michael I (1921–). King (1927–30, 1940–7). He briefly reigned as a child before his father, Carol II, claimed the throne. On Carol's abdication he recovered the throne and played a key role in the 1944 coup which resulted in Romania joining the Allied side. He abdicated under communist pressure in 1947, and returned to Romania after 1989, settling permanently there in 2001.

Năstase, Adrian (1950–). Expert in international law who married into the communist élite before 1989. He joined the National Salvation Front which took charge of the country in 1989 and became Foreign Minister in 1991. From 1992 to 1996 he was President of the Chamber of Deputies. In December 2000 he was asked by President Iliescu to form a government and in the following month became head of the Social Democratic Party (PSD). Foreign policy and economic successes occurred after 2000 but the democratic process was undermined to prevent an effective challenge to the PSD.

Pauker, Ana (1893–1960). Veteran communist of Jewish background who was Foreign Minister from 1947 to 1952 before being purged.

Roman, Petre (1946–). Son of a veteran communist, he played a prominent role in the December 1989 uprising. Prime Minister from then till his mildly reformist aims brought him into conflict with President Iliescu, and he was forced from office by militant coal-miners in September 1991. Roman led the Democratic Party from 1992 to 2001 and held different positions in the governments of 1996–2000.

Stoica, Valeriu (1953–). Lawyer and academic, who served as Minister of Justice (1996–2000) and led the National Liberals from 2000 to 2002.

Stolojan, Teodor (1943–). A state economist before 1989, he was Prime Minister from September 1991 to October 1992. Initially a supporter of president Iliescu, he later joined the National Liberal Party and became its leader in 2002.

Văcăroiu, Nicolae (1950–). An ally of Ion Iliescu under whom he was Prime Minister from 1992 to 1996. He opposed serious reform but this did not prevent him from benefiting from the emergence of capitalism and founding his own bank.

Vadim Tudor, Corneliu (1949–). An outspoken defender of Ceauşescu and many aspects of his regime before and after 1989. With the support of influential ex-communists, he formed the ultra-nationalist Greater Romania Party (PRM) in 1991. His oratorical skills and links with the intelligence world have made him a feared opponent. In 2000 his exploitation of social distress enabled him to win one-third of the vote in the presidential elections, and the PRM has since been the main opposition.

Vasile, Radu (1942–). Prime Minister from April 1998 to December 1999, he helped prevent coal-miners from storming Bucharest in the winter of 1999. Poor relations with President Constantinescu led to his removal shortly after Romania was invited to open talks for EU membership.

ACRONYMS

AC	Civic Alliance
AGVPS	the General Association of Hunters and Fishermen
ANVR	the National Association of War Veterans
AFDPR	the Association of Former Political Prisoners from Romania
AGVPS	the General Association of Hunters and Fishermen
ANCD	Christian Democratic National Alliance
APADOR	the Romanian Association for the Defence of Human Rights
ApR	Alliance For Romania
AVAB	the Department of Control and Anti-Corruption
BBC	British Broadcasting Corporation
BNR	National Bank of Romania
BOR	Romanian Orthodox Church
CADA	Committee For Democratization of the Army
CD	Democratic Convention
CDR	Romanian Democratic Convention
CIA	Central Intelligence Agency
CNAICCO	National Council of Action Against Corruption and Organized Crime
CNSAS	National Council for the Study of the Security Archives
CNSRL	the National Confederation of Romanian Free Trade Unions
CPUN	Provisional Council of National Union
CSAT	The Supreme Council of National Defence
CSCE	Conference for Security and Cooperation in Europe
DCSM	Directory of Military Counter-Espionage (DCSM)
DIE	the Directorate of External Information
DIM	Directory of Military Information

DIMI	Information service of the Interior Ministry (also known as UM 0215)
DSOI	Directory for Supervising Operations and Investigations
EU	European Union
FDSN	Democratic Front of National Salvation
FPS	State Property Fund
FSN	National Salvation Front
GDP	Gross Domestic Product
GDS	Group for Social Dialogue
IAS	State Farm Company
IMF	International Monetary Fund
IRSOP	the Romanian Institute of Public Opinion Surveys
KGB	Romanian Secret Service
NATO	North Atlantic Treaty Organization
NGO	Non-Governmental Organization
OSCE	Organization for Security and Cooperation in Europe
PAC	Civic Alliance party
PAR	Party of the Romanian Alternative
PCR	Romanian Communist Party
PD	Democratic Party
PDAR	Agrarian Democratic Party of Romania
PDN	Party of the National Right
PDSR	Party of Romanian Social Democracy
PNL	National Liberal Party
PNR	Romanian National Party
PNT	National Peasant Party
PNTCD	Christian Democrat and National Peasant Party
PRM	Greater Romania Party
PSDR	Social Democratic Party of Romania
PSM	Socialist Workers Party
PUNR	Party of Romanian National Unity
RFE	Radio Free Europe
SIE	External Information Service
SPP	Protection and Guard Service
SRI	Romanian Information Service
TVR	Romanian Television
UDMR	Democratic Union of the Hungarians of Romania

UFD	Union of Right-Wing Forces
USD	Social Democratic Union
UTC	Union of Young Communists
UVR	Vatra Româneaşca Union

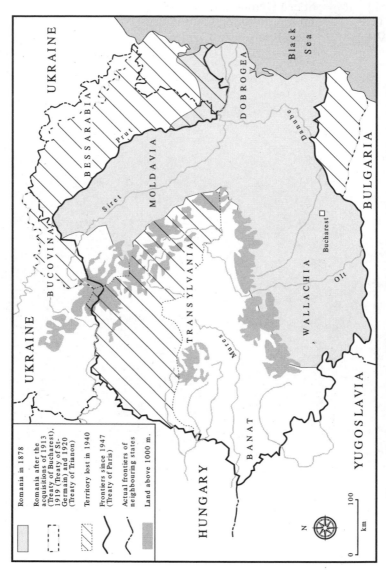

Romania's present-day borders and previous changes (1878–1947)

Romania today: administrative divisions

INTRODUCTION

Many, perhaps most Romanians who will not readily agree about politics manage to find common ground by acknowledging that it is cycles of foreign domination which have prevented their country fulfilling its true potential. Foreign explanations for underperformance in the economic sphere and in developing effective political institutions enjoy widespread popularity. It is hard to deny that Romania has indeed suffered from being in a part of the world which has seen frequent collisions between great powers, local states, and indeed rival social systems. The human and material losses suffered by the country in both the world wars of the twentieth century were immense. But while not ignoring the disadvantage Romania has faced through its sensitive geopolitical location, this book will argue that the long-term problems which have distorted and cramped its development have primarily internal origins.

Romania has never acquired an élite which combines defence of its own position with a genuine and sustained effort to improve the condition and prospects of the population. Romanians have been viewed as subjects rather than citizens by successive regimes of contrasting political hues. There is no doubt that the legacy of vertical dependence and exploitation inherited from foreign rule, particularly in the provinces of Wallachia and Moldavia, cast a long shadow over the independent Romanian state. But these provinces, which made up the core of self-governing Romania from 1859 to 1918, have now been free from direct foreign control for longer than they were under the rule of the avaricious Phanariots, sent by the Ottoman Empire to administer them from the early eighteenth to the early nineteenth centuries.

Romanians often refer to examples of low political standards in high places as ones inspired by the phanariot tradition. But elite strategies based on exploitative relations towards the wider society have acquired a momentum of their own, particularly during the

1

twentieth century. The ability of the privileged few to divert public
resources for private use, or to make calamitous decisions to gratify a
will to power (as under the dictatorship of Nicolae Ceauşescu in the
1970s and 1980s), grew steadily in what had been an era of political
emancipation and improving political standards in most other parts
of Europe. Elites which are strangers to the concept of the public
good have been able to stay in charge by promoting social fragmentation and relations of dependence. Nationalism has been consistently employed as a survival strategy by élites, often weighed down
by records of misrule, to divert popular indignation towards a foreign target.

In terms of exploitation, incompetence and misuse of national resources, the communist regime (1946–89) was the worst that Romania has experienced. But there is plenty of evidence to suggest
that it *intensified* negative behaviour patterns in politics already in existence as well as licensing new ones.

The extrication from communism now involves profound economic, political, and social adjustments. They are almost as systemic
as those which brought the original communist states into being in
Romania and its East European neighbours. Thus, it is reasonable to
assume that currently fashionable analytical categories, devised for
explaining the transition from closed to open political systems in
Southern Europe and Latin America, might not be entirely appropriate for post-communist Eastern Europe.[1] In the burgeoning literature on democratisation, it is often assumed that the transition to
democracy leads naturally to its consolidation once routines and
permanent institutional structures take shape which influence the
behaviour of political actors. But perhaps a majority of newly democratising states are unlikely to reach the consolidation stage. This
may be due to a variety of factors such as conflict over territory or
ethnic allegiance, the absence of well-placed elite figures prepared to
act in a consensual manner, or the failure of socio-economic conditions to improve, thus depriving voters of the incentive to strongly
identify with a pluralist system.

Most of the weakly-implanted democracies in which the danger
of de-democratization is a constant one are to be found in parts of
the Third World where states struggle to assert their authority, or
even to exist, in the face of daunting economic handicaps and

sometimes challenges to their territorial integrity. The multidimensionality of the challenges faced by some ex-communist countries also raises doubts about their ability to remain on a steady path of democratisation. Where the previous authoritarian experience left few political resources which could be used to fashion a democratic successor regime, where the previous democratic role models were absent or uninspiring, or where the manner of the communist state's disappearance was violent or otherwise divisive, daunting handicaps were likely to impede efforts at democratization. Of the East European states which fell under communist rule in the 1940s Romania is one where these blocking conditions were most in evidence fifty years later. The communist regime had been a fully totalitarian one which flattened civil society and regulated the lives of its citizens down to the minutest detail. No previous democratic government had been inspiring enough to act as a reference point for opponents of communism. When, uniquely in East-Central Europe, the dictatorship collapsed in 1989 amid serious violence, dissension about the sequence of events and the emergence of second-ranking communists to shape the transition, polarised the country for much of the 1990s.

The formal break-up of the Romanian communist system appears to have benefited a restricted group of citizens. Some were leading players in the former regime adept at thriving in new times; a much larger group were strategically-placed activists at different levels in the former state apparatus, ready to benefit from the connections they enjoyed with the new power-holders.

Leszek Balcerowicz, a key player in the Polish democratic transition, has argued that at the start of the 1990s, democratising states in Eastern Europe experienced a short and exhilarating period of 'extraordinary politics'. It was one in which '[B]oth leaders and citizens feel a stronger-than-normal tendency to think and act in terms of the common good'.[2] If Romania witnessed such a period of idealism uniting the dictatorship's successors with the population, it was an extremely short-lived one that could be measured in days or several weeks at the end of 1989. The form of government which gradually emerged was not one over which the people were able to exercise some control or one which sought to operate in the popular interest. Instead the post-communist system responded primarily to

the needs of a large élite, regrouping after the collapse of the authoritarian system which had originally brought it into being.

There is plenty of evidence that at first Ion Iliescu, the second-
ranking communist official who became Romania's ruler after the
execution of Nicolae Ceauşescu in December 1989, was looking for
ways to pursue a semi-authoritarian course. Full-fledged liberal democracy appeared too risky and problematic. A façade democracy,
with nationalism replacing national communism as an active source
of legitimacy, fitted in with the country's previous governing traditions. But Iliescu and the post-communists lacked the energy or
vision to try to re-position Romania on an indigenous path. The
catastrophic policy failures of the Ceauşescu era meant that Western
assistance was crucial in order to refloat the battered economy. Also
there was growing awareness within the new ruling élite that the
conditions international institutions laid down in return for aid, especially the transition to a market economy, could be turned to the
advantage of the new economic powerholders and their political
allies. Rather than arrange a compromise with forces on the centre-
right that were slowly regrouping after 1989, Iliescu and his political
vehicle, the National Salvation Front, devised new political and
administrative institutions (or more often revamped old ones) to
consolidate their authority. Not until 1996, when Iliescu and his followers lost both the parliamentary and presidential elections, would
forces committed to substantial economic and political liberalisation
be strong enough to dislodge the post-communist élite.

In 1996, many commentators referred not just to a change of government but to a change of regime. The mistakes and abuses of the
Iliescu regime, and the growing sophistication of sections of the
electorate, meant that it was viewed far more sceptically in the mid-
1990s than at its birth when there was widespread unfamiliarity and
nervousness with the idea of competing parties.[3] Moreover, the international context had changed with the Atlantic democracies being far more willing to bring pressure on illiberal democracies and
support apparently genuine reformers in South-East Europe. But it
soon became clear that in Romania avowed reformers were in office
but not in power. They inherited, and were dependent upon, a state
machine attuned to the needs of the post-communists in charge from
1990–6. It proved difficult to motivate or compel the administrative

machine to carry out reforms. In diplomatic language, the British Department of International Development (DFID), in a 2001 report on Romania, described 'serious deficiencies...in the ability of the administration to formulate, co-ordinate and implement essential policies for economic development'.[4] Parallel structures had been created under Ceauşescu, and in many cases refined under his successor, which meant that there were blocking mechanisms in the judiciary and the security services which thwarted unwelcome change. The 1991 Constitution created a parliament with two chambers whose powers were virtually identical, a recipe for legislative gridlock. These were formidable handicaps; since negotiations with the European Union (EU) to fulfil the terms of eventual membership had begun in 1999, Romania was required to alter its political system, establish the rule of law, rebuild its economy on a new basis, and adopt a vast array of new administrative procedures if accession was to be achieved in or after 2007.

Only a government with clear awareness of what needed to be done, united about the steps to be taken, and showing no fear of upsetting vested interests could have made a significant impact on the broad reform front. Instead Romania was ruled from 1996 to 2000 by a four-party coalition where there was greater mutual suspicion and eventually mutual antagonism than solidarity in seeking to dismantle the legacy of Iliescu and, before him, Ceauşescu. The confrontational rhetoric between pre- and post-1996 powerholders hid the extent to which some parts of the coalition were prepared to accommodate themselves with part of the web of economic and security interests linked to the previous administration. The new government was quickly blown off course, unable to define priorities or agree a programme of action. Key reforming laws were emasculated as much because of internal coalition dissension as the continuing strength of post-communists within the administration.

It is not clear if the outcome would have been significantly different if there had been one united reform party in office, as in Bulgaria from 1997 to 2001. The Peasant Party (PNTCD) and the Liberals (PNL)—the parties most committed to root-and-branch reform— showed an unhealthy appetite for the spoils system. President Emil Constantinescu played a mediating role but at key moments his judgment was questionable and his withdrawal from the electoral contest in 2000 was as serious a blow to reform hopes as any directed by the parties through their infighting. Despite these setbacks, Constantinescu argued that a democratic consolidation was happening. One of its preconditions is that 'a strong majority of public opinion holds the belief that democratic procedures and institutions are the most appropriate way to govern collective life in a society',[5] but during the reformist government's increasingly troubled period in office polls showed mounting nostalgia for single-party and authoritarian forms of rule; an attempt in 1999 to remove the government by means of a mass rebellion of coal miners only narrowly failed. In 2000 fresh elections saw a collapse in the vote of the previously successful electoral alliance, the Romanian Democratic Convention (CDR); its architect and mainstay, the PNTCD disappeared from parliament and soon broke up. Iliescu returned to the Presidency and the Party of Romanian Social Democracy to government. But the Greater Romania Party (PRM), a fully authoritarian force advocating drastic measures against national and ethnic minorities as well as the independent media, had been catapulted into second place.

While élite behaviour patterns, can be criticised, the lack of public pressure for reform also contributed to the contemporary crisis of governance faced by Romania. The country's ability to acquire increasing amounts of national sovereignty, and to recover that sovereignty when it was undermined by Soviet domination after 1945, means that Romanian rulers are drawn from the domestic population and are not imposed from outside. Inevitably, certain mores of society are bound to be reflected in the approach to politics and government shown by the post-1989 political class. The lack of violence as a problem-solving strategy in society is reflected in the political arena. But it has to be acknowledged that less savoury characteristics of the ruling élite may also have their origins in the collective behaviour of Romanian society. Certainly, the inability of groups promoting reform from below to carve out a strong position is due less to obstruction by the state and more to the incapacity of a fragmented and mutually distrustful society to end its own victimisation at the hands of an amoral state.

This book pays close attention to the failure of reform in the second half of the 1990s; it emphasises the scale of the challenge, the strength of vested interests opposed to reform, and the limited vision of those in executive positions. It argues that reformers could have achieved more: by communicating with the population, overcoming their own fragmentation, and mobilising the backing of international institutions to spearhead change at home. But the scale of the challenge was perhaps beyond even higher-grade and experienced politicians, and more united parties. This, it is argued, is due to the continuing damage which the communist system was able to inflict on attempts, in the 1990s, to create a radically different Romania shaped by the values and norms of economic and political pluralism. Accordingly, particular attention is paid to the way that communism socialised two generations of Romanians. Under it decisions were made for ideological reasons that in more pragmatic communist states were influenced by other criteria: private ownership of the means of production was totally curtailed; the removal of bourgeois values and the purging social groups that stood for them was constantly pursued; and finally the creation of a numerically dominant industrial proletariat producing heavy industrial goods which Romania was not really equipped to manufacture on a large scale surpassed normal development goals.

Under communism, civil society was pulled up by the roots. It is widely believed that democratic prospects are enhanced if a range of social organizations broadly committed to expanding citizenship rights are in existence before the transition.[6] But in totalitarian Romania this was impossible. Instead most citizens grew accustomed to being centrally directed by the state. Fear of the state and reluctance to dispute its authority, at least openly, meant that after 1989 there was still a strong reluctance to form or join interest groups, and associational autonomy in Romania was stunted. Moreover, the effects of damaging policies of social engineering pursued under communism left a daunting legacy for a successor regime. Overpopulation on the land was solved at the expense of creating a huge class of worker-peasants located mainly in heavy industrial plants, much of which soon had no future because of the lack of markets for their products.

An already strong dependence on the state was accentuated by the communist era. A leviathan state was created which sought to regulate and control nearly all branches of human activity. But it lacked

capacity and was increasingly brittle, as shown in the way it collapsed in 1989; Ceauşescu's ideological fervour had destabilised the
system. Iliescu and the PDSR (the name of his party from 1993 to
2001) instead revived an older theme in Romanian history since the
achievement of formal independence in 1881: capturing the state as
an end in itself. In the early 1990s the PDSR had been unsure of
how to respond to post-Cold War challenges; it lacked a coherent
programme other than to preserve as much as possible of the old order under a cautiously Western-leaning framework. But it showed
an appetite to occupy the state at all levels: PDSR-elected representatives and their allies in the newly-created business sector sought to
enrich themselves through various forms of mutual support. There
was a deep-seated feeling that state property really had no owner. So
there were no in-built restraints on the plundering of state assets by
well-placed private individuals.

States with which the Romanian government likes to compare
the country—Poland, Hungary, the Czech Republic, Slovakia—also
witnessed such theft of public resources but on nothing like the scale
seen in Romania. This book acknowledges a tradition of diverting
public resources for private use which can be traced back at least to
the eighteenth century and the era of the *phanariots*, and was never
eliminated even during the supposedly egalitarian communist era;
communist politics often proved a screen behind which personal
interests were promoted and wealth diverted for private use, most
notably under the Ceauşescus. Much of the population had grown
accustomed to such behaviour from the successive élites which
ruled over them; except in the province of Transylvania, where the
form of governance was historically based on higher standards, there
were no counter-traditions which could be drawn upon by citizens
keen to limit the power rulers could exercise over them. While the
communist system managed to eliminate democratic practices and
those groups upholding them, it preserved or refashioned other values beneficial for an authoritarian project, one that ultimately
shaded into unrestrained personal rule in the last twenty years of the
communist era. Collective values which downgraded the individual
and made him or her subject to group authority had been instilled
by the Orthodox Church before 1945. Nationalism, after an interlude of Soviet-sponsored internationalism, was rehabilitated and

tailored to suit communist needs; the traditional viewpoint that freedom consisted essentially of freedom from foreign rule and not the right of the individual to dissent from the government or majority opinion, proved extremely useful for a communist system seeking to move beyond Marxism-Leninism to shore up its legitimacy.[7] A new generation of intellectuals promoting implacable forms of nationalism was groomed by the state, and sometimes pre-1945 chauvinists were able to revive their careers by preaching the catechism of Romanian nationalism.

It was of a piece with the particular ruthlessness of the Romanian communist regime that it was able to extract resources from the Romanian past to bolster its rule.[8] Thus longer-term explanations for Romania's lack of success with representative institutions require attention. One important factor uniting the élitist democracy of the monarchical era (1881–1938), the communist regime and its successor has been the consistent need for the state to shore up its authority by maintaining a society dependent on it despite its own poor performance. During the communist era the authorities relied on terror and the threat of coercion to impose their will, but under earlier political systems there was always an effort to promote low expectations and a sense of deference in the population at large. Nationalism was consistently used by all three political systems to divert sections of the population from critically assessing the performance of those ruling over them. An earlier work by the present author argued that the pre-1945 Romanian state was deficient in many of the ways that states normally sought to establish and preserve their integrity and authority: 'As well as an inadequate system of transport and communications, *România Mare* [Greater Romania] proved incapable of providing adequate defence, civil order, a reliable system of justice, a reasonably equitable taxation system, and a framework for industry and commercial activity. The national interest was reduced to safeguarding territorial gains and realising the historic Romanian mission.'[9] When Ceaușescu's audacious policy to transform Romania into one of the world's industrial powerhouses crumbled in the 1980s, he fell back on nationalism and in particular the alleged threats posed by its historic rivals, Hungary and Russia, in order to demand obedience and further sacrifices. Whenever the internal shortcomings of the state, or examples of low standards in high places, became impossible to conceal in the 1990s, threats to territorial integrity—usually from Hungary or the large Hungarian minority in Romania—would be promptly discovered and revealed to a populace by now thoroughly imbued with the main tenets of Romanian nationalism.

Historically, the case can be made that Romanians were prepared to endure worse behaviour from their rulers than their neighbours in other Balkan states. A large number of people related to the state on the basis of dependence. A sense of citizenship has always been weak and, in the context of low-intensity citizenship, democracy has always been feeble. The essence of democracy—participation and a sense of inclusion by citizens—is still largely absent in Romania.[10] The younger generation, who played the leading role in the brief struggle against tyranny at the end of 1989, have largely absented themselves from politics. The continuation of a traditional and authoritarian higher-level education system may be helping to create a younger generation which shares the narrow outlook of the current elite in the bureaucracy, the legal profession and the political world. The need to preserve a relationship of dependence between society and a poorly performing state has always been an elite priority, and evidence for this is not difficult to assemble. The PDSR managed to get away with creating a new private class subsided by public money because of a submissive population. In a gesture comparable to that of colonists giving natives trinkets or alcohol and then divesting them of land and mineral wealth, the PDSR offered concessions to the population, such as share vouchers in companies earmarked for privatisation or the ability to buy their apartments for low prices, while pursuing policies which left them without any long-term material security.

The architect of Romania's exit from communism, Ion Iliescu, has played a key role in legitimising the creation of a new oligarchy, or at least substantially reducing opposition to its methods of wealth-creation. In the eyes of much of the electorate, particularly those living in the countryside and small towns who represent the backbone of PDSR support, he is seen as a morally upright leader against whom no accusations of corruption can be plausibly made. The rectitude of his public behaviour makes accusations that he has smoothed the rise of a large number of dishonest figures in the

PDSR hard to establish. Iliescu's image as 'a genuine man of the people' who can be trusted to look after the interests of ordinary Romanians has been acquired partly thanks to the personalisation of politics. Romanians cannot easily locate themselves on the normal ideological spectrum. When asked to declare, in a 1994 poll, whether they belonged to the right, centre or left of politics, 38% of respondents in the capital replied that they did not know where to place themselves according to these political categories.[11] The desire to make a political choice based on the personality of the competitors rather than what they stood for, appears to be ingrained. Antipathy towards Iliescu lay at the root of many of the protests in the early 1990s by those who felt that the revolution had been stolen; still, to many more living in small towns, rural areas and cities that depended on a single state–run industry and wishing for a benevolent autocrat, he was a reassuring figure. One of the faults of his successor Constantinescu was a perceived inability, when problems needed to be solved, to impose his personality decisively. The importance of the personality factor in politics stems from the weakness of parties and the failure to distinguish between competing programmes. It means that a system based on respect for procedures and democratic institutions can easily be undermined or thrown aside by a populist style of politics in which an individual offers 'salvation' on the basis of his own personal qualities; perhaps it is not a coincidence that the name on which the men who overthrew and executed Ceauşescu could agree for the successor movement to the Romanian Communist Party was the National Salvation Front.

LEEDS METROPOLITAN UNIVERSITY LIBRARY

The restoration of social and economic inequality and the refinement of relationships of social dependence coincides with external efforts to strengthen democracy in Romania and promote good governance. Many international agencies and institutions of global governance are trying to promote reforms which might result in a sustainable political and economic future for Romania. There has hardly been another period in Romanian history when external forces have intervened in its affairs in such a non-exploitative way. It is also possible to argue that aspects of International Monetary Fund policy towards Romania have left the country worse off, but in general the aid programmes of the World Bank, the EU and, in many instances, the IMF are designed to strengthen the capacity of the

Romanian state and its ability to play a full role in transnational organizations like the EU and Nato. Numerous programmes have
sought to promote a public service-oriented bureaucracy, shelter
vulnerable groups such as Roma, unemployed workers and subsis-
tence-level peasants from the downside of the economic and social
transition and, above all, promote a robust democracy.

Romania, ruled for most of the twentieth century by contrasting
regimes united in their desire to promote an autonomous and firmly
national form of political development, is now influenced by powerful external forces with their own specific agenda. The core Atlantic
democracies and the transnational organizations they influence are
promoting democracy in line with competitive market economies.
Political and economic pluralism are seen as two of the most crucial
mainstays of the globalization process. The external forces seeking to
promote the integration of Romania into an international system of
politics and economics assume that the structures and procedures of
core Western democracies are the most appropriate ones for a country like Romania. Integrating Romania into 'mainstream Europe' by
means of EU membership is probably the key undertaking. The EU
mission in Bucharest is probably the most important international
presence in Romania, perhaps even outstripping the US embassy in
importance. Huge amounts of non-reimbursable aid are being channelled to Romania in the first decade of the twenty-first century to
prepare for its membership of a body striving to create a new European federation of states.

Britain's Department of International Development (DFID)
baldly declared in 2001 that 'EU accession is the key driver of reform'.[12] If reform is taken to mean creating a law-based state, entrenched human rights, inclusive citizenship and high standards of
behaviour among elected representatives, public officials, and the
new business élite, there is much truth in that. Without the induce-
ments and security offered by the EU, what incentives would the
Romanian élite have to strengthen democracy and governance generally? How secure would the existing democratic safeguards be?
Romania's experience indicates that external engagement is important for strengthening a fragile democracy in a country where there
are no shortage of reluctant democrats in positions of influence. External pressure alone will not work without social groups prepared

to act as domestic advocates and sustainers of a reforming strategy promoted from abroad. There is no sign that such domestic constituencies are in positions of influence, and sometimes it is possible even to doubt their existence.

A modernisation strategy that is profoundly alien to the values of the national élite is likely to fail if nearly all the pressure is coming from outside. The international officials promoting alien concepts like public service, self-limiting rule, transparency and consultation are essentially transitory, and many of them may not even be aware of the long tradition whereby institutional forms acquired from the democratic heartlands of the West quickly become hollow façades behind which authoritarian and unjust practices continue to flourish. The EU is unlikely to remain a long-term advocate of Romania's integration if the short- and medium-term results of its engagement are disappointing. The ties binding the country to Western Europe are simply too slender. Similarly, NATO's readiness to invite Romania to open talks to join might not be an inspired decision if efforts at civil and military reform remain sluggish.

It came as a relief to many when, in 2000, the PDSR agreed to implement the terms negotiated by its predecessor allowing the EU, along with the IMF and World Bank a major say in shaping the country's medium-term economic strategy up to 2006. However, the relief might have been tempered with caution if there had been greater awareness of longer-term trends in Romanian history. Influential Romanians who see the possession of power as an end in itself have prided themselves on their ability to outwit powerful outsiders who have wished to impose 'alien ways' on them, from the Ottomans to the Soviet commissars. Perhaps only a diminution of Romanian sovereignty to allow external agencies drawn from countries with good public services to rebuild each government department and agency from the bottom up would enable the EU to impose its particular set of values on the administrative machine in Bucharest. But Brussels has little appetite for such in-depth involvement with a candidate country's institutions. It is not unduly cynical to suggest that the primary incentive to cooperate with the EU is the unprecedented amount of funds for structural reform that would be disbursed in the coming years, but if the funds make only a slight amount of difference to the Romanian state's performance and the values underpinning it, there is little to keep the EU engaged. And its rulers, still drawn from the post–communist élite, may have even less reason to accept recommendations for maintaining a democratic momentum. It is likely that where external intervention fails to mobilise a supportive domestic constituency, it will fail altogether. Only if institutions of global governance were to decide to impose a semi–protectorate (which has only happened in contemporary Eastern Europe following prolonged local unrest) could they hope to effect a transformation with a democratic process lacking a strong inner momentum.

While one may be sceptical about Romania's ability to strengthen its engagement with democracy, some important progress has nevertheless occurred during the years since the end of communism. Authoritarian tendencies have been checked at different times. In 1990 popular mobilisation in favour of democratisation, however thinly spread, probably limited the scope of post-communists to create a *de facto* one-party state merely paying lip-service to pluralist arrangements. A lively print media with a strong investigative side holds the government to account more effectively than opposition parties. There is a growing familiarity with complexity and tolerance of dissimilarity; conspiracy theories to explain a wide range of events no longer have the hold on the public imagination they appeared to have in the early 1990s. Peaceful transfers of power occurred in 1996 and 2000, and the results were not disputed in any significant quarter. Above all, perhaps, the ability of anti-minority forces to manipulate the politics of ethnicity appears to have declined substantially. The moderate behaviour of the Democratic Union of Hungarians in Romania (UDMR), even when faced with severe provocation, gave ultra-nationalists less excuse to depict the voice of the Hungarian minority as the enemy within. Public reaction was muted when the UDMR joined the government in 1996 and when it signed a pact of cooperation with the PDSR in 2000.

Time may even show that the 1996–2000 government left some positive legacies in different areas of reform, even though its record was ultimately one of failure, and that not all its successors were interested in promoting dependence or otherwise behaving in an oligarchical manner. But the preference for simulated change, or stop-go reform, remains strong. This means that Romania is likely to retain standards of government which will leave it ill-equipped to grasp the opportunities presented by EU expansion eastwards. Countries which quickly adopted a radical and comprehensive economic reform programme in the early stages of the transition, and then systematically implemented far-reaching institutional changes, are clearly those with the best chance of breaking free of the legacy of the past, an admittedly difficult feat. Romania was hampered by the strength of vested interests from the former times, which found the rules of politically and economically pluralist societies alien or incomprehensible. The preference for agreeing to recommendations from international bodies hoping to assist Romania, while being in no hurry to carry them out if they disrupted élite behaviour patterns, was evident in the 1990s and is likely to remain a predominant one.

The possibility of Iliescu's party seeking to resurrect a project allowing for a single party to exercise a monopoly of control within a pluralist context should not be discounted. What used to be known as the Mexican-style solution (until the defeat of the ruling party there in 2000) consisted of 'an entrenched dominant party with corporatist tendencies ruling over a partly democratic society in which there is limited, tolerated opposition and a weak independent sector but little real democratic culture'.[13] This scenario may be a more probable one in Romania than the consolidation of democracy. It might be more fruitful to compare it with countries like Mexico and Brazil where tight-knit oligarchies with a deplorable record of misrule have sought to muffle popular discontent by encouraging relationships of dependence and promoting aspects of political culture which encourage passivity and resignation. A good example occurred on 14 July 2002 when the PSD mayor of the Moldavian city of Bacau threw a birthday party, providing enough food and refreshments for tens of thousands of guests. It was a scene straight out of a novel by Gabriel Garcia Marquez in which the Latin American oligarch briefly allows the peons on his estate a tantalising share of the good life. The President condemned the mayor for behaving like 'a medieval lord...who called the poor on his birthday to give them a few crumbs', but unless he was blind, Iliescu would have known that similar riches were being accumulated by other PSD officeholders all over Romania.[14]

Instead of comparing Romania with Poland or Slovakia, comparisons with other ex-communist countries where ruling élites have enriched themselves from public funds while closing off outlets for effective protest and renewal might help to deepen understanding of the Romanian trajectory; Angola springs to mind as do some of the ex-communist states in Asia.[15] Descriptions of Luanda with the élite cruising along dilapidated roads in the latest BMW and Mercedes cars evoke some uneasy parallels with Bucharest.[16] But even if the competitive elements of Romanian democracy assert themselves, its ability to consolidate itself will be undermined as long as the economic situation remains so depressing. The 1930s demonstrated the difficulty in Europe of sustaining a pluralist political system against a background of sharply falling living standards. A 1994 United Nations report argued that the enormous spread and depth of economic decline among the former communist countries of Eastern Europe since 1989 had exceeded in magnitude the catastrophe that engulfed the capitalist economies in the 1930s.[17] By 2000, 92% of Romania's 6 million pensioners were living below subsistence level.[18] Its health indices are among the poorest in Europe with only 3.9% of GDP being allocated to health care services in 1999 (the average for EU member states is 8.5%).[19]

The experience of Latin America and indeed of Romania in earlier phases of its history shows that only at rare moments does the populace have the willpower or energy to impose its demands on the political agenda when it is such a struggle to survive simply from day to day. Accordingly, it may not be in the interests of a kleptocratic élite to sponsor improvements in living standards if one outcome is that the population will act more resolutely to ensure better forms of governance. One of the most serious obstacles in the way of better governance in Romania is the very lack of public pressure for reform. People are not united on the basis of mutual trust but only when forced by necessity. This has been frequently said of southern Italy but it is true also of Romania. Both regions suffered foreign domination and exploitative rulers for long periods, and the resulting intense social mistrust stunted civic traditions. Robert Putnam has explored the failure of the civic community in southern Italy;[20] by contrast he found in Northern Italy 'norms of reciprocity and networks of civic engagement'.[21] These had their counterparts in Romania, among the Saxons in particular, and in cities like Timişoara.[22] But this reservoir of social capital was much depleted by the end of communism, when most of the Saxons were on the point of leaving for Germany. Communist leaders drawn mainly from the south had already gone to great lengths to dismantle the civic bonds to be found in Transylvania and, in the eyes of some commentators, to balkanise it by changing its demography and deepening social dependence on the state.[23]

This book argues that the PDSR-led regime is the latest in a long line whose primary objective has been to reinforce vertical relations of domination and personal dependence and discourage social solidarity.[24] The fact that such a process goes hand in hand with an attempt to create pluralist institutions suggests that in many ways the democratising experiment lacks substance. In the following chapters we seek to explain why cynicism and alienation have been the preferred postures of Romanians towards politics irrespective of the political systems the country has known in its 150 years of independent existence. We see how a lack of civic engagement and vertical relations of dependence have made political misrule the norm and not the exception, on how, having been the most regimented of the states in the Soviet bloc before 1989, Romania is on the way to becoming one of the most unequal states in Europe. A new oligarchy, ironically with roots in the communist era, has grown up which possesses few social obligations or commitment to the wider common good. It has important political leverage acquired through its closeness to the party which has controlled Romania's post-communist evolution for all but the period 1996–2000; it has also benefited from the survival of institutions such as the various intelligence bodies and other networks of power which have only been partly reformed since 1989. Small, well-placed groups in the security apparatus and the foreign trade sector were able to acquire sizeable wealth even in the midst of Ceauşescu's equalizing communist dictatorship, and they have reinforced their power in alliance with politicians and other entrepreneurs by diverting public wealth for private use. Domestic forces committed to building a strong and transparent democracy in which such abuses of power have no place, do exist, but they are weak and there is no sign that they will grow in strength and confidence in the years ahead. International engagement with Romania to create institutions that serve the public good that will enable the country to be part of the Euro-Atlantic integration process has had only a limited impact on the quality of governance.

1

DEMOCRACY CONSTRAINED
BY BACKWARDNESS, 1866–1945

A self-governing entity known as Romania has existed since 1866, and the size of its territory was to double after the First World War. For nearly all of its history the country has known systems of government which have concentrated power in relatively few hands. At times Romanian citizens have paid a high price for the unrepresentative nature of their government. The failure-rate of attempts to check abusive practices and promote reforms that boost the legitimacy of the political system has been high. Revolts by groups who feel provoked beyond endurance have usually been unsuccessful in displacing or modifying an unjust system.

There is no single explanation of why the quality of governance in Romania has been low even compared with other states in a part of Europe often seen as a byword for political misrule. But it is worth taking as a starting-point the pre-independence experiences of the different regions comprising Romania. The character of government and this patterns of deep inequality in the relationships between the powerful few and the mass of the population had an impact on economic and social relations, long into the independence era.

A legacy of backwardness

Wallachia and Moldavia were the principalities which comprised the original Romanian state known as the Old Kingdom (the *Regat*), in existence from 1866 to 1918. The evidence we present shows that the political and economic systems prevailing in these territories before 1866 acted as a dead weight, retarding the modernisation of the young state and preserving a massive gulf between the ruling few and the mass of the population.

Foreign control of a territory is usually not an experience that helps to prepare its inhabitants for self-government. When people have been politically marginalized and denied the chance of shaping their own environment even at a rudimentary level, they have thereby been denied valuable opportunities that can widen the pool of leadership from which a new state can find its rulers. If resistance to the sharp experience of occupation and alien rule is wide and even transcends class barriers, it can create a sense of solidarity between different social groups that continues in the independence era. But the territories making up the *Regat* (the Old Kingdom) lacked the formative experiences from which a sense of common patriotism might have emerged.

In common with most of South-Eastern Europe, they were under Ottoman domination from the fifteenth to the nineteenth centuries. South of the river Danube the Bulgarian and Serbian empires had been destroyed and, along with territories inhabited by Greeks, Albanians and other south Slavs, had been swallowed up by the Ottoman empire.[1] However, the Romanian lands did not become provinces ruled by Turkish governors. Moldavia and Wallachia followed a different path of development from their Ottoman neighbours, with Constantinople exercising a form of indirect rule rather than outright colonization. Autonomous princes paid tribute to the Sultan and stayed fully within the Ottoman political orbit, and the local nobility (*boierime*) survived as the ruling élite. The Danubian principalities avoided Islamization and occupation by Ottoman armies; the princes and nobles (*boieri*) were the ones who exploited the common people to preserve their own customs and privileges. Vestigial solidarity was preserved by their shared Orthodox religious faith.

The system of indirect control was modified early in the eighteenth century as Russia and Austria pressed against the northern frontiers of the Ottoman empire. Imperial control over the principalities was then tightened. In 1714 Constantin Brancoveanu, the prince of Wallachia, was executed in Constantinople on the pretext that he was ready to go over to the Russians; in 1711 the Moldavian prince Dimitrie Cantemir had actually taken this step. Henceforth, Greeks occupied the thrones of Moldavia and Wallachia. They were known as Phanariots (after Phanar, the Greek district of Constantinople) but many would also come from Greek families in the principalities. The period of Phanariot rule lasted from 1711–14 to 1821 and during that time eleven families provided candidates for seventy-four different reigns.[2] Leading offices were sold to the highest bidder, who than needed to raise enough taxes during his reign to pay back his debts, bribe Ottoman officials, and accede to the demands of the Sultan. Since the average reign was short, the fiscal burden on the population became extremely heavy.

No institution represented the interests of the common people. The Orthodox Church also comprised part of the exploitative system, along with the great monasteries which needed regular funds for their upkeep. Gypsy slaves were owned by the monasteries as well as by the nobility, a system that was not abolished till the 1850s. This was bound to have a traumatic effect on their descendants.[3] The Phanariot era formally ended in 1821 when the Ottoman empire reinstalled native princes, but the long era of systematic rapacity cast a dark shadow over the modern Romanian successor state. The corruption of state officials or dispensers of professional services is widely thought to have its origins in that regime. 'Phanariot' is a term of abuse that has frequently been flung at politicians since 1990 whose corruption is felt to have exceeded the normal bounds.

The road to independence

A watershed occurred in 1829 with the signing of the Treaty of Adrianople granting Russia a virtual protectorate over the principalities that was to last until the Crimean War.[4] Since 1812 Russia had already absorbed the territory known as Bessarabia, lying between the Dniester and the Prut rivers, and a part of the medieval kingdom of Moldavia. From 1829 the principalities were freed from the Ottoman commercial monopoly. Western capital, quickly followed by Western ideas, started to arrive and according to a later Romanian thinker, Eugen Lovinescu, Romania could at last now embark upon a process of Europeanization.[5] With the Romanian ports on the Danube opened to world commerce, the Organic Statutes of 1831–2 gave the principalities their first constitutional documents. This reform was sponsored by an enlightened Russian governor Count Paul Kiseleff, (the only Russian with a major thoroughfare in the Romanian capital named after him). It attempted to codify relations between the *boieri* and the peasants but this soon proved to be to the advantage of the former.[6]

In 1830 the Romanian oligarchy still clung to Middle Eastern cultural patterns: nobles wore flowing kaftans and turbans, and had little education or knowledge of the outside world.[7] But the intrusion of the West soon changed that. Young *boieri* were sent to Paris to be educated. French and Austrian furniture began to adorn their parents' town houses, but Western cultural acquisitions did not displace Levantine habits. Also, the split between the oligarchy and the peasantry was turning into a chasm, and would not narrow significantly even after a small group of Western-oriented *boieri* and intellectuals mounted an uprising in 1848 and controlled Bucharest until a Russian army crushed the revolt in 1849.[8] The '1848ers' promised economic emancipation but the high *boieri* were assured that it would not be at their expense.[9] The event which started Romania's drive for independence thus contained the double-standard to be found in later rhetorically radical movements at least up until 1945: verbal commitments to social emancipation were not accompanied by a necessary willingness to alter the structures that perpetuated injustice and exploitation.

The prospect that any part of present–day Romania could be self-governing, let alone united with Romanian-speaking neighbours in a common destiny, appeared slim. Nevertheless, the progress to Romanian independence, in stages between 1856 and 1881, was largely peaceful. This was thanks largely to the negotiating skills displayed by the first generation of Romanian leaders, drawn from intellectuals and the lesser nobility. By depicting Romanians as an outpost of Latin culture in the east and a potential field for the exercise of French influence, they won the backing of Emperor Napoleon III for their cause.[10]

In 1859 the union of the Danubian principalities was realised with French support and without antagonising Britain, both territories choosing as their prince Alexandru Ioan Cuza. France was persuaded that union was the best way of preventing Russia from controlling the mouth of the Danube and linking up with its South Slav brethren.[11] Cuza's seven-year reign will always be remembered for the sweeping land reform it introduced to solve the agrarian problem. The Agrarian Law of 1864 was meant to guarantee to each peasant direct ownership of a plot of land, thus creating a prosperous and independent class of small proprietors.[12] Thoroughly alarmed, the *boieri* determined to remove Cuza. They formed the Liberal Party, whose vision for the country did not include a socially emancipated population. Its goal was the narrowly political one of a unified and independent Romania with ethnic Romanians in charge.

In 1866 Cuza was removed in a coup and the curtain came down on perhaps the only genuinely radical political interlude in Romania's history as a state. The political vacuum was then quickly filled when Prince Charles, a member of the Catholic branch of the German Hohenzollern family, accepted an invitation to ascend the throne. Charles's forty-eight-year reign began after a plebiscite in April 1866 in which all but 197 out of the 686,193 votes cast were in his favour.[13]

A promising début: constitutional monarchy

The decision of the Liberals to look for a foreign prince was a typical move by élites in charge of fledgling Balkan states that were seeking legitimacy. Much faith was placed in monarchs whose origins were foreign because they were viewed as more disinterested in their approach to material wealth and power than local subordinates and capable of rising above factionalism. The 1866 Constitution was closely modelled on that of Belgium, a country widely felt to have made spectacular progress since its formation in 1830. Liberals expressed the hope that Romania could soon become 'the Belgium of the east'. But the 1866 document contained articles dealing with property, elections and local government, not found in the Belgian prototype, which reflected the illiberal views of the new order.[14]

Charles of Hohenzollern (Carol) enjoyed a successful reign as prince till 1881 and then as king, dying in 1914. Exercising the considerable powers granted to him by the constitution with increasing confidence, he regarded foreign and military affairs as his special domain. Carol led a combined Romanian and Russian force to victory at the battle of Plevna in 1878, thus ending the Ottoman presence immediately south of the Danube.[15] Romania became an internationally recognised state in 1881, but relations with Russia were permanently soured when the latter retained control of the mainly Romanian-speaking territory of Bessarabia, which most Romanians saw as an integral part of the Romanian homeland.

A monarch who became a guarantor of continuity and was respected abroad brought much-needed stability to Romania. The military remained largely separate from politics, and thus no praetorian tradition developed as it did in Serbia after 1900 and in Bulgaria after 1918. Carol was also prepared to allow capable and even independent-minded figures to exercise power on his behalf. The dominant figure for much of the first half of his reign was Ion C. Brătianu. His Liberal Party took shape in 1875, its chief rival being the Conservative Party: the differences between them can be overstated but the two certainly had opposing views on agriculture and industrial development. The Conservatives believed Romania's vocation to be as an agricultural country, whereas the Liberals believed in a diversified economy in which industry would have a steadily increasing role. Many of them believed in the desirability of state intervention in economic affairs.[16] Conservatives and Liberals had much the same foreign policy which centred around consolidating independence in a contested part of Europe 'where the vital interests of three empires converged'.[17]

The king alternated the two parties in office. When one was asked to form a new government, almost its first task was to organize elections. The state machine was mobilised to ensure that a comfortable majority was secured. This facade democracy drew increasing resentment from among intellectuals. Vasile Alecsandri, seen during his lifetime as the national poet of Romania, described the regime in 1886 as 'a stupid comedy played by stupid actors before a naïve public'.[18]

Political differences were not usually pushed to the limit. Definitely aiding stability was the fact that the population was remarkably homogeneous from an ethnic and religious standpoint. In 1899, 92.1% of the population of 5,956,690 were ethnic Romanians of the Orthodox faith.[19] But there were compact Romanian populations across the frontier in Bessarabia and, above all, in Transylvania, part of the Austro-Hungarian empire. The Romanians were the largest ethnic group in Transylvania, but not only were they denied autonomy by its Hungarian rulers but energetic and ultimately unsuccessful attempts were made to assimilate them. In the nation-building myths of both Romania and Hungary the province of Transylvania held a central place.

Oligarchy and the masses

The peasantry comprised over 80% of the population and of these 85% were illiterate in 1890. However, mass education was not a priority for either party, and income differentials between the peasantry and other sectors of society widened.[20] Despite the 1864 agrarian reform, no self-reliant class of peasant farmers had appeared. The *boieri* used their domination of the local administration to ensure that they kept the best land or cheated on the amounts surrendered.[21] Constantin Dorogeanu-Gherea described the new agrarian order as 'neo-serfdom' under which technically free peasants were bound to their lords far more tightly than before.[22]

In each of Romania's counties (*judets*) the state's local arm was a prefect who brooked no opposition. The state chiefly manifested its presence in the lives of the peasantry through the tax collector, who 'often treated the rural population not as a source of public revenue but of personal revenue'.[23] In 1901 there were 102,560 government employees, or roughly 2% of the whole population, but less than 1% of these received a salary sufficient to allow a middle-class standard of living.[24] Unsurprisingly, no strong sense of public service emerged among this poorly-paid sector. *Smecherie* (crafty dealing) and *bacsis* (bribery) were terms seen as defining the behaviour of certain categories of civil servants as well as their political masters.[25] In Weberian terms, Romania was evolving into a 'patrimonial' rather than a 'bureaucratic' state-nation. Far from having been uprooted, the Phanariot traditions in Romanian public life were merely being updated. No institutions effectively interposed themselves between the oligarchy and the masses or were willing to champion the downtrodden. The king was hardworking and ascetic, but showed no real understanding of the material plight of his people. The Romanian Orthodox Church did little to raise people from their low political expectations and submissive mentality. The 1866 constitution declared it the 'dominant religion', but the political élite determined that it would be subservient to the state.[26] The communists would not find such a church hard to subdue when they came to power after 1945.

During Carol I's reign socially conscious individuals, well-informed about the plight of the peasantry and the state's shortcomings, formulated plans for improvements, but no influential economic or social group was wholeheartedly committed to reform. Theories of democratisation normally view the commercial middle class as the social group best placed to strengthen representative government. A commercial middle class did indeed take shape in Romania from the 1870s onwards. However, it was unable to adopt a progressive role, a primary reason being that urban enterprise was often dominated by an ethnic group seen as alien and unwelcome by the Romanian élite. Ion C. Brătianu was not alone in being alarmed at the end of the 1870s that Jews comprised two-fifths of the urban population.[27] The 1866 constitution denied citizenship to non-Christians, and Jews were forced to seek foreign protection. It was only pressure from the great powers which compelled Romania to grant its Jewish population equal citizenship,[28] but it quietly flouted Article 44 of the 1878 Berlin Treaty concerning minority protection.

The tendency of rulers to scapegoat Jews as 'alien interlopers' was longstanding, and it got a fresh lease of life when minorities grew to be over a quarter of the population in the enlarged state after 1918. It was a tactic which the communists and for a while their successors would be careful not to discard when seeking excuses for the inglorious performance of the Romanian state in economic and social fields. Ethnic nationalism was the unifying ideology of the Liberal-dominated élite under Carol I. The state promoted a sense of patriotism via the new universities being founded, the school system, and the army. Intellectuals and statesmen defined Romania in relation to Western Europe, ignoring its immediate neighbourhood. Brătianu declared in 1879 that 'from the thirteenth century till now, we have been the advance guard of Europe, its bulwark against invaders from Asia. The European states have been able to develop during this epoch because of the sacrifice of others.'[29]

By the latter stages of Carol I's reign Romania was enjoying an impressive economic growth rate. Rates of industrial growth of 6–8% a year (well above the European average) were being registered in the years preceding the First World War, when Romania was starting to export large quantities of oil.[30] Between 1910 and 1920 Romania was fourth in the world as an exporter of wheat and third as an exporter of maize.[31] Bucharest became the largest city in South-Eastern Europe, acting as a hub for the whole region. When completed in 1895, a bridge across the Danube designed to link the

Dobrogea to the rest of the country was the longest in Europe and the second in the world, a symbol of Romania's modest but palpable technological advance.[32]

But progress in communications masked the growing social divide. Brătianu became increasingly authoritarian. The two competing parties were ceasing to stand for different things, both having 'energetic bourgeois and landlord wings'.[33] Romania's great satirical playwright Ion Luca Caragiale wrote: 'Political parties in the European sense of the word, formed by traditions, or by new or more recent class interests, and where programmes are based on principles or ideas, do not exist in Romania.'[34]

The academic and politician Tito Maiorescu branded the Western-style institutions introduced to Romania as 'forms without substance',[35] and indeed the existence of unauthentic institutions that mimicked the civilising practices of more advanced countries from which they derived has been a cause of complaint from his time in the late nineteenth century to the present. Maiorescu was at the centre of a lively debate as to which path of development was the most suitable for Romania. Two broad camps of thought emerged, the Europeanists and the traditionalists, which dominated the intellectual stage till the mid-1940s.

Reformist stirrings and peasant rage

Public-spirited figures were not entirely absent from the governing élite. Spiru Haret, minister of education for most of the time between 1897 and 1910, believed that the agrarian question was primarily a cultural one and he made energetic efforts to raise the low level of rural literacy.[36] But he also acknowledged the economic side of the rural question by trying to improve living standards in the villages: in the early 1900s small rural credit clubs and agricultural co-operatives received government support.[37]

The growth in the number of teachers meant that ideas at variance with the established order began to be widely disseminated in parts of the countryside. In March 1907 peasant discontent boiled over into a violent rebellion, which started in Moldavia and was at first directed specifically against rural leaseholders who were mainly Jewish.[38] Within weeks the revolt spread to Wallachia, where it attained its greatest proportions but the anti-Jewish dimension was lacking. Land hunger and harsh leasing contracts were at the root of the unrest. Village intellectuals—priests and teachers—had already raised expectations. The revolt was particularly fierce in parts of Oltenia where serfdom had been weak and where resentment at worsening conditions was bound to be stronger than in other places.[39] The revolt assumed a critical level when reservists in the west of the country refused to obey the call-up to put down the rebellion in Moldavia. Never before had the Romanian state's authority been so demonstrably flouted.[40] Huge pitched battles took place in subsequent days between peasants and the army in Oltenia, and before the state regained control 11,000 people had been killed.[41]

The Liberals blamed the revolt on 'foreign revolutionaries',[42] but the soul-searching that occurred among intellectuals and, to some extent, the political élite suggested that the foreign alibi was not taken seriously by those who offered it as an explanation to the outside world. In April 1914 parliament approved a bill that would allow universal male suffrage and the expropriation of privately-owned land.[43] Two-thirds of town-dwellers were literate by 1912, but the cause of reform was surprisingly weak in the cities and would remain so well into the future, perhaps owing to the absence of leadership from intellectuals whose outlook was in many instances shaped by careerist and nationalist impulses. The Social Democratic Party, founded in 1893, remained weak. Nationwide it was the teachers who were the most articulate and well-organized group pressing for change. By 1907 they had created their own efficient professional organization which engaged in well-attended public discussions about how their political influence should be used. In 1913, with the election of the rural reformer Ion Mihalache as their leader, the teachers threw their weight behind structural reform in the countryside as the best means of obtaining social justice.[44]

If a relatively homogeneous state of manageable size had survived for another twenty years, would the impetus for reform have resulted in the emergence of an increasingly robust democracy that would have benefited the lives of most of its citizens? Could Romania have gradually evolved towards being a Balkan Denmark where the needs of the overwhelmingly rural population were increasingly reflected in public policy decisions? Or would it ultimately have remained a misgoverned and somewhat riven entity like Italy, where dangerous social tensions were already emerging before 1914?

The First World War and the onset of Greater Romania

We cannot know what would have been the outcome of these efforts to widen participation in public affairs and reduce Romania's glaring social and economic inequalities. The attention of politicians was now increasingly focussed on external matters. In 1913 Romania joined with Serbia and Greece in a struggle, known as the Second Balkan War, to prevent Bulgaria emerging with the bulk of the recently recovered Ottoman territory. This resulted in Romania acquiring Southern Dobrogea from the vanquished Bulgarians (territory it would retain till 1940). This conflict greatly diminished the prospects for regional cooperation among the Balkan states for a long time to come, and promoted instead nationalist political agendas based on irredentism. The prospects for democratic advancement were greatly impeded by the boost given to politics based on national self-assertion and territorial expansion. But these Balkan disputes were merely a curtain-raiser for the First World War. In Romania the king and his ministers actually favoured rival alliances. On 3 August 1914 the Crown Council rejected Carol's proposal that Romania join Germany and Austria-Hungary, and decided instead on a policy of neutrality. Carol I died soon afterwards and his nephew and successor, became King Ferdinand I. He was more amenable to the preference of the ruling Liberals for an alliance with the Britain, France and Russia. The terribly destructive nature of the European conflict was already apparent by the time Romania became a belligerent on the Allied side in August 1916. By the end of that year it had lost three-quarters of its territory and a German army occupied Bucharest.

It is unclear what would have been Romania's fate if the Central Powers had won the First World War. 'Greater Romania' (*România Mare*), the holy grail of Romanian nationalism, was realised when the Allies succeeded in defeating their central European foes at the end of 1918. At the Versailles peace settlement in 1919, Romania was the greatest beneficiary of the victors, desire to create territorially powerful states in Eastern Europe based on pre-existing states (Romania, Serbia) and stateless peoples (the Poles, Czechs and Slovaks) who had fought on their side. It was hoped that large states linked to an Anglo-French alliance system would block revanchist efforts by the defeated powers and contain the menace of the

Bolsheviks who had seized power in Russia in 1917.[45] At Trianon Romania acquired 31.5% of the territory of Hungary (all of Transylvania and two-thirds of the Banat), the Bukovina from Austria, and Bessarabia from Russia. Virtually overnight its size more than doubled. But state and society had been greatly enfeebled by being exposed to a total war which had swept across much of the country. Nearly 15% of Romania's population died in the war.[46] The state's gold reserves had been lost, and both agriculture and industrial production had fallen below the level necessary to satisfy the needs of the population.[47]

Across much of Europe, the war brought a revolution in habits and social relationships. Deference to old monarchies and aristocratic élites was being questioned much more than before. The homogeneous nation-state, legitimised by the victors at Versailles, would be lauded in almost mystical terms by a swarm of nationalist intellectuals. The Romanian sage Emil Cioran summed up the new mood of exultant nationalism: 'It is impossible to envisage a future for nations in the absence of war. Through war, nations become aware of their strength and define their place in the world. The more a nation is tested by war, the more it acquires its vital rhythms.'[48] Such implacable nationalism would slowly incubate in the Romanian body politic during the 1920s and fully erupt in the 1930s as a cause with mass appeal. Uniting areas with different national consciousness, administrative traditions, religious loyalties, and even separate financial, transport, and education systems was bound to be tremendously difficult.[49] Post-1918 Romania now comprised at least four regions which had previously had little contact with one another. A great effort by all would be needed to prevent the emergence of a dangerously fragmented polity.[50] A previously ethnically compact country had become a multi-national entity in which a range of minorities comprised no less than 29.1% of the population (1930 census).[51]

Old habits undermine the new Romania

If the trauma of state-building was to be minimized, a Romanian state prepared to modify its centralizing and authoritarian ethos to encourage the minorities and several million ethnic Romanians to settle down in their new home was required. This would have been nothing short of an effective relaunch of the Romanian state. There were some promising indicators.

The Transylvanian Romanians were a cohesive group largely united behind the Romanian National Party (PNR), and their leaders were aware that the minorities dominated the territory's urban life and could not be ignored or easily disestablished. In 1910 the Romanian population of the major cities of Transylvania had been small–Brasov (28.7%), Sibiu (26.3%), and Cluj (12.4%).[52] The first election held under universal male suffrage gave the PNR and its allies a governing majority. The new government wished to pass a fully comprehensive land reform and open contacts with Bolshevik Russia in order to regularise the frontier between the two states,[53] but on 13 March 1920 the King dismissed it. It had a sizeable parliamentary majority and this act was the clearest of signals that the Bucharest-based élite was going to try hard to govern the enlarged state by traditional methods.

The 1923 constitution, which asserted the ethnic Romanian character of the new state, was bulldozed through by the Liberals. No attempt was made to draw up a document based on cross-party consensus, and instead the 1923 document 'extended the provisions of the Constitution of 1866 to the new provinces'.[54] The king was granted extensive legislative powers, including the right to veto a bill. Parliament turned into an empty shell, failing to act as an effective arena in which different regional, social, and even generational interests could be given constructive expression. Elections did not really express the will of the people but were managed to create an artificial majority for the party whom the king asked to form a government. There was no advance in local democracy which might have compensated for the lamentable conduct of politics at the centre. In 1920 the country was divided into seventy-one prefectures, with the prefects appointed by Bucharest and enjoying absolute control locally. Municipal organs were powerless to defy their writ even if they had the force of local opinion behind them. The prefects even appointed the notaries who administered the villages.[55] For many citizens the only innovation that boosted the image of the state was the agrarian reform carried out between 1918 and 1921, with the primary motive of keeping the Bolshevik contagion away from Romania. The aim behind the reform was often as much to cut minority interests that held large estates down to size as it was to improve the condition of the peasantry.[56] From then on, the government neglected agriculture: no effort was made to consolidate smallholdings into units that could from the basis of an efficient market agriculture. The widespread custom of dividing family farms equally among offspring soon saw the average size of holdings dwindle to an uneconomic level.[57] The limited available capital was directed by government and the banks into industrial channels where better returns could be expected. Export duties on agricultural produce proved a heavy burden.[58] In Romania (as in other Balkan countries) the peasants were forced to bear much of the tax burden even though their *per capita* income was far below that of city-dwellers.[59] This was done by levying light taxes on incomes and heavy ones on mass consumption articles.

Absence of consensus

The urban priorities of a state whose citizens were overwhelmingly rural dwellers was bound to lead to polarization. The Transylvanian National Party (PNR) boycotted the delayed coronation in 1922 of King Ferdinand and Queen Marie, and the Peasants Party (PNT) leader, Ion Mihalache, spoke of the result of that year's elections pointing to 'the oligarchy being in full revolt against democracy'.[60] In 1926 the union of the PNR and the PNT under the name of the National Peasants Party (PNT) promised a more equal political contest. It became the main contender to the Liberals after the demise of the Conservatives. In 1926 polarisation mounted when the Liberals passed a law giving to the party that won at least a 40% plurality a half of the seats, plus a weighted proportion of the remaining seats.[61] This was a law originally devised by Mussolini when he was consolidating his grip on Italian politics before instituting a full-blown dictatorship. But the deaths of the king and Ion I. C. Brătianu within months of each other in 1927 opened up a vacuum which the PNT proved able to fill.

Led by the austere Iuliu Maniu, who had played a prominent role in the events leading up to the unification of Transylvania with the Regat in 1918, the PNT was the only party that could claim to have a nationwide popular base. In December 1928 the most democratic elections in Romania's history were held 'when the decision of the monarchy [the Regency] and the choice of the electorate coincided'.[62] The PNT won 77.76% of the vote and 348 seats out of 387. But within a year the world economic depression deprived it of the revenue which it needed to carry out ambitious changes. The value of Romanian exports slumped as commodity prices tumbled. The PNT was a hybrid party in which the more cautious wing, based on the Transylvanian PNR, was usually dominant. Even without adequate funds, it could have done much to rectify critical aspects of the agrarian problem. Instead, peasants were scarcely to be seen in parliament; between 1922 and 1937 they obtained only 1% of the seats.[63]

The quality of leadership at the disposal of a party given the chance to rectify abuses which disfigure the democratic system is often crucial in determining whether it can succeed. Maniu was a foe of tyranny who never wavered in his commitment to Western democracy even during the onset of fascism, but this incorruptible Transylvanian lawyer was out of his depth in the shifting sands of Bucharest politics.[64] By far his greatest miscalculation was to allow the eldest son of King Ferdinand to ascend the throne in 1930. Carol II, who reigned from that year till 1940, had earlier been forced to waive the right of succession to his father because of his disorderly private life, and it was his seven-year-old-son Mihai who ascended the throne in 1927 on the death of his grandfather. The PNT hoped that, guided by Maniu, Carol would rule as a responsible constitutional monarch,[65] and it was even thought that the return of an adult Hohenzollern to the throne would boost the standing of a government that was losing its way not just because of the economic slump. But Carol II proceeded to act like a Phanariot, concerned with transferring wealth and prestige from the public domain to his private hands,[66] and by the mid-1930s real power was located in a camarilla of his financial cronies.[67] Carol II was a disastrous role-model for a country needing inspiring leadership as the slump deepened and fascism rapidly extended its influence beyond the heart of Europe. He had deserted his regiment in the First World War, and abandoned his wife in the early 1920s to take up with a Jewish mistress, Elena Lupescu, in a country becoming a byword for anti-Semitism.

The failure of the Romanian state to live up to expectations produced mounting impatience. The lack of positions in the bureaucracy to accommodate the professional expectations of thousands of young graduates, who were products of a strongly nationalist education system, created dangerous frustrations, especially among a young generation of urban dwellers whose meagre resources were at sharp variance with their middle-class outlook. Minorities, who were highly visible in the towns and cities of the new territories, were increasingly resented. In 1930 Chisinau's population was 42.2% Romanian, 35.7% Jewish and 17.1% Ukrainian; Cernauti's was 27% Romanian, 37.9% Jewish, 14.6% German and 9.9% Ruthenian and Ukrainian; Cluj's was 34.6% Romanian and 47.3% Hungarian; Brasov registered 32.7% Romanians, 39.3% Hungarians and 22% Germans; Sibiu was 37.7% Romanian, 43.8% German and 13.2% Hungarian; Timisoara's was 26.4% Romanian, 30.4% German and 30.2% Hungarian.[68]

Romania's intellectuals: foes of liberty

Any minority advances in the professional field or the commercial world were often depicted as a provocation to Romanian sensibilities. Well-known intellectuals made or cemented their reputations by legitimising forms of nationalism which insisted that state-building be accomplished on exclusively Romanian lines. There were few branches of learning free from such xenophobia.

In the 1920s Romanian economics were increasingly dominated by the ideas of Mihail Manoilescu, who defended industrialization led by an authoritarian state promoting self-sufficiency and reducing foreign oversight of the economy to a minimum. His ideas had a strong impact outside Romania, especially in Latin American countries keen to shake off North American tutelage, and despite the fact that he died in a communist prison in 1950, even the regime of Nicolae Ceauşescu allowed his work to be mentioned as an important Romanian contribution to the theory of underdevelopment.[69] Manoilescu would have had even more influence as a precursor of development economics if he had not aligned himself first with the Romanian extreme right and then with the cause of greater Germany; in the late 1930s he renounced his previous views to announce that Romania should become a supplier of raw materials and agricultural produce to Nazi Germany.[70] Other intellectuals would renounce or modify their nationalist views according to the dictates of professional advantage or physical survival when communist rule was imposed after 1945.

The first authoritarian wave, represented by Mussolini's Italy and Hitler's Germany, created a favourable impression among educated Romanian youth in the 1930s. Hitler's ability to mop up unemployment, create spectacular public works projects and revive industry in the midst of a global depression evoked much admiration. No such stirring images emanated from the Western democracies, Britain and France, which remained Romania's chief allies up till 1939. Liberal-minded intellectuals were increasingly isolated. Even Nicolae Iorga, the chief populariser of nationalist viewpoints till the 1920s, was outstripped by younger zealots. By 1938 he was heard to complain of Codreanu: 'Who is this young man who is saluted by the youth of this country, who have forgotten their old teachers?'[71] Writing in 1935, Iorga dismissed Hitler as 'the incarnation of an ancient and primitive German tribalism and of an ancient Germanic pagan religion'.[72] But for Lucien Blaga, a Romanian philosopher who eschewed extreme positions, German culture was a catalyst: it 'stimulated native creativity, but did not intrude upon it, in contrast to French cultural influence, which sought to remake the foreigner's culture in its own image'.[73] The most influential member of the intellectual right in Romania was the philosopher Nae Ionescu who, through his newspaper *Cuvintul*, 'exerted a current of opinion hostile to the Western-oriented political parties'.[74] One of his disciples was the young philosopher of religion Mircea Eliade, destined to gain an international reputation once he became a professor at the University of Chicago in the 1950s. Nae Ionescu and his disciples were less repelled by communism than they were by Western-style democracy. Ionescu died in 1940, but it does not take a profound leap of the imagination to see him reinventing himself as an apologist for a communist system with appropriate nationalist tinges if he had lived a few years longer. The Polish extreme right-winger Boleslaw Piasecki, for whom Roman Catholicism played the role of Orthodoxy in an undemocratic Romania, underwent such a metamorphosis in the 1940s when the Soviets plucked him from his condemned cell in return for a pledge that he would promote a Polish brand of Catholicism that was not inimical to Soviet interests.[75]

The renowned playwright Eugen Ionesco wrote in 1945: 'How different everything would have been if those two [Nae Ionescu and

Eliade] had been good masters.[...] If Nae Ionescu had not existed...today we would have a fine generation of leaders between
35 and 40. Because of him they all became fascists. He created a stupid, horrifying, reactionary Romania.'[76]

The rise of the Iron Guard

Conventional party politics held diminishing appeal for growing
numbers of young, mainly urban-based Romanians who were attracted instead by a movement opposed to rationalism, tolerance and
pluralist institutions. Of the many groups, periodicals and individuals
promoting authoritarian nationalism, one assumed predominance. A
fascist movement, the Legion of the Archangel Michael—often
known by the title of its political section, the Iron Guard—placed itself at the head of a nationalist backlash against almost a century of
orientation towards the West.

The Iron Guard was not a foreign importation: it has been described as 'the only "fascist" movement outside Italy and Germany
to come to power without foreign aid'.[77] Although it resembled
mainline European fascism 'with its uniforms and salutes and glorification of the leader', its inspiration was primarily domestic.[78] It glo-
rified the Christian Romanian people, but what made it a magnet
for the discontented and the professionally frustrated was its unrestrained anti-Semitism. The Legionary movement's founder, Corneliu Z. Codreanu, had the charisma and daring to lead a backlash
against 'the mimicry, simulation and hypocrisy of Romanian public
life'.[79] He assailed democracy as a gimmick imported from the West.
This was straight out of the fascist lexicon drawn up in Italy and
Germany, but the strong religious overtones of the Guard's propaganda definitely was not. Priests played an important role in the
movement, especially outside the cities, and no less than 218 of them
were charged with participating in the January 1941 Legionary uprising.[80] The movement also enjoyed significant appeal among urban
workers. The Legionary Workers Corps, founded in 1936, boasted
8,000 members in Bucharest alone.[81] With both the social democrats and the Marxists left in an enfeebled state, the rousing of the urban masses was left largely to Codreanu's movement. The Iron
Guard's popular appeal was shown in earnest at the December 1937
elections. Officially, it got 16% of the vote, six times more than in

1932, but at least one historian is in no doubt that 'the actual fascist vote was well above that percentage'.[82]

During that election campaign the enfeebled PNT, along with a wing of the divided Liberals, signed a pact of non-aggression with the Legionary movement. This has continued to be a subject of controversy down to the present. Historians who do not doubt Maniu's democratic commitment viewed it as a move to avert attacks on the PNT by extreme-rightists during the campaign and to make it less easy for the government to rig the result.[83] Less charitable observers accuse Maniu of giving the Iron Guard 'his moral legitimation', prompting thousands of people 'to vote directly for Codreanu'.[84]

Events moved quickly after the elections of December 1937, which clearly marked the collapse of government by political parties under royal direction: none of the parties around Carol II obtained the 40% of the vote necessary for a parliamentary majority.[85] To buy time and figure out his next move, Carol appointed a minority government composed of two right-wing and anti-Semitic parties, separate from Codreanu's, which had also gained parliamentary representation. The poet Octavian Goga, leader of the National Christian Party, became prime minister and advocated firm alignment with the Axis powers. His deputy was Alexandru C. Cuza, leader of the Christian National Defence League. This eighty-three-year-old academic from Iasi boasted that he already had a distinguished record as an anti-Semite before Hitler was even born; ironically, 'with his white goatee and a long beak of a nose, he looked like a caricature' out of the Nazi Jew-baiting press.[86] During their government's six weeks in office, it passed legislation which resulted in the dismissal of many Jews from public office; Goga also proposed the deporation of a large part of the Jewish population to Madagascar.[87]

The road to dictatorship and war

Fearing that the volatile political situation might slip from his grasp and with his own plans for an authoritarian regime clarified, Carol II dismissed the Goga-Cuza government in February 1938. On 24 February a new corporatist constitution was approved by 4,289,581 votes to 5,843 in a referendum where voting was open and compulsory. The independence of the judiciary and the autonomy of the universities had been suppressed a few days previously and all political parties dissolved.[88] There was now a single party, the Front of National Rebirth, with the king as its chief, his ministers attending parliament dressed in its uniform.

No popular acts of resistance to the ending of parliamentary government were registered in Romania in 1938, perhaps because Romanian democracy had been such a parody of the real thing. The Liberal and National Peasant Parties together challenged the constitutionality of the act of 30 March 1938 dissolving political parties; cooperation between them, which might earlier have prevented the triumph of tyranny, became increasingly noticeable.[89] King Carol, for his part, treated them with care and even their newspapers continued to appear. But he showed no restraint towards the Legionary movement after a last-ditch effort to domesticate Codreanu had failed: in February 1938 he had offered Codreanu the premiership in exchange for the Legionaries' recognition of himself as their 'Captain'.[90] Codreanu was unlikely to jeopardise his credibility by bowing the knee to a corrupt monarch who obstinately clung to his influential Jewish mistress, Elena Lupescu, a woman widely seen as a combination of Messalina and Rasputin.[91] Thereafter Carol resolved to crush the Iron Guard/Legionary movement by force. Codreanu was imprisoned on trumped-up charges in April 1938 and 'shot while attempting to escape', along with some of his chief lieutenants, the following November.

The trajectory of international events following the outbreak of world war prevented Carol II from consolidating his dictatorship. The non-aggression pact signed by the Soviet Union and Germany, which has gone down in history as the Ribbentrop–Molotov pact, also left Romania vulnerable to Soviet expansion. Carol frantically sought to mend his fences with Berlin to preserve his throne. Conditions for the Jews worsened.[92] In April 1940 the Iron Guard was allowed to resume political activity, but with the disappearance of Codreanu and other first-rank leaders in 1938–9 much of its revolutionary dynamism had abated.

Romania was in no position to resist successfully when on 26 June 1940 Russia presented Carol with an ultimatum to hand over Bessarabia (and north Bukovina, formerly part of the Habsburg empire) within twenty-four hours. Romania, which had been describing itself as 'a neutral ally of the Axis', appealed to Berlin for help, but was advised to accept the *diktat* from a state which was Germany's partner in the dismemberment of large parts of Eastern Europe. Much worse was to follow. Transylvania, regarded by millions of Romanians as the sacred hearth of the nation, was partitioned under German auspices. Hitler feared that a war between Hungary and Romania over possession of the territory would interrupt the flow of oil supplies from Romania that were vital for the war effort. One-third of the territory was handed back to Hungary at a settlement in Vienna on 30 August 1940. A disgraced Carol was lucky to escape from Romania with his life. He was replaced by General (later Marshal) Ion Antonescu, a respected soldier who had been closely allied with the PNT in the past and had defied Carol by publicly defending Codreanu and the Iron Guard.

If war had not overtaken Romania and the Carol dictatorship had crumbled within a few years because of its own abundant shortcomings, Antonescu might have emerged as a providential figure capable of bridging the gulf between the democratic and authoritarian camps in Romanian politics. Joining the 1937–8 Goga cabinet as minister of defence, he had made his participation 'conditional upon the avoidance of close links with Germany and he favoured Romania's joining up with Western efforts to prevent Hitler from destroying Czechoslovakia'.[93] But the subsequent course of events was to transform Antonescu's outlook. Stalin's seizure of Bessarabia had reinforced the view that the Soviet Union presented a mortal danger to Romania and that it must join wholeheartedly in a drive to crush its power. The desire to recover all of Transylvania also became an obsession. By the time that the twenty-year-old Mihai, on the throne for a second time, invested Antonescu with full power as Leader (*Conducatorul*) of the Romanian state, the General was convinced that Romania's destiny lay irrevocably with the country best placed to help realise these two goals, namely Nazi Germany.[94]

During the first months of the Antonescu dictatorship Romania was known as the National Legionary State. The Iron Guard was the only political movement openly allowed to function, and the solemn re-burial of its slain leader in November 1940 was followed by a wave of killings of his enemies, Nicolae Iorga being the most prominent victim. A mounting power-struggle between Guardists and Antonescu over the direction of the regime came to a climax in a

Legionary uprising between 21 and 26 January 1941. Many Orthodox priests took part—according to a document of the communist
intelligence service released in 2001, they included the twenty-six-
year-old Teoctist Arapusu who, nearly fifty years later, became head
of the Romanian Orthodox Church.[95] Teoctist was accused of vandalising a synagogue, and indeed much of the violence was directed
against Jews, of whom 120 were killed (according to the Antonescu
regime's own statistics).[96]

Thereafter, the Antonescu dictatorship was a conventional military one. The support of Nazi Germany proved crucial. The Legionaries resembled the Nazis far more closely in their ideology and
methods than did Antonescu, who relied on military officials and civilian bureaucrats. But Hitler, ever concerned with maintaining the
flow of Romanian oil, wished to have a dependable ally whatever his
antecedents. Antonescu, who had Aryan looks and a decisive manner, was already beginning to impress Hitler as the most valiant of the
leaders in the Nazi satellite states and allies. Compared to the vacillating Admiral Horthy in Hungary, the duplicitous General Franco
in Spain and the uninspiring Vichy French leaders, he was someone
whom the Führer found he could work with at all stages of the war.

Romania participated enthusiastically in the German attack on
the Soviet Union on and after 22 June 1941. 'Operation Barbarossa'
was accompanied by various state-sponsored attacks on the Jews. Iasi
had been the stronghold of Romania's anti-Semitic cause: between
26 and 29 June 1941, 3–4,000 of the city's Jewish population were
killed in a pogrom in which Romanian and German armed forces
actively participated.[97] Nearly four months later Romanians were
involved in one of the largest slaughters of civilians during the Second World War following the occupation of the city of Odessa. Resistance had been fiercer than expected, and Antonescu gave the
order to execute 200 people for every Romanian officer killed and
1,000 for every soldier.[98] At his trial in 1946, the Romanian leader
made no attempt to deny giving such an order.

The Germans were present, but it was the Romanians who were
in charge of what became known as the occupied province of
Transnistria, and during the first six months of the occupation, 80%
of the Jews indigenous to the region were murdered by Romanian
gendarmerie, and Ukrainian militia enrolled into the German

security services—a total of some 216,000 people. In one gruesome incident, on 21 December 1941, identified Romanian mass murderers killed 48,000 people with gun fire and grenades.[99]

Yet 300,000 Jews in those parts of Romania known up to 1918 as the Regat avoided concentration camps and massacres; more Jews survived here than anywhere else in occupied Europe. (Apologists for Antonescu, who in the 1990s have caused statues to be erected and streets named in his honour, concentrate on this fact while conveniently ignoring the horrors of Transnistria, or seeking to blame others.) Although they survived, they were subject to 'discrimination, crippling financial exactions, and compulsory labour'.[100] Jews in the Regat survived mostly due to 'the inefficient and corrupt nature of the Romanian administrative system or from Ion Antonescu's decision to postpone and then abandon plans to deport' them, 'rather than from the kindness and courage of the few'.[101] Romania paid a high price for Antonescu's adherence to the Nazi cause. The turning—point of the war proved to be the battle of Stalingrad fought in the last months of 1942 at which the Romanians lost eighteen divisions or almost two-thirds of their forces on the eastern front.[102] By 22 August 1944 Soviet forces had reoccupied Bessarabia and were poised to sweep down on Romania beyond the river Prut; a gloomy Marshal Antonescu predicted that if they did so 'Romania's fate would be sealed for all time'.[103] The following day, back in Bucharest, Antonescu was enticed to the royal palace and removed in a coup masterminded by King Mihai.

This coup mounted in August 1944 proved of enormous benefit to the Allies. According to Albert Speer, who was in charge of German war production, the loss of Romanian oil supplies helped deal a fatal blow to the German military machine.[104] Romania played a far more vital role in the Second World War than in the First in securing victory for the Western alliance. But whereas its territory was greatly expanded in 1919, its fate after 1945 was effectively to lose its independence and have an alien social system imposed on it.

The constitutional monarchy (1866–1938) lasted a little longer than the French Third Republic (1871–1940). Overall this was a lengthy period in which to adapt to the challenges and responsibilities of self-government and create viable political structures. However, social backwardness, economic exploitation and no recent traditions of self-rule proved to be costly inheritances from the past, but the new and untried Romanian state had important advantages not always enjoyed by some of the most successful democracies. Independence was achieved peacefully and not marred by serious internal confrontations. The head of state and the form of monarchical government he embodied were legitimate in the eyes of most of the population. The state possessed no troublesome ethnic or religious cleavages, and during its first forty-five years it avoided troublesome foreign entanglements.

But despite economic advances in the years before the First World War, the quality of government in the *Regat* was poor. Parliamentary institutions were not consolidated on widened. Most of the élite turned their faces against a programme of social emancipation. Literacy was not actively promoted till the 1900s, perhaps because it was felt that an illiterate population was easier to rule. Economic growth was not fast enough to absorb a rapidly rising population. Land reform was postponed, and wealth was increasingly concentrated in a few hands. There were no models of democracy in the region which could have provided inspiration in Romania. Centralized rule based on the model adopted in post–1789 France was felt to be the only suitable model of government. Local autonomy was regarded either as an obstacle to progress or as likely to undermine the cohesion of the state. After 1918 the size of the Romanian state and its population dramatically increased. Although the creation of *România Mare* (Greater Romania) was seen as an inexorable event preordained by history, it had come about as the outcome of clashes between the warring powers over which Romania had little control. There had been no preparation for governing a state which included nearly all ethnic Romanians and in addition a sizeable population of ethnic minorities.

Creating viable democratic institutions in ethnically-mixed Romania would have been extremely demanding, but perhaps not unsurmountable. In natural resources Romania was one of the wealthiest countries in Europe; in 1937 it was Europe's largest oil exporter and the fifth largest in the world. It produced 15% of the world's corn and was the fifth largest wine-producer in the world. Bucharest was the chief South-East European metropolis and the country attracted emigrants from other Balkan states seeking a better life.[105] It was its shortage of social capital and not of material resources which handicapped Romania as it sought to develop. Elites went about the process of state-building in a wrong-headed way. The Liberals imposed the laws of one part of the country, and those who administered them, on a greatly enlarged territory irrespective of huge variations in economic development, social conditions, and patterns of ethnic settlement. After the death of King Carol I the monarchy failed to provide checks and balances. The 1923 constitution was not based on consensus between the major political forces, and this ensured that it would fall victim to the first determined assault on parliamentary government when it occurred fifteen years later. Economic policies failed to reflect the needs of the great majority of citizens eking out a precarious living from the land. Romanian democracy would probably have encountered severe difficulties even if there had not been a great economic downturn at the end of the 1920s. The battle of ideas was being won by anti-democratic extremists long before an unscrupulous monarch, Carol II, closed down parliamentary institutions in 1938. Minorities, above all the Jews, were seen by prominent figures in public life as 'the enemy within'.

If free rather than controlled elections had been allowed in Romania in the late 1930s, there would have been little to stop the Iron Guard coming to power and imposing a nativist dictatorship. As it was, the language of politics over much of Europe was becoming increasingly violent. The Night of the Long Knives and *Kristallnacht* in Germany created an even more powerful impression in a country like Romania where intolerance was already substantially promoted from within.

If Romania had avoided the fate of absorption into the Soviet communist empire and had managed to preserve a neutral status similar to that of Finland, a sense of solidarity might at last have arisen, in the face of danger, which would have enabled a substantive democracy to take shape for the first time.[106] Extreme nationalism was largely discredited, as in much of the rest of Europe. The Liberal and Peasant Parties were the most popular parties in the country in 1945, and a new generation of leaders who had become accustomed to collaborating with one another in the years of dictatorship from

1938–44 might have been able to build a consensual democracy. But if this was the hour of opportunity for Romanian democracy, the trajectory of European politics obliterated it for nearly half a century. Communism distorted Romania's development and made the effort to build free political institutions immensely more complicated than it might have been earlier.

2

RETURN TO UNDERDEVELOPMENT
THE IMPOSITION AND CONSEQUENCES
OF COMMUNIST RULE, 1945–1989

Romanian Communism: from sect to ruling force

Romania may have been in the sphere of Soviet geopolitical power but imposing the Soviet system on the country was no straightforward matter. That the Soviets had no master plan was shown by the way they toyed with creating a nominally independent Transylvania under a pre-war Hungarian prime minister or offering Antonescu his life in return for acting as their puppet.[1] Both men refused, and Moscow was required to propel a small and socially quite unrepresentative group of communists to the helm of the Romanian body politic.[2]

The Romanian left had briefly grown in stature in the pre-1914 years as the country began to industrialise. But its influence waned with the triumph of the 1917 Bolshevik revolution in Russia and the formation of the Soviet Union. Russia's new communist rulers were intent on seizing back the Romanian province of Bessarabia previously in Tsarist hands. A Romanian Communist Party (PCR: Partidul Communist Romaniei) emerged in 1921 which endorsed the policy of the Communist International (the Comintern) to break up states like Poland and Romania which had been created, or else expanded in size, by the Western Allied powers partly to act as a brake on Bolshevik power. The 1924 congress of the Comintern proclaimed the right of minorities to secede from Romania, a stance reaffirmed at future congresses.[3] Perhaps not surprisingly, members of the ethnic minorities predominated within the party. Before 1945 there had only been one ethnic Romanian head of the PCR: Gheorghe Cristescu (1921–4). The others were from the minorities

44

or had been born outside Romania, all being selected by the Comintern. Under Ştefan Foriş (1940–4), a Hungarian, membership of the PCR shrank from several thousand to below 800, and there was no groundswell of support for it within any ethnic group.[4]

The best-known pre-war Romanian communist was Ana Pauker whose trial and imprisonment in 1935 made her internationally known as a popular symbol of heroism.[5] She belonged to Romania's Jewish minority, 800,000 strong in the 1930s. Because of the strength of anti-Semitism, it was difficult for a Jewish militant to rise to the top of the party, and indeed this contributed to the party's marginal position in the 1930s. Nevertheless it was Pauker who was instructed by the Soviets to take control of the Romanian Communist Party (PCR) in 1944. Having spent the war years in the Soviet Union after being involved in an exchange of prisoners between Romania and the Soviet Union, she returned to find a greatly depleted party. Pauker has entered history as a fanatical communist determined to impose Marxism-Leninism on a country which lacked most of the key elements necessary for such a transformation. But a recent biographer has argued persuasively that no other communist leader except Yugoslavia's Josip Broz Tito was prepared to resist the Soviet-imposed line as strongly as she did.[6] She tried to slow down the pace of rural collectivisation that began in the 1940s, and to temper the onslaught on the Romanian bourgeoisie. She facilitated wholesale Jewish emigration from Romania, and tried to protect Lucreţiu Pătrăşcanu, a moderate communist 'who emphasised his Romanian identity over party loyalties'.[7]

In September 1944 Pătrăşcanu had aroused the suspicion of the Russians at the armistice negotiations in Moscow by questioning some of the terms rather than accepting them without demur.[8] Pătrăşcanu was also marked down as a 'chauvinist', a cardinal sin in Stalin's lexicon because in July 1945 and June 1946 he made two speeches blaming Hungarian elements for ethnic tension in Transylvania.[9] His liberal education and undogmatic intellect were viewed as manifestations of bourgeois irregularity and he became increasingly isolated in the party. Pătrăşcanu was a delegate at the Paris peace conference from July to October 1946; one of his colleagues claimed that he was planning to cross over to the Americans until he saw the weakness of American resistance to Soviet demands. He is quoted as saying: 'The Americans are crazy. They are giving even more to the Russians than [they] are asking [for] and expecting. If I go to the American side they may even hand me over to the Russians. I prefer to go home.'[10]

Sovietization

If there is a date when Romania can be said to have passed into the Soviet camp, it was during the three days from 27 February to 1 March 1945 when Andrei Vyshinsky, the Soviet deputy foreign minister, coerced King Mihai into accepting a communist-dominated government. On 28 February, after threatening to revoke Romanian independence unless the king cooperated, Vyshinsky slammed the door of the palace audience room so violently that the plaster cracked and fell.[11] (Vyshinsky had distinguished himself as Stalin's public prosecutor during the trial of 'the Old Bolsheviks' in the 1930s. To him is due the formulation: 'We must keep in mind Comrade Stalin's directive according to which there are periods in a society's existence, and in that of our society particularly, when laws are obsolete and have to be set aside.')[12]

As a sop to Romanian feeling Moscow decided in March 1945 to restore all of Transylvania to its jurisdiction. At the same time it forced through the appointment of a communist-dominated government under Petru Groza, a Transylvanian lawyer and landowner, partly educated in Budapest, who had enjoyed good relations with the Hungarians. He was an anomalous figure whose wealth and social standing enabled him to act as a camouflage as the Soviet grip on Romania tightened.[13] Transylvania's strategic role as the gateway to central Europe from the Russian plains meant that it was prudent to have the region attached to a state which geopolitically was firmly under the Soviet thumb. There may also have been a perceived need to balance the ascendancy which minorities then enjoyed in the PCR with a gesture to satisfy Romanian opinion. In 1945 a Hungarian university, a theatre, an opera house and a radio station were opened in Cluj. A network of Hungarian schools was re-established under state control, followed by state-run newspapers, cultural groups and publishing houses promoting the Hungarian language. Finally, in 1952, a Hungarian Autonomous Region (HAR) was set up covering the areas of Transylvania—a long distance from the Hungarian frontier—where the greatest concentration of Hungarians was to be found. One source argues that Soviet national minority doctrine was the model for this experiment; the HAR was based on a format adopted in areas of the Soviet Union with a mixed population.[14] While remaining subject to the laws of Romania, the HAR had its own administrative organs, was responsible for its own public order, the enforcement of laws, local economic and cultural activity, and a certain degree of economic and financial administration. Leaving aside Yugoslavia, Transylvania was the only part of Eastern Europe fully exposed to Soviet national minority doctrine.

During the first decade of communist rule a ferocious attack was launched against all institutions and individuals seen as representing even a residual threat to the new order. Landowning peasants and wealthier urban groups were divested of their property by outright seizure, currency adjustments and punitive taxation. Members of the old élite were thrown out of their homes or else were obliged to share them with social inferiors (gypsies were billeted with Saxons in Transylvania as part of a levelling strategy).[15] The communists demonstrated their ruthlessness by placing on trial in 1947 the seventy-four-year-old leader of the Peasant Party Iuliu Maniu and sentencing him to life imprisonment (he died in Sighet jail in 1953). Records discovered in the Cluj communist party archives in the 1990s reveal that Maniu's party did much better in the rigged election of 19 November 1946 than official results suggested. The PNT received 42% of the vote in Cluj county as against 33% for the Democratic Popular Bloc composed of the PCR and fellow travellers, this being the best the PCR could achieve even with the might of the state machine and Soviet occupying forces behind it.[16] Alexandru Bîrlădeanu, a leading communist economist, admitted that in Moldavia the communist party did equally dismally; he was one of its candidates and, after reporting the situation to Bucharest, the order was given to take all necessary steps to alter the results in the party's favour.[17]

By 1952 Romania was subject to rigid totalitarian controls. No city resident was allowed to change his or her dwelling without permission, and all movement between towns was controlled by the communist militia. In the early 1950s an estimated 180,000 people had been thrown into labour camps, the most notorious of which was the Danube-Black Sea canal project which claimed thousands of lives.[18] A jail in the far north of the country at the town of Sighet was set aside for the cream of the political élite. Opposition figures among the latter who had smoothed the communist's path to power, such as Gheorghe Tătărescu and Constantin Argetoianu, were swept off to prison once their usefulness had come to an end. Decapitating the political élite and divesting the bourgeoisie of their wealth and status were not particularly difficult tasks in a country where the vast majority of people lived off the land and regarded most politicians as belonging to a separate caste. It was far more difficult to get millions of peasant proprietors to give up their land to the state and enter collective farms. It took thirteen years for collectivisation to be accomplished after the campaign to end landed property (except in unproductive parts of the country) started officially in 1949.[19] Some 80,000 peasants were imprisoned for their opposition. Armed resistance in the mountains continued sporadically through the 1950s unknown to the outside world.[20]

Aspects of political culture conducive to takeover

Even with the help of the Soviet Union, the ability of what had been an extremely small political sect to establish its total power is striking. A large amount of popular submissiveness assisted the communists in their task. Fatalism has often been seen as a determining attribute of Romanian political culture.[21] The Orthodox Church is often felt to be the national institution with the greatest hold over ordinary Romanians. Its tradition of acquiescence to the ruling power meant that it was far less of a headache to the communists in Romania than the Catholic and Protestant churches were to their counterparts in, respectively, Poland and later East Germany. Nichifor Crainic, a right-wing thinker who had hoped that Orthodoxy would be at the centre of a new ruling ideology, concluded by 1944 that his Church had no political orientation of its own and preferred to follow that of the state.[22]

The attitude of the early communist rulers to the Orthodox Church in Romania was subtle and calculating. They saw the majority church as an instrument through which the party could first manipulate and then mobilise society around its agenda of socio-economic transformation. Richard Wurmbrand, an anti-communist

Protestant pastor, recalled attending a meeting in the late 1940s in which Dej reassured an audience mainly of Orthodox clerics that he was ready 'to forget and forgive'—taken as a reference to the Church's well-known sympathies with the Legionary movement.[23] Even though the head of the church Patriarch Nicodim, as a devotee of the royal family, refused to give his blessing to the republic declared at the end of 1947, Dej behaved with a confidence that suggests he knew enough of the mores of the Orthodox Church to be convinced that it was unlikely to become a force of resistance to communism.[24] Viewed in many quarters as suspect, the sudden death of Nicodim early in 1948 enabled the communists to elect a successor who for the next thirty years made the Church compliant to the ruling power. Justinian Marina (1901–77) had sheltered Dej in his church after the future leader had broken out of prison in 1944, but he had also enjoyed good relations with Nae Ionescu, the intellectual driving force behind the pre-war radical right who was a regular visitor to his country parish in the 1930s.[25] Both Dej and Justinian, despite being located at different points on the political spectrum, were committed to indigenous forms of development. The communists repudiated the West, which gave them a degree of common ground with Justinian, head of a church long suspicious of Western interference in Romania.[26] In 1945 the Metropolitan of Transylvania, Nicolae Balan, published an article hailing 'the common Orthodox faith…linking our soul with the soul of Russia, our state with the state of our powerful neighbour…'.[27]

Secular intellectuals were also a group which in many instances the party-state in Romania succeeded in moulding to its own ends. The regime paid intellectuals great attention because it believed that they could play a crucial role in changing the attitude of the population from one of sullen resistance or acquiescence to one of increasing acceptance of the new political realities. Creative intellectuals who were prepared to transfer their allegiance to the party could expect high rewards, while those determined to remain aloof from it could expect heavy sanctions. The prominent writers Mihail Sadoveanu and George Calinescu were among those prepared to endorse the new political orthodoxy.[28] Sadoveanu, who had warned fellow members of the Romanian of Academy in 1942 of the danger of 'the hordes from the steppes', was later seen as an outspoken advocate of friendship with the Soviet Union.[29] Having been president of the Senate under the monarchy, he was vice-president of the Grand National Assembly from 1947 till his death in 1961.

Intellectuals, many with a nationalist background, would be useful tools for the regime when it embraced national communism. Such an era appeared a long way off during the Stalinist years. When Ana Pauker led the PCR (from October 1944 to October 1945), Jewish members were disproportionately located in the ideological apparatus of the party in its cultural, propaganda and media outlets.[30] The best-known of these was Mihai Roller who, as President of the Institute of Party History till the early mid-1950s, tried to remove the national idea from the dissemination of history and replace it with an internationalist (in practice Slavophile) outlook.[31] In the demonology of the regime's early figures that has grown up since 1989, Roller ranks behind only Dej and Pauker. His crime was to emphasise class struggle, as well as international solidarity with Slavic neighbours, especially ones to the east, at the expense of national themes in the study of Romanian history. By comparison figures like Alexandru Nikolski (responsible for the torture, killing and systematic ill-treatment of large numbers of prisoners) have been overlooked.[32] Yet Roller was anxious not to over-emphasise the role of his fellow Jews in the party for fear that it might provoke a backlash. A former party member, Pavel Câmpeanu, recalls a conversation with Roller in which they discussed the case of a young Jewish militant who died in front of a wartime firing squad, shouting 'Long Live the Communist Party'. Roller said: 'This is a real hero but how could I advertise him with such a name?'[33] Jews in charge of ideology and propaganda appeared to act on the principle that it was better to have no martyrs at all than to have Jewish ones. Ana Pauker herself told Georgi Dimitrov, the ex-Comintern chief instrumental in getting her appointed as party leader in 1944, that 'she had an ethnic origin incompatible with the position of a communist party leader'.[34] Pauker never changed her Jewish name, shunned her relations or denied her Jewish origins, but a decision of hers to allow Iron Guardists from a working-class background to join the PCR (held against her at the time of her fall) may have stemmed from a need to disprove the view that the party was overwhelmingly a Jewish-dominated force. Only two Jews were full members of the

Politburo during the forty-five years the PCR was in power. When the ideological line would change in the 1950s and nationalism was rehabilitated, many lost their positions in the ideological sectors of the party and a considerable number emigrated to Israel.

Dej and the emergence of a Romanian brand of communism

Soviet control over Romania was more assured if an ethnic Romanian was placed in charge of a party otherwise still dominated by officials from various ethnic minorities. Gheorghe Gheorghiu-Dej became General-Secretary of the PCR in 1945. From then until 1948 a system of collective leadership existed, but thereafter Dej steadily consolidated his authority within the party. He managed to overcome suspicions in Moscow about his unusual pedigree by showing himself to be a ruthless exponent of policies designed to transform Romania into a Marxist-Leninist state.

Dej (born in 1900) joined the communist movement relatively late in life when already over thirty. He was one of the few bosses of the satellite regimes of the 1950s who had not studied at the Comintern School in Moscow.[35] He was imprisoned in Romania following the Grivita strike involving railway workers in 1933, and was not released till 1944. He had been a railwaymen, and activists from this sector were to play a prominent role in his regime. But despite the legend conjured up by party propaganda surrounding his role in the most serious pre-war industrial unrest, he had actually not participated in the strike.[36] However, his forceful personality and talent for survival enabled him to assume the leadership of the other imprisoned communists. Dej honed his political skills in prison, even managing to influence his gaolers. According to a close associate, he was a good psychologist with a shrewd knowledge of human types, also a mimic and a great story-teller with an amazing memory.[37] During his years in power Dej was popular because of his avuncular, man-of-the-people style. But he had also rarely hesitated to use violence in order to climb to the top. In 1945 he arranged the murder of his predecessor as PCR chief, Stefan Foris, and followed it up by silencing his mother, who was drowned by two of his security operatives.[38] Luçretiu Pătrăscanu became Dej's most prominent victim, being executed after a secret trial in 1954. He also unhesitatingly threatened and used violence to break up what he regarded as unsuitable relationships involving his two daughters: he ordered the execution of one suitor and warned off another with a sound beating.[39]

Dej's ascendancy was complete with the removal of Ana Pauker and her associates on the Politburo in the spring of 1952. This action has often been characterised as a victory for home communists, perhaps imbued with anti-Semitic tendencies, over those who owed their positions to the patronage of Moscow. But the struggle for power within the communist élite was often fuelled by personal conflicts that cut across any divisions between home communists and Muscovites.[40] Pavel Câmpeanu has written: 'Sacrificing Ana Pauker, the Kremlin strengthened the very people who were prepared to confront it... [Her] elimination meant...the victory of a nationalist-orientated Stalinism against the Stalinism of a pro-Soviet orientation.'[41]

After 1952 Dej had a compliant politburo: in 1954 the capital sentence on Pătrăscanu was decided by its unanimous vote, and the court verdict was only pronounced later—a typical example of how justice was carried out under the communist system.[42] Pătrăscanu's trial had been held in secret because of his continued defiance. Dej closely monitored the proceedings through a phone line linked to his office, and he is likely to have heard Pătrascănu's last defiant words before being dragged from the trial room: 'Assassins. History will put you here in this box! You and also your supporters, you servants!'[43] Nearly all Pătrăscanu's co-defendants were Jewish, which added weight to the view which the authorities were seeking to inculcate, namely that Pătrăscanu was really a traitor.

Dej was emerging as Romania's unchallenged Stalinist boss at a time when a collective leadership had been installed in the Kremlin following Stalin's death in March 1953. A process of de-Stalinisation got under way that was increasingly identified with Nikita Khrushchev, General Secretary of the Soviet Communist Party, who gradually manoeuvred to supplant his rivals in the Soviet leadership. Khrushchev's attempt to delegitimise the cult of personality and the terror methods integral to Stalin's rule culminated in his speech to a closed session of the 20th congress of the Soviet party on 25 February 1956. In it he accused Stalin of arresting and deporting many thousands of party members, of executions without trial, and of creating a climate of terror for much of his rule. Dej's composure was shaken by such sensational developments from Moscow, just as his successors' was thirty years later with the rise of Gorbachev. He had used methods similar to Stalin's against the population as a whole as well as against colleagues. A month elapsed before he felt able to read out a shortened version of Khrushchev's speech to an audience of 3,000 who represented the party élite. Note-taking was forbidden and Dej commented that 'thanks to the consistent Marxist-Leninist policy of the Central Committee' the excesses of the personality cult had been eliminated in 1952.[44] But he was well aware that the tendency of the satellites to fall in line with whatever trend emanated from Moscow made him vulnerable. On a personal level his own relations with Khrushchev were never warm and they developed into mutual dislike when his interests and those of the Soviet leadership began to diverge. Dej used to refer to Khrushchev as 'the peasant', and Khrushchev, in his turn, hardly concealed his view that the Romanian leader had outlived his usefulness.[45]

Moving out of the Soviet orbit

Along with the Albanian leader Enver Hoxha, Dej was the only head of a People's Democracy from Stalin's time who was still in place seven years after the Soviet dictator's death. Hoxha had broken publicly with Khrushchev at the 22nd party congress and swiftly took Albania out of the Soviet camp while retaining a fundamentalist form of communism. Unlike Romania, Albania shared no land frontier with any other member of the Soviet bloc and was far away from the Soviet Union itself. But in previous years Dej had surreptitiously taken steps which strengthened his position with Moscow and made it no straightforward matter to bring him to heel.

Along with Dej, Emil Bodnăras, a veteran party figure, managed to persuade Moscow, with which he had close ties, to remove all forces from Romania; this finally took place in 1958.[46] Two years earlier, when Hungary under the communist reformer Imre Nagy, had tried to secede from the communist bloc and adopt a neutralist policy, Romania had been the Soviet Union's most active ally in the crisis. The apostate Hungarian party chief was tricked into delivering himself to Romanian custody, after being promised safe conduct (Valter Roman, the father of Romania's post-1989 Prime Minister, used an old friendship with Nagy stretching back to their days as

Moscow-based operatives of the Comintern, to betray him). Nagy was hanged in 1958 after two years of captivity in Romania.[47]

Dej was able to crack down on dissent at home without attracting the displeasure of the Soviet Union. A second wave of mass arrests occurred, and in July 1958 the death penalty became mandatory for any bid to make the state neutral.[48] Dej was particularly worried that Hungarians in Transylvania would show their solidarity with rebellious compatriots in Hungary and that unrest would spread to ethnic Romanians unhappy with the Stalinist system.[49] In 1959 the Bolyai university in Cluj, a wholly Hungarian-speaking institution founded to signify that the Hungarian minority enjoyed ample cultural rights within the Romanian state, lost its separate existence—many Romanian intellectuals had seen it as an anti-national intrusion. Such a move by Dej was hardly likely to alarm the Soviets, but a real rift with Moscow loomed when Dej showed that he was prepared to defy Soviet economic plans for the bloc of which Romania formed part.

In the early 1960s Khrushchev became increasingly aware of the need for a socialist economic commonwealth to rival the European Economic Community, which had made spectacular strides since its emergence in the early 1950s. In 1962 he proposed that the Council for Mutual Economic Assistance (Comecon) be able to decide the sectors of economic activity on which each member state should concentrate.[50] If Khrushchev's plan to centralise economic planning for the Soviet bloc succeeded, it is likely that its fine arable land would have made Romania a supplier of agricultural produce for much of the rest of the bloc. Such a role did not appeal to Dej, nor probably to the communist party militants, many of peasant origin, who were attached to the idea of swiftly industrialising Romania. Retaining a large peasantry and failing to create a dominant industrial proletariat endangered the prospects of consolidating a communist system which had enjoyed little or no standing in the country up to the late 1940s. Romania fought a successful rearguard action, and at the July 1963 Comecon summit the Soviets and their supporters reluctantly agreed to shelve their plans for economic integration. Romania was demonstrating to the world that it was possible to attain substantial independence in spite of its difficult geopolitical conditions.[51] A number of factors were on the side of the country's leadership. A period of détente followed the 1962 Cuban missile crisis and the Soviet Union was reluctant to crack down heavily on a wayward ally because of the likely impact in the West as well as in newly independent states. The fact that Romania remained firmly orthodox in its internal course reassured the Kremlin. Moreover, the Soviet Union had been sobered by its quarrel with Yugoslavia and during the existence of the Soviet bloc was far less keen to intervene directly in the Balkans than in Central Europe where it felt its core interests lay. When Khrushchev once again attempted to get Romania to fall into line behind Soviet centralism, Dej's response was to get his central committee to pass a resolution on 27 April 1964 which was at once viewed as a virtual declaration of independence.[52] Having been asked by Khrushchev to choose between the Soviet Union and what had been the Soviet model till the end of the 1950s, he chose the latter—which could be summed up as neo-Stalinism at home and Titoism abroad.[53]

Guarded openings to the West

Romania became the first Soviet bloc country to establish independent trading ties with the West. Early in 1960 Dej sent his head of foreign intelligence to London and Paris with a personal message spelling out Romania's intention to shape its economic policy around national concerns and not follow Comecon orders. In the spring of that same year, Romania became the first Soviet bloc country to raise its legations in those two capitals to the rank of embassies.[54]

For relations with the West to blossom, Romania needed to tone down or remove some of the most objectionable features of its political system. Between 1960 and 1964, the number of political prisoners gradually fell from 17,613 to almost nil; henceforth the communist regime found other effective ways to intimidate and control potential or actual dissenters. Under Alexandru Bîrlădeanu, who was in charge of the economy from 1960 to 1965, Romania began to emulate Yugoslavia by developing products for the consumer market and seeking to diversify from heavy industrial production in order to break into lucrative markets in the capitalist West.[55] But simultaneously Dej practised the arts of dissimulation against the West which had proved so successful against the Soviets and their 'peasant' leader Khrushchev. Furious efforts were made to acquire Western economic know-how through industrial espionage; in 1961 an entire meeting of the Politburo and the Council of Ministers was devoted to this subject alone.[56] Duplicity lay at the heart of the system perfected by Dej. Communists insisted on outward conformity but did not demand total subordination to the system, at least until the 1980s when it entered a fully totalitarian phase.[57] Obedience to the leader of the system also took precedence over adherence to the law of the state or to party doctrine. In Romania personal elements transcended ideology to a greater degree than in most other communist systems; old regime figures sometimes survived or even prospered if they showed a willingness to protect Dej and other leading figures. The governor of Dej's prison had treated him leniently: he was later promoted to general and would serve as the prosecuting counsel in the 1946 trial of Marshal Antonescu which led to his execution.[58] It is doubtful if Patriarch Justinian would have risen so highly and fast in the Orthodox Church if he had not assisted Dej when he broke out of prison.[59]

The triumph of the Biggest Zero[60]

Dej died on 19 March 1965 after contacting a rapidly-spreading lung cancer; members of his entourage suspected that he had been irradiated by Soviet agents because of his autonomous stance.[61] One of his last major acts, in 1964, had been to ensure that the Romanian foreign intelligence service shook off direct Soviet supervision. Romania remained the only satellite before 1989 where this was allowed.[62]

At first the prime minister, Gheorghe Maurer, appeared in the strongest position to succeed Dej. This lawyer and longstanding party member had become Dej's closest colleague; he had been closely identified with the policy of seeking independence from the Soviets, but had not been involved in repression.[63] But Maurer was from a bourgeois background and was only half Romanian (his father, a native of Alsace, had been employed as French tutor to the crown prince, later Carol II). By 1965 the communist party no longer had a strong minority presence; many Jewish members had emigrated and Dej had even persuaded Romanian colleagues with Jewish wives to divorce them so as to reduce the Jewish influence within the party. The party had become one of career-oriented workers of peasant background, overwhelmingly Romanian in composition.[64] Maurer was on good terms with the man who had presided over this transformation while in charge of party organization in the early 1960s, Nicolae Ceauşescu, and nominated him as the new General-Secretary, one well-placed source suggesting that he believed he himself could rule through this 'unpolished youth'.[65] Ceauşescu had a stammer, no sense of humour, and found his poor education hard to conceal. But he possessed exceptional willpower and political zeal, and any ambition he may have lacked was made up by his wife Elena.

Ceauşescu was also implacably nationalist and distrustful of the Soviets. In the 1930s, as a country boy involved in communist agitation, he could just as easily have joined the Iron Guard, which would have a much larger working-class membership than its left-wing rival. Ceauşescu's rise up the party hierarchy was assisted by the fact that there were so few young ethnic Romanians with a record of militancy extending back before the party's seizure of power. He was a full member of the Politburo by 1955 when he was aged thirty-seven. His enthusiasm for Dej's autonomist stance guaranteed his rise and after 1955 he was in charge of the growth of party membership. By 1965, 64% of party members were aged under forty, while 99% had entered the party after 1945.[66] Ceauşescu was able to consolidate his authority and clip the wings of his main rival, Alexandru Draghici, minister of the interior and head of the security services after 1952. He arranged the rehabilitation of Pătrăscanu in 1968 in order to remove Draghici, who had played a big role in his destruction. Dej was also denounced for abuses of power. Understandably, there were hopes that Ceauşescu was demonstrating liberal instincts he had never shown in his climb up the party hierarchy, but it soon became clear that he was determined to enter history as Romania's leading communist, and that all rivals, whether living or dead, would have to be cut down to size.

Ceauşescu intensified Dej's foreign policy based on national interest rather than Soviet bloc loyalty, and Romanian nationalism was emphasised with ever greater fervour in order to strengthen the regime's popular standing. In 1966 Romania successfully resisted Soviet plans to strengthen the powers of the Warsaw Pact over the armed forces of its members,[67] and the following year it refused to follow other Warsaw Pact members in freezing diplomatic relations with Israel after the Six-Day War. In 1968 Ceauşescu's image as a reform-minded Marxist received a tremendous boost when he refused to join the Soviet Union and the other Warsaw Pact states in sending forces to crush Czechoslovakia's experiment in liberal communism. However, it was little noticed at the time was the fact that Ceauşescu never endorsed 'the Prague spring' or stated that it was worthy of emulation in his own country. He made sure that the leading reformist tracts published in Prague by Czech party liberals and their intellectual supporters never reached the Romanian press or were even reproduced in the confidential bulletins prepared for party officials.[68] However irritated they might be by Romania's acrobatics, the Soviets knew that Ceauşescu was an orthodox communist who had no inclination to retreat from Marxism-Leninism. Indeed, part of his skill as a leader manoeuvring between East and West was that he knew when to stop short of intolerable provocation.

Deceiving gullible democracies

The West, however, was starting to view Romania as a maverick communist state worth cultivating because it placed limits on Soviet power. In 1968 Tony Benn, the British minister of technology, wrote after meeting Ceauşescu that he was 'very modest mannered, very penetrating in his ability and I liked him'.[69] In that year also, President de Gaulle personally bestowed the *Legion d'Honneur* on Ceauşescu,[70] making it clear to Ceauşescu on that occasion that he was not deterred by the nature of his regime: 'A regime like yours is good and useful but a similar one would be impossible in France or Great Britain.'[71] Such a remark from an influential Western leader would hardly encourage Ceauşescu to liberalise his system—rather, the reverse.

Increasingly convinced that a weak link in the chain of Soviet power had been found, the West invited Romania into institutions that were closed to other communist states. In 1972 it joined the World Bank and the International Monetary Fund, in 1973 it obtained preferential trading status from the European Economic Community, and in 1975 was awarded Most Favoured Nation trading status by the United States, the only Soviet bloc state with such a privilege.[72] In 1978 Ion Pacepa, head of the Department of Foreign Intelligence (DIE), defected to the United States, revealing that 70%

of the commercial attachés in Romanian embassies were intelligence officers and the rest were collaborators with his agency. It was simultaneously a dirty-tricks department and a recruiting centre for agents, landing some big fish such as a French foreign minister of the early 1980s who had been on its payroll for twenty years.[73] From the time Pacepa was debriefed by the Americans, he argued that Romania was playing a double-game towards the West with the complicity of the Soviet Union.[74] He insisted that within the limits allowed by Marxism-Leninism and its treaty obligations under the Warsaw Pact, Bucharest occasionally diverged from Moscow, the aim being to obtain Western technology and loans in order to press ahead with building a communist system.[75] For a communist state the advantageous trading status it enjoyed with the United States placed it in a strong position; Romania was able to obtain high technology goods from there which were denied to similar regimes.[76] At least one academic has argued that the Soviet Union obtained valuable intelligence and economic advantages from Bucharest's close Western ties.[77] Western leaders such as de Gaulle and Richard Nixon who built up good personal relations with Ceauşescu appear never to have tried to secure a relaxation of repression. Speaking to Tony Benn on his 1968 visit to Romania, British diplomats made it clear that no sleep need be lost about the nature of the Romanian system: they 'made the point that the Romanians had never enjoyed any political freedom at any time in their history...and they had not lost a great deal by having a Communist regime.'[78] This attitude was widespread among diplomats from the key Western states towards communist Romania in particular and the Balkans in general.[79]

Communist pharaoh on the Danube

No alarm bells rang in the West when Ceauşescu started to don the trappings of a communist monarch. From 1969 the re-election of the Romanian General Secretary was no longer decided by Central Committee vote but instead by that of delegates at the party congress. This made his removal by close colleagues virtually impossible through normal channels.[80] In 1974 Ceauşecu had himself proclaimed President and was photographed carrying a sceptre. Amid the welter of congratulatory telegrams, a clearly ironical message from the Spanish surrealist painter Salvador Dali, which included the words 'I profoundly appreciate your historical act of inaugurating the presidential sceptre' was published in full in the party daily *Scînteia* on 4 April 1974.[81]

Emil Bodnăras, an active communist since the 1930s and a prominent office-holder under Dej as well as Ceauşescu, enjoyed considerable prestige within the party, and in the early 1970s accused Ceauşescu of having only his own interests at heart and not those of the party.[82] But he shrank from challenging Ceauşescu on the basis of socialist legality, perhaps a telling illustration of how weak were the mechanisms to prevent abuses of power.[83]

Family power and catastrophic policy errors

A turning-point for the regime was Ceauşescu's visit to North Korea in 1971 where he found a brand of communism that suited his character. He determined on his return home to model Romania on key aspects of the fanatical and regimented character of the Kim Il Sung regime. The drive to turn Romania into a low-grade heavy industrial economy was greatly intensified. A huge oil-refining industry was created, even though Romania's shrinking reserves meant that the country lacked the capacity to make this industry profitable. Far more steel plants were created than the country needed.[84] More than ever, ideological goals now surpassed normal developmental ones; by concentrating on bulk rather than quality and exporting to unreliable Third World markets, Ceauşescu hoped to create a society dominated by proletarian values with miners and steelworkers at its pinnacle. The high technology sector was neglected despite an abundance of native scientific talent. No experiments in market economics were allowed; no underground market economy emerged; the service sector was increasingly starved of resources.

Economic experts like Alexandru Bîrlădeanu had been sidelined years earlier, and instead Romania found itself in the late 1970s in the remarkable position whereby it was the dictator's wife who had far more influence over policy than any civil or military official. Nicolae's consort Elena had received minimal education, but it did not stop her from concocting a career as a scientist, acquiring a doctorate in chemical engineering and various honorary degrees on her foreign trips.[85] By 1979 she headed the central committee body for state and party cadres which meant that she controlled every state and party appointment.[86] Recalling Elena, Alexandru Bîrlădeanu wrote: 'Rarely have I met someone who had as many negative characteristics as she had: hateful vindictiveness, stupidity, nastiness, insensitivity and brazenness were the most obvious ones. I don't know how they met up or how this marriage was sustained.'[87]

As power was transferred from the party to the President and a personal retinue dominated by his wife, the past was reinterpreted to justify their personal dictatorship. History was depicted as an inexorable process leading to the triumph of the higher form of society being installed by the *Conducator* (the Romanian word for 'Leader', officially adopted by Ceauşescu in the 1970s). Ceauşescu was described as the practical reincarnation of all ancestral bravery and wisdom from the Dacian kings onwards to Romania's feudal princes, and the more recent fighters for national independence. A claque of intellectuals was needed to sustain such an egregious cult. The most brazen sycophant was Corneliu Vadim Tudor who, in an article published on Ceauşescu's sixty-second birthday in 1980, hailed him as 'our lay God, the heart of the party and the nation, the man for history and eternity whom we shall follow faithfully in all he will do'.[88] The lustre of the *Conducator* was enhanced if it could be shown that he led a country that had always been in the forefront of human development. To that end the doctrine of protochronism was emphasised, insisting that in a number of important fields down the centuries Romanian civilization had preceded the general evolution of Western civilization.[89]

A regime that used nationalism to mobilise and control the masses occasionally allowed veiled references to be made to Bessarabia, under permanent Soviet occupation since 1944. Works of literature appeared in the 1970s containing a sympathetic portrayal of Marshal Antonescu whose forces recaptured the territory from 1940 to 1944.[90] No major industrial plants were ever located in the northeastern city of Iasi in Moldavia just a few miles from the Soviet frontier, perhaps an indication of Ceauşescu's anxiety about the security of the region in the event of deteriorating relations with the Soviet Union. Instead the Moldavian peasantry were encouraged to emigrate to other parts of Romania, especially to cities in Transylvania where ethnic minorities had been especially numerous till the 1960s.

Playing the ethnic card

The Romanisation of Transylvanian cities only became an impera-
tive policy goal under Ceauşescu. In 1968 the Hungarian Autonomous Region was abolished, and 1972 Ceauşescu was speaking
openly of the need to 'work without pause for the goal of national
and social homogenisation in our country'.[91] Policies designed to
create 'a single working people' were viewed by Hungarians as a
barely-disguised attempt to assimilate them at a time when state education in the Hungarian language had been sharply cut back. In the
1970s and '80s the demographic profile of cities like Tirgu Mureş,
Cluj and Oradea, once strongly Hungarian in character, began to be
altered. The demolition of Hungarian districts to make way for
high-rise flats to accommodate the newcomers was described by
Hungarian dissidents as a covert form of the 'systematisation' policy
designed to create a wholly uniform society. Much anger greeted
the decision to assign Transylvanian Hungarian graduates routinely
to jobs in places far away from their own ethnic communities. The
dispersal of young professionals denied the Hungarian community
the services of people who could be effective defenders of their
interests, and in the 1980s many well-educated Transylvanian Hungarians chose emigration to Hungary instead. But a dissident movement also grew up among intellectuals who sought to defend
Hungarian culture by appealing to the doctrine of human rights in
light of the fact that Romania had signed the 1975 Helsinki accords
with their strong human rights safeguards.[92]

Mostly the Hungarian intellectuals who condemned infringe-
ments of minority rights declined to protest at forms of oppression
that involved the entire population.[93] Such introspection would
continue after 1989, hampering efforts to create durable alliances
among exponents of democracy. But sporadic unrest erupted among
mainly Romanian workers in the Jiu valley mines in the 1977, and
among workers in the Brasov tractor plant in 1987, which indicated
that the regime's hold over Romanian workers was slackening.

Socialism in one family, totalitarianism at all levels

Economic improvements and defiance of the Soviet Union had bestowed genuine popularity on the regime during the 1960s.

Ceauşescu's affirmations about the destiny of the Romanian people and the importance of the Romanian past blended well with the outlook of a still largely peasant population. If he had pursued more prudent economic policies, he could have retained a sizeable support base for his regime even after the end of the Cold War. There was no familiarity with opposition politics among the new social groups wrenched into being by the communist state. According to Silviu Brucan, the regime 'enjoyed stability so long as the "unwritten social contract" between the Communist Party and the working-class was strictly observed', one that 'assumed the party's obligation to ensure workers a decent standard of living'.[94] But this contract was torn up by the regime in the second half of Ceauşescu's rule. The building of expensive steel plants and oil refineries led Romania to amass a foreign debt which rose from $3.6 billion to $10.2 billion between 1977 and 1981.[95] Soaring world market prices for the crude oil it had to import for its over-extended petroleum industry exacerbated the debt problem, as did the fact that Romania had to import 80% of the ore needed for its heavy industry; in the 1980s selling Romania's low-quality steel on the saturated world market proved increasingly difficult.[96] In what proved to be a fateful decision, Ceauşescu declared at the end of 1982 that he intended to pay off the external debt by 1990.[97] He accomplished it, but at enormous cost to the economy and the Romanian people. He slashed imports from the West for food, medicines and spare parts, and resolved to export anything that could be sold abroad. Food exports to the Soviet Union were boosted (Romania becoming its chief foreign provider) while strict rationing was introduced at home.[98]

In the 1980s the arbitrary character of Ceauşescu's personal dictatorship was increasingly hard to conceal. A 1981 law permitted imprisonment for mistakes committed in the workplace.[99] After 1984 doctors were asked to medically inspect female workers on a monthly basis and to ask each one if they were pregnant and, if not, why: in March of that year, while addressing the National Council of women, Ceauşescu had insisted: 'Comrade Women, to have children is your patriotic duty.'[100] Ceauşescu believed that a fast-rising population was a necessity if his goal of Romania becoming a major second-ranking power was to be fulfilled. Since 1966 abortion had been illegal and contraceptives unavailable: between then and 1989, 11,000 women died following illegal abortions.[101]

Plans to bulldoze many thousands of villages and relocate their inhabitants in agro-industrial complexes leaked out in 1987; they were part of an Orwellian process to industrialise the countryside in order to create the perfect socialist man and women: a process Ceauşescu dubbed 'systematisation'. Peasants in the Olt land district of southern Transylvania, who had been prepared to endorse the regime during its first decade, regarded the Ceauşescus with contempt and outright hatred by the mid-1980s; some even said 'It would be better if the Russians came'.[102]

Plotting by several officers not imbued with an anti-Russian mentality did occur in 1983–4 but no serious grab for power ensued.[103] However, Ceauşescu was destabilised by the remarkable changes in the Soviet Union from the mid-1980s onwards. Mikhail Gorbachev, the new party chief, wanted to humanise the communist system, make it more efficient, and end confrontation with the West in order that the burden of the arms race on the Soviet economy could be relaxed. He would be prepared to repudiate the Brezhnev doctrine under which Moscow allowed its satellites only limited sovereignty and intervened with force if any of them took a 'counter-revolutionary path'. Ceauşescu might have been expected to hail this development as a vindication of Romania's insistence on national autonomy, but he did not. The Soviet transformation turned Romanian communism, almost overnight, from a maverick form to a grotesque brand not unlike the version seen in the Soviet Union itself during the heyday of Stalinism. Increasing Western attention was focussing on human rights abuses and Ceauşescu's crazed social engineering projects. With direct talks between the superpowers yielding dramatic results, Romania's role as an interlocutor between the Soviet world and the West was no longer required. A discomfited Ceauşescu dropped his role as an advocate of world peace and started to make threatening noises about Romania's aggressive capability. In November 1988, during a meeting with the Hungarian communist leader Karoly Grosz, he claimed that Romania had developed the capacity to produce nuclear armaments while branding Hungary's liberal communism 'a mortal danger for international communism'.[104]

Except for the communist party, no national institution produced dissidents willing to distance themselves publicly from the regime's destructive policies, excepting the Writers Union and the universities. Medical doctors colluded with the regime in incarcerating dissidents in mental hospitals where they were often destroyed by the treatment they received.[105] Privileges and carefully modulated intimidation encouraged intellectuals to stay quiet and sometimes even police their professions on the regime's behalf. In November 1989 the appeal of Mircea Dinescu, a dissident poet, for a general strike of writers was ignored by his colleagues.[106]

Orthodox Church compliance

The Orthodox Church was the only major national institution whose inner life had not been destroyed by the party in order to conform fully with communist norms. Under the 1948 Constitution it was stripped of its title as 'the dominant church', and land it owned became state property, but the subjugation of organized religion to an irreligious state was less onerous for the Orthodox than for other churches. At his death in 1977 Patriarch Justinian left 10,000 parishes adequately staffed and two or three applicants for each place at the seminaries.[107] Important protection had been afforded to monastic life at least until the end of the 1950s.

Critics argue that the Church allowed itself to be used by a regime which never faltered in its belief that religion was an instrument in the exploitation of the masses and must wither away if the Marxist-Leninist goal of a completely socialist state were achieved. Supporting evidence for this view is provided by the fact that the new working class housed in urban high-rise settlements were not subject to an active Orthodox ministry and went largely unchurched.[108] Indeed, despite the doubling of Bucharest's largely Orthodox population, only one new Orthodox church was built there between 1948 and 1989.[109] The Orthodox hierarchy's reluctance to cater for the religious needs of the new working class enabled Protestant denominations and the Jehovah's Witnesses to make a growing number of conversions in the housing estates that ringed all Romanian cities by the 1980s.[110] When the megalomania of Ceauşescu resulted in the razing of historic churches in the 1980s to make way for a new city centre personifying the leader's fantastic vision for Romania, the Orthodox hierarchy remained silent. Nor were any protests registered when Ceauşescu earmarked up to

10,000 villages for destruction in order to make the collectivised peasantry an extension of the urban working class by being dependent on the state for all its needs.[111] The destruction of the peasant world, from which Romanian Orthodoxy had derived much of its vigour and identity, became a real possibility as the regime entered a radical totalitarian phase in the 1980s.[112]

Ceaușescu used nationalism to ease the trauma of homogenising the population into one working people. But even though Orthodoxy was a badge of Romanian distinctiveness, the regime did not see the majority religion as central to national identity. The promotion of atheism did not slacken under Ceaușescu, who lacked any residual attachment to Orthodoxy. Teoctist Arapasu, Patriarch from 1986, declared at Easter 1995 that 'God permitted communism so that it could be conquered by faith'.[113] This view echoes the one heard in Russia that the sin of submission to the atheists is nobler than martyrdom if the survival of the Church can thus be assured.[114] But the Orthodox defence that communism was part of God's plan and the reaction of the Church was in accord with God's intentions is treated with disdain by anti-communist intellectuals. They believed its vigour would have been affirmed more clearly by saying No to the state, despite the price in repression and hardship, rather than by acting as the confessional arm of an irreligious state.[115]

Party regulars challenge Ceaușescu

Belatedly, opposition to the regime built up instead among some of the top officials whom Ceaușescu had relegated to obscurity. Silviu Brucan, a former hardline Stalinist and top official in the Dej era, voiced dissent publicly in 1987. He appears to have enjoyed a certain degree of protection in American and Soviet policy-making circles, which explains his ability to travel to the West in November 1988. From there he was invited to the Soviet Union and received by Gorbachev who said to him that he was in favour of Ceaușescu's overthrow provided that it could be carried out in such a way as to leave the Communist Party as the leading force in the country; he evinced no enthusiasm for intervening in Romania.[116]

On 10 March 1989 an open letter addressed to Ceaușescu by six party veterans was made public to the BBC. Three of the signatories—Gheorghe Apostol, Alexandru Bîrlădeanu and Constantin

Pîrvulescu, a founding party member in 1921—were former members of the central committee or the politburo. The others were Brucan, Corneliu Mănescu, foreign minister from 1961 to 1972, and Grigore Ion Raçeanu, a party veteran. All were quickly placed under house arrest and deprived of their privileges.[117] The letter condemned Ceauşescu's major domestic policies and their effects on society. It asked: 'Why are you urbanising the villages when you cannot assure a decent level of life in the cities? A government which over the previous five winters was unable to solve...the vital problems of the population (light, heating, transport, food supplies) has shown itself incompetent and incapable of governing.'[118] Ceauşescu's minority policies were also criticised: 'The fact that Germans, Hungarians and Jews emigrate en masse shows that the policy of forced assimilation must be stopped.' In a sarcastic tone reminiscent of Brucan's writing style, the six told Ceauşescu: 'You have begun to change the geography of the villages, but you are unable to move Romania to Africa.'[119]

By 1989 Ceauşescu had ensured that the PCR was the largest communist party in the entire Eastern bloc per head of population with 4 million members, but among them, according to Norman Manea, 'it would have been difficult to find a thousand true believers'.[120] However, Ceauşescu never faced direct insubordination until the very end of his rule. The November 1989 party congress was the apotheosis of the regime: the cult of personality was reaffirmed along with senseless economic policies which had despoiled the country.

A social system for which little popular enthusiasm had previously been shown in Romania was imposed by the tanks and bayonets of the chief historic enemy of Romania after 1945. A sect far less representative of society than its communist counterparts in Britain, Australia and Scandinavia was thus catapulted into power. To impose its will Romanian communism had to exercise terror on a gargantuan scale. Aspects of political culture were mobilised to strengthen the communist grip on society: the willingness of the Orthodox Church and many intellectuals to be compliant with a state which protected or advanced their interests is certainly one important factor. But armed resistance to communism continued much longer than in Romania's neighbours—a clear indication that Romania was far from ripe for it. Communist rule was made easier by the absence of strong democratic traditions in Romania, and the regime ensured that continuation of any institutions, such as the Uniate Church, which could inculcate such traditions would not be permitted. It paid special attention to Transylvania, a region which had only been part of the Romanian state for about a quarter of a century and where, it is often believed, the values of the Western enlightenment had made greater inroads among all ethnic groups than in the rest of the country.

Communism would eventually be undermined by calamitous failures in the economic realm. The emphasis on antediluvian heavy industry placed the country on the path of underdevelopment. The economic gap between Romania and Central European states, whether or not under communist rule, widened. Romania was falling behind such states as Greece, Portugal and Spain even before those countries began to enjoy the benefits of European Union membership in the 1980s. Nevertheless the regime, both under Dej and Ceauşescu, encountered less popular unrest than its counterparts in the other large Soviet bloc satellites. A stabilising factor was the creation of a large new working class of often landless former peasants who, till the 1980s, saw life as being better for them in crucial respects under communism than before. The regime tried to make this social element which, known everywhere in the Soviet bloc as *homo sovieticus*, numerically dominant and it almost succeeded. Those in charge of Romanian communism never ceased to appeal to the new Romanians by means of proletarian symbols and values, but increasingly nationalism was used to extract legitimacy and consent from the masses. Regime propagandists characterised the communists as those completing the national liberation struggle embarked upon by heroes previously dismissed as inventions of bourgeois propaganda. Ethnic Romanian solidarity was appealed to by characterising fellow socialist states such as Hungary and the Soviet Union as harbouring ill-will towards Romania. Dej undoubtedly displayed boldness in defying his Soviet masters and breaking free from the Soviet orbit. The duplicity which pervaded Romanian communism enabled him to mislead his Soviet masters, and his successor Ceauşescu repeated the trick with leading Western countries.

If political conditionality had been imposed by the West in return for Romanian access to Western markets and technology, it could have helped to nurture political forces within the ruling party and in society capable of making the transition to democracy far less painful than it would later be. But opposition remained largely stillborn despite the immense suffering imposed on different sectors of society when the Ceauşescu dictatorship entered an openly irrational and fully totalitarian phase in the 1980s. It is not far-fetched to assume that nearly fifty years of political repression will probably impede political activism, and weaken civil society, for long into the future.

The absence of 'socialist legality', and the fact that retribution against a communist who lost in a power struggle often extended to his family as well, meant that party militants were disinclined to challenge Ceauşescu's despotism. For most of his rule he treated the state as his private domain. The highly personal exercise of power witnessed in Romania was more a feature of Southeast European than Central European communist states, and perhaps shows the impact of Ottoman and harsh medieval Romanian forms of rule on contemporary political behaviour. Ceauşescu himself increasingly relied on tradition as a source of his power. He lost touch with the party and alienated his former colleagues who eventually gathered the courage to dispose of him. But not a few of them were carriers of the same behaviour patterns and mentalities as had produced Ceauşescu.

Perhaps the most retrograde effect of the communist era was to create a largely dependent population which got used to receiving most of its material requirements from the state. A person's security and material well-being depended on displaying political conformity. Exercising individual abilities and taking public actions not approved by the state could be extremely costly. This collective trait of dependence on an unaccountable group of rulers had not begun under communism, but during the 1944–89 era it was greatly refined. Inevitably, any democratic system was bound to be seriously impaired that followed such a grim era.

3

COMRADES DISCARD THE IDEOLOGY
BUT CONSERVE THE POWER, 1990–1992

The fall of the Ceauşescus

The events of 1989 which culminated in the overthrow of and execution of Nicolae Ceauşescu and his co-ruler Elena Ceauşescu remain an enigma more than a dozen years after they occurred.[1] One
of Emil Constantinescu's pledges in the election campaign of 1996
was that he would ensure that the truth about a tragic as well as liber-
ating turning-point in Romania's history would emerge during his
mandate. But on being elected President he failed to do so and the
tenth anniversary of the fall of communism proved to be a muted
commemoration which a beleaguered government preferred to get
out of the way.[2] The full story has yet to emerge of events which contained elements of a hastily improvised *coup d'état* and spontaneous
popular revolt, and reconstructing the tense final weeks of 1989
would take more space than is available here.[3] Attention will be paid to
certain aspects of the violent political changeover which had an important influence on the subsequent political evolution of Romania.

The Ceauşescu state possessed more attributes of a totalitarian
dictatorship than any of the other East European party-states. To
proceed towards democracy from the starting-point of totalitarian
dictatorship, without any transitional phase or the supervision of
external bodies such as those which oversaw the introduction of democracy in post-war Germany and Japan, was a formidable undertaking. The more intense the authoritarian experience, the greater is
the presence of an administrative class disinclined to give up the instruments which are the basis of its power and privileges are based.
This was the case in Romania.

70

Ceauşescu undermined his rule by increasingly reserving privileges for an entourage based on his own extended family, thus exposing sections of the political élite to some of the rigours that were the daily lot of most citizens. From 1986 the Securitate's Second Directorate, which monitored the economic situation, was an arena where criticism of the nature of Ceauşescu's rule was being ventilated at senior level. Its head, Major-General Emil Macri, used to arrange lunches with local Securitate chiefs in rural locations 'at which he would vent his anger at the "imbecility" of the President's economic programme' as well as his frustration with the President's wife who was preventing reports about the dire economic situation reaching her husband.[4] Ceauşescu's neglect of the welfare of the mainline bureaucracy may help to explain why the response to his order that popular protests be firmly dealt with was not carried out with more zeal in Timişoara after unrest flared up there on 17 December 1989. For several days hundreds of people had been gathering outside the church of the Hungarian Reformed minister Lazslo Tökes to protest against plans to transfer him to a remote village. He had defied the authorities in his sermons by criticising abuses of power and calling for ethnic solidarity. By 15 December Romanians and Serbs had joined the protest, and the following day 5,000 protesters gathered in front of the PCR headquarters. Shootings began on the evening of 17 December, a determined stand at this point by the security forces against anti-regime demonstrators would probably have produced a death-toll exceeding the official casualty-rate of just over 1,000 killed, making the Tiananmen square repression of June 1989 in Peking appear minor by comparison. But the spontaneous popular uprising in Timişoara—and later Bucharest—was followed by an internal putsch which Ceauşescu was incapable of quelling. A range of political insiders, who intially called themselves moderate communists wedded to socialist legality, formed a National Salvation Front (Frontul Salvarii Nationale: FSN) on 22 December, the day that Ceauşescu effectively acknowledged the collapse of his rule by fleeing with his wife—by helicopter—from the Central Committee building of the PCR in Bucharest.

Enter the FSN

On 22 December the first televised speech of Ion Iliescu, the leading figure among the conspirators, gave strong hints that he remained loyal to his communist roots. He said that the previous leaders 'proclaimed themselves communists. They have nothing to do either with socialism or with the ideology of scientific communism.... They have only defiled the name of the Romanian Communist Party. They have also defiled the memory of those who have sacrificed their lives for the cause of socialism in this country.'[5] Iliescu's commitment to preserving a left-wing monopoly of control was perhaps shown by his decision to bar Corneliu Coposu, the only survivor of the pre-1947 political élite, from entering the Central Committee building where opponents of Ceauşescu had gathered.[6]

On 23 December Iliescu spoke on television about 'terrorists' who would stop at nothing to keep Ceauşescu in power, and he appealed for the television and radio headquarters, as well as the ministry of defence, to be defended. In the days to come several hundred people were killed in Bucharest as fierce fighting engulfed parts of the city centre, but the central committee building and the television headquarters were virtually unscathed while many of the surrounding buildings were damaged or destroyed. If the 'terrorists' drawn from loyalist security units had been intent on gaining the upper hand, they could have cut telephone lines or destroyed the television transmitter. They could also have taken over strategic targets elsewhere, but none of this happened.[7] No 'terrorists' were ever placed on trial, and critics, unable to believe that a longstanding communist like Iliescu could be a harbinger of change, quickly concluded that a bogus mini-war had been fought to legitimize the new power, giving it the prestige of the saviour of the revolution.[8]

The dictatorial duo had been betrayed by General Victor Stănculescu, deputy minister of defence.[9] On 25 December Nicolae and Elena Ceauşescu found themselves before an Extraordinary Military Tribunal on trial for crimes of genocide. They remained defiant, perhaps failing to realise what the outcome of their trial would be, or perhaps assuming that rescue was imminent; Gaspar Miklos Tamas, a philosopher in Budapest of Transylvanian Hungarian origin, later wrote: 'They carried themselves with plebeian dignity, pathetic maybe, but dignity nonetheless.'[10] Once a sentence of death had been hastily pronounced, Elena cried out to the young soldiers designated to be the executioners of both her and her consort: 'Think, children, how for twenty years I was like a mother to you. Don't forget all I have done for you.' But the execution squad did not hesitate to pump nearly 200 bullets into them.[11] An act initially hailed as a purifying one soon gave rise to suspicions that Iliescu and his co-plotters had got rid of Ceauşescu to prevent him from ever testifying against them in open court about their own richly detailed communist past. Thus the violent nature of the regime's demise produced controversy and recriminations which would impede efforts to consolidate a democratic successor right through the 1990s.

It is not altogether unreasonable to view the final struggles within the regime as a clash of two sets of authoritarian values: orthodox communists and some reformers in the Gorbachev mould finally confronted the brand of doctrinaire personal communism personified by Ceauşescu.[12] The aim of those who overthrew and executed Ceauşescu was to abolish the personal rule of the discredited chief executive and not fundamentally to reform the system of government by pressing forward with revolutionary changes. The idea of ordinary citizens taking control of the streets must have been unsettling for orthodox communists used to seeing themselves as the vanguard who carried out the popular will, and it may have been the desire to prevent anti-communist protesters building up a momentum which could have turned them into a force in their own right that caused insiders to act as they did. The first television broadcast made by the FSN leadership on 22 December assiduously avoided the word 'revolution'.[13] Two days later, on 24 December, Virgil Măgureanu read a communiqué of the FSN that triumphantly embraced the term when he declared: 'The revolution has won.'[14]

The FSN described itself as 'the emanation of the revolution', but its actions suggested a movement intent on smothering its radicalism. The rhetoric of revolutionary change was embraced while the goal of a limited restructuring of the political order was never lost sight of. The thirty-nine strong FSN council included army officers, students and intellectuals who had participated in the revolt, but the directing group were people who had been communists right up until the collapse of the regime: Ion Iliescu, Petre Roman, Silviu Brucan, Corneliu Mănescu, General Victor Stăncalescu, Alexander Birlădeanu and Dan Marţian. The FSN council expanded to 145 members in the last days of December but power remained in the hands of Ion Iliescu as its chairman and interim President of the

Republic and Petre Roman as prime minister of an interim government. In the last days of December 1989 the FSN succeeded in consolidating its authority. The old structures of the PCR were taken over while committees of the FSN were set up in workplaces and at the level of each county, municipality, town, and commune. An instruction issued on 12 January 1991 by the FSN council and signed by Ion Iliescu stipulated that these bodies at the central and territorial level 'function as bodies of state power'.

Relatively few Romanians had heard of the fifty-nine-year-old Ion Iliescu. Educated in Moscow for five years in the early 1950s, he had been minister of youth and secretary of the party's central committee in charge of ideology until 1971 when his rapid progress up the party hierarchy was abruptly stalled after he registered some respectful dissent from Ceauşescu's increasingly doctrinaire policies. After that date he held a series of minor party posts: secretary in charge of propaganda in the Timis county party committee and then first secretary of the Iasi county party committee. In the early 1980s he became chairman of the State Committee for Water before being pushed further into obscurity by being assigned a job in state publishing.[15]

Petre Roman, the forty-three-year-old lecturer who would switch from being his political partner to the rival for his job as crucial decisions were taken over the next two years, was the son of Walter Roman, a Spanish Civil War veteran who till his death in 1983 had been a member of the PCR central committee and director of the party's publishing house, Editura politica. Roman was fluent in Spanish and French and held a doctoral degree from the Polytechnical School in Toulouse.[16]

Iliescu and Roman stood by the ten-point programme issued by the FSN on 22 December, which stipulated the introduction of a democratic, pluralist form of government and the abolition of the leading role of a single party; the holding of free elections; separation of powers; elimination of centralised economic management and promotion of initiative and skills in all economic sectors; the restructuring of agriculture and promotion of small-scale production; reorganisation of education; observance of the rights and freedoms of ethnic minorities; reorganisation of trade and a halt to food exports; and the conduct of a foreign policy 'in the interest of the people'.[17]

The emphasis was on technocratic measures to put the country back on its feet. There were few clues in the early stream of FSN pronouncements about how conflicts would be dealt with or how the range of interests clamouring for attention would be accommodated. Iliescu and Roman emerged from a world in which there were no rules for peaceful resolution of conflicts because socialism had led to the abolition of all but the most minor disputes. Iliescu's statements emphasising the need for national unity suggested that he was uncomfortable with the idea of diverging interests, free-wheeling debate, and the legitimate right of opposition groupings to question the basis of his decisions. Given his background this is hardly surprising, and events would also reveal that Iliescu found abandoning the longstanding state tradition of using nationalism to win popular backing difficult. But the ethnocentric character of the FSN only became apparent when it faced overt competition from groups that denied its right to rule.

Initially the multi-ethnic character of the groups that had risen up against Ceauşescu raised hopes that nationalism would not be a defining characteristic of the new Romania. Such hopeful signals prompted Hungary to recognise the new Romanian government on 23 December 1989, the first country to do so, and six days later Hungary's Gyula Hörn was the first foreign minister to visit Romania and see Iliescu. Thus Hungary rendered Iliescu important assistance as he sought to legitimise his authority before the outside world.

Minority rights overshadows the agenda for change

On 5 January 1990 a declaration on the status of the national minorities in Romania was released by the FSN which raised hopes that concrete steps would be taken to accommodate minority concerns. In a key passage, later much quoted, it declared:

> The revolution in Romania, an historic act of the entire people, of the Romanian nation and of the national minorities, attests to the unity and solidarity of all the homeland's sons who have wished freedom and authentic democracy. The bloodshed in common has shown that the policy of national hate-mongering based on a chauvinistic policy of forced assimilation as well as the successive attempts to defame neighbouring Hungary and the Hungarians

in Romania, could not succeed in breaking the confidence, friendship and unity between the Romanian people and the national
minorities.

The National Salvation Front solemnly declares that it shall
achieve and guarantee the individual and collective rights and lib-
erties of all the national minorities.[18]

Individual and collective rights were to be enshrined in a new
constitution and the declaration also promised that a ministry of national minorities would be created to 'provide the appropriate institutional framework for the exercise of the minorities' major rights,
the use of their mother tongues, the promotion of the national culture and the safeguarding of ethnic identity'.[19] One day before, on
4 January, a decree law on local government laid down that in areas
of the country inhabited by ethnic minorities decisions of the state
would be made known to citizens in their own language as well as in
Romanian. Broadcasting in Hungarian and German, curtailed in the
1980s, was to resume.

The government's readiness to allow the Hungarian minority to
play a full role in state affairs seemed to be confirmed by the appointment of well-known Hungarians to prominent official positions. It
should be noted that the various decisions made in the two weeks
after 22 December 1989, which seemed to anticipate a new era in
the treatment of minority affairs, occurred in a hurried and confused
atmosphere and involved a relatively small number of people. It was
earlier rather than later that minority concerns figured prominently
on the FSN policy agenda because Hungarians had organised themselves into a political body which soon showed that it was able to
speak on behalf of a large section of the Hungarian population. The
Democratic Union of Hungarians in Romania (Uniunea Democrata
a Magharilor din Romania: UDMR) emerged on 25 December
1989, having been set up by Geza Domokos, director of the Kriterion
publishing company which had handled the state's falling output of
books published in Hungarian. None of the new Romanian parties
had effectively taken shape when the UDMR was launched. Iliescu
was not yet likely to be receiving submissions about the treatment of
minorities which would conflict with the agenda based on introducing group rights that Hungarians had drawn up. His record between 1990 and 1996 suggests that he did not hold rigid views on

minority questions and that his policy approach was subordinate to the overriding demands of political survival. It was only in January 1990 that political parties began to register officially with the authorities; as for chauvinistic groups, they kept a low-profile as long as public feelings of revulsion against Ceauşescu remained high. On 11 January Domokos assured Romanians that the UDMR 'sets out to achieve the rights of the Hungarians with due respect for the territorial integrity and sovereignty of a free and democratic Romania'.[20] However, warnings were soon being given about the difficulties Hungarians would face in seeking to accomplish their goals. Andras Suto, Romania's foremost writer in Hungarian, warned in January 1990 that 'decades will be needed before the wounds are healed and the nationalism fostered by the dictatorship is buried in the common soil'.[21] Mihai Sora, a pre-1989 dissident from Timişoara who, not long after being appointed minister of education, expressed his support for the re-introduction of Hungarian into schools, warned that the main thing was the attitude of society and its openness, about which he had serious doubts.[22]

From January 1990 there had been attempts to restore teaching in Hungarian to the school curriculum in Tirgu Mureş and Cluj. This involved removing Romanian pupils from schools which had previously been Hungarian, a policy in the hands of a Hungarian member of the government, Attila Palfalvi, one of two deputy ministers of education.[23] In Cluj many Romanian pupils, on finding themselves moved to the old PCR training school on 5 January, took to the streets in peaceful protest along with their parents and teachers. Similar protests arose in Tirgu Mureş but, unlike Cluj, resentment at the way Hungarians sought to overcome their grievances in education merged with other issues to quickly create sharp tension in that city. The Hungarians concerned had miscalculated by taking the initiative in a sensitive area like secondary education where any over-rapid restoration of the pre-Ceauşescu *status quo* could only be achieved by placing Romanians at a disadvantage. The reaction of those Romanian pupils and teachers most directly affected would probably have been little different from that of their counterparts in democratic countries where education has so often proved a sensitive political issue capable of thrusting normally passive citizens into the political arena if the entitlements seem under threat. Also sharp

intra-Romanian disputes arose over how to undo communist injustices where one group of citizens had been seen to benefit at the expense of another set. The clearest example was the bitter dispute
over church property between the Romanian Orthodox Church
and the Uniate (or Greek Catholic) Church which erupted as soon
as the latter was able to worship freely.

Palfalvi was moved from his post on 27 January 1991, but important ammunition had been given to beneficiaries of Ceauşescu's
nationality policies who continued to hold many of the posts that
they had acquired during his assimilationist drives of the 1970s and
'80s. Officials threatened by an abandonment of pre-1989 policies in
Transylvania were not slow to use their access to the media and the
other channels they had for influencing public opinion to generate
fear of Hungarian intentions. The stereotypical image of the arrogant and insensitive Hungarian, which had been reinforced by years
of emphasising the oppressive aspects of Hungarian control over
pre-1918 Transylvania, began to be revived. Time would quickly
show that the dramatic examples of co-operation between two historically rival peoples which made the Romanian revolution such
an uplifting event had barely scratched the surface of suspicions—
those artificially induced and those based on actual memories and
perceptions.

By the first weeks of February 1990 the first clear signs of a
Romanian counter-mobilisation in Romania had emerged with the
formation of the Vatra Româneaşca Union (Union of the Romanian Hearth). This self-proclaimed cultural organisation quickly revealed itself to be a radical nationalist pressure group able to call
upon formidable resources in order both to block Hungarian demands and to depict them as threatening the territorial survival of
Romania.[24]

The FSN becomes a contender for power

The evolution of the FSN from January 1990 onwards was likely to
have shown Ion Iliescu that many Romanians remained strongly nationalistic in outlook and that it was a view he could not afford to
ignore. As the FSN spread out from Bucharest, it absorbed the local
PCR organisation in most parts of the country. Thus in ethnically-
mixed parts of Transylvania the FSN included former party activists

who had first risen to prominence as a result of actions taken by Ceauşescu to marginalise the Hungarian population—the FSN had condemned these in its earliest statements. The FSN clearly found itself in a contradictory position. If it was prepared to honour its promises to Hungarians, this would be at the expense of state and party officials whose co-operation the FSN needed in order to extend its authority across the whole country. Ingenious compromises might have been able to satisfy, on the one hand, Romanian office-holders in no hurry to vacate their posts and, on the other, Hungarians who felt it was time to seek amends for recent injustices suffered at their hands. However, the Romanian political experience, both under Ceauşescu and indeed in earlier times, had not prepared citizens or their political rulers for such compromises. Even in East European states with longer and more encouraging democratic experiences than Romania, the painful exit from communism after 1989 revealed little aptitude for using the techniques of bargaining and negotiation to overcome conflicts.

The fragile consensus between the communist insiders and the dissidents and newly-politicised elements who had briefly found themselves on the same side of the barricades in the anti-Ceauşescu revolt had collapsed by 24 January 1990 when outraged protestors took to the streets to denounce the FSN. They had been infuriated by a change of policy signalled at a meeting of the FSN's council on 23 January when it was announced that the FSN would take part in the election as a political organisation. Having previously declared that it would serve only as an interim government until free elections were held, the FSN now declared its intention to be a challenger in these elections which were due in April 1990. Iliescu claimed that 'pressure from below' had influenced the decision.[25] So a month after being formed the FSN had been transformed from a political caretaker into an active contestant for power. The suspicion that dissidents without a communist party background and members of newly-created parties had about the pedigree of FSN personalities were greatly reinforced by this *volte face*. In response, the leaders of the emerging opposition based on the 'historic parties' issued a statement on 23 January maintaining that the council's decision flagrantly contradicted its earlier promises expressed in its December programme. 'Through this decision', read the statement, 'the

FSN has lost its neutrality and capacity of provisional administrator of power and its credibility before the public opinion. There can be no free elections and equitable conditions for all political formations when the FSN has a monopoly in a clearly totalitarian way on all state levers.'[26]

A series of street confrontations took place between 25 and 29 January 1990 which gave the FSN the upper hand against its opponents, but only after it was prepared to use methods that rested uncomfortably with its self-proclaimed mission of bringing democracy to Romania: calls were made on television for workers to rush to the centre of the capital to protect the government. Unarmed opponents were beaten up on 28 January and the offices of the best-known opposition parties (the National Liberal and the National Peasant Parties) were stormed on 29 January.[27] The FSN was able to rely on shock-troops drawn from the 40,000 coal miners from the Jiu Valley, 350 km west of Bucharest. In the early weeks of 1990 their leader Miron Cozma perfected the technique of the *mineriada*. It has been described as 'an instrument of pressure and intimidation' designed to coerce and punish forces which were felt to be threatening the security and welfare of Romania and its people.[28] The transformation of Romanian society in the communist era had created a political culture dominated by proletarian symbols, and many miners were persuaded that protecting their syndical interests was equivalent to defending the welfare of the nation. The fact that their industry was in headlong decline and required state subsidies in order to survive made popularising such a view among a workforce living in relative isolation and with a strong sense of group solidarity relatively easy.

The journalist Emil Hurezeanu recalled how the miners made their début in the turbulent politics of the 1990s. He was at a Bucharest press conference on 24 January 1990 at which Silviu Brucan, then the *eminence grise* of the FSN, declared: 'Tens of thousands of miners from the Jiu Valley have written tens of thousands of letters in these days, asking that the FSN be a candidate in elections. The miners…are courageous and capable. They know where they are going and we are going to respect their wishes.'[29] On three other occasions in the next eighteen months, the miners showed themselves willing to come to Bucharest *en masse* and threaten or actually inflict violence in order to defend the regime of Ion Iliescu and state-centred economic policies which were seen as guaranteeing them a livelihood.

On 6 February the FSN registered as a political party and soon Ion Iliescu was its candidate for Romania's Presidency. His image as a genuine man of the people—modest in his lifestyle and determined to restore the social contract between ordinary Romanians and the state-proved very appealing. The new élite obviously believed that many Romanians were trusting enough to accept a scenario in which better times were promised while those who had profited under Ceauşescu (other than his immediate entourage) continued to prosper. Silviu Brucan, an influential player in the events of 1989–90, even publicly declared the Romanians to be 'a stupid people' who could easily be directed by those in power.[30] The collapse of the revolutionary front of December 1989 meant that Iliescu was thrown back on the support of former PCR stalwarts, whose outlook in several parts of Transylvania has already been discussed. This development was hardly reassuring for the Hungarians of the UDMR, nor could they gain assurance from the way in which inflammatory television broadcasts had succeeded in sowing mutual enmity among citizens. The events of late January showed that the agencies of manipulation and political control which had enabled Romania to be dominated by unscrupulous leaders had not perished with Ceauşescu. Iliescu's reluctance to yield political power or allow that power to be shared among interests he could not control also revealed important continuities with the past.

Little-noticed amid the pre-electoral turmoil in Romania was the exodus of the Saxons of Transylvania. In Ceauşescu's time about 12,000 a year had left for West Germany after the Bonn government agreed in 1978 to pay DM 10,000 per head for each German allowed to leave. In December 1989 there were still 200,000 ethnic Germans left in Transylvania, and it is estimated that in 1990 half that number left, abandoning Romania for good once the borders were opened.[31] The tenacity which had enabled them to withstand invasion from Mongols, Turks and Tartars ever since King Geza II of Hungary had invited them to defend the eastern borders of his kingdom in 1143 had been crushed by the misfortune which befell the community during the communist dictatorship. Few Saxons

believed that the conditions which enabled them to lead an autonomous, self-regulating existence for centuries could be restored after
the devastation of the previous forty years. One teacher from Sibiu
expressed what may have been a prevailing feeling in 1990: 'You
can restore buildings—even rebuild those that the communists de-
molished—but you cannot change a population corrupted by forty
years of communist dictatorship.'[32] The exodus of a community
which, with the support of a protective German government, could
have acted as a powerful advocate of minority rights was a disquieting commentary on the new Romania and its prospects. The implications were unlikely to be lost on Hungarians, who would have
cause to feel keenly the disappearance of a group which might have
acted as a balancing force between themselves and ethnic Romanians in Transylvania.

Manufacturing inter-ethnic conflict

In a television broadcast on 25 January Iliescu had declared that
'many disquieting phenomena have been brought to our attention
recently from certain Transylvanian counties in connection with
separatist trends which cause tension between citizens of Romanian
and Hungarian nationality'.[33] Iliescu did not specify what these 'separatist trends' were, but the very fact that the country's leader was referring to their existence one month after the fall of Ceauşescu must
have been encouraging to anti-Hungarians seeking ways to block
the granting of minority rights. An unmistakeable sign that the Hungarian minority no longer had the ear of the government came on
6 February when the FSN published its electoral programme. Its reference to minority interests were perfunctory and there was nothing
about collective rights for minorities.[34] As the FSN evolved from a
caretaker government to an active contestant for power, there was
mounting evidence of a retreat from pro-minority declarations issued
after 22 December 1989. Meanwhile school strikes, marches and the
collection of 50,000 signatures in a petition demanding the reinstatement of the Hungarian Bolyai University revealed that some Hungarian political leaders were switching to direct protests as their channels
of communication with the FSN leadership began to dry up.[35]

In the process Hungarians placed far more emphasis on trying to
secure their core demands as quickly as possible than on explaining

their motives to their Romanian fellow citizens. Silviu Brucan (now emerging as an influential commentator) declared on 20 March 1990 that 'the Magyar minority wants to eliminate as a stroke every harmful effect of the assimilation campaign which began in the Ceauşescu period.... The Romanians simply do not understand demands of this kind, and they evaluate all this as extremist.'[36] Brucan's comments were publicised on the day after inter-ethnic clashes had broken out in Tirgu Mureş; the potential for a violent collision had become apparent from the beginning of March. Video-tapes of Vatra Româneaşca rallies in Tirgu Mureş, Cluj and Alba Iulia in late February and early March had shown large indoor audiences being addressed by speakers who denounced the Hungarian minority as irreconcilably hostile and bent on gaining control of Transylvania, and crowds chanting threats against named Hungarian leaders.[37] The Romanian broadcasting media gave plenty of attention to protests over the fate of educational institutions in Tirgu Mureş, involving rival groups of Romanians and Hungarians, which lasted until mid-March. This coverage often reflected ultra-nationalist positions, something that the government belatedly admitted in the wake of fighting in Tirgu Mureş.[38]

The first Romanian protests over Hungarian schools had been in Cluj but it should have been no surprise that it was Tirgu Mureş where ethnic differences flared up into violent conflict. This city (Maros Vasarhely in Hungarian) had been overwhelmingly Hungarian in its character and demography down to the 1960s (according to Romanian census figures, 74.27% of the city's population in 1948 and 73.74% in 1956 were Hungarian).[39] Under Ceauşescu the arrival in Tirgu Mureş of Romanians from the adjoining counties and from as far away as Moldavia led to the proportion of Hungarians dropping to little more than 50%. The state's industrialisation drive led to the 'Romanisation' of other Transylvanian cities where in 1966 largely Hungarian- and German-speaking minorities had made up 35.3% of the population (32.1% of Transylvania's population overall).[40] But the process was more hurried in Tirgu Mureş than elsewhere in Transylvania. By the end of the 1980s many of its Hungarian population felt keenly aware of their relegation. Meanwhile, the Romanian newcomers who lived in new settlements ringing the city had not had time to establish any level of familiarity with the long-term inhabitants; many came from districts where there had been few non-Romanian inhabitants.

Local officials in Tirgu Mureş who had benefited from Ceau-şescu's policy of discriminating against Hungarians were disinclined to cede positions of authority to leaders of the Hungarian community, and there was less turnover in personnel in the administration of the city and county of Mureş than in other ethnically-mixed regions. The replacement of Romanian officials by Hungarians in the overwhelmingly Hungarian-speaking counties of Harghita and Covasna east of Tirgu Mureş may only have heightened fears among the city's recently constituted political élite about the fate that awaited them unless they mobilised to protect their interests.[41] The specific case of Tirgu Mureş may explain why the city's Romanian élite adopted its own survival strategy rather than follow the lead of the FSN which, on becoming a political party, was destined to enjoy less success in the Mureş area than in almost any other part of Romania.

The violence in Tirgu Mureş and its aftermath

Serious violence erupted in Tirgu Mureş on 19 March after minor affrays three days earlier.[42] Widely differing accounts of events were given by local Romanian and Hungarian spokesmen. Moreover, government statements offered explanations that were at variance with one another: causal factors seen as crucial in early statements were played down in later ones and received little credence in the official parliamentary report on the disturbances published on 23 January 1991.[43] It may well be impossible to arrive at a complete and reliable account of the origins of the clashes in Tirgu Mureş, the first place in post-communist Eastern Europe where inter-ethnic conflict spilled over into fatal violence. However, reports filed by foreign journalists in the city indicate that serious violence first occurred on 19 March when a demonstration organised by Vatra Româneaşca turned into a siege of the UDMR offices. The Hungarian writer Andras Süto was badly beaten by a Romanian crowd as he left the building, supposedly under the safe conduct of the chairman of the city council Colonel Judea.[44] The chief aggressors in the crowd were Romanian villagers from Hodac and Ibanesti, 50 km. from the city; in a region where public transport is even more inadequate than in other parts of the country villagers were bused in and out of the city

on two consecutive days. The parliamentary enquiry into the disturbances found that mayors and public functionaries had been involved in transporting demonstrators to Tirgu Mureş on both days.
The fact that no other Romanians living in communities much
nearer to Tirgu Mureş felt the need to head for the city armed with
sticks and knives has convinced one Romanian very familiar with
the area, Doina Cornea, that the violence had been organised by
elements from the intelligence services.[45] Despite the violence of
19 March, 20,000 people assembled for a peaceful rally on the 20th
to protest at the previous day's violence. Romanian flags were
waved as a gesture of loyalty, and citizens from both ethnic communities mingled in the crowd. However, more fighting occurred after
anti-Hungarian crowds assembled and were reinforced by the returning villagers; some of the Romanian organisations represented
at a peace rally had their offices ransacked by nationalist crowds.[46]
Hungarians began to retaliate on this day and, reinforced by defenders arriving from outlying districts including a large number of
Roma, they began to gain the upper hand. At this point army units
responded to a call to end the fighting, which subsided in the city on
20 March, leaving—according to official figures—three dead and
269 injured.

Despite being unable to control events in the city, the government
had a statement issued in its name of on 21 March which was cate-
gorical about what forces were behind the Tirgu Mureş violence. It
referred to Hungarians celebrating the 152nd anniversary of the
1848 revolution on 15 March as producing 'open attacks against the
nationalist sentiments of Romanian people' with 'the state of tension and violent acts' escalating in following days.[47] The celebration
of an event in which Hungarian nationalists had demanded constitutional reforms, liberal legislation and national independence for
Hungary, without taking into account the similar nationalist demands of the non-Magyar peoples, was bound to be resented by
Romanians ready to view it as part of the unchecked 'superiority
complex' of the Hungarians in their midst. But the political aspects
of the celebrations were not stressed, and efforts were made to include Romanians and show respect for Romanian symbols. The
government statement also claimed that the anniversary 'was misused by citizens of the Hungarian Republic who crossed the border

en masse and who hoisted the Hungarian flag on various buildings and at wreath-laying ceremonies, displaying anti-Romanian slogans.'[48] On the same day it was reported that Petre Roman, in a message to the Hungarian prime minister, blamed 'instigators from outside' for the riots: 'We should have expected the Hungarian government to call its own citizens to order and to refrain from...interfering in Romanian affairs.'[49] The 1991 parliamentary report into the Tîrgu Mureş events made did not mention Hungarian visitors as a determining factor behind the violence. It criticised the UDMR for not explaining the nature of its 1848 celebrations more thoroughly, but found that the accusation made in parts of the Romanian media that the UDMR was engaging in an irredentist act had no basis in fact.[50] An admission that mass media coverage (including those of the state television service) had been misleading, not to say inflammatory, came in government statements on 23 and 24 March. On 24 March a government communiqué 'dissociated itself from the mass media accusations against the Magyar nationality population in Harghita and Covasna counties regarding tendencies of separatism...considering them groundless...and it denied news items linking Hungarian state citizens with planned instigations of violence'.[51] Perhaps it is not surprising that both the Romanian media and leading officials advanced external interference as a factor contributing to the violence which occurred in March 1990 when once again the Romanian state was seen to be badly malfunctioning. Unidentified foreigners in the service of the Ceauşescu regime had been accused of responsibility for much of the violence meted out to his opponents during his final days of power.

Besides the role of the media, another cause for criticism which the government had to deal with was the failure of the army and police to respond swiftly to the violence. Helsinki Watch, the human rights watchdog, charged that the police made only feeble efforts to prevent villagers returning on the second day and in some cases waved their buses through roadblocks that were supposed to halt them.[52] Numerous appeals by sixty or seventy trapped UDMR members for local police to rescue them proved of no avail; they arrived four hours after the first calls for assistance, by which time the mob had ransacked the building.[53] On 22 March Gyula Hörn, the Hungarian foreign minister, had complained that Romanian police

and military had been 'watching passively' as the situation deteriorated.[54] When this issue came up at a press conference on 24 March,
Iliescu's reply was evasive: 'We were reproached for not having
taken measures of strength. Meaning what? Resorting to military
occupation of the country?'[55] On 31 March Petre Roman claimed
that the army's low profile stemmed from 'attempts to use the army
against the people before 22 December'. Afterwards 'it was decided
that the army should only interfere to give protection to government and party headquarters, and I can tell you that the military will
never resort to force the way they do in western countries....'[56] The
army had been in a state of disarray since the appointment of General Nicolae Militaru as minister of defence at the start of the year.
This retired officer, who had had contacts with Soviet military intelligence, recalled to active duty thirty other officers, most of
whom had received active training in the Soviet Union. Within an
increasingly unsettled officer corps, a pro-reform group called the
Action Committee for the Democratization of the Army emerged
on 12 February and the next day over 1,000 soldiers and officers
gathered in Bucharest.[57] CADA soon obtained the removal of Militaru, but one of his appointees, General Paul Cheler, commander of
an army division in Transylvania, stayed and openly aligned with
ultra-nationalists from 1990 onwards.

President Iliescu declared on 25 March: 'The current serious political and ethnic conflicts create the impression that Transylvania
may become a serious subject of discussion... We want to state most
categorically that Ardeal and its belonging to the Romanian homeland cannot be a subject of negotiation with anyone....'[58] These
views were echoed by the Romanian deputy premier Gelu Voican
Voiculescu on his arrival in Tirgu Mureş on 22 March to launch a
commission of enquiry into the disturbances. Addressing a public
rally there, he declared ambiguously: 'We ourselves will defend the
country's integrity and never allow anybody to steal a piece of our
fatherland's land.'[59] Such a statement was bound to add to the insecurity of Romanians already inflamed by nationalistic comments in
the broadcasting and print media.

Little noticed at the time but much commented upon later was
the decision of the Provisional Council of National Unity (set up
earlier by the FSN to give its actions a veneer of legitimacy) to

support the creation of a new intelligence service. The decree was published on 23 March and the chief justification for it was stated to be the need to protect Romania from external threats to its security.[60] The rhetoric of senior FSN figures had prepared the way for such a move, with frequent allusions to the Tirgu Mureş events as having been externally inspired. The truth may well never come out, but leaders of the Hungarian minority are adamant that the Securitate and not shadowy foreign agents choreographed the unrest, a view supported by the Romanian dissident Doina Cornea who mentions in her memoirs an example of Securitate involvement at a critical moment in the escalation of the unrest.[61]

Bucharest was probably in little doubt that the friendly relations it had enjoyed with the Hungarian government were unlikely to survive because of the way the events in Tirgu Mureş had been handled. A message to Petre Roman from his Hungarian counterpart, Miklos Nemeth, on 20 March showed the extent to which these relations had deteriorated:

> I am sorry to say that in the wake of the December turning-point the relationship of the Romanian majority with the Hungarian minority has not moved in the direction of reconciliation but in that of confrontation.... To our deepest regret, the Romanian leadership seems ...to subordinate the Hungarian issue to the internal power-struggle, making unacceptable concessions to forces of explicit racial discrimination.... Hungary is greatly concerned over the rise of national ungenerosity, gradually removing Romanian society from the chance of democratic advance and incurring great damage not only for the minority but for the Romanians themselves.[62]

At least the peace held in Tirgu Mureş in the years after 1990, which strengthens the argument that the violence was artificially manufactured rather than being a spontaneous eruption. The role of the media in sharpening ethnic resentments in an atmosphere of personal and group uncertainty was unmistakable. So was the power of rumour in breeding suspicion and confusion among groups long used to relying on informal means of communication: dozens of news-sheets emerged whose chief product was rumour or opinions masquerading as news, and some of these succeeded in placing citizen against citizen on ethnic grounds. Rival national communities proved relatively easy to manipulate by forces intent on promoting ethnic antagonism. Perhaps this was due to the isolation in which they found themselves, to the powerful hold of local élites over them, and to the fact that some community members retained sharp memories of historic wrongs committed against their ancestors by people whom they were now ready to view as ethnic antagonists.

The government's reaction to the Tirgu Mureş events revealed much of the character of the new political order. The rhetoric about Iliescu and Roman standing for technocratic efficiency was shown to be a sham when they could not preserve order in a city located in the very centre of the country, from which reports of trouble had filtered out before 19 March. Secondly, the regime's claim to embody the spirit of consensus was tested in Tirgu Mureş and found wanting. Opposition groups and minority interests were to be included in governing agencies and assemblies only as decorative elements not as forces with a legitimate point of view that would help to shape policy.

Romania's stormy electoral début

Inter-ethnic recriminations were soon eclipsed by bitter controversies among Romanians as campaigning got under way for elections due on 20 May 1990. Opponents of the FSN accused it of seeking to impose a neo-communist solution on the country by pressing ahead with elections a mere twenty weeks after Ceauşescu's overthrow and before its competitors had a chance to organise themselves. From the outset the FSN enjoyed massive advantages over a weak and fragmented opposition. Its position as the dominant force in government gave it control over state assets notably access to printing presses and transportation, and control over radio and television. The last advantage was crucial in a society where television had shaped the outlook of millions of people, particularly the poorly educated living in small towns and villages in remoter areas which received few other sources of information about the world beyond their immediate localities. The totalitarian state had found that rural dwellers were more easily manipulated than other sections of the population, and that television was they key weapon in moulding loyal and uncritical citizens. Anger at the manipulative role of television had caused thousands to demonstrate outside the studios of

'Free Romanian Television' on 4 February 1990, even before events in Tirgu Mureş. The acrimonious election campaign that followed underscored the state media's capacity for bias, distortion and character assassination.[63] Starting on 22 April, the centre of Bucharest had also become a rallying-point for a peaceful sit-in by students, intellectuals and others making up the informal opposition who claimed that former communists were trying to create a democratic Romania in their own distorted image. They demanded that PCR leaders, members of the Securitate, and leading *nomenklatura* officials should be barred from competing in the first three elections for any public office, including the presidency; this was article 8 of a proclamation drawn up by democrats in Timişoara and released on 11 March.[64]

The conviction of anti-government protesters that cosmetic changes were leaving old power structures intact was strengthened when the shape of the 'information service' that was to replace Ceauşescu's secret police, the Securitate, began to be clear in April. The Romanian Information Service (RIS) was to employ 6,000 out of the 15,000 personnel who had belonged to the Securitate up to December 1989.[65] But in the view of vocal critics, statements that the Securitate of old had been abolished were as bogus as the claim that the FSN had no connection with the party that had been the dominant force in Romanian society up till the previous December. However, most Romanians, due to the isolation they had endured for forty-five years, had much narrower horizons. They compared Iliescu's performance not with that of the dissident—turned—Czechoslovak President, Vaclev Havel, or with Gorbachev's, but with Ceauşescu's whose rule had become increasingly arduous for them in the 1970s and '80s. For Romanians unconcerned with party manifestos, Ceauşescu 'the bad father' had been replaced by Iliescu 'the good father'. Under him some of the burdens of daily life had been lightened: supplies of heat and light were restored, peasants were being promised access to private land, rationing was being scaled down despite continuing food shortages, and a full television service was being provided offering entertainment as well as coverage of the exploits of those in power.

The close identification between one party and the state, abhorrent to many urbanised Romanians who wanted a complete break with the past, was not necessarily viewed in this light by less sophisticated people in the villages and provincial towns among whom Iliescu was most tumultuously welcomed on the campaign trail. Romanians had long been used to being ruled by someone in charge of a powerful set of centralised institutions; before as well as during the communist era, political legitimacy had been sought by rulers who promoted themselves as defenders of national security against traditional foes like Russia or Hungary, and the FSN showed every sign of wishing to uphold this tradition. The FSN's readiness to play the nationalist card was shown by the respectability it bestowed on Vatra Româneaşca, which became transformed through well-publicised meetings with Iliescu and Roman from a marginal provincial group into a national political player. The FSN would deal on favourable terms with any group that posed problems for its own opponents. In a bid to mobilise the language and symbols of nationalism when appealing to the public, it struck up an informal alliance with leading elements in the Romanian Orthodox Church, for many Romanians an important repository of national consciousness although it had been tarnished by its close link with the communist regime. Teoctist, the Orthodox Patriarch, had gone into seclusion because of this link, and his re-emergence in the spring after withdrawing an earlier decision to retire paralleled the new-found assertiveness of traditional forces in Romanian political life, whose eclipse had proved equally brief. Leading figures in a re-vamped state and church who had a questionable past to live down and a vested interest in avoiding drastic change struck up an informal alliance. Iliescu was seen on television attending church services, even though he admitted that he was and remained a freethinker.

But perhaps the FSN's most effective means of boosting its patriotic credentials was to deny that its opponents had any. Early in the election campaign the FSN and its allies claimed that the opposition parties were ready to cede Transylvania to Hungary.[66] But Hungarians were not the principal targets of FSN media attacks because of the possibly unfavourable reaction among the correspondents and election observers present in Romania who had not forgotten the events in Tirgu Mureş. The strongest attacks were directed instead against Iliescu's two presidential challengers, Ion Raţiu of the National Peasant Party (Partidul National Taranesc-Crestin Democrat: PNTCD)

and Radu Câmpeanu of the National Liberal Party (Partidul National Liberal: PNL), who had both plunged into active politics after
years (five decades in Raţiu's case) living abroad. They were regularly criticised for having lost touch with the country, and both men
were physically attacked while campaigning by mobs of people who
had been inflamed by media invective in a not dissimilar fashion to
those in Tirgu Mureş.[67]

A broken-backed opposition

Protestations about the communist character of the FSN failed to
gain credibility when neither of the historic parties proved willing to
put aside their factional spirit and close ranks against this danger.
Câmpeanu and Raţiu failed to convince many of the undecided
voters that they could offer Romania anything better than Iliescu.
Neither man possessed the insider knowledge and credibility to
mount a convincing challenge to ex-communists seeking to build a
democracy in their own image. The elevation of such figures
showed the incoherence of the traditional opposition. Until well
into the 1990s it would be composed of personality-based parties
with diffuse programmes, unable to widen its electoral base and so
become an effective political player.[68]

Despite the shortcomings of the opposition standard-bearers in
the 1990 elections, it is hard to see how outright opponents of the
FSN, claiming to belong unambiguously in the democratic camp,
could have overcome their handicaps except over time. At the national level opposition was expressed by the remnants of parties
which had last played a central role in politics in the decades before
communism. Two parties, the National Peasant Party (PNTCD) and
the National Liberal Party (PNL), were hastily reconstituted, the
former adding the suffix 'Christian Democratic'. For over forty
years the activities of what became known as the 'historic parties'
had been completely suspended. The severity of the communist regime had made carrying on even an underground existence impossible. Young Romanians did join the PNTCD and the PNL in 1990,
but these parties found they no longer possessed the social and economic bases which had sustained them between the world wars. The
world of private agriculture, urban business and commerce, and independent religious organisations from which these parties had

derived values, material support and a steady flow of recruits had been shattered in the communist era. At least the National Peasant Party possessed a widely respected leader in Corneliu Coposu, who in the coming years would enjoy a stature and respect extending beyond his party, much to the irritation of Iliescu.[69] Coposu, who had taken the initiative in reviving the PNTCD in late December 1989, was one of the few leading figures to survive the repression which virtually wiped out a whole generation of party activists. He had spent seventeen years in prison followed by another twenty-five years of heavy restrictions upon his activities.[70]

Once campaigning started for the 20 May elections, the historic parties found that little advantage was to be gained from stressing their involvement in politics before 1947 (this may have been why Coposu declined to be his party's presidential candidate). Under the influence of state indoctrination many poorly-educated people, however dissatisfied they may have been in the final Ceauşescu years, associated the inter-war years with exploitation by rural landlords and urban capitalists and were not inclined to vote for any party which might restore such conditions. Most Romanian cities had streets named after Lupeni and Griviţa, where bitter coal-mining and railway disputes had taken place in 1929 and 1933, and been forcibly suppressed by Peasant Party-led governments. Iliescu and his supporters would regularly refer to such events, especially when the opposition was finally able to form a government in 1996. Gradually, it dawned on the more perceptive opposition officials that, although the dictator had gone, the world that had sustained him—along with its structures, mentalities, and customs—somehow lived on. Large elements of the population seemed to have a vested interest in the reconstruction of a modified version of communist Romanian society. Opinion polls after 1989 found that Romanian citizens still had a strongly egalitarian outlook. Between 70 and 74% believed that income levels should be almost equal for all, and in a poll simultaneously carried out by the Gallup agency into attitudes to the market economy there was more opposition in Romania to a sharp reduction in the role of the state in the economy than in any of the countries polled (which included Albania, Bulgaria and the former Soviet Union).[71]

Given the immense handicaps that the historic parties faced in trying to re-integrate themselves with national life, it is not surprising that, being worn down by internal rivalries and suspicions, they turned in on themselves. Younger recruits found that prospects of advancement were blocked by veterans determined to pick up the threads of political careers interrupted in 1940. Such tensions were compounded by members of the intelligence services whose heavy presence in sections of the PNTCD was common knowledge in the 1990s.

The FSN's poll triumph

But for the unwillingness of Radu Câmpeanu, the historic parties would possibly have boycotted the elections, and this in turn would have undermined the legitimacy of the FSN and made the drawing up a new constitution that would enjoy international credibility difficult.[72] The result of the 20 May contest showed that the FSN was the overwhelming choice of the great majority of voters. On a turnout of 86% Ion Iliescu received 85.1% of the vote and was thus elected President of Romania on the first round (a second ballot would have been required if no candidate had got more than 50%). Câmpeanu and Raţiu managed to obtain only 10.2 and 4.3% of the vote respectively.

Meanwhile the FSN obtained 66.31% of the vote in the parliamentary elections, which would enable it to devise a new constitution—the chief task of the two-chamber legislature—largely according to its own tastes. Numerous irregularities in the electoral process were pointed to by election observers and others, but it was clear that the FSN was the choice of a substantial majority of the electorate. Iliescu's paternalistic message and unabashed nationalism was appealing to millions of people, who regarded it as a genuine advance over anything they had been offered by Romanian rulers for a long time. In parliamentary elections, the National Liberals acquired 6.4% of the vote and the PNTCD trailing badly with 2.6%. Even the PNTCD leader, Coposu, failed to gain a seat in his native district of Salaj,—he claimed electoral irregularities.[73] In second place to the FSN was the UDMR with 7.2% of the vote. The ability of Transylvanian Hungarians to maintain a united front enabled the party to put up a strong performance. As for the scattered forces of dissent, they failed to produce a political party capable of mounting a successful electoral challenge. Whereas Vatra intellectuals succeeded in entering parliament, their liberal counterparts who had played a prominent role in the events of December 1989, such as Ion Caramitru and Mircea Dinescu, failed to obtain enough backing in Bucharest where they stood as candidates.

However, the limelight remained focussed on the informal opposition which continued to defy the authorities by remaining encamped in Bucharest's University Square for three weeks after the elections. They had adopted the *nom-de-guerre* of *golani* (hooligans) after Iliescu had described them thus in April. They took their inspiration from the Timişoara Declaration which had been released on 11 March 1990 by young writers and journalists in that city keen to promote human rights and fight for the implementation of democracy. But, unlike Bucharest, Cluj and other cities which had been the scene of fighting in 1989, the embryo citizens movement of Timişoara was able to prevent the FSN from monopolising positions of authority. A situation of dual power existed after January when the leaders of the democracy movement held local elections and formed a city council which set out to improve social and economic conditions and thus had substantial local support.[74] In April 1990 the Timişoara Association suggested that Ion Iliescu and his two opposition challengers should withdraw from the presidential race so that the country could be ruled for two years without a President in the period that a new constitution was being drawn up. According to Nicolae Harsanyi, 'it would have been a chance for Romanians to learn to think for themselves and become less dependent upon powerful personalities who might treat them better than Ceauşescu had done but who were unwilling to offer them significantly greater opportunities to determine their own futures'.[75]

Post-electoral violence and international isolation

The *golani* encamped in Bucharest's University Square were finally removed on 13 June 1990 following a broadcast by Ion Iliescu on that day, calling on loyal citizens to come to the aid of the government. At the same time a similar tent city of dissidents in the Bulgarian capital, Sofia, was unnerving a post-communist regime more moderate than Iliescu's. He also feared that his government's hold over the armed forces was uncertain. On 14 and 15 June thousands of miners from the Jiu Valley arrived in the capital and for the next two days went on a rampage, attacking opposition party headquarters and the offices of civic groups, as well as the Roma or gypsy quarter.[76] Iliescu always subsequently defended their actions. In 1998 he said: 'The riposte of 14–15 June 1990 was an expression of self-defence by the population which saw the institutions which they had voted for under threat.'[77]

In June 1990, without providing evidence, he had warned that the country was facing a 'legionary rebellion', a reference to the extreme right movement of the 1930s. This claim is scarcely credible in view of the fact that his intelligence chief Virgil Magŭreanu had actually arranged for the return of the movement's exiled leader Horia Sima in 1990 and had numerous meetings with him at a safe house provided for Sima in the Danube Delta.[78] At a rally in Bucharest on 15 June, Iliescu Congratulated them on their 'civic awareness', he declared: 'We know that we can rely upon you. When necessary we will call upon you.'[79] He also thanked them for displaying workers' solidarity in face of a plot by forces inside and outside the country who believed that 'right-wing forces should come to power in all East European countries'.[80] Thus the claim that violence involving Romanian citizens had been part of a conspiracy hatched by unidentified forces outside the country was made for the second time by the President.

International condemnation of the government's role in the June 1990 violence was virtually unanimous, and Romania's leaders increased the discomfiture of observers by giving explanations for the events and attaching blame for them which differed sharply from earlier statements.[81] The sympathy and solidarity shown towards Romania in the West in December 1989 gave way to stupefaction and an intense wariness. In the words of one Romanian commentator, the June 1990 *mineriada* was when 'Romania became a strange country' in Western eyes.[82] Economic assistance from the European Community was frozen immediately after the miners' violence, and later Prime Minister Roman's request that Romania be included in the Visegrad group of former Warsaw Pact countries that were pooling their energies in order to speed up the process of integrating with west European institutions was met with a rebuff Roman turned up uninvited at the meeting in Hungary and was only persuaded with difficulty to withdraw from the forum. President Havel of Czechoslovakia felt that the Visegrad partners' agenda would be hampered if they were associated with a country whose level of democracy was regarded with disfavour in the West.[83]

The Bucharest authorities quickly took steps to repair their public image, which suggested that they did not see a return to isolationism as an option open to them—most of all because of the scale of the economic damage inflicted on the country under Ceauşescu. The appointment by Iliescu of a government headed by Petre Roman demonstrated that the authorities wished to develop beneficial economic and political links with the West, albeit on their own terms. The important economic portfolios were filled by men who gradually convinced Western visitors in contact with them of their seriousness in wishing to discard past economic models and press ahead with a rapid liberalisation of the economy. Indeed the Roman government borrowed much of its economic rhetoric from the opposition whose pro-capitalist proposals it had denounced in the spring as an economic sell-out of the country. Privatisation measures were announced in August just as radical as the ones the opposition had promised earlier.

The authoritarian spirit persists

The key test of whether the government was interested in pursuing a policy of political openness would be in the area of local government. In July 1990 Petre Roman began replacing mayors who had been appointed at the beginning of the year with appointees who were clearly loyal to the FSN. The office of prefect was also re-established, the holder being the highest authority in each Romanian county and directly answerable to the prime minister in Bucharest. The appointment of an ethnic Romanian prefect in the overwhelmingly Hungarian county of Covasna produced far more intense protests. Eventually a compromise was reached whereby, in the counties of Harghita and Covasna, mixed pairs consisting of an ethnic Romanian and a Hungarian were appointed as joint prefects.[84] Such a compromise was an isolated occurrence.

The newly-elected government showed itself particularly unresponsive to the demands of the Uniate Church (also known as the Greek Catholic or Eastern Rite Church) for the restitution of between 1,800 and 2,000 places of worship confiscated by the state in

1948 and handed over to the Romanian Orthodox Church. The Uniates were legalised again in 1990, but a new law obliged the Orthodox Church and not the state to restore church property *voluntarily* even though it had been seized by the state.

Another test of the Romanian authorities' readiness to make amends for past injustice towards its own citizens concerned its attitude to King Michael I of Romania whose Romanian citizenship had been revoked by the communists in 1948, one year after he had been forced to abdicate and go into exile. King Michael was expelled from the country again on 26 December 1990 less than twelve hours after being processed through customs and passport control at Bucharest airport without incident.[85] The attitude of the government of a figure who lacked widespread support in the country revealed an insecurity that was at variance with the large electoral mandate it had received in May 1990. (Eventually he was allowed to visit the country, and on his arrival in Bucharest on 26 April 1992 received an enthusiastic reception.)[86]

The September 1991 crisis and the fall of Roman

At the end of September 1991 a renewed onslaught on the capital by coal-miners from the Jiu valley forced Prime Minister Roman out of office. His declared aim of turning Romania into a market economy had divided the FSN. President Iliescu's public endorsement became increasingly lukewarm; the Western-oriented technocrats with whom Roman had surrounded himself were outnumbered by conservative, party-educated deputies with a background in the state bureaucracy.

The 1990–1 Roman government was committed to economic liberalisation, but it failed to see the vital connection between economic reforms and political pluralism. Thus the anti-communist opposition continued to doubt Roman's liberal credentials and viewed the power struggle within the FSN as a personal one between two political chieftains and their respective followers united in a common distrust of true democracy. Adrian Severin, the boldest of the economic reformers, has left a memoir of the Roman government which suggests that the differences with Iliescu over economic policy were real and unbridgeable.[87] He relates conversations with Iliescu at the time in which the President showed his unhappiness with privatisation as a whole in the commercial and agricultural branches of the economy. Severin describes a conversation with Iliescu at the end of July 1990 in which the President declared: 'I don't understand why you are in such a hurry and why you haven't analysed things more carefully before drawing up legislation. These things cannot be decided so rapidly...I don't understand, for instance, how you can think of privatisation. In fact, I don't want that decision taken now.'[88] 'The story of the Roman government', according to Severin, 'is that of a battle between partisans of 'the new' and partisans of 'later on'.[89] Severin complained to Iliescu on 29 March 1991: 'Unfortunately Mr President, you still believe that Stalinism and Ceauşescuism were errors made in applying Marxism-Leninism. We are of the opinion that the only ones who correctly applied the theses of Marx and Lenin were Stalin and Ceauşescu.'[90]

Out of office, Roman spoke on 29 October 1991 of the dangers facing Romania as a result of the survival of the mentality and methods of the Ceauşescu Securitate'.[91] Like Ceauşescu, Roman fell in little over twenty-four hours. The security forces had melted away before the marauders who occupied the parliament building on 26 September 1991. Roman then handed in his mandate to facilitate a political solution to the crisis. He said afterwards that he had had no intention of resigning, but President Iliescu later refused to allow the resignation to be withdrawn. A new caretaker government was then appointed under Teodor Stolojan, finance minister in the first nine months of the Roman government, which parliament duly swore in on 16 October 1991. Roman criticised Iliescu's willingness to negotiate under the threat of force as 'an act of cowardice' which was bound to prove disastrous for democracy.[92] This public breach was the beginning of a power struggle to gain control of the FSN which would split it asunder within six months.[93]

The imperative of unity

One of Petre Roman's last acts as prime minister revealed his capacity for manipulating public opinion rather than channelling it in a responsible direction. On 25 September 1991, while debating in Parliament on the miners' strike that would shortly lead to his removal, Roman suddenly changed the subject and announced that news had just been received that a Transylvanian government-in-exile had been set up in Budapest. A parliamentary debate was immediately called over what Roman described as 'a stupefying action'.[94] But it soon proved to be the work of a handful of insignificant people and no more was heard of it. The existence of a Hungarian threat posing a danger to the well-being of Romania was revived with much greater emphasis in October 1991 with the publication of a parliamentary report into the situation in the predominantly Hungarian-speaking counties of Harghita and Covasna (known as the Szekler counties or Szekler land) in the weeks following the overthrow of Ceauşescu. The report found that Romanians had been subjected to a systematic campaign of intimidation resulting in large numbers abandoning their homes and fleeing the area. Also falling into the category of Hungarian persecution were the deaths of four Romanian members of the Securitate and the militia in the last days of 1989.[95] UDMR deputies, defying the nationalist clamour, pointed out that these members of the security forces had lost their lives not because they were Romanians but because, rightly or wrongly, they were associated with state repression; indeed three ethnic Hungarian under officers were among the dead, the object of popular fury towards a system that repressed everyone. But what had been seen as revolutionary acts of justice in other places where Securitate personnel were killed became anti-Romanian acts in Harghita and Covasna.[96]

The commission appointed by parliament in October 1990 to investigate the situation in Harghita and Covasna produced a report claiming that 4,000 Romanians had hurriedly left the Szekler counties due to an outbreak of intimidation in early 1990. However, Ioan Oancea, the FSN's sole deputy in Harghita, while acknowledging the existence of an anti-Romanian mood in the area at the start of 1990, claimed that many young people sent to the Szekler towns as part of the scheme of compulsory labour direction for recent graduates had left voluntarily, preferring to return to their homes in Wallachia and Moldavia.[97] However, such moderate voices were drowned out in the two-day debate on the report broadcast live from parliament in which FSN deputies competed with ultra-nationalist ones in the expression of anti-Hungarian remarks.

The 1991 constitution and the collapse of FSN unity

The Romanian constitution drawn up by parliament and placed before the electorate for approval on 9 December 1991 embodied the centralising ethos that had been at the heart of state formation in Eastern Europe for more than a century irrespective of the ideological character of the state. Given the insecurity over borders and the internal disunity which led to the collapse of several long-established East European states in 1991–2, the climate was not suitable for a system of government to be adopted which would break up the concentration of power in the capital and allow regions or minorities the control over their own affairs which had previously been denied to them.

The chief architect of the constitution was an obscure academician Antonie Iorgovan who, without any strong public profile, had secured enough votes to be elected as the only independent in the 1990 parliament. The FSN-dominated parliament then duly nominated him to design the constitution.[98] It defined Romania as a unitary state and Article 13 stipulated that the country's official language was Romanian.

The new constitution received endorsement from 81% of deputies, the UDMR voting against it. In the subsequent referendum on 9 December 1991, 78.5% of voters approved the document and 14.1% disapproved on a 69.7% turnout. Only 14% voted yes in Harghita and 21% in Covasna; thus the main Hungarian-speaking counties were the only ones where a No vote was returned.[99]

Nationalist advances

The FSN had received a convincing endorsement for the constitution despite its own widening splits and the collapse of government authority in the autumn of 1991. But the party's hold over Romanian voters would shortly be tested in local elections due to be held to on 9 February 1992 elect mayors, local councils and county councils. For the first time in over fifty years Romanians would also be able to elect, from among their own fellow-citizens, those who would be entrusted with the task of providing effective and accessible local government. The mainstream opposition parties had formed an electoral alliance known as the Romanian Democratic Convention to strengthen their credibility, but by contrast the FSN was in mounting difficulties. Austerity measures had reduced its appeal, and moreover the President was now intervening openly in the party's factional struggles to rally his own supporters, although the head of state was forbidden under the constitution to be a member of any political party.

At each stage of the escalating power-struggle within the FSN, ex-Premier Roman presented himself as the genuine partisan of democracy while casting his chief adversary in the role of the 'nostalgic communist'.[100] But in many eyes it was hunger for political power and not differences over economic policy that lay at the root of the conflict between two erstwhile allies. In Cluj on 29 November 1991 Roman made the promise that 'no former communist party activist or employee of the Securitate will be a candidate on the FSN list in the next election'.[101] But, weeks earlier, many of his own supporters in the FSN had failed to back an opposition amendment to the local government law which would have prevented any PCR activist from being named as prefect or sub-prefect of a county. At the same Cluj press conference, Roman proclaimed himself to be a 'moderate nationalist committed to peace'.[102] However, the FSN produced an inflammatory election newspaper in Cluj, *In Faţa alegatorilor*, impugning the patriotic credentials of its Democratic Convention opponents and, when a second round was held to elect a mayor, it supported the candidate of the Party of Romanian National Unity, Gheorghe Funar. Cluj was the only large populated centre in Transylvania which opponents of the government failed to capture in local elections.

The FSN's national percentage of votes fell from 65% in 1990 to 33% by the 1992 local elections. Further erosion was prevented by its ability to keep control of rural areas, where the influence over voters of local power-holders such as the local police chief, the doctor and sometimes the village priest often counted in its favour.[103] After the local elections the FSN formally split into two rival parties. Petre Roman's control of local FSN branches was sufficient to enable his faction to retain the name and emblem of the National Salvation Front. However, the majority of the parliamentary party went over to the Democratic National Salvation Front (Frontul Democrat al Salvarii Nationale: FDSN), which was less of a political party than a platform designed to secure President Iliescu's re-election. Almost a dozen deputies would also defect to the most extreme of the nationalist parties, the Greater Romania Party (Partidul România Mare: PRM), during the period of political realignment between the local election and the parliamentary and presidential contests due on 27 September 1992. This was a period when ultra-nationalists first emerged in Romania as a distinctive force in their own right rather than as a group operating in the shadow of the ruling party.

Gheorghe Funar, Cluj's newly-elected mayor, quickly became a figure of national prominence thanks to a series of controversial decisions, some of doubtful constitutional legality, designed in his own words to allow the Romanians to be 'masters in their own house'.[104] As leader of the Party of Romanian National Unity (Partidul Unitatii Nationale Romane: PUNR), which had emerged from Vatra Româneaşca, he was the standard-bearer for the segment of the bureaucracy in Transylvania which had benefited from Ceauşescu's effort to impose the will of the majority on an ethnically-mixed province. This élite was above all keen to protect its professional interests, especially at this time when much of the economy was being prepared for privatisation. It did not automatically look to Bucharest for guidance or instruction; indeed there was impatience with the unwillingness of the central state to give wholehearted backing to its ethnic agenda. Funar articulated the view that Bucharest, and the south generally, did not sufficiently appreciate the special needs of Romanians in parts of Transylvania where Hungarians were still numerous or possibly even enjoyed an outright numerical majority. The Cluj mayor's preoccupation with the danger posed by 'anti-national' forces invites comparison with Nicolae Ceauşescu in the later stages of his rule, and in over ten years as mayor he surrounded himself with personnel drawn from his military and security service apparatus who shared his own heightened nationalism. His methods and discourse reveal the extent to which the Ceauşescu era had left its mark on the behaviour and outlook of many middle-aged Romanians who had obtained career fulfilment and security by working for the state before 1989. Funar was the first elected Romanian politician of the 1990s prepared to praise Ceauşescu. In July 1992 he declared:

'The things achieved in the "Golden Epoch" or the "Epoch of Ceauşescu" were ones that the Romanian people are proud of today. They are things which it was not easy for the Romanian people to accomplish in a short period. Unfortunately, Ceauşescu was a dictator who humiliated the Romanian people in various ways:

hunger, human rights, promoting wrong values, closing frontiers, cold dwellings. But from the viewpoint of investment, of buildings, of attitudes relating to independence and sovereignty, he was able to be admired in my view as a good Romanian.'[105]

The September 1992 elections and a new political balance

The month of electioneering which got under way for the parliamentary and presidential elections being held on 27 September 1992 revealed a political landscape greatly altered from that of May 1990. Ultra-nationalists were active contenders in their own right, with Gheorghe Funar fighting a high-profile battle for the Romanian presidency as candidate of the PUNR. Mainstream democratic opposition parties (including the UDMR) had rallied around a single candidate for the presidency, Professor Emil Constantinescu, who appeared more in touch with political realities than the émigrés who had been opposition standard-bearers in 1990. He was a relative unknown who belonged to no party and was chosen only in the summer of 1992, largely at the behest of the PNTCD which had no suitable candidate of its own to put forward.

The electoral alliance known as the Romanian Democratic Convention (Conventia Democrata din Romania: CDR) sought to convince the electorate that a CDR government had the ability to place Romania on the road to economic recovery and social peace. Lacking in its manifesto were any concrete policies for dealing with inter-ethnic relations; if these had been included, they might only have provided an inviting target for the governing side and the ultra-nationalists. However, reunification of Bessarabia with Romania received a prominent place in the manifesto which promised a reformed state based on the rule of law, a President who acted as a 'moderator between social and political forces', a free market economy based on 'large-scale privatisation', a 'social contract' between employer and employee, increased foreign investment, and greater responsibilities for traditional institutions like the church, the army and the schools.[106]

The pro-government forces which had rallied around the Democratic National Salvation Front (FDSN), formed in April 1992, ignored the CDR's campaigning promises. Instead, they revived the charges made against the opposition in May 1990 that it intended to turn the clock back to an era of harsh economic exploitation and that it could not be trusted to safeguard Romania's national interest. Emil Constantinescu declared afterwards that he and his supporters had been accused of five fundamental sins: bringing back the king, restoring landlords, reviving capitalism, selling Transylvania to the Hungarians, and persecuting former communists.[107] Although the CDR campaign was attuned far more to the social realities of Romania than the one in 1990 had been, it overestimated royalist sentiments among the electorate: 'For many opposition figures the king appeared as a messianic figure capable, by a single gesture, of re-establishing not only a normal political life in Romania, but also a new morality....'[108] Of the CDR's candidates 46% were from the PNTCD compared with 18.5% for the Civic Alliance Party, the rest being divided among smaller parties.[109] The PNTCD's phalanx of elderly candidates made it easier for the FDSN to claim that it wished to take its revenge on the country and its blameless citizens for the persecutions its members had suffered in the past.[110]

The result revealed that the familiar values of security and state protection represented by Iliescu still exercised a powerful appeal although his first term had seen a decline in living standards for most of his supporters. He obtained 47.34% of the vote, thus falling short of the 50% that would have enabled him to be elected on the first round. Emil Constantinescu was second with 31.24%; Funar's ability to obtain 10.87% of the vote helped ensure that a second round was held. As in 1990, the President had received resounding mandates in Moldavia and much of the south. His results had reflected those of his party, the FDSN, which had gained only 19% in large towns, 30% in small towns and 35% in the villages.[111] Sharp contrasts also emerged in voting patterns on the basis of ethnic factors. Ion Iliescu did worst of all in ethnically-mixed areas or ones where Hungarians were in a majority. In Transylvania he was nearly 20% behind Emil Constantinescu who had received 42.70% of the vote compared to Iliescu's 23%.[112]

In the parliamentary election, the FDSN emerged as the largest party with 27.71% of the vote, but this was not enough to enable it to govern on its own. The pro-reform forces grouped in the CDR were greatly strengthened when this coalition of avowedly democratic parties came in second with 20.16%, Petre Roman's FSN coming a distant third with 10.18%. The FDSN proved to be the largest party in Bucharest, the south and Moldavia, but in Transylvania there had been a three-way split in the distribution of votes, the UDMR emerging first with 20.5%, the CDR next with 19% and the PUNR close behind with 18% (the FDSN only managing 12% there). In Mureş county the FDSN and FSN polled only 4% each in 1992 compared with 14.2% for the united FSN in 1990. The position was even worse in the city of Cluj where the 1990 FSN vote of 28% collapsed to just 7.36% for its two segments. The Cluj result in September 1992 showed in sharp relief the vulnerability of the FDSN in large populated centres where, due to nationalist rivalries, it was difficult to carve out an appeal based on trust in the president as a symbol of national unity or gradual change. The 28.42% fall in the FSN vote registered between 1990 and 1992 occurred in the most urbanised parts of Romania; in the second round Iliescu forsook the cities and concentrated on remoter agricultural and industrial settlements where his most loyal supporters were to be found. The failure of any party to gain a parliamentary majority enabled him to stress his unifying role in a fluid political situation, and this may have ensured a high turnout of 73.20% in the second round, especially from middle-aged and elderly Romanians, influenced by a lifetime of state paternalism, who feared any uncertainty or interruption of established routines.

On 20.0% of the vote, the CDR fell far short of the parliamentary majority it had hoped for. Constantinescu himself is reported to have said in retrospect that it was possibly better that he failed to win in 1992 because he lacked a competent staff with whom he could have implemented a reform plan for the country.[113] But his own performance was criticised. In 1990 the parties making up the CDR had obtained only 4.65% of the vote, so the 1992 result was a great advance, the best result being in the Banat where the it captured 37%. At last there was evidence that the CDR parties were starting to acquire a social base among certain groups of urban workers as well as among middle-class professionals. But the CDR was gravely hampered by the absence of social forces representing private ownership. New capitalists were in many instances drawn from the ranks of old communists; they relied on the state for protection, and often their ventures were launched by diverting resources from state companies.[114] An emergent group of private capitalists engaged in speculative ventures was hardly likely to be drawn to a coalition committed to a public administration based on a firm code of ethics.

On 11 October 1992 Ion Iliescu was elected for a second term, this time of four years, having obtained 61.43% of the vote as against 38.57% for Emil Constantinescu. The political deadlock resulting from the inconclusive parliamentary result created a situation in which the President wielded considerable power, entrusted to him by the constitution. He called CDR leaders in for talks about a co-alition government, but without offering them terms that made their agreement to participate in government with previously bitter rivals a serious possibility. The FDSN was reluctant to try governing alone and taking responsibility for difficult economic portfolios, which the parliamentary party had few suitable people able to fill. Finally, in November 1992, a non-party government was sworn in under Nicolae Văcăroiu, a senior civil servant in communist times who was strongly committed to a state-led economy. It was sustained in parliament by the ultra-nationalists as well as by the FDSN, whose combined votes gave it a narrow working majority.

The irrational and totalitarian characteristics of the communist re-gime badly damaged Romania and left it ill-prepared to confront the challenges of democracy. The violent replacement of the Ceau-şescu dictatorship and the ability of second-ranking regime figures to shape the direction of the successor regime were bad omens. Consensus and solidarity among the new and old political forces left in the political arena were in short supply. Ion Iliescu and Petre Ro-man showed that they were ready to encourage popular attitudes and reflexes incompatible with democracy-building: inter-ethnic antagonism, suspicion of opposition, and regimentation. They showed little interest in purging the state system of thousands of officials who had loyally served the dictatorship and were ill-suited to oper-ate in a pluralist context. Iliescu's mobilisation of thousands of min-ers to act as his praetorian guard in 1990–1 placed Romania apart from all other post-communist regimes in the region. In terms of external support for integration into mainstream European institu-tions, the country paid a heavy price internationally for adopting such an approach.

The politics of ethnicity had a key bearing on the political struggles of in 1990s. Thereafter it lessened in importance, but ultra-nationalist parties remained permanent players in the electoral arena. If inter-ethnic controversies had not been shamelessly manipulated by Iliescu and his allies, then ethnic antagonism might not have marred the transition to democracy as it did in 1990 and periodically thereafter.

Ideological disputes on classic left-right lines were less important. Romania was the only Soviet-bloc country where the former communist party failed to make a strong showing in the first democratic election—because nearly all the figures who would have been involved in such an enterprise had assembled instead under the National Salvation Front banner. Ideological communists, as opposed to those who used the party as a way to acquire power and privileges, were thin on the ground. The big Jewish emigration, starting in the 1950s, had removed many people prominent in the propaganda wing of the PCR, and thereafter Ceauşescu made sure that anyone whose loyalty was primarily to the party and its message and not to him, was relegated to obscurity.

The apparatus which Iliescu inherited and whose loyalty he was mainly able to acquire was prepared to endure political pluralism as long as its privileged place in society was not undermined. Its willingness to hang on grimly to its privileges was shown by the steps it took in Tirgu Mureş in the first months of 1990. The FSN gradually consolidated its authority once it had become clear that its agenda for change was very limited. Iliescu was committed to having an electoral democracy where voters had the chance to choose a head of state and parties to form the government, but where an oligarchy composed mainly of people who had already been politically active before 1989 could exercise sweeping power without needing to be accountable to any democratic organs.

It was calamitous for Romania that in the first two elections in 1990 and 1992 a clear majority of its citizens showed that they vastly preferred such a guided democracy in which a new élite heavily drawn from the former intelligence services and other privileged groups were able to ignore or undermine the law. Their social outlook had been heavily influenced by a communist regime which reinforced vertical relations of domination and personal dependence and discouraged social solidarity. As a result, the world that had sustained the Ceauşescu dictatorship still lived on and would not disappear quickly. Adherents of genuine democratic change were to be found in large number in Timişoara and later Bucharest. But it would take a long time before they could challenge Iliescu and his acolytes for the top positions in the state, and by that time Romania had been left far behind other comparable states in the drive to escape from underdevelopment and carve out a new future as a would-be member of the European Union.

4

ROMANIA ADRIFT, 1992–1996

Iliescu's management style

President Iliescu and his supporters won the autumn 1992 election by default. As a party the Democratic National Salvation Front (FDSN) had been hurriedly assembled after the break-up of the FSN in the spring of 1992. It was fortunate in facing a low-calibre opposition which lacked even the most elementary professional approach to campaigning. The Romanian Democratic Convention (CDR) continued to make a vital mistake by comparing Iliescu with Ceauşescu. All voters had lived through the Ceauşescu era, and with pre-1989 Romania as their main point of reference, they could see that differences between the two men outweighed any similarities. So the opposition helped to boost Iliescu's image by comparing him with his predecessor.

Despite being a product of the communist era, Iliescu was a different political animal. He remained a self-effacing figure, at least in public, and his lifestyle was modest—his appetite for wealth and high living was kept well under control. His wife genuinely shunned the limelight, so that comparisons with Elena Ceauşescu were totally inappropriate, and the fact that they had no children ruled out any danger of an Iliescu dynasty emerging. Iliescu also retained 'the common touch', which enabled him to relate to individual peasants and workers long after his policies ceased to suit their material needs. Unlike Ceauşescu, he had a thick skin and was able to endure criticism, especially from the independent press which was unsparing in its attacks on him (his composure only slipped once, in August 1992, at Constanta, when he grabbed by the throat a journalist who had been heckling him).

Ion Iliescu possessed some commendable traits not always found in leaders who possess much stronger democratic credentials. As long as his subordinates showed fidelity, he was loyal to them even after they appeared to become a liability for him. Dan Iosif, one of the 'revolutionaries' who rallied to Iliescu's side in 1989, was appointed a presidential counsellor (and was reappointed in 2001) despite being involved in a serious of public quarrely, his only apparent qualification being his unconditional loyalty to Iliescu. Also, Iliescu did not appear to be a vindictive character wishing to settle scores with those who had crossed him. During his second presidential term, he gradually lost interest in a campaign to drive Petre Roman from office by having his financial affairs during his period as premier investigated, and the matter was quietly shelved. He would show extraordinary leniency towards Corneliu Vadim Tudor (hereafter described as Vadim) on several occasions despite the venom of his diatribes. In 2000 he was ready to rescue Adrian Păunescu from political obscurity by giving him an electable place on the parliamentary lists of his party, despite a public attack delivered by 'the Titan of the Carpathians' four years earlier.[1]

The men around Iliescu

But Iliescu's management style during his second term suggests that he had been shaken by Petre Roman's ill-concealed attempt to seize control of the FSN in 1991 and sideline him. Colourless people were appointed to senior positions in the ruling party, which in July 1993 acquired a new name: the Party of Romanian Social Democracy (Partidul Democratie Social din Romania: PDSR). Iliescu's choice of premier in 1992, Nicolae Văcăroiu, was a man destined always to remain in the President's shadow. Oliviu Gherman, the first vice-president of the PDSR and President of the Senate, played a decorative role, allowing Iliescu to interfere in party affairs whenever necessary. Adrian Năstase was the PDSR's executive chairman from 1992 to 1996; this was essentially a backwater position for someone whose quite promising début as foreign minister from 1990 to 1992 might have enabled him to be a more effective prime minister than Văcăroiu. His role was to keep the parliamentary troops in line and ensure that the PDSR's slender voting majority was never overturned. He was ambitious, but unlike Petre Roman he had the patience to bide his time and not try to supplant the PDSR's patriarch who enjoyed genuine popularity with a large segment of the electorate.

In 1992 Theodor Stolojan, Roman's successor as Premier, was the only other person in the PDSR camp with a significant public reputation. In 1992 he let it be known that he would be taking up a position with the World Bank, but if he had been given a free hand by Iliescu to rescue a sinking economy he might have been less inclined to move abroad. In 1996, when a succession of policy failures indicated that someone with Stolojan's economic flair was badly needed, Iliescu turned down the idea of announcing that, if reelected, he would make full use of him.[2] For a while Iliescu relied on Adrian Costea, a Romanian-born and French-domiciled financier whom he first met a year before his 1992 re-election. Costea became an unofficial adviser, and in 1992 he and his wife were given Romanian diplomatic passports.[3] According to Iosif Boda, Costea 'tried with all his might to help Ion Iliescu acquire a new vision and a new strategy to develop Romania'.[4] Boda seems to have been the President's most outspoken adviser. In a series of letters that were printed in a book he published in 1997 on his Cotroceni years, he warned Iliescu that compromise, arrogance and incompetence were threatening the PDSR's hold on power.[5] It was no doubt to Iliescu's credit that he was willing to receive such frank advice, but there is no sign that he felt the need to act on it. Boda has written: 'It wasn't easy to work for Ion Iliescu: the Head of State didn't help you to help him.'[6] Perhaps as a result, Boda spent much of Iliescu's second term as ambassador to Switzerland.

In contrast to Ceauşescu, who had an uncontrollable urge to intervene at all levels of government, Iliescu was willing to decentralise plenty of powers to local potentates, businessmen, trade union leaders (not least Miron Cozma) and managers of state firms whom Andrei Cornea christened 'the directorate' (*directocratii*). He has described a 'Merovingian-type state' where, in return for loyalty, these latter-day barons 'received exceptional benefits and exemptions from the normal law'.[7] By late 1996, when Iliescu was in deep political trouble, Cornea even described the President as 'the weak man of Romania', someone who had become 'the marionette of a corrupt party and its clientele'.[8]

Virgil Măgureanu—man of secrets

The President also gave considerable freedom of action to Virgil Măgureanu, head of the main domestic intelligence service, the SRI. In many ways he was a more skilled political operator than Iliescu, which is not surprising since, unlike the PCR, the Securitate had made use of the skills of political scientists, sociologists and psychologists.[9] Măgureanu was very much left alone by Iliescu to bring order to the sprawling intelligence community and prevent any political skeletons from the 1989–90 period from threatening his hold on power. The SRI employed from 10,000 to 12,000 officers and troops as well as an unknown number of secretarial staff.[10] But Iliescu was shrewd enough to prevent any one figure monopolising the intelligence world. He and Măgureanu may have established an effective partnership at the start of the regime, but in the shifting sands of Romanian politics such alliances all too often turned out to be very ephemeral.

No less than nine different intelligence services existed which were attached to different ministries or, like the SRI, were self-regulating,[11] and no single ministry watched over their workings, which gave infinite scope for infighting, duplication of activities and freelance operations that were incompatible with a democratic state. Some coordination was provided by the Supreme Defence Council (Consiliul Suprem de Apărare a Țării), a collective body chaired by the President, but it enjoyed no constitutional link with Parliament.[12] Eventually, when the prominent role Măgureanu had played in driving Petre Roman from the premiership became clear, regulation of the SRI was introduced, and in June 1993 a Joint Standing Committee of the Chamber of Deputies and Senate for Parliamentary Oversight of the SRI was established by the Romanian Parliament.

Măgureanu had no shortage of enemies within a sprawling intelligence community, which from December 1989 was the scene of a feverish struggle among operatives and former operatives to retain political relevance and influence and above all to acquire material wealth. He displayed *sangfroid*, endless ingenuity and, whenever necessary, ruthlessness in fending off competitors. It is not over-praising Virgil Măgureanu to assert that democracy in Romania was in better shape thanks to his emergence rather than that of any of his rivals, although his controversial role in the 1989–90 era will make him a figure of heated controversy well into the future. According to Cornel Nistorescu (no apologist for the SRI), 'his tactic of combining the scalpel with diplomacy …diminished the risk of the return of a brigade of dark socialists.'[13] His most notable achievement, in the eyes of Dennis Deletant, an alert and well-informed observer of the intelligence scene, is that 'he prevented the SRI from being worse than it could have been'.[14]

During Iliescu's second term, when accusations that well-placed officials were acquiring fortunes by trafficking in influence were widespread, Măgureanu skilfully deflected criticism away from himself. But in 1997 it emerged that he had constructed a sprawling forty-three-room villa in his native village of Giurtelecul Hododului in north-west Romania. He claimed that it had been built through the family pooling its resources. But it soon emerged that he had been able to build it without observing the normal legal procedures.[15] Moreover, the property was the only one in the district with a regular water supply which had been provided free of charge by the state thanks to a decision of the Văcăroiu government.[16] These revelations emerged in 1997 after Măgureanu had stepped down from running SRI.

Hostility to reform at the top

The choice of Nicolae Văcăroiu as prime minister showed how hesitant Iliescu continued to be about the speed and direction of economic reform. He came from a railway background, an occupation where communist influence had been strong, and he went on to make a career in state planning. Unlike the President, he was unable to summon up even vestigial enthusiasm for liberalising the economy. The Organization for Economic Co-operation and Development (OECD) complained in June 1993 that the shift away from state control of the economy had been 'diluted and distorted' in Romania.[17] The timetable for economic reforms during his premiership was constantly delayed, and by 1996 the rate of privatisation in Romania was almost the slowest in any East European country.[18] By the time it had left office in 1996, the government had privatised only 12% of the assets under its control. The government was content to allow the privatisation agency to remain in the hands of the unwieldy Parliament with PDSR notables and supporters sitting on is board as a sinecure. Văcăroiu was probably expressing his true feelings when he declared on a visit to Moscow in July 1995 that he was ready to re-align the Romanian economy with Russia's because Western economic support had been so disappointing.[19] The perceptions hardened in the West that, under him, reforms were agreed to unwillingly and then only to secure funds from international donors which were put to uses other than those intended. During the Văcăroiu years the *leu* was allowed to depreciate. One set of beneficiaries consisted of debtors who had obtained unsecured loans from state banks, since the value of what they needed to pay back was now diminished by inflation. Another was the energy sector which needed to import electricity, gas, oil and a wide range of expensive equipment in order to stay viable. The Văcăroiu government invested much effort in maintaining state monopolies that were notorious for their low productivity and extremely poor quality of service.

RENEL, the state electricity monopoly, became the largest company in Romania after 1990. Legislation passed in that year turned industries that were viewed as strategic arms of the national economy into '*regies autonomies*', borrowing from the French model— maintained out of the public purse but keeping a semi-autonomous status relative to the central state. In 1998 Marius Tinu wrote in *Adevărul*: 'For years now many strategic *regie*…have produced 'strategic' losses of billions upon billions of *lei*, losses converted by the state through subventions…'[20] One of the costliest errors made in Romania after 1989 was the decision to upgrade thermal power plants at a cost of equipment costing billions of deutschmarks, But much of the equipment has lain idle, resulting in a massive increase in the foreign debt.[21] In 1998 a megawatt of electricity cost over $60 while in the West and in Russia and Ukraine it was claimed to cost only half that.[22] Despite a staggering record of incompetence RENEL's management were able, through their close connections with the PDSR, to escape any adverse consequences. The enormous losses continued to be covered by the state budget. Managers and the workforce enjoyed sky-high salaries, an ordinary female employee in being paid more than a cabinet minister's.[23] By 1998 the salaries account of RENEL amounted to 1% of Romanian GDP,[24] and unsurprisingly trade unions and managers formed a united front to prevent any restructuring that would harm their interests. Privatisation was never a possibility under Văcăroiu despite the State Property Fund, an agency set up in 1992 but by 1999 with a remit to liquidate the 47% of state assets placed in its hands. Indeed, it would be resisted under a government more prepared to act on external financial advice rather than ignore it. One journalist branded RENEL and its predecessor the energy ministry, not the central committee of the PCR, as the nucleus of communism in Romania.[25]

In a letter to Iliescu written in May 1994, Iosif Boda warned the President of the failure of the Văcăroiu government to tackle 'the managerial crisis in the public sector':[26] 'The government can be forgiven for not having carried out spectacular privatisations, but it cannot be excused for the fact that it has failed to improve the management of economic sectors financed by the state (this was its principle mission)'.[27] The fact was that the PDSR rewarded its most useful and best-placed supporters with positions in RENEL and other well-paid sectors of the state economy. In return it expected help whenever required. It was widely believed that RENEL would adopt a relaxed view towards late payments from companies enjoying the government's favour but be ruthless in pursuit of those who lacked such an advantage.

The new oligarchy

People previously active in the communist regime who had converted themselves into important economic and financial players in the emerging market economy often benefited through the close ties they enjoyed with those in the state energy sector and other strategic economic sectors. Not a few leading businessmen in the 1990s had been officials in the Department of State Security before 1989. On behalf of the Ceauşescus they controlled the import-export trade, and as well as acquiring a close knowledge of the workings of the capitalist system were able secretly to amass hard currency in foreign bank accounts. Much press attention has focussed on the role in the pre-1989 regime enjoyed by Dan Voiculescu, founder of the Romanian Employers Association and a man with important media interests.[28]

In the early 1990s state banks issued unsecured loans to clients with political influence, who were often able to use the funds in profitable transactions with government departments or state companies.

Bancorex, successor to the communist-era Romanian Bank for External Commerce, lent huge sums on a discretionary basis to clients of the new regime and to state companies which needed constant injections of capital to stay viable.[29] In 1999 when the Bancorex scandal finally burst into the open, it was reckoned that 70% of the credits issued by the bank were non-performing and would be extremely hard to recover (many, in addition, were worth only a fraction of their former value).[30] Low-interest loans advanced in the early 1990s had been devalued for the creditor by the massive rise in inflation during the Văcăroiu years and thereafter. Bancorex had been able to claim enormous sums of public money because of the fear that if it was allowed to fail, it could trigger off the collapse of the entire banking system.[31] Its dubious banking practices also escaped investigation because of the practice of offering free credit to judges, prosecutors and senior police officials.[32]

4.1 billion dollars in non-performing credits was lost to the state between 1992 and 2004 according to the Romanian banking authorities. Bancorex accounted for just over 50% of the losses. But the Banca Agricola, the Dacia Felix Bank, and the deceptively-named International Bank of Religion also added to the toll of losses. Only 13% of the sums lost have been recovered.[33]

After one of the biggest financial scams, involving the collapse of the National Investment Fund in 2000, the government pledged to take quick action against those responsible. But four years later the IMF's resident representative in Bucharest complained that 'the investigation has still not produced any tangible results'. In his turn, the vice-governor of the National Bank of Romania stated that the slow pace of the investigations looking into financial fraud could be due to three main reasons, the investigators' lack of relevant experience, the receipt of bribes, or the use of intimidation.[34]

The failure to depoliticise the economy and carry out proper institutional reforms after 1989 had led to such terrifying abuses. The present generation of Romanians and perhaps the next one too would have to bear the cost unless drastic remedial action was taken. The result of such abuses was that Romanians with genuine entrepreneurial talent, of whom there was no shortage as shown by the rapid growth in small and medium-sized businesses, were usually unable to prosper unless they had good political connections. Instead it was ex-party and Securitate officials who prospered and became even more influential than before by using their connections to obtain credit and buy up valuable assets, such as those in the retail sector, for bargain prices. Many unscrupulous managers of state firms siphoned off company products for their own benefit, and by asset-stripping obtained the wherewithal to launch themselves as private businessmen. There were even enterprising people in the hotel and restaurant world who, before 1989, had been able to acquire wealth by exploiting the shortage economy, and some of them enjoyed spectacular success in the economic jungle which Romania became after 1989.[35] The Păunescu brothers—Gheorghe and Viorel, who had run the Melody Bar, one of the few pre-1989 nightclubs of Bucharest—soon became dollar multi-millionaires, buying up some of the top hotels in the country, such as the Intercontinental which made an annual profit of around $20 million dollars.[36]

There were self-made men who made large fortunes through their own efforts. The best known of these is Gelu Tofan who, after 1989, built up a flourishing road haulage and motor business with an initial loan of $50,000 from a brother in Canada.[37] But anything from 20 to 40% of economic activity in the 1990s took place in the unregulated and untaxed black economy. Smuggling of goods such as cigarettes and tobacco was highly lucrative. In the late 1990s articles published in the Bucharest daily press claimed that Fane Capatina, a notorious smuggler enjoyed remarkable access to circles of power. Cornel Nistorescu has written:

> Fane Capatina is a man from the gypsy mafia...he has his men in the Military Prosecutor's Office and he can send police officers to buy him cigarettes and beer... Many officers, prosecutors, lawyers, judges and MPs also, know him. The truth is that the gypsy mafia had almost reached close to...Iliescu and to... Văcăroiu... They reached the people who used to meet the top people every day and the uncrowned kings of Bucharest nightlife every evening'.[38]

It has even been alleged that smugglers employed cabinet members to enforce the law against their rivals. Zaher Iskandarani, who acquired a monopoly of the import of Camel and Monte Carlo cigarettes, was also able to thwart his arch-rivals, the Nasser brothers, by enlisting political help. Elie Nasser was jailed amid huge press publicity in 1993, but his brother Mike went to Virgil Măgureanu to seek his release. In 1998 the newspaper *Evenimentul Zilei* published a transcript of the discussion which had taken place between them five years earlier. Măgureanu was informed by Nasser that army officers had been paid $1.3 million for their cooperation, whereupon he supplemented cigarette smuggling with arms dealing, apparently with the knowledge of the SRI intelligence service.[39] Iosif Boda, alarmed at such high-level collusion, claims to have urged Văcăroiu in 1993 to remove the head of the customs service and the financial guard. Văcăroiu replied 'Leave them be, leave them to compromise themselves.' 'But why do we need compromised people?', Boda asked.[40]

The PDSR and the nationalists

It would have been normal if the PDSR had hoped to accomplish in the political world what tycoons—many with roots in the Ceauşescu system—were attempting in the worlds of business and finance. During 1994 Adrian Năstase made efforts to turn the PDSR into a party of state. Technocrats who had joined the government on the basis of their expertise were pressurised into becoming party members, and even senior bureaucrats were pressed to join. The principle—which had proved so harmful when applied before 1989—that the state should be governed not by functionaries but by militants was once more revived.

But the PDSR's reach was not equal to its political ambition. It became a flabby party lacking an active inner life. *Dimineata*, the party daily, was read by Iliescu and he ensured that funds were found to keep it afloat despite its tiny circulation, but its turgid columns failed to rally the faithful. In a letter he wrote to the President in the summer of 1995 Boda complained that many of the PDSR's local leaders were 'of very weak quality', some being 'businessmen of dubious character'.[41] Such businessmen could also be found in the PDSR parliamentary party, which may explain why no law was ever passed by Parliament to restrict the financial activities of its members.[42] Parliamentarians also enjoyed immunity from prosecution for all but the most serious offences, turning the chamber in Bucharest into a modern equivalent of medieval churches where refugees from justice could seek sanctuary. Others elected for the PDSR were able to enjoy a lucrative double income by sitting on the boards of state industries and banks.[43]

Occupying 12% of parliamentary seats, the nationalist bloc of parties held the fate of the Văcăroiu government in its hands. The

PRM, the PUNR and, to a lesser extent, the Socialist Labour Party (Partidul Socialist al Muncii: PSM) were rewarded with diplomatic posts, administrative jobs in ethnically-mixed areas, and prefectships. For over a year, in 1993–4, Romanian state television was run by Paul Everac, a writer known for anti-Western views and his nostalgia for the pre-1989 times.[44] Iliescu (who kept a tight grip on Romanian state television) made this appointment and in March 1993, on the occasion of the first congress of the PRM, sent a cordial message to its leader Vadim Tudor, the most extreme of the post-1989 nationalists. Silviu Brucan claims that Vadim was a creation of Iliescu, who 'brought him into the light, encouraged him to launch *România Mare*, received him at Cotroceni, and enabled him to appear frequently on television'.[45] In 1992 Vadim had urged his followers to support Iliescu's presidential bid even if he believed the President's record contained some big mistakes. The PRM supported the government when it faced a parliamentary vote of no confidence in March 1993, but there was speculation that its condition for such backing was that Romanian prefects would be appointed in Harghita and Covasna to end the anomaly whereby each post was split between a Romanian and a Hungarian.[46] The dual authority formula was ended on 26 March 1993 when two Romanian prefects were appointed. According to one UDMR deputy, the government's response to requests that these prefects should be Hungarian was: 'Find us two Hungarians prepared to sign their applications for FDSN membership.' This was a revealing indication of the FDSN's shaky support within the Hungarian community.[47]

Adrian Năstase, the PDSR's parliamentary leader, had attended the same Bucharest high school as Vadim and viewed him 'as a big kid easy to manage'.[48] By contrast Gheorghe Funar, the PUNR leader—who as mayor of Cluj demanded virtual autonomy from Bucharest—was viewed as a major irritant. Until his emergence the determination of the centre to regulate local government down to a very minute level had been one of the constants of Romanian political life irrespective of what kind of regime was in charge. The PUNR, through the accident of holding the balance of power, had turned this convention on its head. In August 1994 three of its members were admitted to the government. The PDSR had long resisted demands from Funar's party that it be allowed to share the fruits of office, but Năstase as chairman capitulated after the PUNR threatened to defeat the law on privatisation which Western creditors viewed as a vital test of Romania's commitment to reform its economic life.[49] The high-watermark of extremist influence in the Văcăroiu government came on 20 January 1995 when the PUNR, the PRM and the PSM signed a pact of co-operation with the government—of which Oliviu Gherman made the nonsensical statement that the protocol with parties that had openly praised the dictatorship was 'an expression of the democratic nature of Romania's political life and meets the increasing demands of contemporary European life for…an approach consistent with the highest international standards'.[50] Several ministries, particularly those of the Interior and Foreign Affairs where PRM influence was already noticeable, received a further influx of activists, the interior minister Doru Ioan Tărăcilă being particularly well-disposed towards the PRM.

Slow emergence from international isolation

Teodor Meleşcanu, foreign minister from 1992 to 1996, inspired more confidence among Western observers of Romania than did Văcăroiu: his low-profile, professional approach to his job won him respect. Romania had competent ambassadors in Washington— Mihai Botez, the former dissident in 1994–5, followed by Mircea Geoana—but this was far from being true of other important foreign capitals. The appointment as ambassadors to countries such as Germany or Austria of Moscow-trained holdover from the communist era (nationalist ideologues or else low-grade backers of the FSN) suggests that foreign relations were still accorded a low priority in Cotroceni. The Bucharest daily *Adevărul* wrote on 22 April 1998: 'In all the world's civilized countries, the best people are selected for diplomacy. Unfortunately for us the Ministry of Foreign Affairs has become a sort of elephant's graveyard to which various political failures are sent, compromised individuals who need to be lost somewhere.'

Romania's reluctance to enforce the increasingly severe United Nations sanctions imposed on Serbia from 1992 onwards shows how careless it could still be of its international reputation. What Western intelligence services knew for some time already was carried by the press when Petru Mihai Bacanu claimed in *România líbera* (10 August 1995) that the Văcăroiu government had permitted oil to flow to Serbia in contravention of UN sanctions. Indignant official denials followed, but on 7 March 1998 Virgil Măgureanu, who was now launching a career in politics and had set up his own party, declared at a press conference that the Supreme Defence Council, then headed by President Iliescu, had approved a decision to send 8,000 tons of gasoline and almost 40,000 tons of diesel fuel to Serbia.[51] Between October 1995 and February 1996, General Ion Pitulescu, then head of the police general inspectorate, had carried out an investigation into the smuggling of fuel to Yugoslavia. The fact that he was allowed to proceed with it made him doubt that President Iliescu had been involved, and indeed on 13 September 2000, while in Washington, Iliescu would deny that any smuggling had been undertaken with the knowledge of the government.[52]

In the report which Pitulescu handed over to Premier Văcăroiu, evidence was provided to show that large-scale fuel smuggling had been carried out by high-ranking officers of the SRI intelligence service—following the orders of their chief Virgil Măgureanu. Military prosecutors dragged out investigations till 2000, when they reached the conclusion that SRI officers had no case to answer. The investigation was then taken up by civilian prosecutors investigating claims of money-laundering allegedly perpetrated by French-based companies belonging to Adrian Costea. At a press conference on 3 August 2000 Pitulescu claimed that the oil smugglers operated through nine firms, purchasing 200,000 tons of fuel mainly on the international market with credits of $150–200 million provided by Bancorex. The fuel was sold to the Serbs at five times the market price which, according to Pitulescu, enabled Măgureanu and his accomplices to make anything up to $500 million from the operation.[53] The most glaring evidence of what many had long suspected—that under Iliescu top officials running state institutions used their positions to make vast fortunes—did not leak out until he had left office. Following the outbreak of warfare in ex-Yugoslavia, Romania began to be seen, rather unexpectedly, as an island of stability in the Balkan maelstrom, and presumably to improve its image Meleşcanu insisted that Romania belonged not to the Balkans but to Central Europe. Nevertheless the Bucharest press persistently complained that problems remained unresolved because of the Balkan mentality of those in high places.

Whatever region Romania belonged to, under Iliescu it was one of Slobodan Milošević's closest allies until the mid-1990s. It was to Serbia that Iliescu made his first official visit abroad in 1990. Unlike other European states, Romania was reluctant to express any public condemnation of the massive human rights violations with which the UN and other agencies were charging Milošević and his subalterns in the war zone, as they sought to create a Greater Serbia from the ruins of Yugoslavia. Bucharest refrained from severing political and diplomatic ties with Belgrade, and on 5 April 1994 Milošević was able to pay an official visit to Romania. When receiving his guest President Iliescu said: 'Our relations are positive from every point of view.'[54] The attitudes shown at specific moments towards Moscow as well as Belgrade showed how real was the temptation for neo-communist backsliding. In April 1991 evidence that Iliescu was still far from certain whether to align with the West even opportunistically was provided when Romania became the only former Moscow satellite to sign a comprehensive treaty of friendship with the Soviet Union. This gave Moscow an effective veto over any Romanian alliance with a Western country, and if it had not been abrogated by the collapse of the Soviet Union six months later it might have placed Romania more firmly in the Soviet sphere of influence than it had been before 1989. Such flirtations with Russia led Iliescu's political and media opponents to redouble their accusations that his five years as a student in Moscow in the 1950s had left him with deeply ingrained communist habits which made him incapable of bringing Romania into the family of democratic nations.[55] The muted response of the Clinton administration in Washington, which spent much of its first term trying to work out a coherent response to the crisis in Yugoslavia, lessened any inhibitions Iliescu might have had about drawing closer to neo-communist forces at home or abroad. In 1995 there was little adverse reaction in the West to the signing of a protocol with parties that openly promoted dictatorship, a crackdown on minorities, and nostalgia for the communist era. Richard Shifter, the US State Department's co-ordinator of policy for Southeastern Europe, showed little concern about the PUNR's entry into government: 'We have other things to worry about. This is a problem Romania has to sort out itself.'[56] Alfred Moses, appointed US ambassador at the end of 1994, described ultra-nationalism as a peripheral question, and argued that it was not just in Romania that extremists enter government.[57]

Iliescu hoped that Romania could benefit from Western economic and diplomatic support while retaining its freedom to shape its own internal approach to democracy. Breakthroughs started to come early in Iliescu's second term. The restoration of Most Favoured Nation trading status by the US Congress in October 1992 was followed by the signing on 17 November of an association agreement with the EU. These were the first major diplomatic successes obtained by Romania since 1990. A strong effort was put into gaining entry to the Council of Europe (COE) whose Parliamentary Assembly, set up in 1949, is the most widely-based pan-European forum. Admission is an important badge of respectability for post-dictatorial states like Romania, given that the Council's chief aims are to protect human rights and democratic freedoms. Romania was given special guest status in February 1991 after Hungary, Poland and Czechoslovakia had been granted full membership, and it finally gained admission in October 1993. The UDMR opposed entry, arguing that Romania's record towards minorities did not entitle it to a place;[58] Hungary was unenthusiastic, but in the end refrained from using its veto to keep Romania out.

Reservations in the COE about Romania's commitment to its core values persisted. From 1993 to 1997 its *rapporteurs* visited Romania every six months to assess progress in observing human rights. Confidence in the Iliescu regime's handling of the issue was not helped when the operating manuals of the interior ministry's counter-intelligence department, known as UM 0215, were leaked to the press in March 1994. These revealed that it was monitoring the movements of political figures and journalists; also that information about Romanians living, working or studying abroad, about employees of foreign firms in Romania, and about foreign residents was gathered on a routine basis. The interior minister Doru Ioan Tărăcilă was summoned before the relevant parliamentary commission to provide an explanation.[59] But it is more likely that the displeasure shown by Măgureanu's SRI about UM 0215 trying to take over some of its intelligence prerogatives was a more effective curb on its activities. Rivalry among different power centres in the sizeable archipelago that constitutes the Romanian intelligence world has benefited democratic forces, which have received useful information as one agency has sought to checkmate the other. But it is naïve to assume that the successors to the Securitate can be restrained from undermining Romania's fragile institutions simply because of the endemic rivalries between them. The Council of Europe also regularly expressed concern at the highhanded way the Iliescu regime treated elected local government officials. During the President's second term 133 elected mayors, 116 of whom were politically independent or from opposition parties, were dismissed from office.[60] The PDSR government viewed local government as a transmission belt for carrying out the decisions arrived at in Bucharest,[61] and the prefect appointed to each of Romania's forty-one counties closely watched the activities of elected local officials, especially if they were drawn from the opposition.[62] A slight brake on the power of the prefects was introduced in June 1996 when a new law laid down that a mayor could not be dismissed unless a binding legal ruling had been provided by a court.

Within the Council of Europe and also the Organization for Security and Co-operation in Europe (OSCE) Romania and Hungary were at opposite poles in the debate about striking a balance between minority freedoms and internal self-determination; on the one hand and state power and authority on the other.[63] At the March 1992 OSCE conference in Helsinki Adrian Năstăse, then foreign minister, had complained that the OSCE process was onesided in its approach to minority issues and seemed to his government to be concerned only with emphasising the rights of minorities and the obligations of states in which they lived.[64] The Romanian position, as advanced at OSCE and other international gatherings, was to emphasise not so much the state's obligation towards minorities as the responsibility of minorities to respect the territorial unity of the state in which they lived and to be loyal to it. Romanian delegates insisted that minority rights were enshrined in states' own constitutions as well as in international agreements.

The strengthening of Romanian democracy

The Romanian decision to align with mainstream European institutions was of benefit to a fragile democratic process. First, the SRI was placed under parliamentary scrutiny in 1993 when a commission made up of nine members of all parties represented in both houses of Parliament was established to supervise its activities.

Secondly, a vigorous independent press emerged during Iliescu's second term, and harried the government more successfully than the opposition parties seemed able to do. It campaigned against corruption and exposed collusion between leading political figures and the newly-wealthy who had prospered through illegal means. *Ziua* (The Day) relentlessly pursued Iliescu on account of his political career before 1989, his role in the upheaval in December of that year, and the ruthless measures he took to strengthen his grip on power in 1990–1. The most successful newspaper, *Evenimentul Zilei* (News of the Day), acquired a large circulation by mixing a diet of sensationalist news with hardhitting criticism of the Iliescu regime. Its ownership structure made it immune to economic pressure from the government, and its revenue was acquired through circulation rather than advertising. As well as permitting a free press to scrutinise government actions, the regime ended the monopoly of the state television service in electronic broadcasting. Perhaps it assumed that its economic backers, who had obtained their wealth through collusion with some of its chief figures, would dominate private television. This started to happen in the late 1990s with some alarming effects, but stations like the BBC World Service were able to obtain licences. By 1996 fifty-three private TV stations were broadcasting, with the largest reaching 46% of the country and 72% of the urban market.[65]

Non-governmental initiatives from abroad were also important in encouraging citizens to stand up for their rights and create a range of effective voluntary bodies which would strengthen democratic civil society. The Open Society Foundation, brainchild of the billionaire financier George Soros, was particularly active in this and it was careful to concentrate not only on larger projects for democratic enhancement but also on small-scale initiatives. These non-governmental initiatives are often ignored when a balance-sheet of external intervention in post-communist states is being drawn up, but there is no shortage of evidence to suggest that in Romania they may have been crucial in sustaining democratic values in the first half of the 1990s.[66] At that time NGOs played an active role in promoting a free media, monitoring local and then presidential and parliamentary elections in 1992, and encouraging the government to show greater respect for human rights. The Iliescu regime was susceptible to international pressure in these areas, and sensed that it could give ground without undermining the basis of its rule, perhaps assuming that the opposition was in no position to loosen its hold on power.

The factionalism which became a noticeable feature of the regime may also have been healthy for democracy. Perhaps in order to reduce the chances that he would ever suffer the same fate as Ceauşescu, Iliescu created state bodies with near-identical functions which often sought to neutralise each other's effectiveness. This parallelism extended from the two-chamber Parliament to the justice arena and finally to the sprawling intelligence community. But there was also a downside. The untidy distribution of power, particularly in intelligence, left open the possibility that functionaries might abuse their position by attacking opponents of the regime. In March 1995 the weekly *22* revealed that the essayist H. -R. Patapievici, an eloquent critic of the Iliescu regime, had been under surveillance,[67] and it emerged that the operative questioning Patapievici's neighbours about his political beliefs belonged to the Presidential Protection and Guard Service.[68] Another outspoken critic of the Iliescu regime, Ioan Petru Culianu, had died a violent death under mysterious circumstances in Chicago in 1991, and the shortlived Patapievici affair raised uncomfortable echoes.[69]

A similar case which came to light at the same time as Patapievici's had a more satisfactory ending. Mihai Razvan Ungureanu, later a minister of state in the Foreign Ministry in the late 1990s, and then a history lecturer at Iasi University, complained to the parliamentary commission for the oversight of the SRI that he was being harassed by one of its operatives. In contrast to the Interior Ministry which controlled the SPP, the SRI promptly announced on 16 March 1995 that the operative in question had been dismissed.[70]

Normalisation of Romanian-Hungarian relations and Euro-Atlantic integration

By the mid-1990s the Iliescu regime could no longer afford to be linked to unsavoury incidents that might create unwelcome parallels with its internationally reviled predecessor. Opportunities were now opening up to enjoy closer contacts with the West which, as well as raising Romania's profile abroad and winning the regime domestic popularity, might also increase the flow of assistance to a failing economy.

In January 1994, when NATO announced a co-operation prog-ramme with prospective new members called the Partnership for Peace, Romania was actually the first former Soviet bloc state to join. This established a process of reforming the Romanian military and bringing it closer to the model of armies in long-established de-mocracies, Greater civilian control was asserted, several hundred hardline nationalist officers were retired in 1995, and professional competence was given a higher priority than in other parts of the state.[71] In early 1996 invitations were extended to former Warsaw Pact states to join NATO, and Romania applied in April that year. The leading states in NATO appeared to have reached the conclu-sion after the war in the former Yugoslavia that Eastern Europe could not be left in a security vacuum.

There was also growing interest, especially among US officials, in the stability of the former communist states bordering ex-Yugosla-via. A US-inspired bid to end the conflict in Bosnia had culminated in the Dayton Peace Accord of November 1995. The need to isolate nationalist hardliners in Bosnia and promote moderate forces capa-ble of arranging compromises across the various ethnic divides was at the centre of the strategy identified with Richard Holbrooke, a former US assistant secretary of state. The architect of the Dayton Accord realised that the success or failure of the initiative depended in part on efforts to delegitimize conflictual nationalism in South-East Europe. It is probably no coincidence that the criticism made by US Ambassador Moses on 22 February 1996 of the presence of ultra-nationalists in the Romanian government came shortly after a visit to Bucharest by Holbrooke to discuss with Romanian officials the aims behind his Bosnia peace plan.[72]

NATO made it clear that a candidate nation's chances of joining the Western military alliance depended on its performance in de-mocratising its society, reforming its economy, settling differences with adjacent states and restructuring its military in accordance with Western democratic standards. Romania's credentials for NATO membership were weaker than those of most other applicants. Its political rulers may have dropped Marxist-Leninist rhetoric, but they appeared to be settling into an oligarchical form of rule; the transition from communism was proving painful and slow in the economic realm; and, above all, the failure of bilateral treaty negotiations with Hungary, Ukraine and Russia, and the delay in normalising relations with Moldova, suggested to many NATO planners that Romania might be a consumer of security rather than a provider of it.

The need to normalise relations with Hungary was seen as particularly pressing. Both states had applied to join NATO at almost the same time, but NATO was not interested in acquiring new members locked in dispute with their neighbours. Encounters between Romanian and Hungarian state officials in the early 1990s never got beyond deputy foreign minister level. In Bucharest deep resentment was shown when Geza Jeszensky, the Hungarian foreign minister, said in August 1990 that the Romanian government should admit that Romania is a multi-national state. The Romanian foreign minister had described this assertion as 'something that does not correspond to reality but might serve revisionist objectives pursued by the current Hungarian foreign policy *vis-à-vis* Romania'.[73] This broadside was delivered in the same month that the Hungarian prime minister, Joszef Antall, made his controversial statement that 'in spirit' he was the prime minister of 15,000,000 Hungarians throughout the world'.[74] Nevertheless, the seventieth anniversary of the 1920 Trianon peace treaty by which what had been two-thirds of Hungarian territory passed to its neighbours was used in Budapest to show that Hungary had come to terms with its past by firmly rejecting irredentism. All six parties represented in parliament issued a statement, on this occasion expressing support for the 1975 Helsinki Final Act's ban on the unilateral alteration of frontiers by force; the statement declared that the present borders were a component of European stability 'irrespective of being just or unjust'.[75] However, Romania remained unimpressed by such declarations as long as Hungary insisted on its right to speak out on behalf of its co-nationals in Transylvania. The firmly-held Romanian view at that time was that the situation of the Hungarian minority in Romania was a purely internal matter and could not be subject to discussion between Romanians and Hungarians.[76]

Eventually negotiations for a bilateral treaty with Romania were re-started by the left-of-centre government of Gyula Horn, elected to office in 1994. The significance both parties attributed to the treatment of minorities and to guaranteeing the status of the border between the two countries had long delayed progress. Romania insisted that any treaty must contain a clause whereby Hungary ruled out any peaceful revision of the frontier, but Budapest, while ruling out any forcible border changes, refused to agree to this for as long as it felt that the Hungarian minority in Romania suffered from a lack of civil rights.[77] In the summer of 1996 an unexpected breakthrough occurred after the Horn government rashly endorsed a declaration at a Budapest summit of Hungarian minorities that the survival of Hungarian communities outside the state could only be assured by autonomy and self-government.[78] There was a hostile reaction from US officials, and suddenly Hungary's admission in the first wave of NATO expansion did not appear so certain after all. A nervous Horn government, which had said earlier that it saw no point in resuming treaty negotiations till after the November elections in Romania, made a *volte face* and asked for them to be resumed on 11 August 1996. Three days later it was announced that the text of a bilateral treaty was practically finalised and would be ready for signing in mid-September.[79] Compromise was reached on the Council of Europe Recommendation 1201 on minorities which Romania had refused to incorporate in the text of a bilateral treaty since this might have been seen as giving approval to the idea of political autonomy for minorities. Bucharest withdrew its objections as long as it was made clear that the joint interpretation of 1201 should neither refer to collective rights, nor force the two sides to grant any autonomy statute on ethnic grounds.[80]

Nationalists rebel as social hardships increase

The prize of being inside the Western military umbrella, seen against the alternative of isolation, concentrated the minds of two intractable neighbours who had hitherto been unable to reconcile their differences. Although arguably Hungary made more concessions than Romania to secure a bilateral treaty, the document was strongly attacked by Gheorghe Funar, the PUNR leader. He charged Iliescu with 'jeopardising the future of the Romanian people and the national unitary state and its territorial integrity' and demanded his suspension from office.[81] The PUNR was ejected from government on

2 September;—Iliescu must have became aware that his own image could be only harmed by an alliance with this party. The PRM had already been ejected from the coalition a year earlier. As for Vadim, he had been unhappy with the PRM being offered only three state secretaryships and one post of prefect.[82] Relations were inflamed with the release in September 1995 of volume 5 of an official history of the Securitate, which contained documentary evidence suggesting that in the late 1980s Vadim was urging 'the competent authorities' to step up their campaign against Radio Free Europe and involve him and his close ally Eugen Barbu in it. This followed leaks to the press, widely believed to have come from Măgureanu (with Iliescu's approval), accusing Vadim of having been a Securitate informer.[83] It was not long before Vadim counter-attacked. In an October edition of *România Mare*, under the pseudonym 'Alcibiade' which he regularly used in his contributions, he accused Iliescu of having assassinated Ceauşescu in cold blood, of having gypsy origins which he was unable to conceal, and of having sold out to the Jews. Stung by these allegations, the PDSR withdrew from its alliance with the PRM on 19 October 1995.[84] Indeed it is hard to see how the alliance with extremists benefited Iliescu's political career or his long-term reputation. Without it the Văcăroiu government would probably have been defeated in parliament long before 1996, followed by early elections, and if these had been won by the opposition it is likely that President Iliescu would have benefited from the unpopular measures a weak opposition government would have had to take. If no party had had an overall majority, he might have been able to entice part of the opposition to coalesce with the PDSR. As it was, an alliance with extremists damaged the President's international standing and prolonged the life of a failing government which gravely harmed Iliescu's popularity at home. Iliescu received little credit abroad for a bilateral treaty viewed as long overdue, and delayed because of his willingness to ally publicly with local ultra-nationalists. A pre-election spending drive in which wages were allowed to outstrip inflation brought the government into conflict with the IMF. In the absence of structural reforms, international creditors were unwilling to provide large amounts of funding to cover the gap between domestic production and consumption. But it was attempts to manipulate the foreign exchange market on

behalf of its favoured supporters that resulted in June 1996, in the IMF withholding a final tranche of a stand-by agreement signed in 1994.

The Iliescu regime's increasingly pro-Western orientation matched the popular mood, as polling surveys indicated, but it failed to recover popularity among a population weighed down by mounting hardships. The average monthly salary in early 1996 was US $110, the second lowest in the region. The majority of the population spent 60% of their income on food, the price of many basic commodities, above all foodstuffs, equalling or exceeding prices in Western Europe. Malnutrition and inadequate heating led to an explosion in the incidence of tuberculosis, which was reported in 1996 to be ten times higher than the European average and approaching Third World levels.[85] Romanians had also emerged from an unusually severe winter in which millions of people had suffered owing to a breakdown in energy supplies widely blamed on state inefficiency.[86] By 1996 there was little left of Iliescu's reputation as a leader able to protect his ordinary supporters from the rigours of moving to a semi-competitive economy.

The taint of corruption

In 1993 the government had responded in an incredibly relaxed manner to the rise of a pyramid-savings operation called Caritas, which enabled investors to obtain an eightfold return on their money within three months. An estimated 3–4 million Romanians—a fifth of the adult population—enrolled in the scheme, parting with around $1 billion—equivalent to half of all state spending in 1993. The lack of attractive investment rates from the banks and the ravages of inflation, which had reached 314% for the first nine months of 1993, meant that there was a huge amount of personal capital looking for a quick return. The PDSR's awkward political ally, the PUNR, had thrown its weight behind the Caritas venture—which was based in Cluj, the stronghold of its leader Gheorghe Funar. The amount of revenue flowing into the city's coffers as a result of Caritas's success gave Funar access to funds which counterparts in other cities lacked. Iosif Boda wrote to Iliescu in 1994 after the Caritas scheme crashed: 'I think you must politically decapitate Funar.'[87] But the response of the state authorities to the affair was confused. Romania had no legislation to protect consumers, or indeed the state itself, from a scheme into which hopeful investors had channelled a large part of the country's liquid assets before Caritas started to default on repayments in October 1993. Government inaction reinforced the image of Romania as 'a soft state' whose leading officials had only the shakiest grasp of long-term planning or crisis management.

In a land of low expectation the failure of many small investors to recoup their winnings when Caritas ran out of funds did not result in widely-predicted violence. It might at least have been expected to destroy the reputation of Funar and open the eyes of most supporters of the PUNR to the fact that the party was engaged in dubious economic practices while sheltering behind the cloak of nationalism. But many citizens were prepared to judge him not on his record as an economic housekeeper but on his ability to satisfy the collective emotional needs of a large swathe of the population susceptible to nationalist appeals. The Romanian press criticised Caritas for offering poorly-educated citizens the prospect of wealth without working for it, reinforcing a sense of personal dependence and sapping individual initiative. But those press outlets which saw Caritas as an irrational phenomenon soon became scapegoats, at least in nationalist eyes, blamed for the shortcomings of a scheme which, in order to remain feasible, needed to attract investors at a rate that could not be sustained by the adult Romanian population.

Nevertheless, much of the press continued to publish serious allegations about the exchange of favours, deception, fraud and outright theft by business figures seen as connected to the PDSR. The abandonment of a number of Romanian merchant ships and their crews in foreign ports during 1995 was widely publicised. The fleet had been privatised and sold off in controversial circumstances some years earlier, and it later emerged that the companies running the ships had obtained a loan of $118 million from Bancorex to carry our necessary repairs. In 2000 Traian Băsescu, then minister of transport, claimed that the shipowners had abandoned the ships rather than do the repairs, and pocketed the loan. He named as accessories individuals holding senior positions in the local administration of the port of Constanta.[88] The collapse in February 1996 of the Banca Dacia Felix, post-1989 Romania's first private bank, was particularly damaging to the government. It had huge debt, and tens of thousands of savers lost their deposits. Its co-founder Sever Muresan, a tennis star of the 1970s, who was allowed by the Ceauşescu regime to settle in France and return to Romania annually.[89] When it emerged that Ioan Sima, another co-founder, had been placed on the state payroll as an inspector in Transylvania after being banned from holding another banking sector position, and that his co-director had been sent to Atlanta to represent Romania at the Olympic Games, it appeared beyond dispute that the regime was more interested in defending *nouveaux riches* who had fallen on hard times than ordinary citizens.[90]

Boda warned the President in a letter eighteen months after his re-election of the 'increase in numbers of those who believe you are guilty for "covering up" large-scale corruption', and that 'the Văcăroiu government has the image of one implicated in large-scale corruption. The truth of the matter doesn't count. It is the perception that exists in the public mind.'[91] Boda was far from being alone in pointing out the tendency of PDSR notables to be surrounded by bodyguards and to drive around in motorcades with sirens blaring and other traffic often forced to move out of the way.[92] It all had an alienating effect as did the decision, as local elections approached, to stage a number of stunts involving well-known Romanian sporting personalities. A lavish state wedding was organized for the Olympic champion gymnast, Nadia Comaneci, in April 1996. The occasion, attended by 700 guests mainly drawn from the new élite, was financed by the Paunescu brothers (see above, page 118), who were then at the pinnacle of Romania's new economic oligarchy.[93] The other big name promoted by the PDSR was the former international tennis star Ilie Năstase, who agreed to run for mayor of Bucharest on the party ticket. The President described Comaneci and Năstase as 'the most important Romanians of the last fifty years'. Năstase had no obvious qualifications to be mayor and it looked as if the ruling élite was testing Silviu Brucan's thesis about the Romanians being 'a stupid' people reconciled to hardship and ill-luck almost to destruction.

Filip Antonio, wrote in *România líbera* in 1996: 'The ruling party knows that after fifty years of communism, and by having a quasi-monopoly of national television, it can afford to fool that part of the electorate that makes no effort to think.'[94] Perhaps the clearest example of the depth of the PDSR's contempt had for many of its own supporters was its appointment as health minister, in 1992, of Iulian Mincu who had been a personal physician of Ceauşescu and closely linked to pre-1989 plans to reduce the food intake of the population, especially the elderly.[95] Under Mincu Romania's health care system declined further as resources were used in ways which failed to benefit citizens facing increasing levels of ill-health and a declining life-expectancy. Cornel Nistorescu, writing after the PDSR's ejection from office, pinpointed the arrogance bred by power in a hardhitting observation:

The other day, I happened to see a villa belonging to another member of the Văcăroiu cabinet. Another caricature of a villa, built to match the principles of a thick-skinned person. And probably built with construction materials gathered by the family over the years and paid for with money coming from the monthly salary. And when you think of all the villas erected by the big guns over the last seven years, it is not the bad taste that strikes you most, but the fact that all the clients of those in power talked pompously about the country and democracy, but cared for none but themselves. They desperately fought to gather fortunes and gave Romanians nothing but flavoured doughnuts.[96]

Electoral defeat

The derelict appearance of much of Bucharest revealed a capital starved of funds by the state. An incompetent mayor from the opposition ran the city from 1992 to 1996, but many *Bucuresteni* blamed the government (which had withheld funds from cities with opposition mayors) for its plight—a sign of growing political sophistication. Năstase, the sporting legend, was rejected in the local elections by Bucharest voters, who voted overwhelmingly in favour of an austere and uncharismatic lawyer, Victor Ciorbea. Attempts to present Năstase as a dynamic outsider capable of tackling corruption were unavailing as the press revealed the extent of his own business interests in Romania. The PDSR—which, as the FSN and FDSN) had done well in the capital in 1990 and 1992—was left with only 16% of Bucharest's council seats. The result was a damning verdict on the Văcăroiu government. The elderly and poor—normally the backbone of the PDSR—abstained from the poll in large numbers, having been worst hit by the collapse in energy supplies the previous winter. The PDSR had hoped that the voters would punish the opposition parties who had run most big Romanian cities since 1992 without conspicuous success. However, many voters blamed the government for starving them of funds. Only in the countryside, where voters usually rely on the political news put out by state television, did the PDSR retain a sizeable part of its former vote. The PDSR only won a single city, Galaţi, and in the vote for county councils the CDR scored higher (17.8%) than the PDSR (16.9%). But the turnout had only been 56.47%, and the voting for local mayoral and district and county council elections produced different results for the two main rivals which suggested that the outcome of the more crucial elections due in the autumn was really anyone's guess.[97] One sign of PDSR nervousness was the decision not to raise the threshold of votes for entry into Parliament from 3 to 5% (as earlier intended). This was a sign that the PDSR still felt dependent on the ultra-nationalist parties (none of which was likely to poll more than 5% given their poor showing in the local elections).

The PDSR's aggressive and negative campaigning intensified speculation that it was prepared to commit electoral fraud in order to overturn the electorate's verdict on its years of power, and the November 1946 elections, stolen by the communists exactly fifty years earlier, were frequently invoked as a model. Several charges were made. The League for the Defence of Human Rights (LADO) and Pro-Democracy, the two long-established electoral monitoring bodies, expressed fears that PDSR members had been placed in charge of many voting districts which gave them the final say in deciding election results. There was also concern about the sudden emergence of 'phantom' monitoring organizations, which had obtained most of the places available to monitors in districts where the PDSR's popularity was in decline. There was even disagreement about the size of the electorate: figures ranging from 15 to 17 million people had been published. Finally, the PDSR's method of conducting opinion polls produced enormous controversy: under the guise of conducting polls, party employees reportedly telephoned several hundred thousand voters and while quizzing them propagated negative views about the opposition.[98] Reports appeared in the media that the PDSR had planned to steal the election through computer fraud and that the stratagem had been foiled thanks to the intervention of Măgureanu.[99] The veteran political commentator Şerban Orescu has commented that Măgureanu, who had obtained his doctorate in communist times on the subject of manipulating the masses via the media, was an expert in guiding public opinion, and this story may well have been disseminated in order to strengthen the SRI boss's position at a time of unpredictable political change.

Iosif Boda in his memoir of the years when he worked for Iliescu, has described how previously close sustainers of the President were growing disillusioned by his uninspiring approach to government as his second term neared its end, and Măgureanu's criticism of Iliescu not long after his defeat suggests that he was one of them. In 1994 he was behind the setting up of the New Romania Party, for which the front man was Ovidiu Trāsnea, reputed to be the supervisor of Măgureanu's doctorate.[100] This party was widely seen as an insurance policy for Măgureanu in case his position at the head of SRI became untenable.

Such manoeuvres indicated clearly that the PDSR was becoming factionalised and fragmented, with Iliescu unable to provide any clear direction. In order to collect the 100,000 signatures needed to nominate him for the Presidency, his supporters (in this case county prefects) had to pressurise state employees in bodies like RENEL to back his nomination.[101] There had even been rumours that Iliescu might run for re-election independently of the PDSR, but on 29 August 1996 he finally accepted the nomination as its official candidate. At the same time he insisted that the PDSR nominate better-quality parliamentary candidates than before—ones who were 'incorruptible, energetic…and able to speak at least one foreign language'.[102] This was a poor reflection on the current state of the parliamentary party. However, the President did not veto a single candidate, and the big PDSR personalities, against whom there were specific allegations of corruption, remained high on the lists as candidates. The press alleged that leading PDSR barons, like Vasile Văcaru, had gathered dossiers on their rivals (he was head of the parliamentary committee on the security services) which, by means of virtual blackmail, made them irremovable.[103] Certainly for Iliescu to allow his party to go into the campaign in such a disorganized fashion showed extraordinary complacency. Many in the press and opposition parties insisted that his candidacy was invalid because Article 81 of the Constitution bars a person from seeking more than two terms in office. He contended that his first term in 1990–2 should not be taken into consideration since it began before the adoption of the new Constitution in 1991. The Constitutional Court ruled on 9 September that Iliescu's candidacy should stand, but it is a body over whose composition the President had exercised considerable influence.[104] The opposition depicted Iliescu as someone with authoritarian instincts who had been unwilling to sever ties with Russia, when it was still communist, in 1990–1. The accusations degenerated into racist abuse, as when the newspaper *Ziua*, echoing Vadim, claimed that Iliescu was of Russian Gypsy origin (a family history allegedly supporting such a claim being published in its 28 October issue).

The PDSR fought a bad-tempered and unimaginative campaign. It revived claims that the CDR would restore the monarchy and landlords, and sell Transylvania to Hungary.[105] Ion Cristoiu believed that the PDSR's approach could be summed up as 'Yes, we are swine, but those in the opposition who want to take over are even bigger swine.'[106] This tactic flopped, according to Cristoiu, because voters had grown more sophisticated and were at last starting to think for themselves. Certainly his hard-hitting and irreverent newspaper *Evenimentul Zilei* had raised public awareness about the misdeeds of the powerful. The PDSR's Gheorghe Dumitrascu complained bitterly in the Senate on 6 November that the party had made a big mistake in allowing the press to develop freely[107]—thus echoing Adrian Năstase's earlier criticism of the press and independent television, including the BBC World Service, an indication of how uncomfortable the PDSR was with the existence of media freedom. On the campaign trail Iliescu received a hostile or lukewarm reception in places where he had been acclaimed in the early 1990s. In Craiova, often seen as one of Romania's 'red towns', he was booed by several hundred people and had to leave the city's theatre by a side entrance. His record was no longer that of a man who upheld social justice and shielded the people from the harshest winds of economic change, but of an out-of-touch leader under whom an unproductive and corrupt ruling class had shot up. The Dacia Felix bank collapse, the Caritas scandal of 1993–4 when the state stood immobile as millions ploughed their savings into a fraud-ulent pyramid banking game, and the prospect of another harsh winter in which the state was no better equipped than last time to maintain heating and light, left him vulnerable to opposition attacks. Petrol shortages and the explosion of food prices were difficult to explain, but they became impossible to justify in the eyes of former PDSR voters who saw *nouveaux riches* and 'mafia' elements avoiding daily hardships because they enjoyed the protection of powerful politicians or compromised judges—protection that Iliescu had promised in 1990 would be the right of every hard-working citizen.

Anatomy of Romania's 1996 electoral shift

On a sunny 3 November 76.0% of Romanian voters cast their bal-lots—a very high turnout by East European standards, and the results showed a radically altered political landscape. Iliescu was ahead on 32.25% of the vote, but Emil Constantinescu was close behind on 28.21%. The CDR leader could rely on the support of the PD-led electoral alliance, the Social Democratic Union (Uniunea Social Democrata: USD) whose leader Petre Roman had obtained 20.54% of the presidential vote, and the UDMR. However, what under-mined Iliescu's chances in the second round on 17 November was his poor relationship with the nationalist bloc.

The results of the parliamentary elections were even more disap-pointing for the government. The CDR and USD had a small par-liamentary majority, which became a safer one when the UDMR was added. The PDSR had lost one-third of its support, its vote in the lower house falling to 21.52%. The fall might have been steeper but for widely-reported incidents of alleged fraud: in Braila 15% of the electorate voted on the 'special list', open to those away from their place of residence, and around 16% of the vote in this county was annulled. In some counties there was a big discrepancy in the vote parties received for the two houses of Parliament. In Arges it is hard to understand how the PRM could have received 19,000 votes for the Senate but 28,899 for the Chamber of Deputies, the PDSR 83,000 for the Senate but 105,800 for the Chamber of Deputies, other than through fraud.[108]

A breakdown of the results by IRSOP (Institute for Researching Romanian Public Opinion) showed that the PDSR had lost because of a switch of allegiances among social groups that had been a key to its electoral success in the early 1990s; among workers the most numerous social category, the PDSR, slumped to 21% (its decline in the south-western city of Resita, where the Văcăroiu government in 1994 had ignored mass protests against the misconduct of factory managers and the local administration, was emblematic). From urban voters, the PDSR only obtained 16%: maladministration and corruption were hard to disguise in the cities, above all in Bucharest where the PDSR was left with only 5 of 29 lower house seats.[109] The PDSR lost much support in former strongholds around Bucharest, such as Prahova and Dimbovita, and in the cities of Moldavia, places where the private media had sparked the growth of informed public opinion that could not easily be manipulated by the state. In western counties from Satu Mare to Timiş the PDSR's decline accelerated; these *judets* were open to external influence, and the official ending of the quarrel with Hungary allowed 'ethnic' issues to be drowned out by 'normal' ones in the electoral contest. This was also true in Transylvania where in most counties the USD overtook the PDSR. Gheorghe Tinca, the minister of defence, was rejected by the voters of Cluj, a final verdict on the PDSR's strategy of concealing a poor record by promoting personalities. Only in isolated rural areas of the east and south, small industrial towns dependent on a single employer, and provincial towns dependent on state television for political views, did the PDSR vote remain firm. Danut Dudu, writing in *Monitorul*, argued that poorly educated voters thought it better to live in poverty than risking the danger of civil war (a possible outcome of a CDR victory according to some in the PDSR). Ironically the regions of the east and the south, where such views were prevalent, had few minorities and had not witnessed street upheavals in December 1989. But people in isolated parts of Moldavia and Wallachia feared change and displayed a natural conservatism.[110]

President Iliescu entered the decisive second round with a flimsy electoral base. Except for the PSM and his own party, no other party backed his candidacy. He claimed that it would be possible for him to co-operate with an opposition-controlled parliament and government, but his behaviour in the days after 3 November suggested otherwise. Speaking in Alba Iulia on 9 November, he stoked nationalist feelings and warned of the danger that the UDMR could pose to national security.[111] His supporters also claimed that an attempt was being made to overthrow the leadership of the Orthodox Church, with the involvement of the opposition. The priest Simeon Tatu, a PDSR deputy, raised the charge probably in a bid to halt the swing to the CDR by Orthodox worshippers.[112] But it was clear when the second round results emerged, that appeals to religious and national sentiment by the PDSR, had no impact. In 1996 it was far less easy to trick Romanian voters by rumours or diversions than it had been in 1990–2. A humbled Ion Iliescu conceded defeat when it was clear that he was unlikely to get more than 45% of the vote. He did not return to Cotroceni; his new role in politics was as the PDSR senator for Bucharest.

Iliescu's provocative statements about the UDMR showed that he was not a point of balance in inter-ethnic relations as he had always contended. He made them at a time when he was under no pressure from ultra-nationalist parties, which had toned down their chauvinist rhetoric, aware of how unpopular it had become with even some of their supporters. As for the UDMR, it had adopted as its presidential candidate its most moderate and fluent parliamentarian, Gyorgy Frunda, who improved the UDMR's image for many Romanian voters. Iliescu had demonstrated how out-of-touch he had been with public opinion by his own excursion into the deep waters of nationalism. But at least he retired with a degree of grace once his fate at the hands of the voters had become clear; if the transfer of power had been disputed, it would have cast a dark shadow over Romanian democracy. As leader of the opposition in the Senate, the ex-President would now have to show if he was capable of a more constructive approach to inter-ethnic relations than he had shown in the final stages of the election campaign.

5

'IN OFFICE BUT NOT IN POWER'
CONSTANTINESCU'S HONEYMOON, 1996–1998

The CDR makes itself electable

One of the new President's advisers has related that on their first day in the Cotroceni presidential palace after it had been vacated by Ion Iliescu the staff 'breathed hostility' towards Constantinescu and his team.[1] Perhaps they expected to be promptly dismissed, which was normal practice in Romania when there was a change of power at the top.[2] Certainly their demeanour indicated that the victory of the opposition had been totally unexpected. The triumph was also a surprise to those in the Romanian Democratic Convention (CDR), who had previously assumed that the Iliescu regime would hang on to power having ensured by underhand means that a peaceful alternation in office would be difficult. The reputation of the CDR had slowly improved in the eyes of the electorate, and by 1996 Romanian democracy was sufficiently strong for its collective will to count.

Although the CDR was an umbrella which contained eighteen organizations, the PNTCD was indisputably in command. The CDR had a coherent and unified message, shaped around clear ideas: the right to property, anti-communism, moral probity, honesty and steadfastness were continually emphasised.[3] A solid bloc of voters, albeit still in a clear minority, was motivated by such a moral agenda, and the PNTCD's image of rock-like incorruptibility seemed to provide a convincing foundation for it. Opposition from millions of citizens who felt that they were beneficiaries of the enforced egalitarianism of the communist era had declined in intensity. Workers who had protested in the 1990 elections against the opposition parties had subsequently become disappointed with the Iliescu regime, and at least in the cities previously loyal voters were beginning to

142

scrutinise its record far more sceptically than before. The 'Contract with Romania' at the centre of the CDR's electoral manifesto, which promised that definite steps would be taken within a 200-day period to improve the lives of different categories of citizens, undoubtedly went down well. It raised expectations and changed the view that the CDR, if elected, would rule on behalf of revenge-seeking and frustrated citizens intent on turning the clock back to 1945. The promise that 15,000 'specialists', whose talents had been ignored by the PDSR, would be drafted into key posts to start a process of national recovery, above all in the economy, proved an exciting image, particularly for the young. It was an effective campaigning slogan for Emil Constantinescu whose stature had grown since his inauspicious political début in 1992. Four years later he was a familiar figure, increasingly trusted for his perseverance, approachability, and awareness of the realities of life in Romania. He came from a village in Arges county, in the Carpathian foothills, which had been the scene of long-drawn-out opposition to the communists in the 1950s. His entry into political life came through the Civic Alliance, a body that galvanised pro-democracy forces in the first half of the 1990s. From 1992 he had been the political apprentice of Corneliu Coposu, who felt that a non-party figure stood the best chance of dislodging Iliescu. By encouraging him to move from the university world to that of politics, Corneliu Coposu appeared to have done a great service to the country.

Internationally events appeared to favour a change of government in Romania. Belated but decisive American intervention to end the war in Bosnia in 1995 was a setback from which the Yugoslav national-communist regime of Slobodan Milošević (with whom Ion Iliescu had maintained a discrete alliance) would never recover. Due to increasing Western involvement in South-Eastern Europe, power appeared to be swinging away from ruling ex-communists in a changing geopolitical environment. But one should not be misled by the scale of Constantinescu's victory; in fact power was lost by the PDSR rather than decisively gained by the opposition.[4] Complacency, growing remoteness from the population and a series of major policy failures and tactical blunders marked Iliescu's second period in office. As well as forfeiting the backing of his powerful domestic intelligence chief, Virgil Măgureanu, he lost the committed support of several capitalists who had previously acquired wealth by exploiting their connections with his regime.

George Păunescu, one of the most controversial members of Romania's new moneyed class, helped to finance Emil Constantinescu's presidential bid, according to one Constantinescu ally who later broke with him. On 10 August 1996 Valerian Stan, Constantinescu's campaign manager, claimed that he was sufficiently alarmed to demand an explanation from his chief political advisers. Costin Georgescu, later Măgureanu's successor as head of the SRI, admitted that an overture had been made to Păunescu, although a donation offered by a company linked to Sever Muresan, implicated in the Dacia Felix scandal, had been rejected. Alarmed that an unacceptable compromise had been made with forces whose wealth was evidence that Romania had taken a wrong turning after 1989, Stan resigned as Constantinescu's campaign manager.[5]

The coalition takes shape

In full public view the CDR had already made a dramatic compromise with the Democratic Party (PD), which was drawn largely from youthful members of the former *nomenklatura* who had been receptive to the winds of change blowing from Gorbachev's Russia in the 1980s. Several leading lights of the PD had been among the most implacable opponents of the CDR parties in 1990, but in 1996 it was clear to both the CDR and the PD that neither could hope to gain a hold on power without putting aside past enmities. It is likely that the willingness of the two to cooperate enabled the PNTCD, especially, to present a more reassuring image to moderate left voters, but—as the Bucharest press noted in the post-electoral period—the tensions between the PD and the PNTCD could barely be covered up as they strove to put together a workable coalition. Indeed, it would have been extraordinary if Petre Roman had not felt profound frustration at being driven into third place by Constantinescu, a man with no experience of government. The elders in the PNTCD who made a fetish of their victimisation under communism muttered publicly about having to cohabit with former communists.[6] Shrewdly the PD chose six ministries which would not be directly involved with unpopular economic measures. Roman himself remained outside the government, choosing to become president of the Senate. The new government also included representatives of the Hungarian minority. Some PNTCD notables felt that this was a premature decision for which the Romanian public had not been adequately prepared,[7] but no popular outcry resulted and for the next four years the UDMR would usually be the least disruptive member of the four party coalition, which also involved the PNL (the Liberal junior partners of the PNTCD in the CDR).[8]

The CDR contingent filled nearly two-thirds of the parliamentary seats belonging to the coalition, and most of them belonged to the PNTCD. It was therefore Coposu's party that effectively had the right to nominate the prime minister, but there was no obvious candidate for this exacting position. Although Coposu had devolved power to the local branches, it had not resulted in the swift rise of talented people fit for heavy government responsibilities. Instead there was evidence in a number of counties that control was concentrated in the hands of small cliques who did not see their primary goal as encouraging public-spirited and competent people to ascend quickly in the party. But even if there had been a clear choice of candidates to head the government, the President would almost certainly have made his own choice either from inside or from outside the party. His choice created no strong dissension inside the PNTCD, but for many it still came as a surprise.

Ciorbea and Constantinescu

Victor Ciorbea had only been a member of the CDR since 1994. But his victory in the Bucharest mayoral election of 1996, the party's first real election victory, was a crucial point in his favour. He was forty-two years old, and originated from the commune of Pocor, which according to 1997 World Bank statistics was the poorest district in Alba county.[9] He obtained a law degree from Cluj and later a doctorate from Bucharest University. Here was a sign of the upward mobility that had existed under communism—it is difficult to imagine someone from the same disadvantaged background hoping to rise in the same way during the 1990s when educational and career opportunities for bright young people from a poor rural background effectively vanished.

Before 1989 Ciorbea had worked in the highly politicised field of justice as a judge and a prosecutor. But no evidence has emerged to suggest that he had abused his position or collaborated with the communist authorities beyond what was normally expected of someone in his position. In 1990 he had stood as a candidate in Alba for the Democratic Party of Workers, one of many satellite parties then formed by the FSN, and for the next few years he played a prominent role in trade union affairs, a diversion from his previous career path. From 1990 to 1993 he was President of the National Confederation of Romanian Free Trade Unions (CNSRL), which was then see by the independent press as pro-communist.[10] By contrast its chief rival, Fratia, headed by the lorry-drivers chief Miron Mitrea, was a favourite of the CDR and frequently invited to public meetings at the headquarters of the Group for Social Dialogue. Ciorbea has claimed that he actually succeeded in removing a lot of communist-minded officials from key positions in the CNSRL, turning it instead into a trade union recognisable as such to anyone in the West (and foiling an attempt by Iliescu to create a tame trade union body).[11]

The CNSRL and Fratia merged in 1993. The previous year, both Ciorbea and Mitrea had been on the electoral list of the Convention of Social Solidarity, founded by Claudiu Iordache who had become a FSN dissident because, among other reasons, he believed that Iliescu's party was turning its back on ordinary Romanians. But in 1994 Ciorbea lost out to Mitrea in a power struggle to control the union federation. He then founded the Democratic Confederation of Free Trade Unionists and threw in his lot with the CDR (while Mitrea was enticed to join the PDSR, where he made a swift rise). A coldly realistic view would be that Ciorbea joined the CDR on the rebound because previous failures meant he had nowhere else to go. But it could be argued that like many other Romanians he had been on a voyage of political discovery since 1990. Once in the CDR, he had no difficulty in articulating the core aspirations of the opposition alliance. The CDR had little presence in the trade union world and Ciorbea undoubtedly was a significant catch. But the authority of the President and of some PNTCD elders was bound to be increased by the appointment of an inexperienced premier like Ciorbea with no support-base inside the PNTCD. Ciorbea has indeed characterised his role during his sixteen-month premiership as being that of 'a moderator' rather than an active decision-maker.[12]

In November 1996 he does not appear to have imposed conditions which would have increased his freedom of action, and he would later concede that he had been wrong to cease being mayor of Bucharest and accept office on such a precarious basis.[13]

By appointing an unblemished outsider as head of government, Constantinescu was sidestepping the political parties, which remained among the most unpopular institutions in public life, and thereby boosting his own authority. But the President himself was in many ways unprepared for the awesome responsibilities that had fallen on his shoulders. Emil Constantinescu was a geologist whose parents were professional people who had risen from a peasant background during the last decades of the monarchy. His roots were mainly in Oltenia and 'before 1989—like millions of Romanians— he had been a communist party member', holding routine party posts at faculty level, 'one of those "passive" party members who neither resisted nor served the regime with enthusiasm'.[14] As rector of Bucharest University from 1990 to 1992 he defended his students, notably during the 1990 *mineriada*.[15] Constantinescu had not been active in politics during those years, perhaps a bonus given the unpopularity of the opposition parties at that time; Instead he had been active in the Civic Alliance (AC), the most visible civic group aligned with the movement for greater democracy. Ana Blandiana, the poet who was the AC's guiding figure, acted as a champion of Constantinescu, and her support, along with that of Coposu, had enabled him to emerge as the electoral standard-bearer of the CDR.[16] Unattached to any of the CDR's parties, he was promoted in its electoral propaganda as a symbol of unity.

However, he came to office without ever having performed any major executive role,[17] and such a President would need talented and watchful advisers. Zoe Petre, his chief of staff between 1996 and 2000, will be a contested figure long into the future. By appointing a woman as his second-in-command, the President was challenging deep-seated Romanian prejudices which had prevented women from playing an active role in public life except in distorted conditions, such as those existing when the Ceauşescus were a dyarchy of power. *România Mare* effectively lampooned the President by suggesting in its cartoons that he was the tool of this masterful lady; indeed, on television she usually appeared more decisive and lucid than her boss. Yet Zoe Petre had shown considerable determination in sustaining Constantinescu's candidacy in 1992 and 1996 when his chances of success had not appeared great, and in 1997 she got her reward, being singled out as one of the few intellectuals who had adopted a disciplined and long-term strategy to try to bring about overdue change in the country.[18]

Reconciliation is the watchword

On 19 November 1998 Emil Constantinescu was reported as saying that one of the biggest mistakes of his administration was that after its electoral victory it failed to reveal the inheritance of its predecessor.[19] If the mistakes of the Iliescu regime had been delineated, Ciorbea and his backers in Cotroceni might have been more realistic about their chances of turning the situation around, at least in the short term. Perhaps an early admission to the Romanian public that the road to recovery would be long and that considerable hardship was unavoidable might have cleared the air and shielded the government from much recrimination later. He faced a difficult choice during the first days of his mandate when PDSR notables arrived at Cotroceni to inform him that the state of the public finances was much worse than official figures suggested. This meant that public officials could not be paid in December 1996 unless the incoming government borrowed further, and Constantinescu reluctantly asked for a parliamentary ordinance to be drawn up to that effect.[20] With the hold on power of a multicolour coalition none too secure, there would have been risks in mounting an offensive against the vanquished regime and its luminaries. Constantinescu, was probably wise to resist any temptation to open criminal investigations against Iliescu for his role in the events of December 1989 and the subsequent miners' incursions in 1990 and 1991. Such a course would have been perilous since Petre Roman and some in the PD had been close to the heart of power at this time.

The President was quick to lower expectations among his own supporters about any restoration of the monarchy. A Romanian passport and eventually some of his property were restored to ex-King Mihai, who in the late 1990s refamiliarised himself with a country he had been forced to leave in 1947. The ex-king also acted as an effective ambassador for Romania in 1997 during the drive for

NATO entry, but in January 1998 Constantinescu stated unambiguously that there would be no referendum on the monarchy for as long as he was President.[21] He also made an early retreat from the position, strongly adhered to by the CDR, that former members of the communist *nomenklatura* should not hold important positions in public life while democracy was being consolidated. This was point 8 of the 1990 Timişoara Declaration;—which Constantinescu, speaking in that city seven years later, effectively repudiated. He argued instead that the criterion for holding public office should not be a communist or non-communist biography but a person's ability to carry out vital responsibilities.[22] On 15 November 1997, when he argued that Article 8 of the Timişoara Declaration was 'no longer applicable', it brought harsh criticism from Constantin (Ticu) Dumitrescu, head of the Association of Former Political Prisoners (AFDPR) and a CDR parliamentarian.[23] However, the President was in tune with the national mood, and his pragmatic approach to this sensitive question probably reflected majority opinion within parties officially linked to the CDR. But evidence has been presented to suggest that even before the election he was willing to be especially conciliatory to the great bulk of those who had been involved in the Securitate before 1989. Şerban Orescu, in a critique of his presidency, recalled an interview which Constatinescu gave to Emil Hurezeanu at Radio Free Europe in 1994 in which, from memory, the future President is claimed to have said: 'If the Democratic Convention comes to power, then it is going to consider those who worked for the former Securitate as ones who did nothing other than their duty under the old regime, and who defended the interests of the state... even a regime like the Democratic Convention is going to take this into account and, as such, is not going to change anything in their activity!'

Hurezeanu, one of the doyens of Romanian journalism after 1989, removed this passage from the broadcast version of the interview, thinking he was thereby assisting Constantinescu. Two days later an irritated Constantinescu phoned, asking 'Why did you cut out that passage?' He was told, 'Mr Professor, I thought I was doing you a favour by deleting it.' 'No, on the contrary, you did me no favour', Constantinescu replied.[24] Emil Constantinescu may have concluded that he and the CDR only had a chance of coming to power if a public statement was made that they should not be seen as deadly enemies of the network of interests making up the old Securitate. In the capitalist West it was not unknown for parties of the left to make such public declarations where vested interests opposed to a transfer of power to avowed socialists are entrenched in the state. But the new President had opportunities to place the sprawling intelligence community under greater democratic accountability, but he was slow to take them up. The Supreme Council of National Defence (CSAT), the only body to coordinate the activities of the nine state intelligence agencies in Romania, was left unaltered. Chaired by the President, it has no constitutional link with Parliament and indeed was set up in 1990 before the promulgation of the Constitution. Writing in 2001, Dan Pavel judged that the President 'didn't have the political will, or the courage, or the democratic vision to subject the CSAT to a democratic transformation'.[25] If the CSAT had been disbanded, he would have been forfeiting powers but ones that could have been gravely misused by an illiberal successor.

At least Constantinescu always made a determined effort to argue in public that the biggest threats to Romanian national security were internal in origin rather than external. He associated national security with the defence of democratic values and the need to assert the rule of law when it was flouted by economic forces which believed that they were entitled to defy the authority of the state.[26]

Slaying the dragon of corruption

Constantinescu appeared keen to bring to account hitherto untouchable groups which had looted the Romanian economy when, on 7 January 1997, he announced a full-scale offensive against corruption. He appeared on television to announce the creation of a National Council of Action Against Corruption and Organized Crime (CNAICCO). This was the first of several high-profile addresses in which he emphasized the moral danger and subversion of democratic values posed by corruption, and the need to switch from a parasitic and exploitative capitalism to a growth-generating one which did not forget its duty to contribute to the public good.

To be effective inspiring words needed to be backed up by action. The first big fish to be hooked was Miron Cozma, the Jiu Valley miners' leader. One week after his arrest on 10 January Andrei Cornea remarked that Cozma had 'exercised a veritable politico-economic blackmail on the former government, contributing to the growth of unproductive subventions and...to our present economic impasse'.[27] On 27 March Cozma was sent to trial for organizing the violent events of 24–6 September 1991. Shortly beforehand, the President had characterized him as 'a person who, for almost six years, was allowed to defy all the institutions of state with the tacit agreement of the former political leadership'.[28]

Corruption generated strong passions (as well as contradictory attitudes) among the Romanian public, and Constantinescu's crusade against it raised huge expectations. He was not helped by the decision later the same month of Nicolae Cerveni, a lawyer and PNL parliamentarian, to defend in court the two heads of the Dacia Felix Bank who faced serious criminal charges. In 1996 Cerveni had also agreed (until dissuaded by Constantinescu) to defend Zahar Iskandarani, who faced charges of defrauding the state of large amounts of revenue through cigarette smuggling.[29] Even worse, another PNL parliamentarian, Viorel Cătarama, who had been perhaps the chief financial contributor to the President's campaign fund, had recently suffered an embarrassing economic reverse;[30] his SAFI investment fund crashed in 1996, with many thousands of depositors losing money,[31] but because there was no legislation to protect investors, Cătarama faced no liability, and even became head of the Senate's powerful economic committee where he would exercise great influence in the years to come. But the presence in the CDR of senior figures whose, actions appeared to undermine the CNAICCO initiative did not affect popular faith in it. Constantinescu enjoyed steadily rising poll ratings, as did Ciorbea; in June 1997, according to a poll of the Romanian Institute of Public opinion Surveys (IRSOP), these stood at 67 and 62% respectively; 69% of the population were highly satisfied with the measures the government had taken to combat organized crime.[32]

These figures are striking because during the previous four months the government had started to implement what it called a programme of shock therapy. On 31 January 1997 Ciorbea said that he had been left with no option but to do this: the previous government had 'bought social peace at an immoral price, that of the destruction of the economy'.[33] Prices for energy and food were completely liberalised between February and May, and prices in the shops for a wide range of commodities roughly doubled in the first quarter of the year. Businesses suffered greatly from the slump in domestic demand and sky-high interest rates. Average living standards were expected to drop by around 20% in 1997, and this in a country where the average wage was not much above $100 a month.[34]

A centre-piece of the new policy was a plan to reduce the budget deficit to 4.5% of GDP, a level necessary to boost foreign confidence in the economy and hopefully attract the foreign investors who had ignored Romania hitherto. The 1996 official deficit was 5.8% of GDP, but various forms of hidden subsidy probably pushed this above 10%.[35] To achieve budgetary stability, it was necessary to remove subsidies not only on basic staple goods but on loss-making industries. Very powerful lobbies had successfully defended their privileges in the Vacaroiu years, and these needed to be neutralised if the ruinous practice of pouring huge amounts of state revenue into loss-making state activities was to be ended. In April 1997 the government designated for closure ten unprofitable state enterprises which had accounted for 7.5% of the losses of the entire state budget.[36] This package of measures was elaborated after consultations with the IMF and the World Bank. Ciorbea even showed his keenness by raising oil prices on 1 January 1997, instead of on 1 February, the date agreed by the cabinet (although simultaneous social protection measures were not yet ready).[37] IMF and World Bank representatives were impressed by the seriousness with which Ciorbea was approaching the economic situation, and the IMF offered a new loan in the hope that the Fund's seal of approval would attract international investors. In May 1997 the London *Economist* appeared in no doubt that Romania's new ruling team 'have set about remaking Romania's economy, its polity, even its values, with almost Bolshevik zeal'.[38]

Bringing the Hungarians in from the cold

The growing popularity of the coalition in the first half of 1997 was even more striking because during this time the Romanian state appeared willing to adopt a far more positive attitude towards the Hungarian minority. The UDMR, which at various times had alienated most sections of Romanian politics and even produced calls for its total suppression, was now in government. In May the educational and local administration laws were amended, giving minorities the right to be schooled in their mother tongue at all levels as well as the right to use their language in court and in the local administration. The government had already published plans to introduce bilingual signs in areas of minority settlement, and a Hungarian consulate was to be opened in Cluj in the summer. These measures produced no public outcry, and even the nationalist parties and the PDSR found it hard at first to rouse their supporters to protest in large numbers (in April 1997 the PDSR initiated a censure motion against the Ciorbea government for ceding to 'autonomist and separatist intrigue').[39]

The rapprochement between neighbours and historic rivals was marked by a series of high-level visits. It was to Hungary that Adrian Severin, the new Romanian foreign minister, paid his first official visit. Hungary's backing for Romanian entry to NATO was confirmed, and a range of initiatives to strengthen defence and economic co-operation was announced. In his March 1997 visit to Budapest, Premier Ciorbea emphasized the importance of economic and military co-operation. He made clear his hope that the relaunching of the Romanian economy would be aided by Hungarian investment and Hungary's greater experience of market economics.[40] This marked a change from the Iliescu era when the government was reluctant to encourage investment from Hungary, and nationalist parties viewed such investment as tantamount to the re-colonization of the country and discouraged it in the parts of Transylvania where they had influence. But when Hungary's President Arpad Goncz paid a state visit to Romania on 25–27 May 1997, he found that there were 800 companies with mixed capital drawn from both countries operating in the Tirgu Mureş area alone.[41]

Ciorbea shared a strong personal commitment to improving Romanian-Hungarian ties at the human level. He spoke of his own friendly contacts with Hungarians while at school, at university and serving in the army. He sent greetings to Hungarians in Romania celebrating their national day on 15 March, and by allowing state officials to participate in the festivities, thus established a precedent.[42] The significance of the gesture is clear when one recalls the historical events in questions, for this date commemorated the 1848 revolution led by Louis Kossuth, who had refused to recognise the existence of a Romanian nation in Transylvania. Conflicting nationalists neutralised each other's bid for freedom in a territory in revolt against the imperial rule of the Habsburgs. Avram Iancu, the leader of the Romanian 1848ers in Transylvania, appealed to the Hungarians 'to understand that weapons can never decide between you and us. Fate put us in a homeland so that together we can strive to improve it and enjoy the results.'[43] A century and a half later, Ciorbea's bid to carry fellow Romanians with him as fences were mended with Hungary and its co-ethnics living in Romania were strengthened by the fact that he came from Iancu's locality in the Apuseni mountains, still viewed as a cradle of Romanian nationalism.

However, foresight and tact are needed in defusing sensitive interethnic issues; otherwise the intended benefits can be lost. If a reminder of this axiom were needed, it was provided in March 1997 when Ciorbea outlined a two-stage process whereby a Hungarian section would be established at Babes-Bolyai University in Cluj followed by the creation of a separate Hungarian-language university.[44] This was condemned outright by the left-nationalist bloc of parties, but it also divided opinion within Cluj's main university, which had played a moderating role during the nationalist tensions provoked by the city's controversial mayor. But one pro-rector threatened to resign while another backed the right of Hungarians to their own university; Romanian and Hungarian student associations adopted different positions; significantly, the Cluj branches of the main parties in government soon expressed their unhappiness about Ciorbea's move.[45]

For changes in this highly sensitive area to gain acceptance great skill in conflict management was needed, but little was shown by the government. Ciorbea took his stand without consulting the university's rector Andrei Marga, whom he would normally have considered an ally. Possibly the government had decided that a process of prior consultation would enable a coalition opposed to the Hungarian university to be mobilised, but its haste and failure to prepare public opinion left the government isolated, and a retreat was announced: after meeting university leaders President Constantinescu announced that one university would survive but with Romanian and Hungarian sections. Eventually, on 21 October 1997, when the Hungarian Prime Minister was visiting Bucharest, the Romanian government expressed its willingness to see a Hungarian-language university founded in a part of Transylvania other than Cluj.[46] The university question periodically disrupted relations between the UDMR and its coalition partners, but it only threatened to blow the coalition apart once, in the autumn of 1998 (see chapter 6).

During the next four years the UDMR acquitted itself well in the bear-pit of coalition politics. It concentrated on obtaining definite policy goals rather than advancing personal or group ambitions. These often seemed the primary concerns of many of the actors in Romanian coalition politics during a stormy period which would result in ruined reputations for several parties and their leaders. So at a very difficult moment in Romanian public life the UDMR moved to the mainstream of politics and often performed a stabilising role in a fragmented and chaotic political atmosphere. By not regularly demanding concessions from its partners as a price for staying in government and by largely staying aloof from the politics of patronage, it largely succeeded in burying its negative image in the eyes of Romanian opinion-formers and a large segment of the electorate.

The algorithm principle

A poll carried out by the Centre for Urban and Rural Sociology between 16 and 24 August 1997 posed the question 'How long can your family sustain the current reform programme?', to which the response of 23% was one year, of 24% between 3 and 5 years, and of 21% around 5 years. These figures suggest that a large segment of the Romanian population did not have the fatalistic and short-term attitudes often found in underdeveloped states—of living from day to day and not having broad horizons. But the dominant coalition parties did not share this willingness to show restraint and curb appetites. Powersharing after 1996 was characterised by 'the algorithm principle' whereby many thousands of positions, from cabinet portfolios down to prefects, directors, heads of offices, inspectors, heads of research institutes and so on were assigned on the basis of the electoral strength of the ruling parties. The CDR's rhetoric about drafting in 15,000 specialists soon faded away as the main parties invested valuable time and energy in filling the state apparatus with their own supporters.

From its time in office in 1990–1 the PD had acquired a retinue of political clients in the state sector—administrators, technicians, managers and directors of companies—whose interests it wished to safeguard. But there were many others looking for state protection who saw the arrival in office of the PNTCD as a golden opportunity to ingratiate themselves with a party lacking in experience but with jobs at its disposal. From the start of 1997 when he became editor of *Evenimentul Zilei*, Cornel Nistorescu offered sometimes brilliant daily insights, in his editorial columns, into the pressures which politicians unused to the corridors of power faced and how they frequently lost their way. He described the scene on the night of Emil Constantinescu's victory: '…All sorts of people were crowding at the door of the fresh President…all sorts of PDSR cronies insinuated themselves. A few months ago some of them could be seen around the PDSR leader…and now…they were shouting "We won, we won". During that outpouring of joy, nobody found the time to throw them out…there were businessmen among them…Most put their eggs in two or more baskets…being on good terms with everybody, so that they might say "I was by your side" to whosoever emerges as winner. It is the petty world of pilferers always crowding around those in power, the meal-ticket, and the flashlight.'[47]

Gabriel Tepelea, the first vice-president of the PNTCD, said on 14 April 1997 that the party had been flooded with applications for membership and that it was going to 'analyse these applications in light of the professional and moral prestige of the candidates. To accept these people *en bloc* would undermine the base of the party.'[48] But a month earlier Tepelea had declared that the PNTCD was prepared to enrol ex-members of the PUNR 'if among them are men keen to rekindle Transylvanian traditions'.[49] The eighty-year-old second-in-command of the PNTCD appeared to have forgotten that the PUNR had been promoted in 1990 by the FSN and the Securitate in order to prevent the PNTCD from ever again counting for anything in Transylvania. Given the lack of contact between different levels of the party, it was not difficult for many opportunists to shelter under the PNTCD umbrella. Indeed, in June 2000 Mirel Tiriuc, a PNTCD stalwart who had resigned from the party on being appointed head of the stocks and shares commission, expressed his dismay in an open letter at the 'unbelievably numerous parasites' who had flocked to the party, and the need for their removal.[50]

Perhaps an even greater problem was the unwillingness of the PNTCD seniors to delegate to experts and promote them quickly to positions where their specialist knowledge might make a difference. Elena Stefoi wrote in 1997 that 'many PNTCD representatives sincerely believe that years spent in prison are an alibi to cover up inefficiency and legislative nonsense'.[51] She was referring in particular to elderly figures who until 1989 'used to pass their time standing in queues to buy milk, roaming about Bucharest markets or engaging in nostalgic…conversations…Few had any expertise in market economy problems or had been in a position to run a staff of twenty and make sure they were paid'.[52] But these were people who, on flimsy evidence, insisted that they were capable of handling all sorts of urgent tasks. Their doyen was Ion Diaconescu, Coposu's successor as president of the party, who was also President of the CDR and President of the Chamber of Deputies.

Only with difficulty did the Civic Alliance (AC) persuade the CDR parties to agree that the wisest course would be to appoint a government of specialists (rather than elected politicians) with the expertise that hopefully would enable reforms to be carried out. The AC presented dossiers with appropriate names but its president, Ana Blandiana, reckons that they were virtually ignored.[53] She turned down the position of ambassador to UNESCO, having long expressed a preference for operating in the civic arena at home. Zoe Petre has claimed that at least half the staff in the president's office came from an AC background, but Blandiana contends they were just nominal members who jumped on the civic bandwagon to take part in the auction for posts.[54]

There was disappointment among CDR stalwarts when ex-officers who had been part of CADA, the military reform movement of 1990, remained marginalized; outrage grew when it emerged that officers implicated in the repression of 1989 were still being promoted. CADA officers could not easily have been integrated back into the army so that they could work effectively with officers who had kept their heads down in 1990 or else actively worked with the new power. But by 1998 Gabriel Andreescu, a founder and moving spirit of the Romanian Association for the Defence of Human Rights (APADOR), was in no doubt that the principle of 'anti-selection continues to determine appointments to important public positions'.[55]

Bold remedial measures to improve the economic health of Romania needed the single-minded attention of the new rulers, but the elevation of the algorithm principle to the heart of government meant that such attention was often lacking. The decision to devote precious government time to ensuring that Romania would be one of the countries invited to join NATO at the June 1997 Madrid summit which would decide on its first enlargement towards the East also weakened the momentum behind domestic reform.

The NATO chimera

In 1998, now out of office, Victor Ciorbea stated that 'the decision to postpone part of the structural reform programme in order to concentrate on the bid to join NATO' emanated from Cotroceni, and that he regretted having gone along with it; it was felt that radical measures in the macro-economic sphere might provoke industrial unrest which would harm the country's image at a vital moment.[56] Zoe Petre, present at many talks between the President and the prime minister, did not recall ever having heard the President suggest that domestic reform should be postponed till after Madrid.[57]

The warning delivered by the finance minister Mircea Ciumara in January 1997 that 'if we don't accomplish reform in 1997 we will reach the situation of Bulgaria' was ignored.[58] In 1996 Bulgaria had seen the value of its currency collapse amid bank failures and runaway inflation, and the term 'Bulgarianisation' had become fashionable nextdoor in Romania, denoting the fate likely to await the country if reforms were put off or only partially implemented. Cornel Nistorescu, a consistent supporter of reform efforts, could write in May 1997: 'It becomes clear that the reform...hasn't actually started. There was only a sort of vault in January; during the negotiations with the IMF...the state budget was modified to meet the required conditions. But that was all. The passing of the necessary bills was put off again and again. The debts of the biggest companies were forgotten and the 50 companies planned to [be] privatised every week, are sold like in slow motion, or not at all. It is clear that instead of a radical policy, a rather prudent one was adopted....'[59]

Concentrating energies on the race for NATO enabled a disparate coalition to show unity, and at least for some months it would hopefully divert an expectant public opinion from the difficult

economic situation at home. Perhaps Romania might defeat all the
odds and be admitted. The new government only had six months to
meet the criteria for entry after what were seen as six lost years, at
the end of which the Iliescu regime had made a belated and unconvincing bid to be considered a fit candidate for NATO membership. Strenuous efforts were made to convince the world that a stable
and democratic government had been installed which was committed to introducing a free market economy. Civilian control of the
military had been established and, along with Poland, Romania was
seen as having the only army in Eastern Europe able to play a full
role in NATO. Romania was also devoting nearly 3% of its GDP to
defence, twice as much as Hungary and the Czech Republic. The
preponderant role of the security services in Romania before 1989,
and emerging evidence that former Securitate operatives enjoyed
wide influence in political and economic life, were troubling to
NATO. In no other candidate state did such a situation apply, even
remotely. It was possible to put a brave face on it by arguing that the
intelligence services had been less infiltrated by the Soviet secret services than had been the case in Czechoslovakia, Hungary or even
Poland.[60] But this view was doubted by others, notably Ion Mihai
Pacepa, the head of the External Intelligence service until his defection to the United States in 1978.

Virgil Măgureanu, who had been involved in the removal of
Ceauşescu and was one of the chief architects of the Iliescu regime,
remained in charge of the SRI after 1996. Nicolae Ionescu-Galbeni,
the PNTCD elder who chaired the parliamentary commission on
the SRI, stated in early 1997 that Măgureanu would be allowed to
carry on till September when his contract expired,[61] but on 24 April
Măgureanu asked to be relieved of his position. His resignation was
widely seen as an attempt to assuage fears in Western intelligence
circles about including as a NATO member a country where thousands of communist-era security operatives were still highly influential in its sprawling state security field. Măgureanu had steadily
distanced himself from his mentor Iliescu since the latter's star had
waned. He had even defended the good name of the PNTCD's
Corneliu Coposu after Iliescu claimed in April 1997 that Coposu
had been well-known as a collaborator with the Securitate.[62] *România líbera*, for years a daily press scourge of the Iliescu regime, was full

of praise for Măgureanu as he stepped down to plan his entry into politics: 'The positive evolution of the SRI is to the credit of Mr Măgureanu,' wrote Roxanna Iordache.[63] She thought it significant that he had recently claimed to have voted for change because he could not endure any more stagnation. She also repeated his claim that as early as 1992 he had advised Iliescu not to stand for President, and that if his advice had been heeded Romania might easily now be a front-runner in the contest for NATO entry. Măgureanu was adept at bathing a very controversial career in a favourable light. Perhaps his true vocation was in public relations and not in politics, since the New Romania Party which he joined in 1997 failed to prosper even after he renamed it the Romanian National Party. He was a polished TV performer, unafraid of being confronted by an awkward question, and probably no contemporary security chief in the former communist world has been so talkative or seemingly approachable. But his ability to disarm liberal opponents showed that the new government and some of its media allies had rather a naïve approach to the security services and what was to be done with them.

It is likely that such matters were overlooked by NATO because their political significance did not become immediately apparent until the government ran into trouble from 1998 onwards. But in 1997, at the height of Romania's NATO bid, there was an incident which suggested continuity rather than change in relation to the security services. In July 1997 General Ioan Talpes was replaced as head of the Directorate of External Information (DIE), which dealt with external intelligence matters. He had run the DIE from 1991, having previously worked closely with General Ilie Ceauşescu, deputy minister of defence before 1989. Constantinescu, on assuming office, had said: 'Talpes is not going to be changed because he has carried out big services for the country.'[64] But his position became untenable after it emerged that a DIE agent had recruited a Swiss diplomat to spy for Romania.[65] Instead of being sent into obscurity, Talpes was offered three ambassadorial positions—he chose Bulgaria.

Thankfully for President Constantinescu, most international attention was focussed on his efforts to alter Romania's international image by strengthening ties with neighbours from which the country had traditionally held itself aloof. He had accepted the view of one Romanian historian that 'Balkan solidarity is a prelude and not an alternative to Euro-Atlantic integration.'[66] The feelings were reciprocated in Serbia at the end of 1996; crowds demonstrating in their capitals against their communist-inclined regimes invoked 'Bucharest' as a talisman which would hopefully speed the demise of anti-Western rulers. In January 1997 the President sent a personal emissary to meet opposition leaders in Serbia, thus abandoning his predecessor's stance of identifying with the hardline Milošević. Romania stepped up its contribution to the NATO-led force in Bosnia, and in March agreed to contribute to the Italian-led force being sent to strife-torn Albania. Not only was Romania projecting itself as 'an island of stability' in the Balkans but it was hoping that the West would take note of its readiness to keep the peace in its disorderly neighbourhood rather than wait for outsiders to do so. The unanimous vote of the Council of Europe in May 1997 to end its monitoring of the human rights situation in Romania was a sign that the country's external image was at last improving.

Arguments that by including Romania NATO would be better able to deal with serious challenges on its volatile southern rim were attractive, but they ultimately failed to convince the United States and, to a lesser degree, Germany and Britain. Romania had moved from being a rank outsider to a serious contender for NATO membership, but these countries preferred to confine the first wave of expansion to three Central European states. Given the time and energy invested by Romanian leaders, the rebuff was an undeniable disappointment. King Mihai warned, a little melodramatically, that the refusal of Romania's application 'will be seen as a rejection of our entire nation and consequences are bound to follow. The West will have little credibility, not only in my country but in the entire region.'[67] However, early indications suggest that this view is too pessimistic. A poll taken by IRSOP towards the end of May found that only 9% of Romanians were concerned about the country's failure to join NATO at an early stage.[68] This was probably a sensible reaction. The concrete as opposed to symbolic value of joining NATO had never really been properly explained by anyone; it was never made clear for instance what Romania would get in return for spending $3 billion on restructuring its armed forces to bring them into line with NATO's. In the IRSOP poll 29% of respondents blamed Romania's former rulers for any failure to join NATO, compared to 11% blaming the current government. The most influential daily paper argued that 'economically, for Romania to join the first wave of NATO expansion would have been an over-generous gesture by the alliance'.[69] Romania's strongest champions, France and Italy, promised that they would continue to champion its NATO bid. President Clinton also tried to assuage Romanian disappointment at NATO's rejection of its application by paying an eight-hour visit to Bucharest on 11 July. In University Square he declared: 'the door to NATO is open, will stay open, and we will help you pass through it.'[70] If nothing else, this visit showed that Washington realised the importance of providing top-level support to Romania's reformers, perhaps out of a belief that their success could have a stabilising influence in South-Eastern-Europe as a whole.

Even though its poll ratings held up, the government found itself on the defensive even before the decision of the Madrid summit. Social protests erupted as soon as the effects of shock therapy began to be felt. In the spring of 1997 workers in Brasov blocked an important highway after their tractor factory lost its electricity supply because of non-payment of bills. In early June the Jiu valley miners went on strike, many wishing to go to Bucharest to confirm their status as 'a privileged category of the nation'.[71] The forces of order managed to restrain them and prevented any repetition of the 1990–1 events, but the government restored power to the tractor factory in Brasov and passed an ordinance giving workers generous redundancy payments. Cornel Nistorescu wrote on 7 June: 'They are terribly afraid of the people. They take two steps back every time the people raise their voice in anger.'[72] Industrial unrest acted as a disincentive to foreign investment and the rate which had been very encouraging in the first half of 1997 slowed down perceptibly in the second half of the year.[73] But in 1997 as a whole $998 million was invested in Romania, more than double the figure for 1996.[74]

Introspection and dissension

Ciorbea has claimed that he recommended holding early elections in the aftermath of the NATO summit when the incompatibility of the PNTCD and PD was becoming increasingly obvious and the CDR still held a commanding poll lead.[75] But he lacked the authority in Cotroceni or in the CDR for his recommendation to be heeded. His authority over the coalition parties in parliament, a chamber to which he did not belong, was also weak. It was during his government that the problems arising from the 1991 constitution having created two parliamentary chambers with broadly similar powers, each able to block bills from the other, first became serious. Under 'carbon-copy bicameralism' the two chambers often obstruct each other's work by producing vastly different bills that purport to deal with the same problem.[76] A mediation commission exists to reach agreement when the two chambers pass different versions of the same law, but these grave defects slowed down the lawmaking process at a time when many bills urgently needed passing to convince international bodies that in its reform efforts Romania was at last making up for lost time. Allowing the two chambers to check and balance each other was meant to reduce the danger of a return to authoritarianism. However, it is arguable that, the 1991 constitution actually increased that risk by producing an enfeebled parliament which the people (according to countless polls) view with contempt.

The Ciorbea government also found itself thwarted by parliamentary committees which rejected its legislation despite the coalition enjoying a technical majority on each of them. The head of the Senate's economic committee, the PNL's Viorel Cătarama, frequently inconvenienced the government because he believed that it was neglecting domestic capital in favour of foreign interests.[77] George Pruteanu, the PNTCD deputy who chaired the lower house education committee, blocked an education bill which was meant to overturn the 1995 one which many Hungarians felt discriminated against them. He argued that the new one was unacceptable because it allowed Hungarians to be taught the subjects of history and geography in their own language. To the applause of left-wingers and nationalists, he declared in November 1997: 'Right or wrong, this is your country. Your language is spoken in Budapest but your life is here in Romania.'[78] For Pruteanu and his allies educational bilingualism and the danger it posed to national dignity and state security became an obsession, and by contrast they paid little attention to the fact that illiteracy was once again becoming a major problem due to the defects of an educational system starved of resources. Figures issued by the ministry in early 1998 showed that the country's illiteracy rate had risen to 6%, ahead of Bulgaria, Hungary, Poland and the former Czechoslovakia.[79] Such rebellions grew, and sometimes the government's majority existed on paper only. As a result, it often had to resort to passing bills by 'executive ordinances' or decrees which became law, although eventually they would need to be ratified by parliament. At least fifty such ordinances were passed in 1997, which soured relations between the executive and the legislature, and hampered the development of a culture based on political compromise. By 2000 one journalist was clear about the effect of executive ordinances: 'They have turned Romania into a counterfeit democracy where the government rules *de facto* and parliament has a mere decorative role.'[80]

As his political problems mounted, Ciorbea failed to keep open a clear channel of communication with the public. In May 1997 state television schedules were altered to enable him to read out a 22-page statement on the government's programme which took three hours to deliver:[81] a welter of statistics were supposed to be an acceptable substitute for a clearcut strategy and time-table for reform.[82] Ciorbea himself later admitted: 'I was preoccupied with governing and ignored the necessity of having a communications strategy.'[83] Unrepresentative groups were able to sow confusion and to profit from the failure of a government, which had raised huge expectations, to communicate even with its own supporters. A vivid example was provided in the autumn of 1997 when a group of hunger-strikers camped outside the Senate in protest at the government's intention to withdraw a range of privileges which they enjoyed.

Capitulation before vested interests

In 1990 Iliescu had granted to people who had participated in the December 1989 uprising what were known as 'revolutionary certificates', entitling the holders to a range of privileges, income tax exemptions, free public transport and even grants of land: 27,000 of these certificates were issued. According to the 21 December 1989 Association (part of the CDR), most of those who received them were bogus revolutionaries, at least 6,000 having belonged to the police, army or Securitate.[84] Granting 'revolutionary certificates' to such people had been a clever idea of the FSN in 1990 when it was looking for ways of expropriating the revolution from its adversaries, but it was not easy to reverse. A bill drafted by the 21 December 1989 Association which intended to confine certificates to those wounded in the uprising, or to the relatives of those killed and wounded, was publicly opposed by the pseudo-revolutionaries. At a rally in September 1997 they accused the President of trying to get rid of them in order to impose 'a peasant-liberal dictatorship' on Romania—a clear indication of the neo-communist affiliations of some of them.[85] They mounted a hunger-strike, and instead of defying it CDR dignitaries went to parley with them; These included the President himself, who turned up at their encampment at 3 a.m. on 14 October.[86] The next day Ciorbea announced that that the government was giving in to the hunger-strikers' pressure. The law was to be postponed and a special commission set up to check all revolutionary certificates. This effectively killed the issue.[87]

At the start of the affair of the 'revolutionaries' the President had declared: 'In November 1996 we won the elections but we did not conquer power, because a large part of the economic power belonged, and still belongs in good measure, to a mafia-type web of interests which has no connection with the national interest.'[88] This was a very realistic assessment, and suggests that the President only became fully aware of how circumscribed his position was after his election, although he and his supporters had long insisted that the power of the old communist state had remained intact in many of its aspects. Although the task he had assumed of creating a law-based state, in which the power of special interests would be broken, was indeed formidable, not all the cards were in the hands of his opponents. With vigilance and tenacity the Presidency and its political allies could still have reduced the privileges and sense of political immunity enjoyed by forces with their origins in the communist period.

For instance, the President might have thought twice before agreeing to become Honorary President of the National Association of War Veterans (ANVR); up till 1989 all those whom the communists had considered undesirable were excluded from it.[89] Its president was a general who in October 1956, as head of the military garrison in Timisoara, had helped suppress the students demonstrating in solidarity with the revolution in Hungary.[90] A storm arose in November 1998 when it emerged that, at the recommendation of the ANVR, President Constantinescu had decorated, Vasile Ciolpan, governor of the prison in Sighet where ill-treatment of prisoners like Iuliu Maniu and Dinu Brătianu had hastened their end in the early 1950s. Ciolpan, an octogenarian, was not an obscure figure,[91] especially since he had figured in a long-running television series 'Memories of Sorrow', re-telling the story of communist-era repression.[92] It was a black mark against Cotroceni that none of the President's advisers realised the grave error that had been committed.[93] And it was not the only occasion when poor advice would land him in embarrassing difficulties.

By far the most embarrassing retreat made by the CDR during the Ciorbea premiership was the decision taken in August 1997 to fire Valerian Stan, head of the Department of Control and Anti-Corruption (AVAB). This was a sensitive position which involved the monitoring of full-time officials and elected representatives in the government service to ensure that no abuse of office had taken place. Stan's appointment in 1996 appeared to signal that anti-corruption rhetoric would be matched by action. He had belonged to the CADA military reform movement, and after being dismissed from the army in 1990 he was very active in democratisation initiatives. As well as being one of the vice-presidents of Romania's leading human rights watchdog, APADOR, he had been prominent in the Civic Alliance (AC), in which capacity he had worked closely with Emil Constantinescu before their disagreement over the funding of the 1996 CDR presidential election campaign (see p. 144) Nevertheless his appointment by the new President to head the AVAB was an indication that he expected Stan to carry out his job seriously. In June 1997 Stan issued a report which showed that land and state property had been handed over 'in an illegal way' to 5,997 people between 1990 and 1995.[94] Unlike Ceauşescu, who had denied senior party figures ownership of property, Iliescu often granted his supporters the use of 'protocol' houses and flats, many of which had been nationalised by the communist regime without compensation. Thus senior figures were continuing to live in these properties undisturbed despite the fact that some had been regained by their former owners through the courts. During the 1996 elections Petre Roman was shown to be living in 'a protocol' house, paying a nominal rent. The CDR had pledged in that year to close the State

Protocol Agency which owned a great deal of property inherited from the PCR.

Stan's report revealed that so-called 'revolutionaries' had been given land in many parts of the country.[95] State-owned houses, often in exclusive parts of the capital, were also made available to 147 high-ranking figures, including leading lights in the PD—Stan branded all such transactions as illegal. The PD tried to restrain him. Roman reminded his CDR colleagues that, before forming the government, each of the participants had agreed to impose a moratorium on their past actions. In his attempt to restrain Stan Ciorbea placed the AVAB under his own authority and restricted Stan's access to the media. However, in late August Stan reiterated his charges against the PD and on the 28th he was sacked, Diaconescu declaring that his dismissal was necessary for the government to continue functioning.[96] The PD had threatened to break up the coalition unless Stan was silenced.

Caving in made a mockery of the promise given on 12 December 1996 and published in the Official Monitor that 'the Government is going to launch a total war against corruption which is revealed at the highest level'.[97] Roman eventually vacated his protocol home because the benefit of paying a nominal rent was not worth the political damage he suffered as a result. But the PD had proved more ruthless than the CDR in this battle of wills. Ciorbea later described his willingness to sack Stan as the worst mistake of his premiership.[98] The CDR and above all Constantinescu, had thrown away their trump card, their principled stand on corruption. It made no difference that on 26 August a general prosecutor widely felt to have blocked major corruption cases was replaced by one, Sorin Moisescu, who took a far more pro-active stance. Instead of disbanding the State Protocol Agency, the coalition came to appreciate its usefulness and its board was staffed by its own representatives.[99] Instead of disappearing into obscurity, Stan became one of the fiercest critics of Constantinescu's anti-corruption efforts, probably doing lasting damage to the reputation of the President, who in his memoirs accused Stan of being on 'a mission of destruction'.[100]

For an election to have been called on the issue of corruption in high places would have been deeply embarrassing to the PD and would have brought no joy for the PDSR, which was trailing badly in the polls. (In 1996 Iliescu's own reputation for incorruptability had been dented when it emerged that he had illegally bought the house which the State Protocol Agency had lent him while president.)[101] But Ciorbea 'didn't have the courage to confront those who sabotaged him openly, just as he didn't have the courage to escape from the President's guidance... The Christian Democrats gave him their support only in return for his obedience'.[102] Cornel Nistorescu had revealed the defects of Ciorbea's governing style shortly before the crisis which would blow him away erupted: 'Victor Ciorbea doesn't show firmness within the government. The meetings start later than scheduled, some people keep talking on their cellphones or leave during the debates, others argue violently when the Premier, instead of cutting the Gordian knot, tries to settle things little by little, until the hours are wasted. His frequent involvement in minor matters...leaves us no other choice but to stress that a much firmer attitude...is needed.'[103]

Death agonies of the Ciorbea government

Ciorbea reshuffled his government on 4 December 1997, the main casualties being poorly performing PNTCD ministers in the departments of health, education, and finance. At the instigation of Cotroceni, technocrats were drafted in to strengthen the government. The new finance minister was Daniel Daiǎnu, formerly chief economist at the Central Bank and widely regarded as one of Romania's best economic minds. Despite his reputation, Daiǎnu had been blocked by PNTCD elders because he had worked for the external intelligence service after graduating from university in the 1970s, a fact he had never concealed. The new education minister was Andrei Marga who had turned Cluj University into one of the few thriving institutions of higher learning in the country.

The coalition rebirth proved abortive. On 3 December the PD had warned that it was only prepared to grant the technocrats a three-month period of grace to prove their worth. It then voted against a coalition proposal allowing the government to issue ordinances during the parliamentary recess. It was unhappy at not being given top posts in the loss-making state bank Bancorex, which was slowly being prepared for privatisation, or in the Financial Guard.[104] Matters came to a head when Ciorbea let it be known that he would discipline ministers who missed cabinet meetings without good reason or made unauthorised statements on controversial topics. A confrontation then ensued between him and the PD's transport minister, Traian Băsescu, when the latter criticised Ciorbea and the PNTCD and their role in government. The PD had a good tactical reason to provoke a crisis; it was trailing badly in the polls, showing little more than 5% support in some of them. Bad publicity had arisen from a messy internal party dispute between the foreign minister Adrian Severin and his party leader which led to Severin quitting the government on 23 December (see page 195). With state sell-offs planned, the PD was likely to face difficulty in placing its business supporters in key positions and enable them to benefit from privatisation as long as Ciorbea was in charge.

Tortuous negotiations over the December reshuffle, and the three-month death agonies of the Ciorbea government which followed, undoubtedly succeeded in blowing the coalition off course. Quite early in the crisis, on 15 January 1998, Valentin Ionescu, the new minister of privatisation, said that if it went on much longer privatisation would be put back by four months.[105] On 29 January 1998 the PD withdrew from the government when the PNTCD refused to abandon Ciorbea and appoint a substitute prime minister. It then blocked the budget, although the IMF had suspended its loan agreement until it was passed. All attempts at resolving the conflict by Cotroceni ended in failure. One shaky truce brokered by the President collapsed in early February when the PNTCD brought in Wim Van Velzen, a Christian Democrat politician from the Netherlands strongly supportive of Romania's Euro-Atlantic integration bid, to denounce Roman and his party.[106] The PD dug its heels in further when polls showed that it was beginning to recover electoral support (the PRM was the only other party to benefit from the crisis).

Ciorbea finally departed on 30 March after the PNL and younger members of the PNTCD, with their political careers firmly in mind, joined calls for him to quit. Only the Civic Alliance sustained him to the last, and thereby attracted press criticism for prolonging a crisis that had been extremely costly for Romania.[107] Diaconescu, the PNTCD leader, later reckoned that a big mistake had been made in appointing Ciorbea prime minister: 'He had no history in the party and he was also lacking in the experience necessary for such a position.'[108] But the fact was that everyone was in the same position, and

Ciorbea, unlike Diaconescu, was at least prepared to criticise his own failings. He believed that he had been mistaken in stepping down as mayor of Bucharest in 1996, when he believed that he was in a position to transform the face of the capital. But he never really explained why he did not return to the mayor's job. After all, he had not resigned from the post when serving as premier and there were enough like-minded people in the PNTCD to ensure that he could obtain the resources necessary to try to put his municipal plans into operation. Ironically Ciorbea's eventual successor as the city's mayor would be Traian Băsescu, whose informal approach to politics was so unlike that of Ciorbea—whom Silviu Brucan described as 'a religious-style preacher who offered interminable lessons in morality'.[109]

Ion Diaconescu believed that, despite its aggressive behaviour, the PNTCD had no option but to get along with the PD because 'we are both in the same boat'. As captain the PNTCD was about to supply from its own ranks someone whom the PD would soon find more congenial than many on his own side.

Radu Vasile

Radu Vasile did not reflect the anti-communist values of the PNTCD, although he had joined it in 1990, and he had friendly links with parties across the political spectrum.[110] He had somehow risen 'in a party centred around nostalgic octogenarians', which showed him to be a flexible and highly adaptable politician.[111] He was described as 'the least Peasantist of the Peasantists…amenable to all parties and orientations'.[112] These characteristics were revealed at the end of 1999 when Vasile's premiership collapsed amid the same acrimony as Ciorbea's. Afterwards, in the space of one year (2000), he left one party, joined one on the extreme right, and formed another before finally joining the PD. Ciorbea had predicted that Vasile would end up in the PDSR and was therefore not far out.[113] There had been persistent rumours that if Iliescu had won in 1996 he would have appointed Vasile prime minister of a multi-colour government as a gesture of national unity (and perhaps to allow the PNTCD to carry the blame for the financial mess the country was in). Vasile had sniped at the Ciorbea government while secretary-general of the PNTCD in 1997–8 (he would later describe Ciorbea as 'a Trojan Horse' or 'a foreign ingredient' inside the PNTCD).[114] He also quietly supported Senator Pruteanu's hard line on minority education until the latter was expelled from the PNTCD in March 1998. In late 1997 he even declared 'I have begun to lose confidence in political parties', which revealed the populist instincts of someone who had been a university professor of socialist economics before 1989.[115]

Whereas Victor Ciorbea was reckoned by the journalist Emil Hurezeanu to lack the versatility or the craftiness to manage a land where he observed Balkan and Levantine instincts were increasingly to the fore, this could not be said of his successor.[116] Radu Vasile's chameleon-like ability to empathise with the average Romanian meant that his poll ratings were soon higher than the President's. Constantinescu had turned him down for the premiership in 1996 when he was already the best-known Peasantist outside the ranks of the older generation. He then sought to manage the Ciorbea government from Cotroceni 'by phone and nocturnal talks'.[117] But Vasile would not be so malleable. Constantinescu knew it and a rivalry between them developed.[118] It would soon match that between Iliescu and his Premier in 1990–1 and would reach a similar dénouement (though without the violence). Vasile had secured the premiership *despite* Constantinescu, with the active support of young Peasantists in 'the Brasov Group' and covert backing from the PD.

Constantinescu's credibility was now slipping within the CDR. He had sustained an unsuccessful premier long beyond the point when Ciorbea could ever have recovered his position. Yet he had lost the support of the Civic Alliance, previously his most loyal backers, for not defending Ciorbea even at the price of the coalition's collapse. It was said of Ciorbea that he was a helpless 'victim torn to pieces by four camels pulling in opposite directions', but much the same could be said of Constantinescu during the second half of his presidency when he found retaining control over his erstwhile allies difficult.[119] But the poll ratings of both the President and the CDR still held up. A poll taken by the Centre for Urban and Rural Sociology in late February 1997 showed that 45% of respondents intended to vote for him: he was over 30 points ahead of any competitor (Iliescu was on 14%), and with 27.9% support the CDR was only slightly down on the 1996 election result. This poll also showed that while 22.3% of voters had no expectation that the reform process would succeed, 48.8% believed that it would yield positive results after one year. A rapid programme of privatisation was favoured by 54% as opposed to 26.6% who preferred a much slower process; 64% also expected the President to play an active role in government business.[120]

The coalition parties were able to benefit from the electorate's still vivid memories of the PDSR's inglorious period in office. That party remained in the doldrums, having ruled out modernising its programme, and suffering a damaging series of defections as a result. Cornel Nistorescu had confidently predicted in June 1997 that 'no matter how bad things may be in Romania... there will be no bright future for Ion Iliescu's party.'[121] This was a faulty prediction, but at least Nistorescu was one of the few in the democratic camp to spot the rising poll ratings of the PRM led by Vadim Tudor, and draw the right conclusions: 'There is a grain of truth in all that he says... It still remains a burlesque show. But people, out of despair and lacking an alternative, start to trust his words. As the current ruling power drops brick after brick, we must take the Vadim phenomenon more seriously. We achieve nothing by treating him with superior and mocking comments. Vadim, with Funar... and Miron Cozma... will make a famous trio. Outrageous, ridiculous, absurd, but supported by the people's discontent. A deadly remedy.'[122] To the surprise of some, the New Romania Party, with Virgil Măgureanu firmly in charge since at least the autumn of 1997, failed to prosper as trust in conventional solutions began to flag. Măgureanu was an expert in manipulating public opinion—which indeed had been the subject of his doctoral thesis. He was relaxed and plausible on TV chat shows while Iliescu was evasive and spoke in stilted language. Heading a party with 150,000 members, mainly with links to the intelligence community, he had well-placed supporters in every county. His party combined emphasis on the danger allegedly posed by Hungarians to national security with a policy of low-priced food for all Romanians.[123] But it stagnated in the polls, and Măgureanu concentrated on his family's growing web of business interests.[124]

Quis custodet custodes? Tigareta II

Cotroceni and its coalition allies could still benefit from their high-profile anti-corruption drive, but by 1998 the momentum behind it was ebbing. The CNAICCO's report on its activities in 1997 appeared late because the Ministry of Justice had provided it with insufficient information. In February 1998 the President openly stated that because the ministry was dragging its feet it was not possible to speak of 'even a small offensive against corruption'.[125] During a TV broadcast in September he named a tax inspector with the Bucharest fraud squad who had been sentenced to three years in jail, but those advising him had 'messed up the papers' and the man named was still at his post and apparently innocent of all wrong-doing.[126] One undoubted success of the anti-corruption drive was the apprehension, on 3 July 1998, of Petre Isac, a government inspector caught in the act of taking a $10,000 bribe.[127] Isac had been PDSR mayor of Coştesti in Argeş county from 1994 to 1996 and he appeared to have no difficulty ingratiating himself with the PNTCD. As an employee of the Department of Local Public administration he had been requested to provide a *curriculum vitae*, but he was not called to account for failing to do so.[128] A similar display of amateurism had come from the PNTCD when Vasile's government was formed and one Alexandru Bogdan was nominated as minister of agriculture. Bogdan had belonged to several other parties, including the PDSR, before securing a place on the PNTCD's list of candidates in 1996. He had been nominated for agriculture by PNTCD elder Gabriel Tepelea, a choice approved by Vasile who seemed to know nothing of his background despite having been the PNTCD's secretary-general the previous year.[129]

In April 1998, Emil Constantinescu's anti-corruption campaign suddenly suffered what proved a mortal blow when a senior military officer assigned to provide his security were found to be involved in a multi-million dollar smuggling racket in cigarettes. Cigarettes are a lucrative source of income in a country where 21 billion are reckoned to be smoked each year.[130] *Tigareta II*, as the press dubbed the scandal (to distinguish it from a previous cigarette smuggling racket), broke on 23 April 1998 with the arrest of Colonel Gheorghe Trutulescu for allegedly orchestrating the smuggling of 30 million cigarettes to Bucharest's Otopeni airport on 16 April. According to the press, Trutulescu had been entrusted with the President's security on both his foreign and domestic visits (a claim denied by the latter's chief of staff, Zoe Petre). Colonel Ion Suçiu, commander of the military sector of the airport, was also later arrested.[131] The scandal came to light not because of the vigilance of law-enforcement agencies or the CNAICCO but as a result of infighting between rival state security agencies. Trutulescu belonged to the President's Protection and Guard Service (SPP), which had close links with the intelligence and security service of the ministry of the interior (UM 0215). UM0215 had been involved in subverting the opposition in 1990, and Trutulescu and Suçiu had been part of a special military unit charged with the suppression of anti-communist demonstrations at the end of 1989.[132] When it became known that the SRI had secretly filmed Trutulescu's role in the smuggling operation, the press assumed that the scandal broke because of turf wars between it and competitors in the intelligence world. The SRI is the only official intelligence agency in Europe which is allowed to finance itself from commercial activities.[133] In the wake of the scandal the press was able to publish plenty of evidence of the wealth recently acquired by Virgil Măgureanu, director of the SRI from 1990 to 1997.[134]

The President did not come well out of the affair. On taking office he had made only minor changes to the SPP despite its close association with the Iliescu regime,[135] and he was slow to remove its chief, General Nicu Anghel, who resigned long after the crisis had ignited.[136] A President now dubbed by the press as 'the Prisoner of Cotroceni' seemed to know far less about the security services than the PRM; just a few days before *Tigareta II* broke, Vadim Tudor had issued a detailed statement 'about corruption at all levels of state organizations'.[137] On 22 May 1998 the Supreme Council of National Defence (CSAT) decided to restructure UM 0215, which duplicated many of the activities of the SRI. However, two new bodies were created out of it, which increased the number of intelligence services yet further—with the risk that they would easily slip out of government control unless maximum vigilance was exercised. One press source even speculated that a proposal to disband UM 0215 completely had been rejected for fear that there would be a mass migration of officers to the PRM,[138] which already boasted that it had a more efficient intelligence service than any of the state-run agencies. Nevertheless, the latter often supplied it with classified information with the object of undermining its opponents in the mainstream parties.[139]

The President's standing in the polls immediately dropped by 20% after the *Tigareta II* affair and would not recover. A prestigious state visit to the United States, where he addressed both Houses of Congress (a rare honour for an East European leader), failed to revive his fortunes at home. He no longer sounded convincing when he remarked that he was disgusted by the performance of the Romanian political class (when this remark was made in February 1998 at the world economic summit in Davos, it earned a riposte from Senator Vasile Lupu, one of the most capable Peasantists, that he should not have been disgusted because he too was a member of that class).[140] It was hard to maintain confidence in an anti-corruption campaign when it failed to detect wrong-doing among officers who were with the President on a daily basis (Trutulescu had planned to store the cache of cigarettes in the backyard of the presidential palace). Constantinescu appealed to the public in 1998 to contact him directly if citizens had evidence that wrong-doing in high places was being concealed, but there is no evidence that many did.[141] At least the President managed to repair his links with the Civic Alliance which, after receiving a visit from him, affirmed on 20 May 1998 its support for his anti-corruption efforts.[142] But the voice of the AC's estranged vice-president Valerian Stan had greater resonance, and he was given a platform in the daily press for increasingly sharp attacks on the President for departing 'in a significant way from the...promises on which the election campaign was fought'.[143] Even Ciorbea joined the ranks of Constantinescu's critics: by February 2000 he was ready to claim (but without naming names) that the President had kept members of the Securitate in various state institutions during his years in office.[144]

By 1996 Romania had lost seven years of reform thanks to the political stagnation of the Iliescu presidency and the reluctance to break with spending priorities and mind-sets more characteristic of communist times. To have expected the CDR and the newly-elected President Constantinescu to make dramatic progress in overcoming this legacy of failure would have been unrealistic, especially when it is recalled that ex-Iliescu allies, Petre Roman's PD, were to play a prominent role in government.

The degree of unpreparedness shown by the CDR parties during the changeover showed that they were not ready for power; Victor Ciorbea appeared almost as surprised as everyone else when he was asked to become prime minister. The CDR did not seem to realise just how closely the PD was still wedded to an FSN agenda, with more emphasis being placed on the politics of patronage than on identifying the main tasks necessary to start the process of economic recovery and institutional rebuilding, and get agreement on spending approaches, divisions of responsibility, and a timetable for change. Hardly any meaningful dialogue had ever taken place within the PNTCD about policy options, so a ready meeting of minds between it and the PD about what its governing priorities should be was scarcely feasible. Nevertheless, it is striking that the CDR failed to rise to the challenge confronting it and become a single reform movement rather than an electoral alliance.[145] The historic parties remained wedded to their separate agendas, even though the case for an amalgamation was overwhelming. But too many vested interests would have been affected if the political scene had been tidied up and one centre-right party had been formed to concentrate single-mindedly on implementing the CDR programme.

The parties of the coalition and their elected representatives were in a permanent election campaign and it was against each other that they were competing.[146] It was soon clear that no parties with a cohesive internal structure and clear ideological outlook existed on the governing side, except for the UDMR and the PD who were defending, respectively, an ethnic cause and an adaptable segment of the population who had a stake in the old order and wished to be influential in the new one. But the historic parties did not really know which social groups they represented. The initiative remained with the CDR and the President until the autumn of 1997. It was not the failure of NATO to admit Romania that blew the reform off course, nor was it the obstruction or plotting of anti-reform elements within the state apparatus, nor was it even the restiveness of a population facing an unstoppable slide in living standards and unwilling to be the victims of a failed economic experiment. Instead it was divisions within the CDR (often of a petty kind) and a failure to agree a proper plan for reform and agree on a timetable for necessary changes that produced mounting disillusionment with the government by the time of its first anniversary in office. Ciorbea was gone three months after this following a lengthy crisis in which the CDR's numerical strength counted for little against a much more experienced and ruthless PD, which proceeded to wage a guerrilla war against its coalition partners. If the latter had sized up Petre Roman's gameplan sooner, they might have gone for early elections in 1997–8 to try and obtain a majority of their own. The cigarette smuggling scandal which erupted in May 1998 showed how little control the regime had over branches of the state, especially the security services. If the moment had been used to close down agencies and remove officials who were incapable of being reconciled to democracy, then President Constantinescu might have been able to restore his sinking credibility. But it proved to be the point of no return for a floundering President and a disunited coalition which by now had lost the ability to communicate effectively with most of the voters who had placed them in office.

The debacle of coalition rule indeed showed how difficult it was to demolish the harmful legacy of communist rule. But it also suggested that there was a deeper malaise in the approach of Romanian élites to the task of governance. This had undoubtedly been greatly exacerbated by communism, but it had older origins.

6

A BROKEN-BACKED COALITION

External disillusionment

In 1997 Romania found itself in the international spotlight for the first time since 1990, but it subsequently forfeited much of the international goodwill that greeted the overthrow of the Ceauşescus. This occurred when opponents of President Iliescu were brutally assaulted in the streets of Bucharest in 1990, apparently at his instigation. The rapprochement with Hungary, the strengthening of minority rights and efforts to consolidate a fragile democracy appeared to restore some of that goodwill, and on several occasions in 1997 the US President, Bill Clinton, expressed admiration for the Romanian-Hungarian entente as a model for solving inter-ethnic disputes. Speaking at The Hague on 28 May 1997 on the fiftieth anniversary of the launch of the Marshall Plan, Clinton singled out Romania as a country 'where democracy has prevailed over intolerance'.[1] His visit to Bucharest on 11 July 1997 understandably fuelled large expectations.

But the Western organizations which Romania hoped to enter had always made it clear that the success of the bid to join mainstream Europe would depend largely on sustained economic reform. After the painful demise of the Ciorbea government, there could be no doubt that their progress in restructuring the state-led economy had been minimal. Privatisation legislation may have been passed, price controls lifted and the currency freed, but 80% of the economy was still state-run and dependent on public revenue to stay afloat.[2] This would remain the case until late in the coalition's life. Inevitably confidence was eroded in the ability of Romania to cast off its totalitarian legacy and begin to catch up with its Central European neighbours. The European Commission was unenthusiastic about coaxing the country out of its economic sick-bed to prepare for the tough race that all candidate members needed to run to fulfil the accession terms, and in July 1997 it recommended that Romania, along with five other states, be left out of the accession process, due to start at the end of that year, since it was unpredictable when it could meet the terms of entry.[3] In July 1998 a Commission official declared publicly that 'Romania had the worst economic performance of any EU applicant over the past year'.[4] In August relations with Brussels were scarred by the government's failure to submit economic data in time to enable the Commission to publish its annual report on applicant countries; when the data were finally submitted, they included contradictory estimates of the same indicators, produced by different ministries.[5]

But the scene was not entirely gloomy at the Luxembourg summit of EU heads of government in December 1997 it was decided to extend invitations simultaneously to all eleven aspirant members, but to proceed at a much slower pace with those, such as Romania, that fell far short of entry requirements. Further encouragement was offered in March 1998 when the EU decided that the pre-accession states least prepared for entry would receive a disproportionately large share of funds from the EU in the hope that they would catch up with the fast-track candidates.[6]

An unyielding IMF

Romania had some well-wishers in the EU, not least Romano Prodi, prime minister of Italy from 1996 to 1999 and from 2000 President of the European Commission. But the International Monetary Fund (IMF), the external agency most closely involved with Romania since 1989, would not allow its judgment to be clouded by sentiment. In March 1998 it suspended the standby loan agreed in 1997, the fifth agreed since 1989 of which none had been fully paid because of Romania's non-compliance with its terms. An IMF delegation came and went in the summer of 1998 without terms for a new loan being agreed. The IMF was unhappy with Romania's failure to bring down inflation and with the budget deficit of 4.6% which Radu Vasile had recommended on taking office.[7] It complained of budget priorities being distorted by the subsidies flowing out to loss-making state companies, a long-standing complaint. However, some of its own solutions were uninspiring, such as its call for higher taxes, which would not affect the black economy, variously estimated to encompass between 15 and 40% of economic activity. Tax increases were likely to place an intolerable strain on thousands of new companies which had sprung up in the 1990s, and were already reeling from falling demand; a 22.6% fall in real wages in 1997 contributed to a 12.1% drop in the volume of retail trade. In 1999, 190,000 of Romania's 393,000 private companies would register a loss. Yet these companies, though producing only one-quarter of the national wealth, carried two-thirds of the tax burden.[8] Many of them had been set up by people with genuine entrepreneurial drive which communism had thwarted but not destroyed. To impose a crippling tax burden on small- and medium-sized companies, on which the economic future of the country depended, appeared a naïve strategy on the part of the IMF. In the shadow of IMF disapproval, it was difficult for Romania to raise loans at favourable interest rates on international capital markets, and further deterred potential investors. In August 1998 the country's creditworthiness was further damaged by the collapse of the Russian currency, which reduced the attractiveness to investors of countries with economic structures that appeared similar to Russia's. By the end of the year, major international ratings agencies were placing Romania in a high-risk category.[9]

Faced with mounting troubles at home, Prime Minister Vasile blamed foreign intelligence services for creating diversions designed to turn foreign investors away from Romania.[10] This was a clear repudiation of the President's view that the chief threats to Romania's well being were internal rather than external in origin. Nevertheless, Vasile would develop a strategy of trying to reassure the IMF and the EU that bold changes were on the way while at the same time convincing Romanian workers that a safety-net would be provided to safeguard their welfare. In a speech broadcast on 13 April 1998 Vasile pledged to 'put Romania firmly on the road of no-return towards a market economy and democracy'.[11] But despite being more skilled than Ciorbea at political manoeuvring, he could not easily translate good intentions into actions. A primary obstacle was the overmanned bureaucracy which lacked any incentive to make modernisation work and had no fear of sanctions from divided reformers. Serious reform would threaten Romania's bureaucratic culture which was based on postponing decisions, avoiding responsibility, often favouring special

interests, and allowing the operation of parallel agencies to neutralise change.[12] Local officials could sometimes be as obdurate as ones
in the central ministries. Early in his premiership, Vasile had to
make the long journey to Caranşebes in the south-west to persuade
local managers to stop obstructing the efforts of US investors to buy
a local furniture firm.[13] At other times Vasile used the populist card.
In November 1998 he told workers in Brasov that 'Romania is one
of the few countries in the world which produces its own aeronau-
tical equipment and there is no reason to justify the closure of the
industry.' According to one editor, this was a throwback to the
1980s when Ceauşescu would insist that Romania needed to be
self-supporting in key aspects of industry.[14]

Who governs Romania? The case of Renel

Vasile's irresolute approach to underperforming state companies was
shown in his handling of Renel, the state electricity company. In
1990 Petre Roman had set up a range of state companies holding
monopolies in key economic sectors. These monopolies, temporarily exempt from privatisation, were based on the 'regie' concept
imported from France.[15] *Regies* like Renel enjoyed major autonomy
from the state, although it guaranteed their income. A law dating
from August 1990 allowed the administrators of the *regies* to establish
their own salaries.[16] Disclosures in 2000 revealed that executives in
the *regies* received salaries as high as $100,000 and that average wages
were three to five times higher than those in other state firms.[17] In
2000 the President himself revealed that Renel's salaries alone accounted for 0.84% of GDP in 1999 while the company registered
losses amounting to 1% of GDP.[18]

In 1997 the three principal *regies*—Renel, Romgaz and Petrom—
had been given ninety days to come up with a restructuring programme. But thanks to the government's preoccupation with the
algorithm and the lengthy crisis at the end of 1997, nothing happened.[19] In May 1998 Vasile got the agreement of the entire coalition to block Renel's bank account. But on the same day the account
was suddenly unblocked again. The Prime Minister's spokesman
threatened to remove the accreditation of journalists if they revealed
what the premier had promised the previous evening 'when he had
been tired'.[20] Unexplained pressures had forced the government to

quickly reverse a measure long-called for by the IMF. According to *Adevârul*, 'the impact on the government's image and on that of the Vasile team is catastrophic. The government is completely on the defensive against the monopolies and their trade-unions'.[21] This sobering incident revealed the continuing influence of the directors and managers of ailing state industries, known as 'the directocracy' (*directocratii*). They had been a key pillar of the Iliescu regime, and they were still able to prevent their plants and utilities being placed under proper budgetary constraints even in the absence of their patron.

Slow-motion privatisation

The State Ownership Fund (Fondul Proprietar de Stat: FPS) was the body in charge of the privatisation process. Between 1991 and 1996 it sold companies to only eleven foreign investors. In 1997 the Ciorbea government placed it firmly under government control. Its new director, Sorin Dimitriu, was chosen by the President himself. During the communist era Dimitriu had been a middle-ranking manager in the steel industry before serving in Petre Roman's government and then acting as a FPS director during the Vacaroiu years.[22] He had all the hallmarks of a born political survivor, managing to secure a good place on the PNTCD election list in time for the 1996 elections. Constantinescu even lobbied for him to succeed Ciorbea as premier in March 1998 but the basis for his confidence in Dimitriu remained unclear.

The FPS was soon criticised for its sluggish approach to sell-offs. Targets for restructuring changed frequently and were usually not met. Fears of sparking off unrest meant that plans to privatise loss-making heavy industrial firms were shelved. Instead of selling off the large portfolio of firms in its hands and preparing to disappear from the scene, the FPS itself expanded rapidly in 1997–8; imposing new buildings were opened and lots of new staff hired.[23] The only sizeable company sold by Dimitriu was Romtelecom, one of the few profitable state ones. It was sold in 1998—not to a private buyer but to its counterpart in Greece—on terms which the press insisted were greatly to the advantage of the buyer.[24] Dimitriu was finally removed on 19 October 1998. According to one source, only IMF concern over the slow and confused model of privatisation 'was sufficiently strong' for that to happen.[25]

Signs of nepotism in branches of the state crucial for the reform process produced disillusionment about how serious the post-1996 government was in moving Romania in a new direction. Sorin Dimitriu's brother Andrei had been secretary of state in the privatisation agency during the time the former was in charge, and his wife Anca was one of the directors of the FPS.[26] Ion Diaconescu, the PNTCD leader, who had sustained Dimitriu till the last, had appointed an 'unending list of nephews' to key posts in the state administration.[27] The prime minister's wife Mariuca Vasile worked in the Agency for Recouping Banking Assets (AVAB), which was seeking to recover the huge sums looted from state banks before 1996. During 1999 she opposed her superior Ovidiu Grecea, who wished to seize the assets of well-known figures who were debtors to state banks,[28] advocating persuasion rather than coercion. The Vasiles' own wealth became a public issue in late 1999 when it was reported that 'the prime minister's son drives a car that sweeps away "the chicks" in the neighbourhood and which his father, together with the whole family, could not possibly afford to buy with their salaries'.[29]

Four-wheel-drive cars (or *jeepuri*) became the status symbol of the newly-moneyed élite who drove around at weekends in all weathers to show off their powerful machines.[30] Even the main author of the 1991 constitution, the jurist and PDSR senator Antonie Iorgovan, and his immediate family had (according to the press) no less than seven cars. This information appeared in an article which described how in 1995 he had managed to buy a villa in one of the exclusive districts of the capital,—placed at his disposal in the early 1990s— for the nominal sum of $200, a tiny fraction of its current value.[31] Not a few of the Bucharest owners of *jeepuri* had also done well thanks to their close connections with those at the centre of power.

Government adrift

What became known as the Bell Helicopters affair also tarnished the image of leading government figures and drew in the President himself. In 1997 Romania signed a preliminary agreement with Bell Helicopters, a subsidiary of the US firm Textron, allowing it to acquire a controlling stake in a loss-making Romanian aviation firm for $50 million and produce helicopters for the Romanian military. Romania would buy ninety-six helicopters—at a cost of around

$2 billion—and hope to produce more for export.[32] Supporters of the contract argued that bringing large US industrial companies into the country would boost efforts to promote foreign investment, preserve jobs, and impress NATO with Romania's determination to modernise its armed forces in the hope of soon joining the Alliance. However, the IMF and the World Bank argued that the country could not afford such a project.[33]

Opposition to the deal was expressed across party lines, but was led by Daniel Dăianu, the finance minister. In July he refused to put his signature to a cabinet decision approving the financial arrangements, knowing that they would upset his financial targets and lead to unpopular cuts in social expenditure. The defence minister Victor Babiuc, who had championed the helicopter deal, demanded that Dăianu either agree to it or be sacked. The outcome of the dispute was decided by President Emil Constantinescu, who has been an enthusiast for the deal. He argued that the Bell contract was vital for national security and obtained the ringing endorsement of the CSAT (the Supreme Council of National Defence).[34] He took the lead in persuading Vasile and the PNL to withdraw their backing from Dăianu, who was sacked on 23 September. However, the deal fell through once it became clear that international agencies monitoring the Romanian economy were distinctly unimpressed by a contract of which the advantages for Romania were far from clear. Two of the President's most forthright critics argued that it was a sign of his weakness for a quick fix, which had far less to it than met the eye. They cited his assiduous lobbying for a pipeline to come via Romania westwards from the Caspian oilfields when most of the projected routes published in specialist journals made no mention of Romania.[35]

The Tigareta II scandal (see above, pages 173–5) and the Bell Helicopter affair left Constantinescu's anti-corruption campaign in desperate trouble. In September 1998, at the first press conference he had given for months, the President explained that the CNAICCO (National Council of Action Against Organised Crime), set up in January 1997 to combat corruption, had had to begin from scratch: 'Until two years ago nothing had been done. We found only files with newspaper cuttings to be used for blackmail.'[36] He claimed with some justification that progress had been made in cleaning up the banking system; he had refused to allow the ruling parties to control the banks by appointing directors.[37] He even claimed that under the PDSR the banking system had been so mismanaged that 'had the transfer of power only come a month later, we would have witnessed the descent of the banks into chaos and the country's collapse.'[38]

Perhaps if Romania, like Bulgaria in 1996, had experienced a full-blown financial crisis under an anti-reform government there could have been a chance for root-and-branch reform. According to one Western diplomat, questioned in 1998, 'The problem is that the old system did not get sufficiently broken up. Too many of the old relationships survived.'[39]

A judiciary ambivalent about a law-based state

The judicial system, with honourable exceptions, was unenthusiastic about the anti-corruption drive. The Prosecutor-General's office (known as the *procurata*), an institution specific to communist regimes, survived the 1989 revolution. Andrei Vyshinski, the infamous chief prosecutor in Stalin's Russia, had provided the prototype for this role. Prosecutors enjoyed much greater power in the communist judicial process than judges, and in the late 1990s the outcome of a corruption case often depended on which prosecutor took it up.[40] The unwillingness of judges to assert their independence may stem from the fact that the 1991 Constitution does not adhere strictly to the principle of separation of powers. According to one well-known lawyer, judges and prosecutors, classified as members of the magistracy, are 'under the thumb of the executive branch'.[41]

Executive interference was undisguised in the last years of the Iliescu presidency. In 1995 the President condemned as 'unlawful' a series of court decisions ordering the return of nationalised houses and apartments to their original owners, and urged local administrative bodies not to carry them out. From then on the Prosecutor-General filed many appeals against those court decisions, and the Supreme Court, which had previously accepted the lower court's jurisdiction over property restitution cases, quickly reversed its position and held that the court had overstepped its authority.[42] Many of the plaintiffs appealed to the European Court of Human Rights which often judged in their favour.

The difficulty of getting judicial bodies to support an anti-corruption campaign which might discomfit the pre-1996 regime was shown by an incident related by the human rights lawyer Monica Macovei: 'In January, I filed a complaint against the former president, Ion Ilieseu, for committing perjury. In December 1997 Iliescu had testified under oath that in 1991 my client—the Civic Alliance…—compelled the miners to use violent measures to bring down the government. Iliescu testified as a witness during a hearing before the Bucharest Court of Appeal in the case concerning the miners' alleged unlawful actions. Although my client was not a party in the trial, I proved its legitimate interest and requested a copy of Iliescu's sworn testimony. The chief judge refused my request saying, "I don't want to lose my job; what happens if Iliescu gets angry with me? He might again someday be president!" I responded to the judge that he could not lose his job since my request was lawful, the trial was public, and anyway his appointment was for life. Finally, he allowed me to read Iliescu's statement, but I did so under the supervision of the court clerk, who refused to let me take notes. The judge feared any written evidence proving his involvement—even if legal—in the case of Civic Alliance versus Iliescu. Besides demonstrating that judges still do not act independently, this story demonstrates the way that the rule of law is diluted by judges who still fully expect the executive to interfere and who make decisions or act in anticipation of this interference.'[43] The police were little different. In 2000 Cornel Nistorescu wrote: 'There are many police officers you will go to in order to file a complaint. If the complaint is against someone close to the PDSR, it's tough luck. "No dice, as the others are coming in and I'd be finished," they will tell you.'[44]

Exasperated, Constantinescu declared in December 1998 that it was impossible even to speak of 'a small offensive' against corruption. In the same month the justice minister, Valeriu Stoica, argued that the permanent tenure of some judges needed to be removed because of serious cases of corruption and incompetence.[45] But it was the CNAICCO itself that was officially wound up in February 1999 as its lack of success in accomplishing its goal became ever more embarrassing to the President: During its two years of existence economic and financial crime was widely perceived to have 'soared to unprecedented levels'.[46] *Adevarul* claimed that numerous dossiers had been blocked because those implicated were important figures in the PNL or PD. It pointed the finger at the Popescu clan from Dimbovita county, nephews of Ion Diaconescu, who 'plunder and terrorise the country in the name of continuing "the Maniu-Mihalache" line' (these were the two main pre-war PNTCD leaders, well known for their probity).

Confronting totalitarian legacies

The retrograde behaviour of CDR notables was also responsible for the emasculation of another piece of legislation meant to mark a clear break with the past: the law on the access to the files which the pre-1989 Securitate kept on millions of citizens. 70-year-old Senator Constantin (Ticu) Dumitrescu, head of the Association of Former Political Prisoners, a body affiliated to the CDR, had long been associated with this cause. In 1992 the Chamber of Deputies had passed a motion granting access to the Securitate files on MPs and senators, but the Senate then failed to pass it. After 1996 the passing of legislation seemed assured. In March 1997 Dumitrescu tabled a bill which would allow all citizens access to their Securitate files; moreover, the files of individuals holding public positions or elective office would also be in the public domain. A National Council for the Study of the Security Archives (CNSAS) would be set up to administer the documents. It would be modelled on the Gauk Institute in Germany, which between 1990 and 1997 had processed some 3.7 million requests to view files of the former East German Stasi.[47]

The 'Ticu Dumitrescu' law languished for months after it was sent to the government for comment. Not only did the senator criticise the President for displaying a lack of political will, but in September 1997 he implied that certain PNTCD elders feared the publication of their own dossiers and had taken action in consequence.[48] Dumitrescu was disciplined by the PNTCD in 1997 and suspended from it in 1998. Evidence that senior CDR figures wished to emasculate the bill came in 1998 when the PNL's Mircea Ionescu Quintus and the PDSR's Doru Ioan Taracila persuaded the Senate to pass an amendment allowing the dossiers to remain in the hands of the Securitate's successor, the SRI. Access to the files could also be withheld if national security was invoked.[49] In 1999 the SRI also persuaded Parliament to block access to the files of serving Romanian diplomats and members of the intelligence services by invoking national interest.[50]

The utility of opening up the Securitate files was doubted by some who did not necessarily harbour a guilty past. The names of informers could be revealed only if a petitioner was able to prove a violation of human rights, and the law does not provide for any sanctions against perpetrators of such violations.[51] Besides, a large part of the archive was no longer intact. Compromising files had been removed and seven tons of them had been half-burnt in mid-1990 in a botched effort at concealment by the SRI, which became known as the Berevoiesti affair,[52] and it was likely that others had been tampered with. N. C. Munteanu, a journalist with Radio Free Europe, managed to see his Securitate file and thought it authentic, except for the last page, which convinced him that 'dossiers which are going to be presented to the population are not going to be original but a synthesis arranged according to the SRI's own purposes.'[53] Mircea Gheordunescu, the deputy head of the SRI, lowered expectations about the opening up of the Securitate archive: 'You have to bear in mind Romanians are not Germans… The system used in Germany cannot be reproduced here. For a start we have only thirty people to put order in kilometres of files. They have 3,000. Even the way of classification and indexation is very complicated here.'[54]

The CNSAS, the board set up to review access to files, fell victim to political infighting once a pale version of the Ticu Dumitrescu law was finally passed in 1999; the algorithm principle applied to its membership; its eleven members were to be nominated by parties proportionate to their representation in Parliament, serving six-year terms. In the Senate an attempt was made to block the PNTCD's nominee, Horia Patapievici, an anti-communist writer, on the grounds that he was anti-national in outlook. Andrei Pleşu and Mircea Dinescu were attacked because they had been members of the PCR. The law on Securitate dossiers insists that candidates cannot have been communist party members, making no special provision for dissidents or opponents of the communist regime who either quit the party or were expelled.[55] Eventually all three were able to join the CNSAS.

Cotroceni was criticised for adopting a supine attitude to the dossiers. Relations between the President and his civil society allies were also soured by his silence over the Gheorghe Ursu affair.

Gheorghe Ursu had been arrested in 1985 after colleagues in the institute where he worked discovered a diary in which he criticised the regime and mocked its pretensions, and died in prison from beatings after his arrest. After 1997, the director and deputy director of the SRI, Costin Georgescu and Mircea Gheordunescu, both of whom were personal friends of the President, refused not only to return the diary to Ursu's relatives, but also to act when it became public knowledge in 1999 that two of Ursu's killers, both former officers of the Securitate, were working for the SRI in leading positions.[56] The breach between former allies in the democratic camp caused by this affair was shown by an open letter to Georgescu from leading pre-1989 dissidents: 'The fact that eight years after the revolution of December 1989, the authorities shield Securitate activists from their victims' gaze raises a question-mark about the options of the political forces which took over the leadership of the country in November 1996. What should we assume about the director of the SRI (and through him, the country's President) who keep Romania in the "original" position of a country clamouring for participation alongside the community of democratic nations, while showing themselves incapable of lifting a part of the insiders veil of the Securitate.'[57]

At least the annual SRI reports which Costin Georgescu presented to parliament were less bound up with unspecified foreign threats. The report for the period between June 1998 and June 1999 described corruption and the actions of certain unnamed trade-union leaders as posing the main threats to national security.[58] The next one, issued in February 2000, emphased organized crime and arms smuggling. It mentioned the tendency to increase majority-minority tensions on the part of some politicians keen to popularise 'radical orientations' without saying who they might be. But despite these dangers, Romania was described as 'a stability zone'.[59]

Progress in bringing to justice individuals responsible for the hundreds of death which occurred in the December 1989 revolution was slow. On 20 December 1996, at a solemn meeting of Parliament marking the seventh anniversary of the revolution, the President, recently invested, bluntly declared: 'If we don't succeed in establishing the truth about these events in the year ahead, we are not fit to reassemble here on 21 December 1997.'[60] Little was achieved subsequently as General Dan Voinea, a senior official in the Supreme Court of Justice admitted on 15 December 1998: 'If at the commemoration of the hero-martyrs of the revolution, President Constantinescu is not able to say with his hand on his heart that he has respected promises, we procurators are the principle guilty ones, because the dossiers are in our keeping.'[61] Thanks to General Voinea's indefatigable efforts, successful prosecutions were mounted against generals implicated in acts of repression in 1989. On 15 July 1999 Generals Victor Athanasie Stănculescu and Mihai Chitac were accused of ordering troops to open fire on unarmed civilians in Timişoara on 17 December 1989, an act which resulted in seventy-two deaths and 253 seriously injured, and each was sentenced to fifteen years in prison on charges of aggravated murder.[62]

Petre Roman, who had appointed Stănculescu to a senior position in his government in 1990, described the sentences as 'an act of blind vengeance by certain politicians whose interests run totally against democracy and the course of history'.[63] However, in the words of presidential spokesman Razvan Popescu, this statement denied 'the independence of the justice system at the highest level of representation'.[64] The claim of the defence minister Victor Babiuc that 'the two generals themselves did not harm anybody' and 'played a decisive role in the army switchover to the side of the revolution' showed how keen figures in the PD camp were to find extenuating circumstances to prevent justice taking its course.[65] The disagreement and irresolution within the coalition in 1998 over how to cope with the repressive legacy of the communist era gave former and serving intelligence officers the perfect opportunity to go on the offensive. During the first year of Vasile's premiership files were disclosed which sought to discredit coalition figures. Ioan Ghise of the PNL, elected mayor of Brasov in 1996, was accused of having been an informer,[66] and the PD's Adrian Vilau, head of the parliamentary commission overseeing the foreign intelligence service, lost his position after evidence was presented suggesting that he had collaborated with the Securitate.[67] The UDMR's Francisc Baranyi, then minister of agriculture, was forced to resign after a similar disclosure even though he insisted that he had signed an agreement to cooperate at the point of a gun in 1961, that his cooperation had been shortlived, and that he never subsequently caused harm to anyone.[68] Each of their files was leaked by a serving captain in the SRI, Constantin Alexa, who admitted that in the case of Baranyi this was done with the aim of destroying his career.[69] Alexa was dismissed from the SRI and brought before a military tribunal and charged with endangering national security, but he left court a free man in June 1999, having been given a suspended jail sentence—hardly a disincentive to other SRI officials tempted to do the same thing.[70] The PNTCD's Vasile Lupu fought off allegations that he had collaborated with the Securitate as a young man and went on to pilot important reform legislation through parliament.[71] So did Ioan Ghise, who was re-elected mayor of Brasov in 2000. None of the coalition figures who only paid lip-service to reform had their dossiers exposed. The revelations may well have been planned to discredit figures like Lupu who were serious about reform, Vilau in a sensitive political position, and the UDMR which prided itself on being largely free of compromising links with the communist era. The leaks may also have been designed to help rehabilitate left-wingers and nationalists whose careers had been inhibited by the roles they had played before 1989. Their exoneration would prove much easier if the public could be persuaded that anti-communists had feet of clay and were in no position to accuse anyone else of collaboration.

Dennis Deletant has pointed out that both the Baranyi and Vilau cases 'highlighted the lack of precision in the use of the term "informer" in the Romanian media. Its indiscriminate application to anyone who entered into a written agreement to pass information to the Securitate, irrespective of the type of information conveyed, has betrayed a lack of sensitivity in treating the nature of the Securitate into the daily lives of Romanians...'[72] The intrusive nature of the communist state meant that millions of Romanians had been forced to have dealings with the Securitate. To fail to distinguish between levels of cooperation meant that it was relatively easy for beneficiaries of the communist regime to argue that no one was either innocent or guilty since all had colluded with the system. The practice of selectively leaking files on opponents even appeared to have the approval of the prime minister. In June 1998 Radu Vasile said that he had obtained information from the secret services about anti-government moves by some leaders in his own party.[73] This was a remarkable disclosure that made it appear normal for the security services to interfere in party politics. It is perhaps no coincidence that the dossiers of PNTCD figures leaked in 1998–9 all belonged to the prime minister's opponents.

With the coalition divided, much of its reform programme blocked and diluted, and unrepentant supporters of the former communist regime flourishing in business and starting to regain influence in politics, it is not surprising that nationalism quickly revived as a valuable political commodity. In early 1997 the UDMR's György Frunda had warned: 'If things go wrong [for the government], it is the Hungarians who are going to be blamed.'[74] The PD in particular confirmed this judgement by consistently taking an anti-minority position to deflect criticism against it for being part of an increasingly unpopular government. During the last months of the Ciorbea government, its parliamentarians had voted against, or refused to sustain, government ordinances designed to allow the use of Hungarian in government institutions. The PD voted against Ordinance 22, which therefore failed to obtain the Senate's approval on 22 March 1998, with the result that bilingual inscriptions and notices put up in hundreds of localities would have to be removed;[75] and sources from inside the PD (which was by now outside the government) maintained that their action was a warning to the UDMR on account of its fidelity to the Ciorbea government.[76] Roman's party, on this and other occasions, showed that it considered the UDMR representatives to be vassals who should not have the audacity to play a front-rank role in Romanian politics. Early in 1998 it was difficult to remember that a foreign minister from the ranks of the PD had said only a few months earlier that the stability and security of Central Europe depended on sound Romanian-Hungarian relations.

The UDMR: a constructive force in government

Whether or not there would be a state-funded university employing the Hungarian language proved to be the most problematic question with an ethnic dimension in the lifetime of the coalition. For the UDMR it was an absolute priority, since they feared that in its absence the Hungarians would slowly but surely lose the intellectual élite without which the minority would be unable to renew itself culturally. According to a poll carried out in Transylvania during the summer of 1998, only just over 13% of Romanians believed that such a university would have a positive impact on inter-ethnic relations, while exactly 50% thought the consequences would be negative or very negative.[77]

In 1959 the Hungarian state university in Cluj had been absorbed into the chief Romanian one in the city, one of the first acts by the communist state to terminate the collective rights which the minority had been granted after 1945. By 1997 the amalgamated university, widely known as the Babes-Bolyai university, had eighty-one sections, of which twenty-three had teaching in Romanian and Hungarian, eight in German, and one (social assistance) catering specifically for the Roma minority.[78] In March 1997 Victor Ciorbea, as prime minister, appeared to pave the way for a state-funded Hungarian-language university being founded in Cluj when his government introduced an 'urgent ordinance' modifying the 1995 education law to allow the establishment of universities with instruction in minority languages.[79] But he had to retreat in the face of criticism, not least within his own party, the PNTCD. Opposition to minority-language universities encompassed a broad spectrum of Romanian opinion; it was fuelled by the media and opposition parties, university figures joined in, and organisations supposed to be pillars of enlightened civil society also became involved.

At the height of this dispute, on 3 September 1998, Bela Markö declared that from then on the UDMR would act 'in conformity with our own program and the interests of our electors'.[80] This was a shift away from the more consensual attitude the party had shown in March 1998 at a time of Romanian coalition infighting when Markö had said that the UDMR would 'not insist that its demands be implemented immediately' because 'the most important thing on the agenda now is to ensure the passage of the budget in parliament'.[81] There was strong pressure not to move on this issue from the Council of the Representatives of the Union, the mini-parliament of the UDMR which has no counterpart among the Romanian parties. So, as other situations of inter-ethnic tension have shown, a high level of inner party democracy can occasionally jeopardise a pragmatic stance, allowing more radical voices to come to the fore. According to Alina Mungiu-Pippidi, a demand by radicals that the UDMR quit the government, because of an apparent breach of faith

by its coalition partners was only resisted with the greatest difficulty.[82] On 30 September 1998, just two hours before a UDMR
deadline for quitting the coalition, the government agreed to the
establishment of a 'multi-cultural' Hungarian-and German-language
university to be called Petöfi-Schiller, thereby defusing the coalition
crisis. A legal framework for creating such a university was supposed
to be drawn up, but by the time the government left office just over
two years later little had been done.

The PD: Trojan horse of the coalition

The PD was easily the most troublesome member of the four-party
coalition during all its phases. This was at last publicly admitted in
January 2000 by Traian Băsescu, the transport minister, who had became exasperated with the tactics of his leader, Peter Roman. He
had told Petre Roman that 'he could no longer afford to continue a
duplicitous policy…we ought to assume our share of both the ac-
complishments and failures of the government. Certainly, this duplicity (to criticise the government from within for image purposes)
has been catastrophic for the party.'[83] The PD opposed government
efforts to halt the spiralling losses of the state farming sector, which
had been thoroughly mismanaged during PDSR rule. It had originally backed an agreement made with the World Bank that assistance to modernise agriculture would be provided if most of the
large state farms were wound up or privatised. The accord had been
signed on 1 July 1997, but three months later the PD tabled a motion saying that the pig and chicken farms were 'of strategic importance' and should not be privatised.[84] The person behind this *volte
face*, Triță Făniță, not only chaired the Senate's agricultural commission but was a powerful figure in the grain-exporting business, and
by frequently threatening to defect from the PD (he eventually
joined the PDSR in 2000), he extracted the backing of Petre Roman for preserving the state's considerable farming interests. Before
1996 the government had instructed state banks to cover foreign
debts and afterwards Făniță lobbied hard to have them rescheduled.[85]
François Ettori, the outgoing representative of the World Bank,
criticised such delaying tactics as harmful to reform in an interview
with *Adevărul* on 11 April 1998, and was quickly reproached by the
PD for having the impertinence to interfere in the internal politics

of Romania. Roman's motives for backing Făniţă were political; he wished to avoid alienating any part of the PD electorate (which was more in favour of state intervention in the economy than the CDR's) in case it jeopardised his presidential chances in the 2000 elections, and to keep the party firmly behind him, he had also cracked down heavily on any perceived dissent.

On 22 September 1997 the Romanian political world had been rocked by allegations by the foreign minister, Adrian Severin, that documents in his possession proved that the editors of several important daily papers were working for foreign secret services. But most attention was reserved for his claim that two of the current party leaders were spies who had been financed by intelligence services from abroad.[86] Such accusations of spying and intrigue had been rife in Romania since 1989, but they had normally only been made by fringe politicians. The President asked the CSAT to confirm or reject Severin's allegations and in December 1997 it announced that they were groundless, but Severin refused to retract them and resigned. The government had lost a figure who enjoyed credibility among the Western politicians he had met while a delegate to the Council of Europe or as foreign minister because of his enlightened views on minority issues and strong commitment to Euro-Atlantic integration. But his allegations did nothing to advance Romania's integration hopes, probably the reverse. Severin was eventually expelled from the PD along with his fellow senator, Adrian Vilau. On 19 November 1998, at the meeting of the party's national coordinating committee to decide his fate, Vilau openly accused his party leader of having served a foreign power, something which much of the press assumed had been behind Severin's original disclosure, although he never named names.[87]

Only a few PD figures were prepared to halt the trend in the PD of becoming 'more and more a Petre Roman Party'.[88] In an open letter to his leader, Senator Radu F. Alexandru complained of 'multiple faxes setting out the line local branches needed to adopt', of 'people summoned to Bucharest for "ideological training"', of 'the intimidation and discouragement of some of the leading figures in the country', and 'the messages of "support and solidarity" sent to Roman'.[89] The aggressive tactics within the coalition at least helped to divert attention from the condition of the PD. During the month when his critics were expelled, Roman announced that the Vasile government was being given a three-month deadline to improve its performance, otherwise the PD would quit by 4 March 1999. According to one Bucharest editor, the PD wished to be: 'the one party to be taken into account to join any future government...It remains in the coalition but flirts with the PDSR. It remains with the parliamentary majority but often votes with the minority...It promotes democratic ideas and principles, but opposes...privatisation in the most important sectors...Roman criticises the lack of reform but he forgets that he has ministers in the most important economic ministries and 19 secretaries of state and heads of *regie*'.[90]

Society loses patience with the coalition

Emil Constantinescu appeared to be stating the obvious when he declared on 4 September 1998 that 'the experience of the last years shows us that there is not a bigger enemy of reform and well-being than a political class found in permanent dispute'.[91] Infighting, not only within but between parties, virtually prevented ministers with a non-party technocratic background from carrying out their plans. The President had brought in a number of technocrats after the failure of party nominees to make an impression in ministries such as education and health, an approach which enjoyed media backing. An editorial in *Adevărul* argued: 'We need to have a government of apolitical technocrats chosen on professional criteria which for 6 months or a year is separate from political agitation.'[92] But it was sometimes hard for ministers with no party background to obtain parliamentary support for legislation. Moreover, their presence was resented since it disrupted the algorithm process. Even the PNTCD showed irritation. Its deteriorating relations with the forces of civil society, which Coposu had brought into the CDR, suggested that it was a state-oriented party just like the others. Miklos Bakk, a Cluj-based political scientist, argued in 1999: 'The historic parties actually love the state and see society as dependent on it...They do not conceive intermediate levels between the state and society, such as regional autonomy or the principle of subsidiarity...The PNTCD is not a Christian Democrat-oriented party but a state-oriented party.'[93]

The best-known technocrat was Daniel Dăianu, finance minister from December 1997 to September 1998. His presence was resented by the PNTCD old-guard. He had voluntarily admitted his connection with the Securitate twenty years earlier as a young graduate recruited into Pacepa's foreign intelligence agency. In March 1998 he had helped draft a communiqué, signed by himself and two other technocrats in the Ciorbea government, highly critical of standards of behaviour in political and administrative institutions: reform was 'becoming a simple pretext for negotiating seats of power' and it was necessary to solve 'not just a simple political crisis but a deeper one, a crisis of principles...and in the end identity'.[94] Dăianu was replaced on 23 September 1998 at the request of the Liberals who had earlier nominated him. Their reasons were 'insufficient promotion of liberal policies in public finances, delays in reorganising the Ministry of Finance, and poor communication between the minister and the party leadership'.[95] But the real reason was Dăianu's refusal to back the bell Helicopter deal, which he believed would be ruinous for Romania.

The media was assiduous in exposing evidence of low conduct in high places, even when the evidence was far from watertight. Having been a champion of democracy in the early 1990s, much of the daily press started to criticise the coalition in a strident and populist fashion. Some newspapers even flirted with chauvinism as past of a circulation battle for a pool of readers, which was shrinking as a result of the recession. Private television channels also provided an outlet for populist frustrations. To the fore was Antena 1, the highly lucrative electronic counterpart of a national newspaper chain called *Jurnalul National* which attracted big sales by promoting bingo games and sensationalist reporting with a strong nationalistic edge. Antena 1's regular Marius Tuca show subjected coalition politicians and liberals from civil society, who were foolhardy enough to appear on it, to a kangaroo court of invective and denunciation. By the end of the 1990s Antena 1 had the biggest viewing audience of any Romanian television station. Mounting social distress gave plenty of ammunition to the government's critics. The country had the worst infant mortality rate in Europe. Between 1990 and 1995 the female fertility rate fell by over a quarter, the reduced family size being a sure sign of generalized economic hardship.[96] The Bucharest office of the UN Development Programme (which produced the previous statistic) also found in a report issued in 1997 that the income of 34% of

Romanian families was insufficient for their current needs, for 37% it covered only essentials, and for 21% it did not assure a reasonable standard of living.[97] The June 2000 report of the UN Development Programme provided further evidence of worsening social conditions. Describing the situation in 174 states regarding living conditions, *per capita* income, life expectancy and educational conditions, Romania ranked 64, far behind Slovakia (40), Hungary (43), and Poland (44) and even behind Bulgaria, which was in 60th place.[98]

Half way through its term, the coalition appeared to have lost touch completely with much of the electorate. In October 1998 the PDSR overtook the CDR for the first time since the election.[99] More worrying was the rise in support for the extremist PRM which scored 16% in a December 1998 poll.[100] According to repeated polls, politics remained the most despised profession in the country and Parliament the most vilified institution. Politicians were seen increasingly as a separate caste with no interest in protecting the common good, and ever anxious to find ways of benefiting themselves materially from elected office. Midway through the government's term, it was indeed clear that most of the CDR deputies, particularly the newer ones, were interested in advancing their own personal ambitions and not in the welfare of their constituents.[101] Cornel Nistorescu, with his often acute sense of the popular mood, showed how parliament and citizens were becoming estranged from one another: 'Beyond their conventional politeness, people have the same feeling of contempt for their MPs as they once had for the party activist who used to go to the provinces with a lot of fuss. And the Romanians, who have long practised the art of duplicity, give him a warm welcome, and once they get home they curse him... The Romanian MP increasingly shows he doesn't consider himself an individual working for his community, but a lucky guy who has to solve his own problems, or the problems of the clique he is part of. The phone calls to intervene in sell-off matters, in the distribution of commercial premises or to arrange for privileged treatment are not made in front of people, and few traces are left behind. But people talk about them and do not forget a thing.'[102]

In November 1997 President Constantinescu had reassured Romanians that 'towards the end of next year things will improve'.[103] In the same interview he insisted: 'It is no longer the case of a generation of sacrifice, but of a tough but shortlived period whose benefits will appear soon.' He never explained the basis of his optimism, and many Romanians would probably have agreed with Cornel Nistorescu who wrote on 27 December 1998: 'We haven't had such a bleak year since the days under Ceauşescu.'[104] Indeed many Romanians were starting to believe that life for them had been better under communism; a poll in November 1998 found that 51% held this view. More ominously 73% believed that the state needed to be run in an authoritarian manner by a single leader.[105] Even unconditional backers of democracy were losing heart. Horia Patapievici, whose writing scornful of the PDSR gave heart to the opposition before 1996, wrote in November 1998: 'Men for whom the entire intellectual opposition struggled for six years have succeeded in less than two in crushing any illusion that Romania might be saved *by them*.'[106]

It is not clear whether the ruling parties appreciated the width of the gulf opening up between them and voters they had previously regarded as their backers. Before the 1996 elections Mircea Ionescu Quintus had been asked if the leaders of the historic parties realised what would happen if the strong hopes which public opinion has invested in the PNTCD and PNL were dashed. After a moment of reflection, he replied: 'If we do not satisfy the hopes of public opinion, our parties will be finished.'[107]

The mishandling of the Jiu Valley miners

Long before receiving the verdict of the voters, the CDR and the other coalition parties were almost overwhelmed by a political challenge which, like the events of 1989, was a combination of a popular rebellion and a putsch carried out by well-placed individuals who had access to the levers of power. In January 1999 the government was faced with another revolt by the coal miners of the Jiu Valley, 350 kilometres west of Bucharest. In the early 1990s their leader Miron Cozma, acting in concert with more influential figures, had perfected the technique of the *mineriada*. It has been described as 'an instrument of pressure and intimidation' designed to coerce and punish forces which were felt to be threatening the security and welfare of Romania and its people.[108] Cozma had numerous charges hanging over him, but the police in Tirgu Jiu, when asked why no effort was ever made to arrest him, explained that they did not know his address.[109] Cozma's arrest in January 1997 was one of the few de-cisive actions of the Constantinescu presidency. He was placed in custody on charges of endangering national security, stemming from the fourth *mineriada* that had led to the toppling of the Petre Roman government in 1991.

While Cozma was awaiting trial in the autumn of 1997, what ap-peared to be an imaginative attempt was mounted to end the disrup-tive role the miners had periodically exercised in politics. Miners were offered generous redundancy terms to stem the losses from an industry that was failing due to the obsolescence of its equipment, bad geological conditions and declining markets. Severance fees var-ied in proportion to work experience with the least experienced of employees receiving six months' wages and qualified miners taking home twenty months'. According to Ministry of Work and Social Protection estimates, by 22 September 1997 approximately 84,000 workers had received a total of $140 million in severance payments ($100 million of this was disbursed to 45,000 miners).[110] A work-force estimated at 41,500 in 1997 had been halved within a year to 21,750.[111] According to Premier Vasile, a large part of the credits re-ceived from the IMF and the World Bank in 1997–8 was spent on miners' redundancy payments,[112] but neither these international bodies nor the government had set up the necessary social prog-rammes—for job re-training and new job creation—to enable the miners to find an alternative livelihood.[113] With 75% of the active population of the Jíu valley engaged in mining there was no alterna-tive work locally, and it is hardly surprising that, in the absence of any law preventing the miners from returning to their old jobs once their redundancy money had been spent, many did just that. Hopes that they might invest the severance money in small businesses in their home areas (many originally came from Moldavia, the poorest region in the country) were fantasies, and showed how out-of-touch politicians were with local realities.[114]

In December 1998 Premier Vasile announced an austerity programme that had as its centre-piece a number of mine closures estimated to result in a 37% reduction in mining activity.[115] Western creditors had refused to provide any more financial aid unless subsi-dies to loss-making industries were drastically cut immediately, and the government was in no position to argue. A fresh stand-by loan from the IMF was urgently needed with repayment of a debt of nearly US $2 billion due in the spring of 1999. The government was gambling on the presumption that the miners' ability to rock the political establishment was a thing of the past. The strong public sympathy that had once been felt for workers involved in a dangerous occupation had eroded as their wage rates continued to exceed those of most other groups of workers. Vasile made good use of the media to argue the government's case. Ministers refused to go to the Jíu valley to meet miners' leaders, an act which would have been seen as an abdication of state authority.

But the position of the two-year coalition was acutely weak. Cozma had been released in July 1998 after the judge reduced the charges he was facing in connection with the overthrow of the Roman government in 1991 to a secondary one and gave him a sentence that matched the time he had already spent in custody. This perfectly illustrated the problems reformers faced in seeking the cooperation of state officials, groomed in the communist era, to remedy major abuses. Judge Dinu Marin, who had tried Cozma, began his working life as a lathe-operator and obtained upward mobility by joining the militia. His political loyalties were revealed when, already a judge, he spoke at a large public rally in Bucharest in favour of Iliescu's presidential re-election in 1992.[116] Back in charge of the League of Jíu Valley Miners, Cozma was now also vice-president of the Greater Romania Party (PRM) which was mounting an offensive against the government as its poll ratings rose above 15%.[117] In a speech in August 1998 which became known as 'the Proclamation of Cimpia Tirzii', Vadim issued threats of violence against the Roma and the leadership of the Hungarian minority party, the UDMR, threatening rule by firing-squad and mass detention of his opponents in a football stadium.[118] He also used his media outlets and Parliament, where to an incredible extent he was able to flout normal conventions. In November he claimed that the President and his family had salted away $100 million and that he intended to jail him for life if he ever got to Cotroceni.[119] In December he tried to impugn the reputation of the President by claiming to be in the possession of the personal diary of Rona Hartner, an actress living in Paris, proving that he had had an affair with her and was supporting her with public money.[120] Both parties denied the affair, and graphologists from the Ministry of Justice concluded that the actress's personal journal was not in her handwriting.[121] But although the evidence for such a charge was extremely threadbare, the smear seemed to have its intended effect. Vadim had a much more effective public relations machine than Cotroceni, and nobody in Romania could match his ability to spread rumour and distortions of the truth. If through the Rona Hartner affair Vadim meant to persuade a large section of the Romanian public to welcome a new *mineriada*, he certainly enjoyed some success.

The fifth mineriada

Cozma called the Jíu Valley miners out on strike on 4 January 1999, and on 18 January a march on Bucharest by an estimated 10,000 miners got under way. President Constantinescu proclaimed that 'the time of miner-led rioting is over', but the march gained an alarming degree of support in the villages and towns of Oltenia that it passed through.[122] Mircea Dutu was one of many journalists who observed that all along the miners' route 'the population enthusiastically joined them, attacked the police force and openly expressed their dissatisfaction with the rulers and their action.'[123] Other journalists believed that the local shows of solidarity with the miners showed that the Romanian people 'have a soft-spot for the haiduk' (the type of popular outlaw found in the Balkans before 1800 of whom Cozma was felt to be a modern incarnation).[124] But most commentators gave contemporary explanations for the crisis of authority. Cornel Nistorescu wrote: 'People no longer support tough attitudes and authoritative commands. A large number of towns face overall economic bankruptcy and are on the verge of turning into real social bombs if they can no longer hope that their endurance now will pay off in the future.'[125]

Unemployment had risen at the end of 1998 to an unprecedented 10.6% of the active population, but according to Laurentiu Dumitrascu, a PNTCD deputy who observed the miners' march over several days, activists from the PRM and also the Socialist Party (PS) played an active role in stirring up the local people as the marchers filed through their areas.[126] He and journalists on the spot reported that men commanding the miners had mobile phones and maps, and Viorel Oancea, secretary-general of the Ministry of the Interior, declared that 'behind the miners are men trained in the arts of war'.[127] Opponents of the PRM claimed that many of the miners had been given military training by PRM members from intelligence and army backgrounds. Valeriu Stoica, the Minister of Justice, was the most prominent official who alleged that the PRM had been engaged in an attempted *coup d'état*. Stoica cited a letter which Vadim Tudor had addressed to the miners in which he instigated the people to side with the strikers, appealed to PRM activists to assist them, and proposed the creation of a Council of the Revolution.[128] At a special sitting of Parliament on 23 January he promised the PNTCD and the PNL a 'mother of battles', declared that 'revolutions create their own legal bases', and appealed to the army to disobey orders and 'fraternize' with the population.[129] The power Vadim exercised was shown by the timorous reaction of parliamentarians at a 20 January meeting of the Senate where he arrived flanked with bodyguards; only the Hungarian UDMR was prepared to challenge his barking invective.[130] Three days later Bucharest was rife with rumours that a coup was unfolding, a view which the Hungarian Senator György Tokay voiced openly.[131] The press reported that directors of state television who aligned with the opposition actually made preparations to welcome such an eventuality.[132]

A large force of 6,000 police and gendarmerie was routed by the miners on 21 January at Coştesti where around 1,500 of the former were disarmed and captured.[133] This caused panic in government. Intelligence about the miners was inadequate or non-existent, with leading SRI officials in the area of unrest taking sick-leave as the crisis unfolded. On 28 January the head of the SRI, Costin Georgescu, reproached officials responsible for monitoring the miners' protest for failing in their duty.[134] Gabriela Adameşteanu, editor of *22*, argued in the 26 January-1 February edition that the battle of Coştesti was clear evidence that the President and government 'do not control the institutions of state, particularly the Interior Ministry and the secret services'. Many of the troops were conscripts untrained for riot situations. Little or no provision of food or shelter was made for them, while the miners received supplies without any hindrance. According to *Adevărul's* Cristian Tudor Popescu, 'not one gendarme or soldier was motivated in this confrontation, nor did they see the miners as an enemy. Orders "from Bucharest" were seen not as measures to safeguard national security but as the desperate attempt of rulers to save their own skins at the price of the blood of others.'[135]

It was the attitude of the officers commanding the government forces that gave rise to the most comment and concern. The tactics of Gheorghe Lupu, the general in command of local forces, brought a chorus of criticism that he had deserted his men and given orders that cleared the way for the miners' advance. On 25 January he was charged by a disciplinary council with breaking military rules.[136] His superior, the deputy interior minister, resigned on the same day, and the interior minister Gavril Dejeu had resigned on the day his forces were routed at Coştesti. To Cornel Nistorescu and other commentators the entire sequence of events confirmed once and for all that the government was in office but not in power. He wrote on 25 January: 'I have repeatedly warned of the shady manoeuvres of the generals and colonels in the top echelons of the Ministry of the Interior and the General Police Inspectorate...the police leadership managed to preserve intact its militia mentality... The way the state was defended in the Jiu gorge and at Costeşti perfectly matches the way loyalty was defended in the cigarette, coffee and liquor deals.'[137]

The prefect of Rimnicu-Valcea, Nicolae Curcaneanu, who was captured during the disturbances, blamed the rout at Costeşti on the absence of a stable central command, the presence of too many generals and colonels, and the failure to provision troops.[138] An exultant Cozma suggested that 'the government should make us [the miners] gendarmes because we proved that we are very good, even better than the ones we faced.'[139]

On 22 January, after several hours of talks at an Orthodox monastery in Cozia, an agreement was signed between Premier Vasile and Cozma which was sufficiently advantageous to the miners for them to halt their march and return home. The agreement was brokered by the Orthodox Church, a national institution widely felt to be above political strife. It was a humiliating climbdown for a government whose head was forced to go back on his promise not to negotiate with someone who, according to President Constantinescu, 'for almost six years was allowed to defy all the institutions of the state with the tacit agreement of the former political leadership'.[140] In a revealing admission, Premier Vasile said on 27 January, while on a trip to Germany, that the government had no alternative but to sue for peace: 'According to Government information, if the miners had reached Bucharest, over 80,000 rioters would have been in the city…Under these circumstances, the city would have turned into a battlefield and the Government would have had to leave … the police would have been outnumbered as only 1,000 gendarmes were in Bucharest, most of whom were recent recruits… [the peace of Cozia] was practically the only solution.'[141] The peace of Cozia bought time for the government, and at the same time exposed divisions in the ranks of its militant opponents. Most of the miners seemed content to accept the economic gains offered to them and go home, but there was a sense of betrayal among the socially disaffected elements who had attached themselves to the march. Romeu Beja, Cozma's deputy, was imprisoned for several hours by local gangsters who had terrorised the Rimnicu Valcea district on learning that Bucharest would not after all be at their feet.[142] It has been argued that Vadim was all for pressing on to Bucharest but could not persuade Cozma to agree to this high-risk move.[143] From this point on, divisions between the two of them became increasingly open as the Cozia deal slowly saw the initiative pass from those ready to supplant the government.

Post-mineriada anxieties

When trying to assess the significance of the fifth *mineriada*, commentators often drew negative parallels suggesting that Romania was moving towards a condition that placed it among the most lawless and poverty-stricken nations in Europe. Dumitru Tinu's editorial in *Adevârul* of 25 January was typical: 'If nothing is done properly, the threat of anarchy will become a general one and Romania is going to jump beyond the stage of "Bulgarisation" towards that of Albanisation.'[144] But there were encouraging developments even at the height of the miners' rebellion. The response of the trade union movement gave cause for hope. Marin Condescu, leader of miners outside the Jiu Valley, refused to sign an appeal of solidarity with Cozma even in the face of physical threats, and disassociated himself from the strike.[145] The railway workers' union postponed a long-planned strike, evidently out of fear of being linked with Cozma's action.[146] Bogdan Hossu, head of the large Cartel Alfa union confederation, was particularly forthright in his condemnation: 'The continuing protest action by the miners will bring damage not only to the Jiu Valley but to the entire population of Romania since investors will flee a country marked by such instability.'[147]

The Romanian media, particularly the daily press, adhered to high professional standards in covering the strike often in the face of actual and threatened violence from miners and other protesters. The regular flow of news prevented the spread of rumours and distorted information which could have produced a situation of general panic and confusion. While Cozma still remained a threatening influence, editorial writers were prepared to stick their necks out and call for his arrest and strong measures against his extremist political backers.[148] On 29 January the President told around seventy reporters who had covered the miners' unrest that the information they provided reached him far from promptly than that of the intelligence service.[149]

It was perhaps the muted behaviour of the main opposition party, the PDSR which prevented the initiative falling into the hands of the extremists promoting the miners action. Ion Iliescu and his party had drawn much closer to Vadim and the ultra-nationalists since losing office in 1996, and the possibility that they would coalesce in a future government was not ruled out by the PDSR's leader.[150] Towards the end of the crisis the PDSR criticised the government for taking revenge on the miners, but on 19 January it rejected a PRM request to hold a joint rally in Bucharest and publicly appealed to the miners not to come to the capital.[151] Perhaps crucially, on 21 January, with government authority in tatters after the defeat inflicted at Costeşti, it showed solidarity with Vasile and his beleagured ministers,[152] and joined all the parliamentary parties at Cotroceni (except for the PRM) in signing a communiqué calling for social calm and a compromise solution.[153] The PDSR may well have calculated that it did not stand to gain any advantage by helping to remove a weak government that was likely to be defeated in elections by the year 2,000, in a doubtful constitutional manoeuvre which would only remind foreign governments of the unconventional circumstances in which it had acquired power in 1989–90.

Outside the areas along the route of the miners' march, public opinion also remained calm. No public rallies were held in support of the miners. Cornel Nistorescu believed that despite being oppressed by poverty and insecurity 'the silent majority of Romania's population instinctively felt that order was preferable to chaos.'[154] The first poll taken after the start of the unrest showed a fall in Vadim's popularity rating from 18 to 12% and that of his party to 12% with the main coalition force, the CDR, top at 34%.[155] A poll conducted immediately after Cozma's arrest on 13 February found that 59.66% of respondents believed his behaviour during the fifth *mineriada* had been an attempt to undermine the power of the state (with 27.62% taking a contrary view).[156] Perhaps an eloquent sign of underlying stability in the face of the mounting social crisis was the sight of thousands of Romanians patiently queuing in the January frost to pay their taxes (to avoid penalties for late payment).[157]

The biggest test the government faced was how to recover the initiative from Cozma, Tudor and their supporters. The first move against them was the suspension of Vadim from the senate on 27 January for thirty days, later followed by a Senate vote to remove his immunity from prosecution. The Interior Minister Valeriu Stoica expressed willingness to go even further. He pointed out that Article 37, paragraph 2, of the 1991 Constitution defines extremist parties and the circumstances in which they can be prohibited and he called for the PRM to be outlawed if it was found to have violated the Constitution. His own views on the matter were unambiguous: 'If the healthy segment of the Romanian people does not react immediately against this danger, a collapse is possible. The rise of Hitler and Mussolini are well-known. The events of the Jiu Valley show that he [Tudor] is capable of playing the same role.'[158] But most of Stoica's colleagues were not as forthright, and those newspapers which had opposed the miners' action were mostly sceptical about this course, believing that the PRM could quickly re-emerge under a new name.[159] There was much greater media backing for the retirement from the bench on 29 January of Judge Dinu Marin, who had allowed Cozma to leave prison in June 1998 after reducing the charge he faced to a minor public order offence. Stoica was widely defended from criticism that he had violated the independence of the judiciary by forcing Marin to resign. Newspapers like *Adevărul*, normally critical of the government, drew attention to the conspicuous wealth Marin had acquired despite his small salary.[160] The state had appealed Marin's decision in the Cozma trial and on 15 February the Supreme Court reinstated the original charge of endangering national security, and sentenced Cozma to eighteen years in prison.[161] Two days later Cozma was arrested at Caracal following a violent clash between police and 300 of his supporters as he attempted to lead a new march on Bucharest. A sixth *mineriada* was stopped in its tracks, but the muted end to the miners' protest produced accusations from the opposition that the government had but pressure on the judiciary to deliver a verdict appropriate for the moment.[162]

The success of the police in capturing Cozma was also linked to the initiative of the new interior minister Dudu Ionescu on 10 February to introduce an amnesty bill for deeds committed by the army and the militia in December 1989. Several deputies alleged that the bill was meant to increase the motivation of security force commanders to carry out orders to deal firmly with rebellious acts by miners.[163] Viorel Oancea, an Interior Ministry official and former mayor of Timişoara, the birthplace of the 1989 revolt, was demoted by the minister after criticising his initiative.[164] The weekly journal *22*, seen as the flagship for the forces of Romanian civil society, was especially critical of the amnesty proposal, but its role in the crisis period had underlined civil society's weakness. According to Horia Patapievici, perhaps the best-known liberal intellectual in Romania, the turnout at pro-democracy demonstrations in Timişoara on 21 January and Bucharest on the 22nd 'shows that the numbers effectively supporting a protest against an attempted coup were worryingly small... What we describe as civil society is in fact a fractured organism.'[165] The announcement on 23 February that in the absence of Cozma the Jiu valley miners' union had signed a new work contract halving the salary increases agreed at Cozia was the clearest indication that the emergency was over.[166]

Preoccupation with the escalating Kosovo crisis meant that the miners' revolt received limited attention in the foreign media. But the reflex of finding foreign explanations for domestic ills was never far below the surface. On the eve of the Costeşti violence. Vasile Alexe, a regular columnist in *România libera*, speculated that unnamed foreign interests wishing to destabilise the entire Balkans were behind the revolt.[167] The view was supported by Ion Diaconescu, the elderly leader of the PNTCD, who demanded in its aftermath that 'all those acting in the interests of foreign powers should be eliminated from the ministry of the interior'.[168] The SRI reports from districts affected by the unrest backed up views persistently expressed in the print media of suspicious activities on the part of Russian embassy officials at the height of the unrest (although, having acquitted itself poorly during the crises, the SRI may well have been seeking to boost its own image by pandering to anti-Russian prejudices).[169] *România líbera* also drew attention to a possible Middle Eastern involvement, carrying an extensive dossier on 6 February documenting the undeniably close contacts which the PRM leader enjoyed with the Iraqi and Libyan regimes.

Premier Vasile declared on 27 January: 'The Western world understands that in Romania the state institutions are still fragile and that the danger of communist forces taking over power is real.'[170] But commentators opposed to communism nevertheless reproached the West for being influenced by cultural prejudices in its tardy reaction to Romania's problems. The view of Bazil Stefan in *România líbera* of 11 February was not altogether untypical: 'I fear it is the old Western prejudice towards Eastern Orthodox countries, prejudice which denies them the chance to move on to capitalism, democracy and modernity and which fixes the "borders" of Europe at the line of demarcation between the Roman Catholic and Protestant countries on the one hand, and Orthodox ones on the other.' Other commentators with the same political outlook preferred to see Romania's predicament as arising from the inadequacy of its political culture. Gabriela Adameșteanu complained that Romanian political culture had a fatal predeliction for populist solutions, believing that the slogan 'The only solution is another revolution' was a standard reflex throughout its modern history. She even claimed that 'in Romanian history coups d'état appear with greater frequency than any other kind of event'.[171] Dan Pavel, a prominent political scientist exhorted, 'Let us re-invent Romania.'[172] The Russian expert Martin Malia's verdict on the destructive impact of Soviet rule on the new Russia may have had some applicability to Romania in the late 1990s. He talked of 'an institutional abyss' being 'the legacy of a leviathan Soviet state which, when it collapsed, left behind only administrative and economic rubble devoid of the judicial, accounting and police procedures necessary for a modern society'.[173]

Different editors expressed alarm that the incapacity of the state was fuelling a powerful sentiment against Bucharest.[174] Cozma himself articulated anti–Bucharest feelings when seeking to justify his actions.[175] In an editorial entitled 'A Separatist Leader, Cozma the Romanian', *Adevărul's* Cristian Tudor Popescu warned that Cozma's defiance had powerful separatist reverberations: 'Here is a Romanian who declares that he doesn't recognise the central authority of Bucharest, something which the UDMR has never done, not even through its most aggressive representatives. "If the gentlemen from Bucharest make their laws, then we are going to make our syndical justice," says Cozma.'[176] Popescu had earlier warned that the socio-economic crisis was degrading Romanian national unity and was capable of producing 'a velvet separatism' in which it was Romanians themselves, not any troublesome minority, who would take the lead in reducing the hold of Bucharest over them.[177]

The government failed to regain the initiative after its first year in office had proved so disappointing. The main focus of conflict was transferred from the squabbling coalition parties to the President, and to a prime minister determined not to be treated as an underling by Cotroceni. Reform was bound to suffer when personal infighting exacerbated the failings of the government system in Romania. Little noticed at the time, President Constantinescu made a significant admission in September 1998 that there was no bigger obstacle to reform than such infighting. Previously it had been an article of faith for everyone in the CDR to blame the communist past, and the survival of men and ideas from that era in positions of power, as the primary cause of Romania's difficulties. Here was an admission that the coalition was contributing in a significant way to the scale of the country's problems.

Soon the national perception would increase that the corruption and arrogance of power which had led to the electoral downfall of the PDSR were traits shared in full measure by its successors, especially those who had shouted loudest about the faults of the Iliescu administration. The print media in particular ventilated these views. The political élite was viewed as a separate caste with its own appetites and agendas, increasingly blind to the common good. Romania is not the only country where newspapers which may have played an effective role in promoting democracy have turned against those who try to put it into practice when the results have failed to meet their expectations. But it was the extremist fringe of Romania which increasingly capitalised on popular discontent. Vadim Tudor's Greater Romania Party (PRM), written off in 1996, forced its way to the political foreground within two years of the election in which it got less than 5% of the vote. Polling evidence showed that most voters were now starting to regard the Ceauşescu era with nostalgia rather than repulsion. Support for authoritarian solutions was on the rise.

In the first months of 1999, during the rebellion by mine workers from the Jiu valley, Romania was very nearly taken over by the PRM and former members of the security services who had swelled its ranks. The security forces of the state were outmanoeuvred and overwhelmed in two humiliating encounters. For how long the Council of the Revolution proclaimed by the PRM in January 1999 would have lasted is unclear. The attitude of the West would have been critical. The EU had reluctantly allowed Romania to join the enlargement process, even though it would manifestly be unfit for entry for years ahead. But all the evidence suggests that NATO would have been as reluctant to intervene militarily in Romania in January 1999 as it had been in December 1989.

The forces of civil society committed to democratising Romania were of little use in countering a new authoritarian power-grab. Previously the mainstay of the democratic opposition during the first half of the 1990s, the Timişoara movement and the Civic Alliance became pale shadows of their former selves during the years the CDR were in government. While it had few vocal or influential defenders in the media or in civil society, hostility towards the prospect of a PDSR comeback, hopes that direct EU assistance would boost the troubled economy, and enjoyment of the trappings of office gave the government a residual motivation to stay together to complete its four-year term.

7

TIME RUNS OUT FOR CONSTANTINESCU

No fresh start after the Mineriada

Only with the greatest difficulty had the government prevented the miners from seizing control of Bucharest. If they had prolonged their march in January, it is difficult to see how they could have been stopped, since the army might well have refused to obey any order to fire on them.[1] After the *mineriada* relations between the officer corps of the army and defence Minister Babiuc were clearly strained.[2] An uneasy peace descended after Miron Cozma's arrest on 17 February. But the government was unable to restore either its authority or the popularity it had enjoyed up to a year before. Confirmation of this weakness was shown by the fate of its efforts to have Vadim Tudor arraigned before the courts.

In 1998 Gheorghe Funar, his close ally, claimed that the PRM's influence in both the state prosecutor's office and the Ministry of Justice had prevented Vadim's arrest.[3] On 20 January 1999 the former was at last prevailed upon to start proceedings against Vadim after he had sent an incendiary letter to the miners attacking the President and the head of the Senate. It was announced that he would face trial on charges of instigating violent actions and undermining state authority—under the Romanian Criminal Code these are crimes punishable by a maximum sentence of life imprisonment and forfeiture of all assets.[4] On 23 March the Senate lifted Vadim's parliamentary immunity under which he had sheltered since his election in 1992.[5] The way seemed clear for him to appear in court to answer at least some of the eleven charges then pending against him. But no further action was taken. On 10 September 1999 the Bucharest Appeal Court ruled that it was not competent to decide whether the PRM should be outlawed; both the justice minister and a range of human rights groups had requested that this should be done on the grounds that it had violated constitutional provisions forbidding incitement to racial hatred.[6] At least the PDSR was prepared to distance itself from Vadim's party after several years of fraternal cooperation; in February 1999 Iliescu declared that he would only establish a coalition with parties that respected the Constitution.[7]

The state's weakness in the face of extremist activism was shown in relation to a publication even more virulent than those linked to the PRM. *Atac la persoana*, published by Dumitru Dragomir, specialised in xenophobic articles against Jews, Roma and other minorities often using the crudest and most insulting language. In the 7 September 1998 edition of the magazine an article appeared, under the by-line 'Swastika', stating outright that on the streets of Bucharest too many Jews were to be seen—'potential soap'. The article produced international protests, and on 7 September the minister of justice asked the Procurator General to intervene and stop the publication's 'national-chauvinist propaganda', but it continued to appear.[8]

Romania and the Kosovo conflict: the coalition's finest hour?

In the spring of 1999 domestic events were eclipsed by the conflict in Kosovo. NATO's aerial campaign against Serbia, beginning on 24 March, gave Romania leverage in international relations which it had not possessed for many years. NATO required military facilities from Romania as well as Bulgaria in its drive to force Slobodan Milošević to give meaningful autonomy to the Albanian majority in Kosovo and halt ethnic cleansing Romania's strategic importance increased as a protracted aerial war got under way and plans for a ground invasion of Kosovo were hastily drawn up. The importance of the South-East European flank to NATO's security, previously underestimated by most NATO planners, seemed vindicated by the Kosovo war.

On no other major policy issue had a previously fractured government shown so much unanimity, at least in public. On 22 April Parliament approved NATO's demand for unlimited use of Romanian airspace. Victor Babiuc, the defence minister, declared on 30 April: 'Romania's interests are divergent from those of Serbia today... We have only one solution and one answer: to be alongside and together with NATO.'[9] On 27 April General Constantin

Degeratu, chief of the Romanian general staff, was equally firm: 'Romania must support NATO in solving this crisis in Kosovo until the end.'[10] Even Iliescu's party abstained in the parliamentary vote on granting the requested access to airspace rather than take a stand that might jeopardise its links with NATO if it returned to office after the elections due in 2000.

The government's impressive support for a high-risk NATO campaign, which was slow to achieve any of its aims, stemmed from a desire to advance Romania's chief foreign policy goal of entering NATO during the Alliance's next round of enlargement. The prospects for this had diminished since 1997; Strobe Talbott, Deputy US Secretary of State, declared in November 1998 that 'Romania has regressed a great deal, which proves it was not ready to join NATO and it is still not ready to do so.'[11] Bucharest now had an unexpected opportunity to show that the country could be a key provider of security on NATO's south-eastern flank. This pro-Western orientation also stemmed from fear of Russian intervention in the Balkans on the side of Serbia. The strongest pro-NATO statements from Romanian officials came in the wake of the April 16 vote in the Russian *Duma* endorsing the call for a union between Russia, Belarus and Serbia. Official anxiety and that of much of public opinion derived from the belief that Romanian security—and possibly independence—might be threatened if a historic adversary like Russia were to establish itself as a regional power in the Balkans.

On 18 April Romania denied Russia the use of its airspace for humanitarian flights to Serbia,[12] and on 23 April gave its backing to the oil embargo announced by NATO to deprive Milošević of fuel supplies. It was encouraged in this by a similar degree of support for NATO actions from Bulgaria: the two neighbours closely coordinated their responses to the Kosovo crisis, a rare instance of cooperation between them. But it was relatively easy for Bulgaria, by comparison with Romania, to accede to NATO's request for assistance from friendly but non-belligerent states. A reformist party, the Union of Democratic Forces, enjoyed a commanding parliamentary majority, and despite being a fellow South Slav nation there was no tradition of active friendship with Serbia. Indeed the two states had been involved in four wars against each other between 1885 and 1945 over the disputed territory of Macedonia. Romania was in a far less advantageous position. The coalition's parliamentary majority was shrinking by the week owing to defections, and the failure of the government's reform programme meant that it lacked the authority needed to rally support for a controversial foreign policy decision. Moreover, Serbia was perceived in the popular imagination as an ally of Romania, indeed the only one of its neighbours against which it had not fought a war. Some historians questioned this rosy view of bilateral relations, but it was one articulated in the press and the electronic media where hostility to NATO's action in Kosovo was orchestrated.[13] In much of the Romanian media NATO, not Belgrade, was blamed for the hundreds of thousand of ethnic Albanians streaming out of Kosovo.[14] NATO's bombing of bridges over the Danube cut off trade between Romania and Serbia and isolated it from markets in Western Europe.[15] Already, in the early 1990s Romania had lost up to $3 billion after joining the embargo against Iraq, hitherto one of its chief trading partners. No compensation was offered by the West; nor was Romania compensated for its heavy losses resulting from the embargo against Yugoslavia after 1992.[16]

A public opinion poll published on 22 April showed that only 1% of Romanians supported NATO's military campaign to get Serbian forces to withdraw from Kosovo,[17] and during the conflict much of the press and several private television stations expressed virulently anti-Western views.[18] President Constantinescu tried to defend his government's stance on 16 April, saying: 'For our country there is no other strategic option… I have placed Romania on this firm road because in her history Romania has suffered too much owing to the equivocal positions adopted by her leaders, and owing to their hesitations and change of directions….'[19] For one of the few national editors to support the government's line, it was a refreshing contrast with past equivocations when major moral issues were at stake. Sorin Rosca Stănescu wrote: 'For the first time, the representatives of the Romanian nation abandoned, after so many years, the road of duplicity. … They showed by their loyalty to Western democracies and the North Atlantic alliance…that people's freedom isn't negotiable in the market place…but is defended, even if there are costs.'[20]

In the statements and speeches made by Western leaders during the conflict there were indications that a historic change in the West's relations with the Balkan states might be occurring. Several important figures talked of creating a common security umbrella and integrating the region economically with the rest of Europe. Madeleine Albright, the US Secretary of State, claimed 'the security of countries bordering Yugoslavia' to be 'as important as that of NATO countries themselves'.[21] In an address to the American people President Clinton contrasted Serbia with Romania: 'Who is going to define the future of this part of the world [the Balkans]... Slobodan Milošević, with his propaganda machine and paramilitary forces which compel people to give up their country, identity, and property, or a state like Romania which has built a democracy respecting the rights of ethnic minorities.'[22] The British prime minister Tony Blair, while addressing the Romanian Parliament on 4 May, referred to Romania as 'an exemplary partner and future ally'.[23] At the fiftieth anniversary NATO summit, a stabilisation plan for the Balkans involving a substantial injection of Western aid was outlined by Joschka Fischer, the German foreign minister.[24]

Romania and Kosovo: a missed opportunity

In the spring of 1999 the rhetoric of Western leaders towards a region normally seen as peripheral to their interests was full of promises to undo the neglect of the past when cynical decisions were made that strengthened the forces of dictatorship in the Balkans while doing little to strengthen European security. Romania's unequivocal position of support could be contrasted with the position of Hungary and the Czech Republic, which officially entered NATO in April 1999 and were found to be lukewarm about the whole Kosovo operation. It is not unreasonable to argue that Romania, while enjoying its unexpected and shortlived leverage in international relations, could have asked for concessions from the West in order to take an unpopular stance. It was also risky. If the NATO operation had resulted in stalemate or in a humiliating retreat from the skies above Kosovo and Serbia, then front-line allies like Romania and Bulgaria would have been in far greater jeopardy from a vengeful Serbia than the major Western participants. The Macedonian and Greek governments received economic concessions in order to support the NATO operation in Kosovo despite the anti-war mood among their populations (the Albanians of Macedonia excepted).[25] There is no available evidence to suggest that Romania was prepared to make support for NATO's controversial mission in Kosovo conditional on obtaining such concessions.

What could Romania have reasonably asked for? It was the first country mentioned in the declaration issued on 26 April 1999, at NATO's fiftieth anniversary summit promising further expansion.[26] But early membership of NATO would surely have been regarded as out of the question as long as it failed to fulfil the economic conditions for membership, and the battered state of its economy and infrastructure also ruled out a quick acceptance of its application to join the EU. But focussed and immediate support to improve the performance of the economy would not have been an unreasonable request. In the 1970s the offer of cheap credits by the EU had enabled the newly democratic Spain and Portugal to create a climate that enabled free politics to sink firm roots. The post-1948 Marshall Plan had transformed the economic prospects of West European countries shattered by war.

Before any offer to assist NATO had been made or accepted, Romania could reasonably have asked for assurances that it would be compensated in full for its economic losses resulting from the war. A concerted effort by both down-river Danubian states to obtain firm guarantees on this issue would probably have earned the respect of hard-headed officials in the NATO and EU bureaucracies. Similarly, both Bulgaria and Romania might have earned respect from policy-makers alarmed by the vitality of nationalism in their part of Europe if they had argued that their national interests required a contented Serbia, which should also be assisted to break free from dictatorship. If Romania and Bulgaria had linked their well-being with that of the ordinary citizens of Yugoslavia and pressed NATO to offer sizeable humanitarian assistance to Serb civilians after the war, they might have raised their status in the eyes of their own domestic opinion and of other Europeans horrified at seeing ordinary Serbs being punished for the sins of Milošević and his ruling circle. And there might never have been a better time than the Kosovo war for Romania to press its case for the International Monetary Fund (IMF) to revise its lending terms. The IMF's obsession with macro-economic stability had forced the Vasile government to raise taxes and cancel tax breaks to foreigners.[27] A high tax environment had driven thousands of legitimate businesses to ruin and stimulated the black economy, which the EU estimated may have accounted for 30–40% of GDP in Romania by 1999.[28] The IMF's decision to award a massive loan to Russia in April 1999 with few of the restrictions normally attached to countries like Romania was surely a response to the tough bargaining position that Moscow set out during early stages of the war. Constantinescu could have gone over the heads of the IMF to plead with Clinton and Blair to facilitate a new IMF strategy designed to encourage the emergence of an economically active middle class in Romania; the coalition suffered at the polls for presiding over the decline of the country's fledgling middle-class.

Last but not least, the Romanian government had nothing to lose by asking President Clinton for an extra 50,000 green cards or work permits to enable Romania to benefit from the labour shortage in large areas of the booming US economy. Such a concession would have cost the United States little. People living in unemployment blackspots like Hunendoara, Neamt county, and Reşita whose feeling of hopelessness was making them receptive to nationalistic propaganda might then have been more appreciative of the government's stance on Kosovo if it had opened up opportunities to work abroad that would have transformed their wage-earning prospects. It would have eased the distress of a percentage of the industrial workforce for whom there is little prospect of secure employment and opened up the welcome possibility of remittances flowing back to Romania from America to stimulate the economy. It might even have been a fitting reparation given the fact that a sizeable portion of Romania's technocratic and scientific elite was now working in research establishments in Seattle and California's Silicon Valley.

Before the Kosovo crisis President Constantinescu had given signs in interviews and speeches that he understood the unsentimental nature of the West's relationship with Romania and the region of South-East Europe. In 1997 he declared that the West had 'betrayed those fighting for democratic change...Today our illusions have ended. we understand clearly that we cannot talk for real with the West, except in terms of profit and mutual interest.'[29] In May 1998, while on a visit to Canada, he had accused the West of treating Romania 'with arrogance and sometimes even contempt'.[30] But the bitterness with which he expressed himself on 13 July 1999 revealed deep frustrations with Western *realpolitik* and one can speculate that by now he regretted not having attached conditionality clauses to Romania's participation in the NATO campaign against Yugoslavia. After visits in rapid succession by Western VIPs, he declared on 13 July: 'Every day personalities from NATO and the EU come to Bucharest and tell us that during the conflict we behaved like a member state of NATO. But nobody offers us security guarantees or speaks about the recovery of our losses due to the embargo [on trade with Yugoslavia]...While we are patted on the back and congratulated, our losses mount day by day.'[31] In the six weeks since the end of the war, the Romanian President had discovered that President Clinton's declaration on 12 April that the West 'should try to do for South-Eastern Europe what we helped to do for western Europe after World War II and for Central Europe after the Cold War' was not going to be backed up by action.[32]

The Stability Pact: less than meets the eye?

The Stability Pact for South-East-Europe, agreed on 10 June by the foreign ministers of the leading Western countries, was going to be a very pale version of the Marshall Plan. Madeleine Albright's declaration on 10 June that 'Europe has to pay for the reconstruction of the Balkans' contrasted with the attitude of Germany's Joschka Fischer.[33] He made it clear on his visit to Bucharest on 8 July that the Stability Pact should not be understood as a means of granting material and financial rewards for economic losses. Instead the aim of the pact was to promote 'economic development opportunities in the region on a long-term basis'.[34] German caution was perhaps understandable since Germany, the richest EU state, would have been contributing the most to any Balkan Marshall Plan, given that the United States had made it understood that its contribution would mainly be to fund the actual military campaign in Kosovo.

Afterwards Romania was left with two concrete assurances from NATO countries. The British premier Tony Blair had promised, when addressing the Romanian Parliament on 4 May: 'At the meeting of the European Council in Helsinki in December, Great Britain is going to support an invitation being extended to Romania to begin negotiations to join the EU.'[35] Britain's hitherto lukewarm attitude to Romania's membership application was being replaced by a more committed stance. But no amount of moral support from the

West could enable Romania to meet difficult accession terms if an economy, unable to recover without massive external intervention (not just financial but involving a transfer of management skills and practices to the bureaucracy), continued to decline. The second assurance to Romania and other multi-ethnic states in the region was that no change of boundaries was planned in Yugoslavia as part of an eventual peace settlement. So a Kosovo taken out of Serbian control, and placed under UN jurisdiction until the exact nature of its relationship with Yugoslavia was determined would not be a precedent for Transylvania or any other mixed region in East-Central Europe which had changed hands several times in the last eighty years.

Kosovo prompts a PDSR comeback

At the outbreak of the Kosovo conflict Ion Iliescu had warned that it would lead to 'an escalation of revisionist designs that might question existing borders in East-Central Europe'.[36] During the conflict the PDSR in Timis county, directly adjacent to Serbia, maintained close links with Milošević's party.[37] Its ratings continued to rise, and during the Kosovo conflict it established a commanding lead over the CDR. This was despite the revelations appearing in the daily press about the plundering of Romania's largest state bank, the Romanian Bank of External Commerce (Bancorex), when the PDSR had last been in office. Between 1990 and 1996 Bancorex had lent huge sums on a discretionary basis to failing state companies and clients of the Iliescu regime, which then pumped enormous amounts of taxpayers, money back into it.[38] The Bancorex affair was one of the darkest stains in the history of post-1989 Romania, but an increasing number of citizens refused to make any distinction between the pre- and post-1996 regimes in regard to corruption. Until mid-1999 both the Ciorbea and Vasile governments diverted budget revenues to keep Bancorex afloat out of a genuine fear that a general collapse of the financial system might follow. In July 1999, when the decision was taken to close down Bancorex after it had issued $1.2 billion in non-performing loans, the scandal was seen to be as much one of the Constantinescu era as of its predecessor.[39]

The public's jaded reaction to the Gabriel Bivolaru affair was another indication that the PDSR no longer needed to worry about its past record. In 1996 'Bibi' Bivolaru had been accused of illegally obtaining credits to the value of 20 billion lei from the Romanian Bank of Development and of committing forgery and fraud. To insure himself against legal action, Bivolaru obtained a good position on the PDSR's electoral list and in 1996 was elected to Parliament, which but him beyond the reach of the law.[40] For three years the PDSR blocked attempts to lift Bivolaru's immunity. His fellow PDSR parliamentarians (led by Adrian Năstase) even accompanied him to the State Prosecutor's Office in 1997 as a gesture of solidarity;[41] perhaps some of them feared that if Bivolaru were abandoned 'they would be next in his shoes'.[42] But in the changing public mood the PDSR finally agreed to support the lifting of Bivolaru's immunity in March 1999.[43] Increasingly disoriented, many voters were prepared to blame the government for all their ills even though the evidence that its members were responsible for major graft, on the scale of that seen before 1996, is far from compelling.

It is relatively easy to appeal on nationalist grounds to voters whose political outlook is shaped by poverty or the fear of it, and this is what the PDSR did after 1996. As before, the UDMR was the PDSR's chief target. On 17 October 1998, at a meeting in Cluj of PDSR leaders from Transylvania under the chairmanship of Ion Iliescu, a declaration was adopted, part of which read: 'The UDMR's policy is imbued with nostalgia for the criminal Vienna diktat and is aimed at the premise of achieving the dismemberment of the Romanian state'.[44] The PDSR was in competition with the PRM to capture the nationalist vote in Transylvania which had been without a secure home since the effective break-up of the PUNR in 1997–8. In 1999 the PDSR enjoyed a breakthrough in a province where it had always been weak by effectively absorbing Vatra Românea̧sca, the chief exponent of Romanian nationalism there.[45] Adrian Năstase, the second-ranking leader of the PDSR, found no difficulty in fanning national insecurity. He seized upon the Hungarian government's support for autonomy in the Yugoslav province of Voivodina as a sign that Hungarian revisionism was emerging as a threat to regional security.[46] In July 1999 he even predicted a 'hot autumn' in Transylvania, arguing that socio-economic frustrations could bring ethnic antagonisms to the surface.[47] In the same month, PDSR Senator Radu Timofte (appointed head of the SRI eighteen months later) claimed, without offering any supporting evidence, that radical Hungarians had formed paramilitary units in Transylvania.[48]

Constantinescu at bay

Despite his tumbling poll ratings, the President seemed determined to run for a second term, but he was no longer able to impose his will on the government as easily as he had done in Ciorbea's time. Radu Vasile enjoyed more popularity in the polls. In August 1998 he had reacted with scarcely disguised annoyance when, for the first time, the President used his constitutional prerogative to chair a cabinet meeting.[49] By May 1999 Vasile was able to veto the President's proposal that Theodor Stolojan (prime minister in 1991–2 and with a good reputation as an economist) join the government as a chief economic adviser.[50]

Vasile was a better communicator than Constantinescu. His rough-and-ready colloquial style brought him closer to the average voter than the President's rather aloof and sorrowful manner of speaking.[51] He might even have made a good prime minister in the opening stages of a transition to democracy if consensus rather than confrontation had reigned among the foremost political forces, but Romania lacked the good fortune of states such as Poland, Hungary and Spain. Vasile developed a normal relationship with the opposition, facilitated by his good links with the PDSR and some of the nationalists before becoming prime minister.[52] A diminution of party warfare also enabled the 1999 budget to be passed in February unlike previous years when it had not been approved till the late spring.

The IMF adds to Romania's woes

The budget was a tough one, allowing for a deficit of just over 2%. GDP had slumped by 5.4% in 1998 and a further contraction was expected in the next financial year. The balance of trade was the worst in nine years, and investment had dropped by 18.6% compared with the previous year.[53] The IMF was reluctant to restart talks for a new stand-by accord with the government until it showed results in the areas of banking reform, closure of unprofitable mines, and privatisation.[54] But in May 1999 Romania was required to pay out almost $610 million to service a foreign debt of $800 million which had been incurred under very disadvantageous terms in the early 1990s. In June an additional $480 million had to be paid while the country endured monthly debt service payments of $156 million.

With the central bank scarcely able to cover such heavy withdrawals, it seemed almost impossible for Romania to avoid defaulting without IMF support. In the first two months of 1999 the value of the lei fell by 10% in relation to the dollar and a major financial ratings agency increased the level of economic risk for investors in Romania from B+ to B-.[55]

On 22 April 1999, in the midst of the Kosovo conflict, the IMF agreed to a further standby loan to Romania worth around $500 million.[56] In the West it was seen as a reward for the support Romania was extending to NATO, but this view is hard to justify. Further negotiations over the summer would show that the IMF continued to insist on tight credit and high tax policies, which were bound to depress economic activity. Such a deflationary approach is at variance with the one adopted towards Spain and Portugal when they were emerging from dictatorship in the 1970s: cheap credit and low interest loans to businesses were offered to 'jump-start' growth, and the purchasing power of the consumer was promoted in various ways. However, the view that developed economies needed relatively large budget deficits in order to import requisite technology, rebuild their infrastructure and promote growth was more widely accepted before the onset of economic neo-liberalism in the 1980s. Daniel Dăianu, writing in 1999, argued that a temporary and moderately large deficit was acceptable especially if it was kept in mind that Romania's level of outstanding debt, 35% of GDP, was relatively low. The figure for France and Germany by contrast was 60% and for Italy over 100%.[57]

When the agreement for a $547 million loan was finally reached in August 1999, the IMF insisted that Romania must raise an additional $475 million from private sources before the second tranche could be released. Vasile complained in July that the IMF was constantly imposing new conditions for the resumption of lending; Romania, he argued, was being treated far less generously than Russia or Ukraine and 'has been put in the same basket as Pakistan'.[58] IMF disfavour meant that Romania was seen as a high-risk area for investors and lenders and therefore, in order for the second tranche of the IMF loan to be released, another loan had to be raised at punitive rates of interest. This would further eat into the country's shrinking revenues and make it ever more dependent on international assistance to fund its budget provisions. Thus a vicious circle was maintained.

In July 1999 the President stated that Western governments and agencies should heed Romania's specific needs rather than imposing broad conditions often with disregard to local circumstances.[59] A punitive tax regime, along with primitive accounting methods unchanged since the communist era, would threaten many small- and medium-sized firms with bankruptcy. One American law firm with interests in Romania complained at the end of 1998 that 'instead of building a middle class, Romania's tax laws are destroying the nation's modest entrepreneurial class'.[60] Gradually pressure from the EU helped to reduce the mountain of regulations impeding private commerce. The EU was also aiming through the Phare programme to stimulate small and medium-sized businesses, sometimes with low-cost credits as well as training, and an injection of technical know-how. But IMF insistence on tight credit and fiscal constraints to fight inflation had proved fatal to many such businesses. Coordination between international agencies with reform agendas to prevent such contradictory outcomes was clearly lacking. In the era of the Balkan Stability Pact, this applied not just to Romania but to the region in general. Western initiatives to promote stability and economic growth were undermined by the difficulties of coordinating the work of different international agencies; by turf wars between them; and by the fluctuating commitment of countries which had initially pledged to invest time and money in reconstructing the region.[61] More immediately, lack of coordination between the executive and the legislature was a pressing problem for the Vasile government, which was increasingly pushing legislation through in the form of ordinances or decrees rather than as bills. Article 14 of the Constitution stated that 'in exceptional circumstances, the government may adopt emergency orders',[62] but by 1 September 1999 more than 300 ordinances had been passed, exceeding the 1998 figure of 220, the previous record. However, organic laws could not be passed as emergency rulings, with the result that legislation in vital areas, such as regulating property ownership, languished in Parliament for years.[63] The bicameral Parliament's clumsy procedures and the loss of the government's majority in the Senate by 2000 created this legislative blockage, but within the government regular contact between key players was lacking. Radu Sârbu, in charge of the privatisation drive from 1998 to 2000, openly declared at the end of 1999: 'I could not see Radu Vasile unless he called for me, and during the last year we met only four or five times.'[64/65]

Privatisation's new lease of life

Sârbu, a former physicist, was one of the few longstanding PNTCD members to make a strong impact in government. Because of his successes as director of the FPS in Cluj county he was appointed at the President's behest as its national head in October 1998. He quickly decentralised the operations of the FPS and responsibility for selling off most companies was devolved to county branches. Salaries were also based on performance.[66] During his first four months in the post, the number of companies privatised was double that during the last nine months when Sorin Dimitriu was in charge.[67] At a press conference marking the end of his first year in office Sârbu claimed that his goal was to complete the privatisation process by the end of 2000. He predicted the dissolution of the FPS within that period; half the county divisions would be closed and most FPS staff dismissed by mid-2000 before closing the FPS at the same time as elections were due in November 2000. 'Its disappearance', Sârbu promised, 'will mean the consolidation and relaunching of the Romanian economy on another ownership basis.'[68]

Under Sârbu the goals of the FPS were broadened. The need to raise revenue by the sale of large companies was supplemented by the desire to make contracts that would result in long-term investment and prevent failing enterprises from being a drain on the economy. Anyway, some auctions of companies only involved one investor, which meant that the sell-off price was low; a storm of protest ensued from this, and by September 1999 two-thirds of contracts made in the previous year had become the subject of litigations. Sârbu made an enemy of politicians on all sides by refusing to allow elected politicians to enter FPS premises, or to be members of the administrative boards in charge of companies earmarked for sell-off. These tough tactics were meant to end the trafficking of influence, that was felt to have been a hallmark of the FPS before Sârbu's time. But politicians and especially their allies in the media proceeded to vilify Sârbu and his close officials, claiming that they were profiting from a process that was bringing 'ruin and damnation' to Romania. In his haste to reach his sell-off targets, Sârbu did cut corners. Due to hostility from Parliament and the courts, his targets became increasingly unrealisable. 47% of state assets had been placed in FPS hands when it was set up in 1992, but by September 2000 only 37% of those assets had been sold or wound up.[69] The PDSR and PRM raged at 'strategic' companies being sold for what they claimed was less than their market value, a lack of transparency in sell-offs, and alleged corruption.[70] Arguably no public figure had been the object of such fury for disrupting deal-making between politicians and businessmen since the time of Elena Ceauşescu, who was known for keeping her husband's underlings on a very tight leash. The fact that Sârbu was the chief hate-figure of the coalition suggests that he had been effective in shaking up politico-economic system where reform was usually only an empty ritual.

Deposing Vasile

Inevitably Sârbu's energetic measures, designed to effect a drastic slimming down of the size of the state, generated hostility within the government, starting at the very top. The AVAB checked his financial affairs, along with three other PNTCD members of the government, all of whom were seen as foes of the prime minister. Since Ovidiu Greçea, head of the AVAB, was a close associate of Vasile's, it was normal for the press to assume that Vasile was masterminding these investigations.[71] In September 1999 the influential daily, *România libera*, urged his replacement by Sârbu, saying that 'the country needs a Transylvanian Prime Minister—young, firm, pragmatic and at the same time with clear…moral principles'. It claimed to have learnt 'from reliable sources' that Cotroceni and the PNTCD leadership planned to change the prime minister and 'bring forward a personality opposed to Balkanism'.[72]

This scenario duly unfolded immediately after the close of the EU summit in Helsinki on 14 December 1999 when attention was focussed on the EU's decision to invite Romania to begin accession negotiations. On the same day the PNTCD announced that it no longer had confidence in Vasile and was asking its ministers to leave the government. Soon more than half the ministers quit, but Vasile refused to go and was dismissed by presidential decree. This action was widely seen as being of doubtful constitutional validity: the Constitution allows the President to fire a minister but says nothing about the prime minister.[73] Şerban Orescu has claimed that Vasile had the right to appoint successors to the vacant positions which had arisen.[74] The defiant prime minister only stood down in exchange for being nominated to the presidency of the Senate,[75] which became vacant after its holder Petre Roman became Foreign Minister in the new administration. But Vasile's enemies in the PNTCD blocked this move and he was quickly expelled from the party. He then formed a new party with ten parliamentary supporters before eventually joining the PD.

Vasile's political outlook was so adaptable that he could easily have found a place in any of the main competing parties. This was also true of many politicians who migrated back and forth across the political battle-lines as the exhaustion of the coalition parties (excepting the UDMR) opened up the prospect of sizeable realignments. The schism in the PNTCD left the coalition without an effective majority in the Senate. The doubtful constitutionality of Vasile's dismissal weakened the government's legitimacy and its ability to govern a restive population.[76]

Mugur Isărescu and Romania's EU application

Two PNTCD prime ministers in a row, deserted by their party, would eventually leave and form rival ones—Ciorbea's Christian Democratic National Alliance (Alianţa National Crestin Democrat: ANCD) had already been in existence since the spring of 1999. The PNTCD's reduced credibility was shown by its inability to impose its own candidate as head of government. Instead this task was entrusted to the governor of the central bank (National Bank of Romania: BNR), Mugur Isărescu. No one had held a key public position for longer than Isărescu who had been at the helm of the BNR since 1991, and developed good relations with parties across the political spectrum. In particular he had been praised for his ability to shelter the currency during periods of crisis. Indeed his steadying hand at the BNR had provided badly-needed stability for an economy otherwise lacking a strong reform momentum. But it remained to be seen if in government he was capable of controlling a fractious coalition often preoccupied with the spoils of office. The early indications were promising: he enjoyed good relations with the President, who gave him his strong backing, and the PNTCD seemed willing to give him the space to implement economic reform. As for the PD, its divisions were increasingly out in the open, which reduced its capacity to make trouble for its partners.

One of Isărescu's achievements was to bring order to cabinet meetings. Under Vasile meetings were held in an atmosphere laden with cigarette smoke with mobile phones constantly in use and ministers conducting their own separate discussions with each other. Isărescu banned smoking and put an electronic force field around the cabinet room which prevented mobile phones operating. He also turned the talkativeness of ministers to his advantage. Having developed a good understanding with the cabinet secretary, he would ask amid the din whether there was any objection to a particular item being carried. When no response was heard, he deemed the item approved. When Băsescu, usually the most obstructive of the ministers, asked what happened to a particular item of business, Isărescu would reply that it, and other items, had been approved much earlier. These tactics of an outwardly mild prime minister were successful, and proper cabinet meetings, in which Isărescu's authority was seldom challenged, became the norm. Isărescu's elevation coincided with an unprecedented degree of public support for Romania's application to join the EU. Its President Romano Prodi, while on a visit to Bucharest on 12–13 January 2000, was optimistic about his hosts' chances of accession. He urged investors to be less sceptical about Romania, saying that 'in a few years...to invest here will be like investing in Germany, France or any part of Europe'.[77] He also declared: 'I don't see a possibility of failure for Romania in the accession process unless Romania decides to stop it'.[78]

Romania's conditional support for NATO in the Kosovo conflict had revived backing for its EU membership ambitions among several West European leaders. An important indication that the EU was serious about proposing Romania for entry came on 26 October 1999. Günther Verheugen, the EU Commissioner for Enlargement, proposed the establishment of a working group composed of representatives from the EU, the IMF and the World Bank, as well as other financial institutions and Romanian experts. It would work alongside the Romanian government to map out and then monitor a medium–term economic strategy to be implemented over the next seven years.[79] The Verheugen initiative got the immediate backing of the government and eventually even received the grudging assent of the PDSR. Inevitably Romanian sovereignty was infringed under an arrangement which gave the EU a big role in mapping out a candidate member's medium–term strategy, but a temporary reduction of control over economic strategy formulation was preferable to insolvency and long–term decline. Even in the nationalist camp there were surprisingly few cries that Romania was in danger of succumbing to a Brussels version of the external economic control exercised by the Soviet Union until the mid-1960s; what undoubtedly softened opposition to the Verheugen initiative was the readiness of the EU to provide substantial financial grants to enable Romania to reach EU standards on a wide range of key indicators.

On 15 February negotiations with the European Commission formally got under way, and by mid–March Romania had submitted its medium-term development strategy for the period 2000–6. This was accompanied by a declaration of support from all heads of parties represented in Parliament, as well as employers' organisations and labour unions. Isărescu persuaded the PDSR to endorse a text committing Romania to adopt and implement community legislation, clearly define property rights, and speed the shift to a mainly market economy; it is unlikely that a Prime Minister from the ranks of the CDR parties could have done the same. Verheugen saw the strategy, as he stated on 20 March, as 'guaranteeing that the efforts to meet EU membership terms will continue even if there is a change of government'.[80] On 17 April the PDSR, easily the hot favourite to replace the current coalition, ruled out having Romania's large ultra-nationalist fringe as coalition partners. This was after a warning by Verheugen in February that Romania's accession chances would be adversely affected if such elements joined a future government.

EU pressure for reform bears fruit

The increased presence of the EU in policy-making had a number of beneficial effects. After being criticised by Brussels for the neglect of nearly 190,000 children in state care, the government quickly introduced a better system of provision.[81] Strong EU pressure also led to the passage of a law on 8 December 1999 granting security of tenure to high-ranking civil servants, many of them appointed after the 1996 elections.[82] The law was designed to promote a civil service ethos, allow the disengagement of party politics from strictly administrative functions, and provide a clear division of responsibility between officials themselves. These were seen as minimum steps needed to create a civil service committed to economic reform.

Most ministries are considered to lack competent and motivated officials, as well as access to resources to step up administrative capacity. Bureaucrats with long service who are distrustful of change remain entrenched in several ministries, such as finance and foreign affairs; moreover, the appointment of qualified and able staff to these ministries has not kept pace with the departure of the nucleus of staff of this calibre for better-paid employment in the private sector. With the exception of a small number of ministries, the turnover of staff in middle and senior positions in the bureaucracy is high. Thus the continuity necessary for introducing improvements often does not exist, and planning had become a luxury. As a result, proposed laws were often poorly researched and not always well drafted. If Romania was to succeed in adopting new laws right across the policy-making process and attain to norms established in existing member states, administrative reform had to proceed without delay. But the press was sceptical if the life of the 2000 law on Public Functionaries would extend much beyond the term of the government which sponsored it.[83]

There was consternation on the left at EU insistence that property rights trampled upon in the communist era must now be respected and restitution provided if Romania was to make progress in the entry negotiations. On 25 August 1999 a law designed to compensate former home owners for the loss of their property was passed by the Chamber of Deputies. It gave them six months to file claims for restitution. It provided for the return of homes or apartments or else compensation through bonds and shares in profitable companies, or cash payments from special funds over a period between five and twenty years.[84] One opposition amendment that was accepted prevented the eviction of tenants in seized property who became formal owners in 1995 when the government allowed millions of householders to buy their homes at reduced prices.[85] However, the PDSR vowed to overturn the law on being returned to power.[86] Adrian Năstase, the party's senior vice-president, declared on 24 August that the government wanted to restore pre-World War II rule by a narrow oligarchy.[87] Inter-ethnic rivalries were also stoked up;[88] Ion Iliescu declared on 30 August that under the new laws many Romanian tenants would be evicted by former Hungarian owners and that a form of 'ethnic cleansing' would ensue in several Transylvanian towns, the centres of which would be completely owned by minorities.[89] The head of the keyholders association (representing those who benefited from communist-era expropriations) even claimed that it would lead to the separation of Transylvania from the rest of Romania.[90] Parliament only passed the Law for Illegally Seized Buildings on 16 January 2001 and in a compromise form. Claiming that restitution claims might swallow up half the total budget, the PDSR persuaded the PNL to allow former owners or their descendants, who would be due for monetary compensation, to receive treasury bonds or shares in newly privatised companies instead of cash. Confiscated buildings used by the state, political parties or NGOs were to be exempt from restitution, although owners would be entitled to some form of compensation. This amendment prevented the restoration to their former owners of state schools which had previously been owned by Hungarian churches.[91] Overall the question of property rights remains unsettled with abundant scope for future conflict.[92]

A law to dissolve state-owned farms and return farmland and forests to former owners enjoyed an equally tortuous parliamentary journey. Known as 'the Lupu law', having been championed by the PNTCD senator, Vasile Lupu, it sought to build on the 1991 law which returned a maximum of 10 hectares of farmland to former owners. Several million Romanians became owners of farms, and private farming covers 85% of agricultural production. But at 1.6 hectares the average farm size was barely enough to support a farmer's family. Despite the richness of much Romanian land, productivity is low because many private farmers cannot afford quality seeds or fertiliser. Nor do they have access to the larger national market, since the links between state farms and food-processing companies remains strong.[93] The 1991 law also restricts the purchase, sale or leasing of land which the state has returned to private hands. The World Bank encouraged the government to remove these restrictions and increase the amount of land that could be restored to former owners. This, and plans to encourage the one-third of farmer aged over sixty-four to retire and to provide young farmers with cheap loans to buy their land are seen as necessary steps to end the depression in Romanian agriculture.[94] Lupu's law proposed to increase the amount of land that could be restored to former owners from 10 to 50 hectares per person, but for much of 1999 the PD was only willing to restore a maximum of 10 hectares.[95] It appeared that the National Salvation Front had reemerged as a *de facto* entity committed to preserving as much of the state-led economy as possible. In the autumn of 1999 the government managed to get the Lupu law debated in a joint session of parliament where it still had a precarious majority. On 9 November 1999 parliament finally adopted a law on the restitution of farmlands, forests and pastures, allowing restitution of up to 50 hectares. It is likely to affect between one and four million families, but there are real doubts as to whether it could ever be the basis for a viable private system of agriculture.[96]

Isărescu's approach to government

In what was to be the last year of the coalition's life Isărescu emphasised that his chief concern was to promote economic recovery to halt the decline in living standards and strengthen Romania's EU bid. Whether much progress could be registered would depend on the leeway the ruling parties were prepared to give him. With Petre Roman now installed as foreign minister, the PD was more concerned with restoring its tarnished image abroad than in aggressively pursuing its own interests within the coalition. But Isărescu must have been aware that in an election year the ruling parties would be keener than ever to secure state funding for favoured schemes and districts. His ability to persuade them to curb their appetites for the sake of the national interest would be an acid test of his skills.

Relations with the IMF would continue to be of central concern. On 13 December 2000 it removed Romania from a group of high-risk countries which, it was thought, would have difficulty in paying their external debts (the country had successfully paid $2.5 billion that year). However, it froze the $547 million standby credit agreed in August 1999, making clear that it was unwilling to release a second round of credits or negotiate a further lending round until after the budget had completed its parliamentary passage. IMF vigilance stemmed from a fear that election-year pressures would result in a large budget deficit. It probably still recalled that in 1994–5 a large part of a loan given when the PDSR was in office was diverted towards shoring up uncompetitive industries, and it may well have been determined not to allow anything similar to happen again.[97] Isărescu was particularly concerned to try to boost exports, which had fallen by 6% in 1999, and foreign investment which in the first three-quarters of the year amounted to only $145 million. In January the tax rate on corporate profits was lowered from 38 to 25% and the value-added tax was cut from 22 to 19% on selected products and services.[98] Further efforts were made to try and simplify an accounting and tax-raising system which had caused not a few foreign companies to abandon efforts to invest in Romania. In May 2000 negotiations with the IMF for a fresh standby loan were successfully completed, but despite his public commitment to good governance Isărescu found establishing his authority over the machinery of state to be difficult.

Victor Babiuc's reluctance to quit as defence minister after he left the PD in February 2000 disrupted government for several weeks: once again narrow party interests had apparently prevailed over wider considerations in a key area of government. Isărescu initially positioned himself above this conflict, but increasingly he would find it difficult to avoid taking sides as the political temperature warmed up as elections approached.

The failure to bring wasteful public spending under control proved damaging. A power-struggle ensued between the government and the monopolies controlling the energy sector, known as *regies*. In the spring of 2000 Isărescu refused to approve several requests from them to raise charges for important products and services.[99] Constantinescu told journalists on 6 April that it is 'inadmissible' for the state utility monopolies regularly to raise prices while paying enormous salaries.[100] But when the main trade union in Renel took the government to court over its blocking of wage increases, the Bucharest Appeals Court ruled in favour of the workers[101]—yet another example of the unwillingness of the courts to endorse the government's reform policies by their decisions.

Isărescu at bay: the FNI scandal

Mugur Isărescu's credibility rested primarily on his widely-perceived image as a guarantor of financial stability, but a crisis at the end of May 2000, which brought the financial and banking system to the verge of collapse, tarnished his reputation and helped to derail eleventh-hour efforts by the CDR parties to salvage their reputations. Between 1996 and May 2000 five private banks were declared bankrupt, and against this background savers and investors were attracted instead by the mutual fund market. In contrast to the private banks, only one mutual fund, SAFI, had collapsed, in 1996. By 2000, 345,000 investors had total assets of more than $191.7 million in the area; one company, the National Investment Fund (FNI), accounted for 87% of the investors and 75% of the sector's total assets. Following a newspaper article alleging that a change in valuation rules was likely to lead to a decrease in the value of the FNI's assets, large sums began to be withdrawn from it, and when the FNI withheld payments to depositors, panic increased and the managers fled the country. Confidence in the rest of the financial sector plummeted and there was a flood of withdrawals from Romania's leading bank, the Commercial Bank (BCR).

The collapse of the FNI affected around 300,000 investors, and angry depositors were soon besieging government offices demanding compensation. Anti-government feeling intensified following the arrest of Camenco Petroviçi, until recently President of the CEC, Romania's largest state savings bank. Petroviçi, a member of the PNTCD, was accused of having signed a contract guaranteeing CEC investments in the FNI without informing the CEC administrative board.[102] The CEC connection was used to encourage people to invest in the fund by assuring them that their money was guaranteed by the state.[103] With backing from the IMF, Isărescu succeeded in stemming the panic and halting the run on the BCR. In a radio broadcast on 30 May he warned of 'a financial plot', but the press took up this claim and allegations were made that BCR depositors had been contacted by phone about its imminent collapse; however, no supporting evidence has emerged. But there were also allegations that a group of well-placed 'inside' investors had been alerted about the parlous state of the FNI which enabled them to withdraw their investments in time. Many newspapers acquired some names and printed them; they included Sorin Ovidiu Vintu, founder of the FNI and of another investment fund, Gelsor, who had sought to carve out influence by founding newspapers and sponsoring parties and leading public figures.[104] Vintu was placed under official investigation, but denied these charges. However, it was less easy to dodge hard evidence that many FNI local branch office heads were former officers of the SRI, or the Securitate—at least six such figures were named in the press.[105] As with the *mineriada* in the winter of 1999, the SRI seemed to have no idea about how to react with the media appearing better-informed than its own chiefs.

There was no evidence that Mugur Isărescu was in any way involved in the FNI affair, but in the ensuing months he was singled out by angry protesters who claimed that FNI investments had been guaranteed by the state and that as central bank governor from 1990 to 1999 he must have known about what was going on and should have done something about it. This was in fact not the case. The central bank was not responsible for the commercial contracts concluded by banks, nor was it required to regulate or monitor investment funds.[106] The attempt by his cabinet colleague Traian Băsescu (running for the Bucharest mayoralty in local elections) to link Isărescu with a 'banking mafia' added to the prime minister's discomfiture.[107]

Iliescu shrugs off the Costea affair

When the FNI crisis erupted, another political scandal which appeared to threaten the left's electoral prospects was already under way. A team of French investigating magistrates had been in Romania since 4 May investigating the whereabouts of some $58.3 million misappropriated in Franco-Romanian business deals. The man at the centre of the affair was the fifty-year-old Romanian-born Adrian Costea, who had lived in France since 1973 and held dual French-Israeli citizenship. Costea was placed under arrest in France for twenty-six days in 2000 when investigations into money-laundering were started.[108] He denied wrong-doing concerning the disappearance of Romanian state funds. The bulk of the missing money had come from Bancorex, till 1999 Romania's second largest state bank and closed down in that year after a report—as mentioned above (p. 220)—which showed that since 1990 it had issued $1.2 billion in non-performing loans. Razvan Temesan admitted that he promoted Costea's business dealings while head of Bancorex in the mid-1990s.[109]

The French judges were investigating why diesel oil to the value of $5.5 million imported by Costea to Romania in 1995 and paid for by Bancorex had never reached its destination. They questioned leading figures in the PDSR about the mechanisms which enabled Bancorex to issue unsecured loans for vast amounts of money during its years in power. This enabled political aspects of the affair to come to the fore. Costea had been an unofficial presidential adviser to Ion Iliescu from 1991 to 1996 and both he and his wife were given Romanian diplomatic passports.[110] In 1996 he arranged the printing in France of large amounts of campaign literature for Iliescu's re-election; he also printed, in English and French translations, two books carrying the President's name as author which were meant to boost his image outside Romania.

In 1997, after Iliescu's electoral defeat, Costea moved on and played an important role in setting up and financing the Alliance for Romania (ApR), a break-away party from the PDSR led by Teodor Meleşcanu, foreign minister from 1992 to 1996.[111] In 1999, despite Costea's previous closeness to the PDSR, President Constantinescu made him an adviser and extended Costea's right to carry a diplomatic passport. Constantinescu did not deny his links with Costea, which were not extensive. But Iliescu and Meleşcanu initially denied having close links with Costea. When facts were unearthed weakening such claims, both men, now rivals for the presidency, accused each other of allowing Costea access to the corridors of power. In two interviews broadcast by a Romanian television station on 16 and 17 May, Costea insisted that he was able to acquire influence with the two post-1989 Presidents because he unveiled convincing plans for attracting foreign investment and improving Romania's image on the world stage. Angered by the attempts of both Iliescu and Meleşcanu to minimise his influence, he issued detailed accounts of how close his links with them were. He claimed that Iliescu's campaign team in 1996 was selected largely on his advice, and that the ApR was formed as a result of meetings he arranged in France the following year with Meleşcanu, whose expenses he had paid.[112] As a result, in a statement issued on 13 May, Iliescu admitted having known Costea since 1991 and that his presidential office used him as an adviser until 1996, claims which he had earlier denied. But he insisted that he never granted Costea favours or gained materially from the relationship.[113] To add to Iliescu's discomfiture, the Romanian customs service announced on 14 May that it was investigating possible fraud relating to the import of ten lorry-loads of campaign material which Costea printed to assist his 1996 presidential bid. Customs had no records of any duty having been paid, an offence that could carry a sentence of between two and seven years in prison. Costea announced that he planned to sue the PDSR to recover the cost of the material.[114] French judges had begun investigating Costea after receiving an anonymous letter from Romania detailing serious wrong-doings. It was widely noted that Virgil Măgureanu, head of the Romanian National Party (PNR), had predicted on 31 January that 'an extremely feverish electoral season will come, with blows below the belt and dirty moves.'[115] The former SRI boss made no secret of his political ambitions, and Iliescu stood in the way of their realisation. In August 1999 he had been quoted as threatening to release information on politicians, claiming that those in question 'have already compromised themselves'.[116]

The Costea affair illustrated the power derived from access to sensitive information gathered by state intelligence agencies before 1989 and how feeble the law was in regulating this area. In the event Iliescu was virtually untouched by the Costea affair. Responsibility for the contract for election material was successfully passed on to underlings and he never faced a court appearance in either Bucharest or Paris.[117] Once he was re-elected, the Romanian authorities ceased co-operating with the French judicial authorities and even demanded the return of documents previously lent to them. The main casualty of the Costea affair turned out to be the ApR and Teodor Meleşcanu, who had been running in second place to Iliescu in the polls for at least a year—he had appeared to be a formidable challenger capable of attracting support from centrist as well as left-wing voters. But he acquitted himself poorly in the Costea affair, and defections from the ApR would soon relegate the party to the margins of politics.

The Kosovo crisis was a sharp test for the Romanian government, forcing it to show how committed it was in practice to Euro-Atlantic integration. However, the government passed it well. It

could have extracted concessions from the West in return for its
willingness to share the risks of over burden with NATO, but there
is no sign that it tried to do so. Instead it faced a populace overwhelmingly hostile to NATO's military action: its unpopularity
grew, and popular hostility hardly diminished despite evidence of
EU commitment to throw its weight behind Romania's membership bid. At least it was the PDSR and not the PRM which was the
beneficiary of the CDR's difficulties. Corruption allegations center-
ing around the Costea affair failed to impede Iliescu's return from
the electoral wilderness. But the PDSR did not hesitate to stir up
nationalist passions, especially in Transylvania, to prevent the PRM
from overtaking it. It was a sign of the opposition left's readiness to
play the ethnic card at a time when it had few economic incentives
to offer voters whom it wished to draw over to its side.

Coalition disunity was once again on full display in December
1999 when the prime minister, Radu Vasile, was dismissed in a move
of doubtful constitutionality. The new prime minister Mugur
Isărescu was a non-party technocrat and as such was seen by the EU
as a figure able to prepare Romania for accession. In the last year of
the coalition's mandate external pressure was the chief stimulus of
reform. Already, under the Verheugen initiative, Romanian sovereignty was infringed through an arrangement which gave the EU a
large role in mapping out the medium-term strategy of a candidate
member. The willingness of the PDSR to accept this arrangement
showed how significant amounts of EU aid could sweep away nationalist complexes.

Important reforms were passed as a result of EU insistence that
Romania adhere to norms designed to ensure a minimum level of
governmental effectiveness and economic justice. One designed to
strengthen the neutrality of the civil service and reduce the ability of
governments to pack its upper reaches with its own supporters succeeded in becoming law by 2000. A rougher passage awaited one
designed to restore private property to former owners, but the Law
for Illegally Seized Buildings was eventually passed early in 2001.
But there was every indication that parties like the PDSR, in spite of
paying lip-service to these measures, had little desire to stand by
them. The instinct to be modern and pro-Western in rhetoric while
adhering to a monopolistic and authoritarian approach to politics
remained strong a decade after the 1989 revolution.

8

TAKING THINGS TO EXTREMES
THE 2000 ELECTIONS AND THEIR OUTCOME

The June 2000 local elections

The first serious electoral test which the CDR and the PD would face after nearly four years of unfriendly cohabitation in government came with the local elections of June 2000. The coalition had transferred power and resources to the localities,—a move unprecedented in Romanian history—to strengthen its bid for EU membership. Prefects can only now dismiss a mayor if a binding court ruling has been provided. A law on local public finance introduced in January 1999 enables local government to receive 50% of income tax as well as a large share of the revenues earned by the local branches of the national privatisation agency. In another break with precedent the government showed itself willing to sanction its own mayors against whom serious corruption accusations had been made. Before being arrested on corruption charges in February 2000, Marin Lutu, the PNTCD mayor for Bucharest's Fourth District, was stripped of all party offices.[1] But the electorate seemed determined to punish the CDR. Even the PNL thought it prudent to keep its distance from the PNTCD and run separately. The two forces, the PNL and PNTCD, won roughly 1.2 million votes compared with 2.7 million in the 1996 local elections. In the mayoral contest the PNTCD-dominated CDR fell to fifth place—the only city of significance which it won was Timisoara. The PNL did slightly better with 9.06%, and captured four large cities. The biggest surprise was the ability of the PD's Traian Băsescu to capture Bucharest, previously a CDR stronghold. The PDSR had seemed poised to win, but in a tight second round fight Băsescu finished slightly ahead. His reputation as an administrator capable of getting things done eclipsed that of being a troublesome member of the government, and the willingness of CDR voters to support him decided the outcome.

The party of the nationalist ultras, the PRM, received just over 5% of the vote. But this figure masked strong performances in individual centres, particularly the city of Cluj where Gheorge Funar, the anti-Hungarian mayor, won 47% of the poll. A Hungarian challenger was in second place, but to prevent the second round turning into an ethnic confrontation he decided to retire. In the run-off Funar faced a CDR candidate who received the backing of all other parties, including the PDSR. This was a rare sign of solidarity against an extremist threat.[2] But it was not enough to stop Funar, who was narrowly elected for a third term.

In the county council elections the PDSR obtained 27.37%, significantly lower than the 40% it regularly obtained in opinion polls. This contest was felt to be the most accurate mirror of the parliamentary elections, since both were fought under the same boundaries. But the failure of the ApR to obtain more than 8.53% of the vote brought relief to the PDSR.[3]

Constantinescu's bombshell

It was hard to see how the CDR could be durably reconstituted as an electoral alliance unless the PNTCD decided to cede its primacy in the coalition and allow the Liberals much more influence. Emil Constantinescu might have used his remaining authority in the PNTCD to encourage it to think in such terms or at least to seek the replacement of its elderly and completely discredited chairman, Ion Diaconescu. But instead he appeared on television on the evening of 17 July to announce that he would not be a presidential candidate in November. The decision appeared to have been taken at short notice because as recently as 30 June he had announced that he would indeed run for a second term.[4] His withdrawal also seems to have been made without consulting leading figures in the CDR, which had sustained his two previous runs for the presidency.[5] In his 17 July address Constantinescu declared: 'When I launched myself in the fight against corruption, I discovered in Romania a mafia system in which a web of front organizations was backed by the highest state institutions.... We live in a world where everything is for sale— principles, ideologies, parliamentary secrets. My place is not in this world.'[6] It was unheard—of for a Romanian ruler to renounce power voluntarily in the way Constantinescu had chosen. Sceptics suggested that his withdrawal was a temporary ruse, but much of the press hailed it as a moral and disinterested act.[7] The President insisted that it was irrevocable, and that he would not even stand for Parliament to give him immunity from prosecution, a pointed reference to the conduct of his predecessor Ion Iliescu.[8]

Constantinescu must have been influenced to make this decision by his low standing in the polls (he had failed to get much above 20% for more than a year) and perhaps by the thought of the hostile reception awaiting him on the campaign trail. It seems to have been facilitated too by the existence of a credible successor very much in his own mould. An effective partnership had developed between the President and Prime Minister Mugur Isărescu since the latter's appointment in December, and on 30 June Constantinescu had described Isărescu as 'the best premier after 1989 and one of the best Romania has ever had'.[9] It seems that he had talked with Isărescu before his broadcast to try and persuade him to enter the presidential race. The PNTCD, despite being stunned by Constantinescu's withdrawal, soon gave its public backing for a presidential run by Isărescu—who declared on 31 July that he would make his intentions clear the following month.

Constantinescu may well have assumed that the CDR could be reconstituted behind an Isărescu candidacy. The PNL, at the initiative of its first vice-president Valeriu Stoica, had been seeking to put together an alliance with the ApR, but the talks were proving difficult and there were signs of unrest inside the PNL about an alliance with the left. But, the President seems to have done little to pave the way for a CDR revival. In his election broadcast he promised to relaunch his campaign against corruption in high places.[10] However, he spent the four remaining months of his presidency largely in seclusion or on foreign visits.[11] If Constantinescu had fought on, it is entirely possible that his second round candidacy would have provided sufficient momentum for the PNTCD to rise above the 10% threshold necessary for electoral alliances to enter Parliament. The threshold was double that of 5% set for individual parties (recently raised from 3% in a bid to exclude smaller groups) because the PNTCD preferred to run in tandem with a group of smaller parties in an alliance known as CDR 2000 (launched on 1 September 2000). The belief of the PNTCD that parties like the Party of the Romanian Right, two ephemeral Ecologist parties, and Ciorbea's ANCD could provide enough extra votes to exceed this very high threshold for entering Parliament suggests it had become somewhat cut off from reality.

Suicide of the centre

Other moderate parties made blunders that enabled anti-system forces to garner immense electoral capital when the elections were held. The Alliance for Romania (in disarray since its leader Meleşcanu had become embroiled in the Costea affair) set unacceptably hard terms for an alliance with the PNL. The Liberals presidential candidate Teodor Stolojan enjoyed much higher ratings than Meleşcanu, who stubbornly held out for the top post; negotiations foundered in July and by August 2000 the ApR's poll rating had collapsed from 14 to 6%. Meleşcanu and Stolojan enjoyed credibility among a large section of the PDSR electorate. Both had acquitted themselves relatively well in the service of Iliescu before 1996, while shielding themselves from some of the excesses and blunders of his rule. So a chance to unite the pragmatic left and centre-right was effectively thrown away here. An agreement between the PNTCD and the PNL to reunite behind a Stolojan presidential bid with Isărescu as the prime ministerial nominee might still have enabled the CDR parties to retain their own core vote while making inroads on the left. Indeed, *Evenimentul Zilei* had launched an appeal on 21 July 2000, backed in subsequent days by a strong response from readers, for a Stolojan-Isărescu pact, but it was ignored by their political sponsors.

Diaconescu of the PNTCD pronounced the CDR dead on 1 August when he turned away two PNL emissaries with the words 'It's dead...It's dead. What is there left to talk about?'[12] Education minister Andrei Marga was snubbed by his colleagues when he called in late July for the creation of a 'PNTCD-Liberal reform coalition'.[13] The chances of a reconciliation were dashed when the PNL agreed to put on its electoral lists members of a left-wing think tank who had been theoreticians of reform of the socialist system and had created in 1999 the Social Liberal Initiative to promote the candidacy of Stolojan, someone who had already made the journey from the technocratic left to the centre.[14] But a walk-out had occurred of old-guard Liberals in which Senator Dan Amadeo Lazarescu was to the fore (they refused to endorse such a 'flagrant deviation towards the communist left', but it emerged in April 2001 when the CNSAS released Lazarescu's Securitate file that, in return for being allowed to attend conferences abroad, he had been an assiduous, and paid, informer before 1989).[15] The Liberal revolt was contained, but it justified the PNTCD in refusing to cede the Liberals a strong position within the CDR. Meanwhile, the feuding within the CDR only boosted the appeal of the candidates who projected a strongman image (Iliescu—and Vadim), one that was most at variance with sterile parliamentarism. It is clear that important figures in the once-united CDR regarded the first round of the presidential elections as a US-style primary that would decide which of their candidates would go forward to face Iliescu in the deciding round. Zoe Petre, for instance, declared in early August that the CDR 2000 would support Stolojan in the run-off if Isărescu failed to make it.[16] Except for journalists, such as Sorin Rosca Stănescu, there was no public recognition that rival technocrats contending among themselves might be completely upstaged by a rogue challenger who would show how much they had lost touch with the national mood.

At least Stolojan sought to harness the anger of the electorate at the abundant shortcomings of the political class. He had some claim to be viewed as an outsider since he had been in government for only one year (during his premiership in 1991–2); after this he worked for the World Bank which sent him to the Central Asian republics that had formerly been part of the Soviet Union. After 1998 he worked for the Tofan group, one of the few large Romanian companies not associated with speculative practices or dominated by members of the old *nomenklatura*.[17] The one black mark against Stolojan was that during his premiership he had nationalised hard currency bank deposits (preventing their withdrawal until their value had greatly depreciated thanks to inflation). The plundering of state banks by those in high places had created a liquidity crisis and in turn compelled Romania to obtain loans at disadvantageous terms: when announcing his candidacy, Stolojan pointed out what most politicians preferred to remain silent about: one-third of the national budget was now spent on servicing the external debt.[18] Another hefty budget segment went on paying the arrears of debts to the state of state-owned companies and Stolojan promised to introduce a new set of priorities under which education and health care would receive greater spending.[19]

Isărescu did not officially enter the presidential race till 11 October, and his late entry enabled him to argue that he was devoting more attention to his duties as head of government than to politicking. But he also had good reason to keep his distance from what by now was the most unpopular party in the country; the PNTCD was backing a candidate visibly ashamed of the quality of those sustaining him.[20] He stressed the importance of continuing with the privatisation process and the reform of the public utilities and financial institutions, hardly a manifesto designed to fire the country with excitement. According to Silviu Brucan, he was too detached and his language too sophisticated for him to make a strong popular impact in the time available.[21] He was soon the subject of effective smears by the PRM concerning his alleged role in the FNI and Bancorex scandals.

Grassroots alienation at danger level

The reluctance of the conventional parties to campaign in the enthusiastic way they had done in 1996 meant that the public stage was often dominated by FNI depositors noisily demanding compensation for their lost investments. Evidence suggests that the protests were not altogether spontaneous, but had been cleverly orchestrated by the PRM; when Cornel Nistorescu invited some of those who had been protesting at the launch of Isărescu's candidacy to come to his office to explain their case so that he could then publicise their points of view, 'they vanished as if by magic'.[22]

The PRM was also able to exploit indignation arising from the murder in September 2000 of one of its members, Virgil Sahleanu, a union leader in Iasi who had led protests against the sale of the Tepro engineering plant in the city to a Czech company which, as it turned out, was on the verge of bankruptcy. This sale had raised angry passions long before the murder of Sahleanu: during the previous November, Tepro workers had carried portraits of Ceauşescu at a 10,000-strong trade-union rally which ended in clashes outside the prefecture in Iasi.[23] In the light of such scenes it is not altogether surprising that a poll (carried out by CURS and the Romanian Academic Society) produced the following answers to the question: 'When in the last 100 years did things go better for Romania'?[24]

	%
Before World War I	4.2
The inter-war period	13.5
The Dej years	4.6
1965–79	34.3
1980s	18.4
After 1989	8.5

Double the number of respondents believed life had been better for them in the 1980s than it had been after 1989 and a majority, 52.7%, believed that life was better for the Romanians under Ceauşescu than at any other time in recent history. This poll confirmed that the communist era remained the chief reference point for most Romanians: details of that time, such as the endless queuing for scarce basic commodities and a television output largely devoted to the public duties of the Ceauşescus, had faded from memory. In 2000 the all-important fact was that 44% of them lived on an EU average poverty wage of $4.30 a day.[25]

Nearly a month after this poll was released, deputies and senators defied the advice of their leaders and voted to increase their own salaries by 16%; the turnout was one of the biggest recorded for a vote in chambers marked by chronic absenteeism.[26] Coalition deputies were usually among the worst absentees; summoned to vote by mobile phone, they either turned up late or not at all. By 2000 it was necessary to announce a final vote on a bill one week in advance for a majority to be present.[27] The PDSR, by contrast, was far more disciplined and had a good attendance record, and those with their own businesses (among whom were many from the PD and PNL) attended more often. It is not surprising that voters often saw their electoral representatives as a separate caste ever ready to indulge their appetites and protect their positions. Dumitru Tinu reflected the public mood when he wrote in *Adevărul*: 'There is no money to add a few more percentage points to the salaries of doctors and teachers, but without the slightest hesitation they [the politicians] vote tens of billions for limousines, mobile phones, foreign trips, office equipment, more secretaries and advisers, useless trifles, bodyguards'.[28] In May 2000 the historian, Florian Constantiniu even made a comparison between the politicians of the 1980s and those of the democratic era, which was unfavourable to the latter.

In the 1980s the poet Gh. Dumitrescu wrote an article for the journal "Vatra" mocking party activists...symbolised by 'Comrade Gusa' and 'Comrade Ceafa', both of whom were uncultivated and arrogant. ... Comrade Gusa and Comrade Ceafa have turned into Deputy Gusa and Senator Ceafa. Comrades Gusa and Comrade Ceafa were more fearful of abuses. They were afraid that their petty theft (10 kilos of meat bought...at a small price from the party shop, a feast given at a party rest home) might be denounced by a rival or by an ill-meaning informer of the Securitate. They were still afraid of someone. Messrs Gusa and Ceafa are afraid of nobody. Parliamentary immunity ensures their impunity. They travel abroad, have expensive cars, have villas built, go to football matches when they should vote on important laws that are necessary for the country. Nobody punishes them. The voters? The Romanian voters are probably the most backward in Europe as regards their political culture. Backward and resigned.[29]

Poll after poll revealed a complete lack of public confidence in the parties (77%) or parliament (74%), the figures in brackets being the results of a poll by the Metro Media Institute in 1999 and perfectly in line with many others.[30]

In democratic Romania it appeared difficult for individuals to improve themselves by hard work and regular behaviour. An IMAS poll carried out with Romanians over the age of twenty-eight in February 1999 asked the question: 'How have today's rich made a fortune?' Of the respondents 38.2% believed it was through their connections with the powerful; 37% that it was through receiving government help to start a business; and only 6.3% put it down to hard work. In answer to a further question 'Can a person get rich by honest means in present-day Romania?' 69.6% said 'No' compared with 29.3% who answered 'Yes'.[31]

With a two-thirds majority of parliamentarians required before one of their number could be arrested or prosecuted for any offence, the impression grew that Parliament was a haven for individuals wishing to evade justice by acquiring parliamentary immunity. This impression was further strengthened by the fact that individuals had to contribute large sums of money to be adopted as a candidate. The minimum campaign contribution expected by the PDSR and PNL was $4,000 (four years' earnings for an average Romanian).[32] Cristian Pîrvulescu, head of the Pro-Democratia Association, claimed in 2001 that the first place on a party slate was put up for sale, with a candidate having to pay a large sum in hard currency to obtain an eligible place. One candidate on the CDR 2000 slate admitted having paid $10,000 to get on to the slate of an ecology party that belonged to this alliance.[33]

The reputation of politicians was further harmed by the tendency of a great many to migrate from party to party, which suggested that personal ambition took precedence over programmes, ideology or principle, and encouraged the view that parties were loose combinations of ambitious individuals keen to capture the state for their own advantage.[34] In 2001 a leading daily published a list of fifty-seven parliamentarians elected after 1989 who had transferred to other parties.[35] Thus, a party that could show a contrast with the self-serving behaviour of the established ones was bound to be taken seriously by an angry and confused electorate. On 1 September 2000 Cristian Tudor Popescu published an editorial in *Adevârul* entitled 'Let us Learn Hungarian' contrasting the level of internal democracy of the Romanian parties with the UDMR, and arguing that the Hungarian minority force had much to teach the Romanians in this respect. However, Romanians were unlikely to be tempted to support the UDMR, even if its champion was a journalist who normally published articles hostile to that party. The only other party which seemed to reject the oligarchical approach to politics favoured by the rest was another force which traded on an ethnic appeal: the Greater Romania Party (PRM). Figuring prominently on the PRM's electoral lists were several of Romania's best-known folksingers; Ilie Ilascu, who had been a political prisoner in the hands of pro-Russian separatists in Moldova since 1994, and a higher proportion of women candidates than in any other major party. There were also figures deeply involved in communist-era repression, corruption before and after 1989, and attempts to undermine democratic institutions, as well a gallery of candidates condemned by human rights organizations for their anti-semitic, anti-Roma and anti-Hungarian views, chief among whom was the party's leader Corneliu Vadim Tudor.

But even for nominally mainstream voters vaguely aware of the PRM's extremist pedigree these were often not big enough deterrents against supporting Vadim. The PRM's principal advantage was that it had not been formally in power since 1990, and could therefore claim that it had not been responsible for worsening the conditions of life of ordinary Romanians and had a clean pair of hands.

Paradoxically the rural, elderly and poorly-educated sections of the population who had voted disproportionately for Ion Iliescu in 1990, 1992, and 1996 now emerged as a strong factor for stability. Previously they had been seen as a barrier to democratisation, content with paternalism and unlikely to object to a revival of fully authoritarian rule. But in their conservatism they were increasingly seen as a firebreak preventing further advances by Vadim; for several years opinion polls had suggested that their loyalty to Iliescu was unshakeable whatever accusations were made about his record in government.

The liberal forces standing between the individual and the state and grouped under the banner of Civil Society were unable to offer a convincing alternative to the unpopular parties. Adrian Severin argued in February 2000 that civil society was reduced to a few NGOs which were only surrogate clubs for the frustrated who feared running for election or assuming the responsibilities of government.[36] The best-known liberal NGO, the Civic Alliance (AC), had frequently intervened in politics but was discredited because of its close association with the CDR and Cotroceni. Marches, which the AC called or participated in when democracy seemed threatened on 22 January 1999 and on 7 December 2000 (due to the rise of Vadim), attracted pitifully few people.[37] By contrast, the General Association of Hunters and Fishermen (AGVPS) was able to mobilise far greater numbers in a large march in Bucharest in September 1999 in protest at government policy on hunting.[38] Adrian Năstase happened to be the president of the AGVPS, a sign that the PDSR had closer contact with civil society than the parties which sometimes invoked it as a mantra.

Ana Blandiana has recognised that by pledging support for an increasingly unpopular President and a weak Premier like Ciorbea, the AC used up a lot of its national credibility.[39] At the May 2000 congress of the AC, Valerian Stan announced his resignation. He harboured not only disappointment but hostility to various senior

figures in the CDR not least Constantinescu.[40] Blandiana feels that
his tactics in 1997 of challenging the PD over the acquisition of protocol houses were ill-advised and she asked him then to concentrate
on much more substantial corruption matters.[41]

In 2001 Ana Blandiana stepped down as head of the AC to concentrate on building up the Memorial to the Victims of Communism, a museum at Sighet occupying the same building as the prison
which housed elite figures from 1948 to 1955, which is seen as one
of the finest memorials in Europe to the victims of tyranny. In 2001
Ana Blandiana stepped down as head of the AC and was replaced by
Şerban Radulescu-Zoner, a PNL deputy from 1992 to 2000 who is
widely felt to have kept his integrity in that period (he initiated a bill
intended to confiscate the wealth of state officials who had defrau-
ded the banks in the 1990–8 period and he had served a lengthy
term as a political prisoner before 1989).[42]

The inability of the forces of liberal civil society in Romania to
handle criticism was illustrated in March 2000 when Dan Pavel, one
of the regular political commentators of its weekly journal *22*, was
banished from the paper without being informed in advance of his
dismissal. His offence was to have accused the leading lights in the
GDS—Andrei Plesu, Mircea Dinescu and Gabriel Liiçeanu—of being good liberals but poor democrats who believed themselves more
equal than others before the law.[43] Squabbling intellectuals in their
ivory towers had little influence on the national mood. The young—a
category whom reviews like *22* had regularly saluted as potential re-
deemers of the nation—were about to cruelly disappoint their liberal admirers.[44] A warning that they were not a group instinctively
drawn to the path of Western individualism had already occurred
with the publication of a poll in February 2000 taken among students: this showed that young people, who had had little experience
of communism, still expected the state to provide them with material support for education (99%) and student accommodation (82%)
as well as food and other basic requirements (42%).[45] Graduate unemployment was emerging as a serious problem, exacerbated by the
virtually impossibility for Romanians of all ages to seek work abroad
because of visa restrictions. By January 1999 a quarter of all the unemployed had received university or high school education,[46] and
65% of students were ready to emigrate because they saw no chance
of getting on in Romania.[47] But with this route effectively blocked

except for winners of the lottery for a coveted green card to enter the United States, it is hardly surprising that some among them were attracted to political extremism. Ironically it was an American cultural import—rap music, as popularised by the performer Eminem—which may have contributed to the supportive youth environment for extremism. The violence and iconoclasm of many of the lyrics to be found in rap music matched Vadim's violent and uninhibited rhetoric. Indeed homegrown rap bands—BUG-mafia, IQ Sapro and Morometzii—soon emerged to cater for a growing local musical craze. During the election campaign unemployed young people, with little more to do than sit in cafés for most of the day, could watch Vadim dominating the media airwaves with rap music playing in the background.

The new look PDSR

Fading memories of the PDSR's record in government and a widespread conviction that the party could be no worse than the outgoing coalition boosted Iliescu. He repositioned himself as a centrist and moderniser ready to make alliances with former opponents in the political centre. Discreet overtures were made to the PNL and even to the UDMR; from June 1999 Iliescu had urged his cohorts to refrain from displaying 'a bitter attitude' to the Hungarian minority or to Budapest.[48]

In October 1999 an alliance was signed between the PDSR and the main Roma party, representing a large disparaged group which the PDSR had usually spurned.[49] The reaction from the Romanian populace was as muted as that which greeted the news of the entry of the Hungarian UDMR into the government in 1996 (suggesting that stereotypes about the ingrained anti-Roma feelings among Romanians may need some revision). Also, six trade union leaders were able to obtain electable places on the PDSR's electoral lists[50]—a calculated gamble by the PDSR to try and draw the unions into its orbit.

Gestures designed to calm fears about the party's intentions if returned to government were made to the West by its premier-designate, Adrian Năstase. After a trip to the United States in August 2000 he repositioned his party's economic policy by insisting that market reforms offered the only chance for Romania to develop in a normal way. He promised that the PDSR would not be profligate with public money and would respect the medium–term economic strategy drawn up earlier that year by Isărescu, mainly in conjunction with the EU.[51] In 2001 Romania would hold the presidency of the Organization for Security and Co-operation in Europe, and Adrian Severin, just appointed chairman of the OSCE's parliamentary assembly, joined the party on 4 September. This former Foreign Minister, once a strong critic of the PDSR, now believed that it had evolved from being 'an ideological party to a party of interests'.[52]

Iliescu got a surprising endorsement from a prominent media analyst long regarded as a foe of what he stood for. Dan Pavel had warned in an editorial written in August 1999: 'If they come back to power, they are going to do what they did before...A centralized statist bureaucracy will be kept on', one that would 'safeguard the interests of...corrupt managers...and a nationalist oligarchy of interests'.[53] But by September 2000 Pavel was far more relaxed about the prospect of a PDSR comeback. He believed that 'in reality Iliescu's party has an honourable record...in opposition'. It had played a full and constructive role in the life of parliament; 'Of the 2,225 interventions in parliament between 1 September 1997 and 1 July 1999... 1,049 were from the opposition, of which 708 belonged to the PDSR. Whoever studies them with care will notice that the majority of these interventions were constructive and rational.'[54]

It is not surprising that statements such as that of US Senator Joseph Biden while on a visit to Romania in September 1999, that he thought it would be a setback for Romania if Ion Iliescu returned to the presidency, were heard far less frequently abroad.[55] Iliescu began to recover some of the prestige which he had briefly enjoyed at the end of 1989; in 1997 he had seemed finished as a leader, with the PDSR county branch of Galaţi openly proposing that he be 'kicked upstairs' to become the party's honorary president,[56] but by 1999 the polls were clearly in his favour thanks to the poor record of his successors. In May 2000, on announcing his availability as a presidential candidate, he had declared: 'Despite advice coming from persons close to me to withdraw to a position that is more comfortable, I feel that my physical powers have not left me.'[57] On this occasion he said that the PDSR was not willing to replace 'the pork-choppers of the ruling party with the pork-choppers of his party', and that the party list nominations would no longer be made 'bureaucratically' but 'on the qualities of the people'. The Romanian word for pork-chopper is *fripturist* and it means an unprincipled political careerist—hence this was an admission that in the past the PDSR door had been wide open to *fripturisti...* The case of the notorious Bibi Bivolaru who obtained parliamentary immunity in 1996 under the PDSR banner was well known, and Iliescu asked his party to ensure that those who ran for Parliament on the PDSR ticket should file a statement of their financial situation in order to avoid another 'Bivolaru' case.[58] But despite these fine words it soon emerged that large sums of money had to be handed over for an aspiring candidate to obtain a secure place on the PDSR's lists.[59] Room was found too for an avowed nationalist of pre-1989 vintage, Adrian Păunescu. Unease was felt in some quarters over the electoral alliance formed between the PDSR and the Romanian Humanist Party (PUR), the political vehicle of a controversial entrepreneur, Dan Voiculescu, who had acquired much of his power-base through working in the foreign trade companies controlled by the Securitate before 1989.[60] An advocate of economic policies favouring domestic capital over foreign rivals, his main source of influence probably came from ownership of a range of media outlets, the flagship being Antena 1—Romania's most popular private TV station and strongly nationalistic in its treatment of politics.[61]

The PDSR used Voiculescu's media outlets to lash out at the FPS, Radu Sârbu becoming a hate figure in the campaign; on 14 November the Senate passed a motion demanding that all privatisation measures be frozen until a new government was sworn in. But in general the PDSR's message was one of national reconciliation, and its tone was not extreme. This meant that none of the major contenders for office was prepared to give full voice to the frustrations of the millions of voters whose personal circumstances had worsened after 1996 and who had not experienced Iliescu's earlier term of office as any sort of golden age.

The PRM taps into mass alienation

The fact that a large portion of the electorate was deeply unimpressed by the both the government and opposition alternatives presented an unparalleled opportunity to the PRM. Having been in opposition for almost the whole of the 1990s, it could disclaim all responsibility for the misrule which had characterized that decade. Critics might say that the PRM had in fact exercised great influence from behind the scenes, and carried weight in key ministries, which it had used to sabotage any genuine attempt at reform. But many Romanian voters were hardly in the mood to listen to warnings about Vadim's record and where he might take the country if elected. Some young people who saw him as unbalanced were still prepared to vote for him, either because they wished to take revenge on the older generation or for the sake of adventure or mischief-making.[62] The PRM's manifesto was carefully drawn up to reflect the frustrations and hopes of ordinary Romanians who felt themselves exploited or ignored by the political class in faraway Bucharest. Since September 2000 Vadim had been promising the following measures:

— the immediate liquidation of native and foreign mafias operating in Romania;
— the destruction of prostitution chains and illicit drug networks;
— seizure of large fortunes acquired through fraud and their transfer to a National Fund for Savings which would relieve the suffering of Romanians in dire poverty;
— the public trial of persons guilty of acts of genocide against the Romanian people;
— the taking of all necessary measures to repatriate $4 billion deposited by Romanians in foreign banks;
— dissolution of the State Ownership Fund and a rethinking of the whole privatisation process;
— a referendum on whether the death penalty should be instituted for paedophilia and child murder;
— establishment of a Committee for the Investigation of Anti-Romanian Activities, as well as expulsion from Romania of all persons guilty of sabotage, espionage and advocating the territorial division of the country;
— lowering of the price of food, drink, medicine and school supplies;
— eradication of the scourge of Gypsy criminality, primarily by educating the representatives of their community, but also by creating workplaces for them.
— reinstatement of the authority of the Romanian state in Harghita and Covasna counties;

— acceleration of the 'historical and irreversible-phenomenon' of peaceful unification with Bessarabia and Bucovina.[63]

In the eyes of Romanians who believed that their rulers and their business cronies were creaming off the wealth of the country while fear and poverty stalked the streets, many of these measures seemed overdue. The fact that Vadim promised a six-month period of dictatorship for his new broom to sweep away the refuse of the old regime did not reduce the appeal of his message, despite a hostile response from the media. It was in the last week of campaigning that polls showed Vadim to be in second place to Iliescu, well ahead of the rival candidates fielded by the ex-CDR parties,[64] which appeared to surprise all his competitors except the PDSR. Adrian Năstase had warned in August that Vadim's appeal was being greatly underestimated,[65] and indeed he was the only senior figure willing to go on the offensive against Vadim in the campaign, arguing that his draconian ideas to restore the authority of the state contravened 'European ideals'.[66]

The press closed ranks against Vadim as it became clear that he was capable of staging a major electoral upset. His extreme statements were reprinted, and his close links with the Ceauşescu regime pointed out along with the fact that his entourage was full of former PCR activists, Securitate officials and members of the militia.[67] It was somewhat ironic that newspapers now sounding the alarm had helped prepare the ground for the PRM's populist assault by exaggerating the defects of the outgoing government—*Adevărul* is the one that immediately springs to mind. Perhaps it had dawned on editors like Cristian Tudor Popescu that they would no longer be able to criticise the President with impunity if Vadim was installed in Cotroceni; on that very matter Anghel Stanciu, a vice-premier of the PRM, declared on 29 November that 'journalists who sold out to the west' might be sent to work in forced labour camps.[68]

But if the press thought it could puncture Vadim's bubble, it was mistaken. Readership levels were low in Romania, which is why newspapers had sometimes claimed the same nationalist turf as the PRM in a bid to boost their sales levels. Most voters acquired their knowledge of the news from television and increasingly from aggressively populist channels like Antena 1. This was a medium where Vadim was the undisputed master. He had started off the presidential race with a public recognition level as low as 35% compared to Iliescu's 99% and Isărescu's 50%. But, according to the sociologist and poll-ster Alin Teodorescu, his television appearances greatly sharpened his appeal;[69] his endless stream of oratory, his shock tactics and his colourful wordplay put him in a league of his own. Since 1990 he had perfected a form of written communication with Romanians through his weekly newspaper, which proved even more effective when it was transferred to the television screen. His demonisation of opponents, his insistence that only he could defend core Romanian values, and his identification of multiple threats that endangered the very existence of Romania repelled not a few Romanians, but far more were mesmerised by his performance, especially during an election period.

Vadim delivered his most uninhibited television performance to date on 21 November on the state television channel. All the main presidential candidates (except the UDMRs) had gathered in the studio for a debate, with the rules of engagement carefully negoti-ated in advance. What happened might have been predicted given the way that Vadim had flouted the rules of Parliament and even of the courts in order to give full play to his king-size ego. He swept aside the moderator and denounced the PD challenger Petre Roman, an old enemy, in the crudest terms, claiming too that his father had been a Russian agent who had been ready to dismember Romania. Roman tried ineffectively to block the tide of invective; Isărescu and Iliescu stayed outside the fray and only Stolojan tried, with some success, to stand up to Vadim.[70] The editor of *Evenimentul Zilei* wrote immediately afterwards that this was the first moment when the Romanian electorate had been able to 'get the measure of Corneliu Vadim Tudor's madness'.[71] Such a performance, he argued, was bound to produce a fall in his popularity.[72] But Romanian politics had fallen into such disrepute, and its main practitioners enjoyed such poor standing, that Vadim could not easily repel voters alienated from the *status quo* as long as he expressed their frustrations. Attempts to brand him as an 'extremist' were similarly unconvincing: a political spectrum stretching from the far left to the radical right did not re-ally exist in Romania and most voters were scarcely aware of such a spectrum or were interested in placing themselves upon it. A poll car-ried out in early 2000 asked the question: 'Some people feel more to the right, others more to the left in politics. Which position suits you?' No less than 41.8% of respondents said the question was of no importance to them and 17.3% said they just didn't know.[73] It follows then that accusations of left or right 'extremism' are thus likely to have had meaning to only a small section of the population. Amid widespread confusion over the difference between 'extreme' and 'moderate' political behaviour, and against such divided and lacklustre opposition, the PRM was bound to make an impression. It promised immediate action to solve problems of poverty, injustice and personal insecurity for which no other party had bold answers. Vadim cleverly portrayed himself as a regular citizen, 'an active Christian' who only 'knows four destinations: home, the Senate, the Party, and the printing house'.[74] He dismissed claims that he was an extremist, saying that if anyone could prove it, he would quit politics. He showed his innate skill as a manipulator when he said: 'What does extremism really mean? These are just words against me. Show me a person of any nationality whom I harmed. There is no one.'[75]

The PRM received an additional windfall on the eve of the election when the CNSAS published a list of candidates who had collaborated with the Securitate. The list included the leader of the PNL, Mircea Ionescu Quintus, but nobody from the PDSR or the PRM. It was well known, at least within the media, that the PRM was full of former Securitate figures and their willing collaborators (Vadim had praised them in the past for carrying out what he saw as their patriotic duty), but in October the PRM had simply refused to hand over its candidate list for verification by the CNSAS.[76] That no action was taken against it is not surprising given the weakness of the Romanian state in so many areas. But the fact that the CNSAS was able to publish even an incomplete list of candidates linked compromisingly with the former regime can only be viewed as gross interference in the electoral process. It confirmed the worst forecasts made when the much-disputed Ticu Dumitrescu law on access to the Securitate files was passed in 1998 that it would be used to rehabilitate oppressors and besmirch proponents of democracy.

Romania's new electoral landscape

Of all eligible Romanians 65.31% voted in the presidential election of 26 November. Iliescu was ahead of his rivals, but Vadim was only

8 points behind him, having obtained a vote more than six times greater than in 1996. For a precedent it was necessary to go back to the Depression years of inter-war Europe to find an extremist party enjoying such a giant electoral leap. In the parliamentary election the PRM's vote was less high, at 19%, but with the elimination of other formations (including the PNTCD-controlled CDR 2000 which failed to reach the required threshold), the party ended up with almost a quarter of the seats in both houses of Parliament.

Adrian Năstase correctly identified the huge support for Vadim as 'a form of protest against the entire political class, an anti-system vote'.[77] The PRM had made striking advances in nearly all parts

RESULTS OF ROMANIAN PRESIDENTIAL ELECTIONS, 26 NOVEMBER 2000

	Votes (%)
Ion Iliescu (PDSR)	36.35
Corneliu Vadim Tudor (PRM)	28.34
Teodor Stolojan (PNL)	11.78
Mugur Isărescu	9.54
Gyorgy Frunda (UDMR)	6.22
Petre Roman (PD)	2.99
Theodor Meleşcanu (ApR)	1.91
Others	2.87

RESULTS OF ROMANIAN PARLIAMENTARY ELECTIONS, 26 NOVEMBER 2000: CHAMBER OF DEPUTIES

	Votes (%)	*Seats (%)*
Party of Romanian Social Democracy (PDSR)	36.61	45.32
Greater Romania Party (PRM)	19.48	25.68
Democratic Party (PD)	7.58	9.48
National Liberal Party	7.48	9.17
Democratic Union of Hungarians in Romania (UDMR)	6.80	8.25
Romanian Democratic Convention 2000	5.04	–
Alliance for Romania (ApR)	4.07	–
National Liberal Party—Cimpeanu	1.40	–
National Alliance (Party of Romanian National Unity—Romanian National Party)	1.38	–
Ex-officio members representing national minorities	–	2.10
Others	11.16	–

ROMANIAN PARLIAMENTARY ELECTIONS, 26 NOVEMBER 2000: SENATE

	Votes (%)	Seats (%)
Party of Romanian Social Democracy (PDSR)	37.09	46.45
Greater Romania Party (PRM)	21.01	26.42
Democratic Party (PD)	7.58	9.28
National Liberal Party	7.48	9.28
Democratic Union of Hungarians in Romania (UDMR)	6.90	8.57
Romanian Democratic Convention 2000	5.29	–
Alliance for Romania (ApR)	4.27	–
National Alliance (Party of Romanian National Unity—Romanian National Party)	1.42	–
National Liberal Party—Cimpeanu	1.22	–
Others	7.74	–

These results were published by the Central Electoral Bureau on 30 November and were published in *Monitorul* on 1 December 2000.

of the country, among all age groups, and in most social categories. These were biggest in regions and among social groups which, in 1996, had strongly endorsed the centrist parties which governed for the next four years. The PRM did best of all in Transylvania and among 18–30 year olds, 33% of whom seem to have voted for it.[78]

Only in Timişoara, the city where fidelity to the anti-communist principles of the 1989 revolution had always been strongest, was a CDR mayor victorious in the June 2000 local elections. Yet by November the same year the PRM had emerged ahead of all its rivals (albeit narrowly) in the presidential and parliamentary elections. It was a shock result, even though it was voters in the small-town and rural areas that comprised the Timişoara electoral district who probably played a key role in strengthening the PRM. Transylvanians could have registered their profound dissatisfaction by abstaining on polling day or endorsing parties with a regional outlook. Many undoubtedly did refuse to vote, but the big swing in support for the PRM suggests that many more were prepared to resort to a radical course to express their alienation from the current state of politics.[79]

Inevitably fears were expressed that the PRM's success might also be due to an increase in inter-ethnic tension. But preliminary evidence suggests that it was acute dissatisfaction with the coalition's record rather than the appeal of the PRM's anti-Hungarian or anti-Roma policies which gained it such strong backing from social

Stopping Vadim 259

groups hitherto deaf to extremist appeals. In 1998–9 Vadim had
held a number of high-profile rallies in Cluj and Tirgu Mureş in
which the invective and threats against those he perceived to be the
chief ethnic foes of the Romanians were far more virulent than
usual, but they produced few electoral rewards for the PRM in the
June 2000 local elections.[80] In November 2000 the PRM failed to
score more impressively than elsewhere in areas of Transylvania
either where there had been past instances of inter-ethnic conflict
and sharply-expressed rivalry, such as Tirgu Mureş or Cluj or where
Romanians might have been expected to feel insecure through
being outnumbered by Hungarians, as in the counties of Harghita
and Covasna.[81]

There is strong evidence suggesting that miscalculations by the
CDR contributed to the PRM's triumph. The sudden withdrawal
of Constantinescu in July 2000 opened the way for the PRM to
argue that the President's anti-corruption offensive had just been
pretence. Vadim made corruption and a strategy for fighting it the
central planks of his campaign, just as Constantinescu had done in
1996. An exit poll carried out on 26 November found that 42% of
voters considered that the first priority of the next government
should be the punishment of all those guilty of corruption.[82] It was
the number one issue for the voters of each of the parties and for no
less than 56% of PRM voters. Alin Teodorescu, the director of
IMAS, claims that when Constantinescu dropped out of the presidential race, he forced approximately 20% of the voters to seek a
new home.[83] If the CDR had united behind a single presidential
candidate with a strong reform message and concrete measures at
the heart of it, it might have preserved most of its base, but in the end
Isărescu and Stolojan retained only 20% of this reservoir of votes,
Iliescu acquiring 10%. If the figures of Alin Teodorescu Romania's
best-known pollster, are to be believed, Vadim gained no less than
50% of the votes that had gone to Constaninescu in 1996.[84]

Stopping Vadim

Having refused to close ranks to ensure a passage into the second
round, the PNTCD and the PNL were left with little choice but to
throw their support behind Iliescu. Some dissident voices argued
that it was better for the CDR and its civil society allies to remain

aloof from the battle since the two choices on offer were equally
unpalatable; indeed it might have been better to have Vadim in
Cotroceni when his power was still relatively limited rather than after he had built up a formidable political movement.[85] But from
Constantinescu down, the outgoing government leaders indicated
that supporting Iliescu was the only course available given the obvious threat which Vadim posed to Romania's fragile democracy.
Iliescu and the PDSR made it easier for their former adversaries to
contemplate what they would have found unthinkable only a few
days before: they ruled out any alliance with the PRM even if
Vadim won the presidency, and reaffirmed their interest in active
cooperation with the centre-right parties that had been returned to
Parliament. Iliescu declared: 'This is no longer about me. It is a very
important moment in which Romanian society has to decide
whether it wants the democratising processes which started in 1989
to continue, if it wants to go further along the road to progress. Or
not.'[86] In a moment of supreme irony, he had to warn pillars of civic
liberalism such as Gabriel Liiçeanu not to speak out too openly in
his favour because 'the people's hatred for them is so great' that they
might stampede towards Vadim.[87]

In the two weeks before the 10 December run-off Vadim pitched
his appeal towards anti-communist voters who had backed Stolojan
and Isărescu. On 6 December, in an hour-long election broadcast recognised even by his critics as a *tour de force*, Vadim tore into Iliescu,
branding him as a willing dupe of Moscow who had betrayed his
country.[88] Iliescu had wisely refused to engage in a personal debate
with Vadim. Instead he reinforced the message that he was the only
figure who could guarantee stability and recovery, branding Vadim
as 'a danger to democracy and the fate of Romania'.[89]

It was unclear how Romanians would vote in the second round
which now made the country the focus of international attention.
Statements issued by President Clinton on 1 December and by the
European Commission three days later expressed concern.[90] Alin
Teodorescu (and no friend of Vadim) argued that Vadim might quite
possibly win the run-off.[91] This was not an unreasonable supposition. The PRM's anti-corruption message was very attractive to
PDSR voters, 44% of whom, in the exit poll mentioned above, had
identified it as their prime concern. Besides, it was unclear to what

extent firmly anti-communist voters in the CDR would transfer to Iliescu. But the closing of political ranks against Vadim was bound to have an effect; he now complained that he was being 'hunted down like a war criminal by the servants of the new world order'.[92] The press now delved even more deeply than before into Vadim's extremist past before and after 1989. On 7 December several newspapers reported that for years he had avoided paying taxes to the Romanian state.[93] The weakness of state authority was a prominent recurring theme in his electoral propaganda and it was now apparent that Vadim himself had contributed to the malaise. But far more damaging was the revelation that in spite of his staunch defence of Orthodox values, he was not himself a member of Romania's majority church. It was discovered that he had grown up in a Baptist family; in statements unearthed from the archives of *Sâptamina*, the paper he wrote for before 1989, he defended the city planning strategy that involved the destruction of historic Orthodox churches.[94] *România líbera* revealed that Vadim continued to have close links with north American Evangelical Protestants, running the story under the headline 'The "Believer" Corneliu Vadim Tudor is quite simply a man without God'.[95]

Such revelations were bound to come as surprise to those who viewed Vadim as a national tribune of the people. The Orthodox Church continued to enjoy a strong following, particularly in Moldavia, and some even detected a religious revival among a section of Romanian youth. Moldavia's leading churchman Bishop Daniel, the Metropolitan of Moldavia and Bucovina, openly called for the faithful to support Iliescu.[96] After a *Te Deum* in Bucharest's main cathedral on 1 December Teoctist, the Patriarch, appealed 'to all of our people, irrespective of their beliefs, to make sure that the country is led by those who have shown balance, not by extremists'.[97]

Romania draws back from the brink

The 10 December presidential run-off resulted in a clear victory for Iliescu, but turnout fell to 57.5%. He got 66.83% of the vote while Vadim obtained 33.17% a result very much in line with poll predictions in the final week of the campaign. Ironically Iliescu got the highest percentage support in the two mainly Hungarian counties of Harghita and Covasna where, respectively, 90.83 and 88.5% of voters backed him. Hence claims that these Transylvanian counties were hotbeds of 'separatism' (ones that the PDSR had endorsed in the past) had surely been totally misplaced. Vadim was the victor in only one of Romania's forty-one counties, Bistriţa-Nasaud, but he polled over 40% in the counties of Alba, Arad, Caras-Severin, Gorj, Maramureş, Salaj, Sibiu and Tulcea. Most of these counties had two things in common: they were geographically isolated from the capital, and the sense of being ignored or exploited by a centralized system was keenly felt, in most of them. Secondly, they were all dependent on industries in decline and thus unable to offer a secure livelihood. The crisis of mining in Gorj county, which included the Jiu valley, is well-known and it is surprising that Vadim polled only 43.31% of the vote there. But in all the rest of them agriculture was the mainstay of the local economy: falling prices for agricultural products, the unviability of many small farms recently returned to private ownership, and the severest drought in over forty years resulted in unrelieved gloom. It is interesting that in several of these countries much of the land had proved unsuitable for collectivisation, and private initiatives (within very strict limits) had been permitted under communism. Alba, Maramureş and Sibiu spring to mind, all in Transylvania. So it was not only in counties transformed by communist-era regimentation that Vadim did well, a worrying pointer for the future. It is interesting that (after the Hungarian counties mentioned above) the two places where Vadim did least well were the capital and Iasi, where he only polled, respectively, 26.17 and 26.11% of the vote. These cities had both witnessed considerable changes after 1989, with the result that an informed public opinion had developed which was not so susceptible to Vadim's rabble-rousing. Timişoara had, by recent tradition, been ahead of these two in its desire for integration with the democratic West; usually the votes of the birthplace of the 1989 revolt ensured that Timis county returned the largest pro-democratic vote. But this time 36.48% of its voters supported Vadim in the second round.

Vadim cried foul, claiming that he had been the real second-round victor, and in a theatrical gesture he lodged a complaint with the European Court of Justice in The Hague.[98] But international monitors concurred that the ballot had been properly conducted, and there was relief abroad that it was Iliescu who was assuming office on 21 December for his third presidential term. As expected, Adrian Năstase, now aged fifty, was installed as prime minister on 28 December. With over 46% of parliamentary seats, the PDSR felt able to govern alone, but the creation of an informal alliance with the UDMR was greeted with relief by the EU. Hungarian support in Parliament was offered in return for ratifying local government reforms strengthening the position of the Hungarian language in areas where it was widely spoken. The PNL also affirmed its cooperation with the government in return for the promise of a serious look at constitutional reform, particularly to clarify the roles of each of the houses of Parliament. But the strength of bipartisan politics would be measured by the extent to which pro-democratic forces could combine to block further advances by the PRM. Năstase's strategy appeared at first to be one of separating PRM parliamentarians from their leader. Senior positions in parliament were given to PRM figures, and PDSR conservatives not appointed to the cabinet were compensated by being given charge of important parliamentary commissions. This raised the danger that PRM and PDSR forces might combine in the future to water down, delay or even throw out laws with which they were uncomfortable.

Western pressure largely accounted for the decision of the PDSR to offer an olive branch to a traditional foe like the UDMR. EU aid to the tune of billions of dollars was on its way and it would have been highly self-defeating if the PDSR had reverted to the churlish habits of government that had earned it discredit before 1996. The CDR had come up against a state machine much of which stubbornly refused to alter behaviour patterns inimical to good government. But its fall had come about primarily through its own deep shortcomings. Poor-quality leadership particularly in the PNTCD, failure to establish an effective partnership with the Presidency, and failure to engage in dialogue with the population or even to keep lines of communication open to its own supporters left it floundering within a short period of taking office. It allowed its reputation to be tarnished by a more cunning coalition partner, the PD, which fought a quiet guerrilla war against colleagues whom it viewed as political enemies. The decision to remain with a broken-backed alliance, even after the long-running Ciorbea crisis when it was clear that differences between the PD and the PNTCD extended beyond personalities, was a fundamental error. The appointment of Radu Vasile as premier helped to smooth over relations between the chief protagonists in the coalition, but only to create inner conflict within the PNTCD and impair relations between Cotroceni and the government. The electorate were surprisingly long-suffering—the CDR was still able to win the Bucharest mayoral elections in June 1998 after eighteen months of falling living standards—but the *dégringolade* at the heart of government stripped away its remaining credibility. The appointment of the technocratic Mugur Isărescu as prime minister after the removal of Vasile in a palace coup brought no recovery in fortunes. Genuine progress in Romania's membership bid to join the EU left most of the populace unmoved. After the deeply unpopular (but courageous) decision to give full backing to NATO's controversial military offensive against the Milošević regime in Serbia in 1999, there was no other opportunity for Constantinescu or any of his appointees to capitalise on foreign policy issues. A sharp fall in support for the CDR would have been inevitable even if it had avoided many of the debacles of the post-1996 period; what turned it into a catastrophic collapse was undoubtedly a serious of gambles based on a faulty assessment of the popular mood and the strength of the PNTCD. Constantinescu's decision to retire seems to have been made in haste and without consulting the forces that had sustained his career. In the absence of a clear successor who could reunite the CDR, it was a reckless move which he will find hard to justify in his memoirs.[99] The PNTCD's refusal to strike a more equitable bargain with its chief partner, the PNL, and then its decision to press on alone with a new hastily assembled alliance backing Isărescu, who ran as an Independent, was the greatest blunder of all. The PNTCD found itself outside Parliament, having achieved just over 5% of the vote.

When Constantinescu made his final election broadcast on 17 November he already appeared a relic from the past. He admitted that he 'had not impressed too many people', but he insisted that after 1996: the war against corruption had yielded results: 3,500 dossiers had been drawn up against persons accused of corruption and involvement with organised crime and around 1,000 custodial sentences had been handed down.[100] But these figures found as little credibility among many of those who had rallied to Constantinescu in 1996 as his earlier claim that he had taken Romania to a post-transition phase in which democracy was being consolidated.[101] His isolation was cruelly exposed on 10 December, as he approached the building in Bucharest to cast his vote for his longstanding foe Iliescu: an irate PRM supporter rushed forward from the crowd and threw paint over him.[102] The press reported that his bodyguards, from the controversial SPP force, stood by as if hypnotised; later the head of the SPP blamed Constantinescu for his men's slow response, claiming that Cotroceni had issued contradictory orders about his security which had impaired their effectiveness. The President's inability to establish control over a force with such a questionable attitude to its duties exemplified the problems he faced during his mandate. The political mood was now ugly, with extremist forces that advocated dictatorship enjoying greater support than in any other European country.

Without the high-level attention the West started to pay to the Balkans after 1995, one cannot say whether democracy could have survived in Romania in the last five years of the century. Elected governments in the Balkans exhibiting the same weakness as the coalitions in office in Bucharest during this time had been brutally replaced in the inter-war period. A sign of the malaise was the formation in October of the National Association of Romanian Officers, whose statutes expressed a desire for the military to play an active political role. This move, indicating a disenchantment with current politics that extended high into the military, resulted in General Mircea Chelaru being dismissed from his post as head of the army on 1 November.[103]

Democracy's prospects now seemed to depend on how successfully the PDSR could work with the EU and other external agencies to rebuild the country's shattered economy. Such a partnership deserves the epithet 'the odd couple'. Up to only a short time before, the PDSR had insisted that state-led economic enterprises dating from the communist period must still have pride of place, and holders of such views still dominated the PDSR benches in Parliament. Democracy's prospects in Romania now seemed to depend on whether or not the PDSR could relaunch itself as a genuinely social democratic force in the way that has occurred in Hungary and

Poland. If the PDSR turns out to be a leopard unable to change its spots, no centre-right alternative waits in the wings. Instead reinvigorated forces of extremism with an anti-Western and anti-minority agenda are in a strong position to fill the vacuum left by successive governments whose reforms have collapsed around their ears.

9

A MESSIAH FOR ROMANIA?
CORNELIU VADIM TUDOR AND THE GREATER ROMANIA PARTY

In June 2001 the front page of *România Mare* proclaimed the Greater Romania Party (PRM) to be 'the most important nationalist movement in Europe'.[1] The party's vote had gone up from just under 4% in the 1992 elections to 19% in 2000. It was expanding while the only other major parties of authoritarian nationalism, at least in Western Europe, were retreating. The Italian Social Movement, the heir to Mussolini's Fascist Party, was disavowing its radicalism and regrouping around a Gaullist position so as to be able to participate in government following the vacuum on the centre-right opened up by the collapse of the Christian Democrats. In France Jean-Marie Le Pen's National Front suffered a disastrous split in the late 1990s, which meant that it could no longer expect to obtain the steady support of up to 15% of French voters.

Romania offers fruitful terrain for a party like the PRM. Parties and movements viewing the nation as a moral unity and with a message that thus transcended familiar class divisions enjoyed increasing success during Romania's first-sixty years as an independent state (1881–1945). Rather than obliterate it, the communists who ruled Romania for the next forty-five years came to terms with the nationalism already so deeply embedded in Romanian political culture, expropriating it to serve the interests of an élite engaged in stupendous efforts to create an industrial state in a mainly agrarian society. Despite the massive policy failures resulting from Ceauşescu's efforts to privilege heavy industry, the appeal of economic and political self-sufficiency remains strong. During the first post-communist decade the failure of liberal political and economic models has helped to erase memories of national communism's critical shortcomings. The opening up of the Romanian economy to external competition and the dismantling of much of its industry has coincided with falling living standards and an even sharper decline in economic activity. By the time of the 2000 elections the credibility of public figures in the political centre-ground, who disavowed nationalist fervour and stood for regional cooperation, appeared to be as low as that of their counterparts in the 1930s. With very little warning a populist advocating indigenous solutions emerged who in the first round of the presidential elections won more votes than all the candidates of the outgoing coalition put together. Without the post-communist left being able to offer a governing alternative to the discredited centrist formations, it is difficult to imagine what could have stopped Corneliu Vadim Tudor from making mass discontent his passport for power.

Many Romanian supporters of Vadim appear to have been unaware of his extremist views and intentions, and were mesmerised by the brilliant orator of his assaults on conventional politicians. But anyone familiar with extremist movements influential in Europe between the two world wars would see obvious affinities with the PRM. It incites anti-Semitism and the use of violence to resolve political problems. It openly advocates dictatorship and promotes a cult of personality around a leader which is excessive perhaps even by inter-war standards. It stands for ethnic purity and promises drastic action against those perceived as the ethnic enemies of the Romanian people, namely the Hungarians and the Roma. It makes up for the absence of a sizeable Jewish population by accusing a large number of public figures of being pawns of an international Jewish conspiracy seeking to destroy Romania. It is hostile to liberalism and to socialism in their international versions. It is deeply suspicious of international capitalism which is seen as intent on destroying the Romanian traditions and lifestyles which it believes to be necessary for the preservation of national identity. It makes no secret of its intention to impose a ruthless authoritarian regime if it should get the chance to rule Romania, and to hasten that moment it is ready to use extra-parliamentary action to subvert the democratic order.[2]

Vadim in the gallery of European extremism

Although it is no exaggeration to describe the PRM as one of Europe's most visible fascist parties, some qualification is required.

In the 1930s a large and influential fascist movement, the Iron Guard, did flourish in Romania. The PRM does not derive its inspiration from that movement even though it is prepared to endorse important aspects of its programme.[3] Instead its reference point is the communist regime which lasted from 1946 to 1989, and in particular the long nationalist phase associated with the dictatorship of Nicolae Ceauşescu. The PRM seeks to build on the work of a regime which boldly combined Marxism-Leninism with the nationalism recognisable by anyone familiar with inter-war Europe. At its heart was a gratuitous cult of personality centred on the ruling couple, Nicolae and Elena Ceauşescu, important aspects of which Vadim has imposed on his own movement.

There is little purpose in undue preoccupation with the question whether Vadim's movement is extreme-left or extreme-right. International opinion has classified it as 'extreme-right'—the same accolade as was given to Hitler's National Socialism and Mussolini's Fascism. But the Nazis, like the PRM today, heavily drew on the revolutionary methods and symbols of the totalitarian left. Hitler never disowned his debt to the Russian Bolsheviks, declaring in 1934: 'It is not Germany that will turn Bolshevist but Bolshevism that will become a sort of National Socialism. Besides, there is more that binds us to Bolshevism than separates us from it. There is, above all, genuine revolutionary feeling, which is alive everywhere in Russia except where there are Jewish Marxists. I have always made allowance for this circumstance, and given orders that former Communists are to be admitted to the party at once. The *petit bourgeois* Social Democrat and the trade union boss will never make a National Socialist, but the Communist always will.'[4]

One Romanian editor warned in 1999 that the PRM represented 'a fascist-communist' threat to Romania.[5] Against a background of democratic misgovernment, the emergence of a movement amalgamating the extremes is perhaps not surprising given the vitality of collectivist traditions on both the radical left and right of Romanian politics. The collapse of the fledgling Romanian centre-right at the end of the 1990s gave the PRM its chance to seek power; 'fascism achieved its most striking results whenever the traditional right was too weak to protect its own position.'[6] In post-1918 Italy, and not long after wards in Germany, voters were prepared to invest their hopes in a new revolutionary movement when the traditional right was found wanting. Ceauşescu may not have revived irredentist claims on Romanian territory or rehabilitated icons of Romanian nationalism such as General Ion Antonescu or Corneliu Zelea Codreanu, but the communist regime made vast efforts to indoctrinate the population with a combination of socialism and nationalism. This greatly assisted Vadim in carving out a popular support-base.

Ceauşescu was hardly an innovator in jettisoning the internationalist baggage of Leninist socialism; before him, Stalin, had injected Russian nationalism into Leninism.[7] Charles Maurras, the French reactionary, politically influential almost throughout the first half of the twentieth century, long ago recognised that there was a 'form of socialism, when stripped of its democratic and cosmopolitan accretions, which would fit in with nationalism just as a well-made glove fits a beautiful hand'.[8] Thinkers and (less often) activists of both left and right could sometimes find surprising common ground by advocating revolution against bourgeois society and the values it stood for. At the turn of the twentieth century, Georges Sorel helped to prepare the ground for a synthesis of left and right based on a glorification of violence and contempt for the existing order. His book *Reflections on Violence* led to the creation of Italian revolutionary syndicalism which fed into Italian fascism.[9] In the late 1930s Henri De Man, head of the Belgian Socialists, recommended a reconciliation between left and right in order to construct a new order that rejecting parliamentary government under bourgeois supervision.[10]

It is doubtful if Vadim has ever heard of Georges Sorel or Henri De Man—his repertoire of ideas is fairly limited—but his style and methods are comparable to those of Benito Mussolini, the progenitor of Fascism, who was certainly influenced by Sorel and in turn influenced De Man. He was a journalist who spent half his life serving the cause of the left in Italy before deserting it, at a time of wartime patriotic fervour, to pioneer fascism. Like Mussolini, Vadim is an expert propagandist able to capture and hold an audience by using the different mediums of communications available to him. Like Mussolini too, he was a single-minded agitator who evaded justice and escaped control of the governing classes who thought they could manipulate this turbulent figure for their own ends. Both were greatly assisted by their adversaries who were often weak and opportunistic.

Post-1918 Italy and post-1989 Romania were places in which rules for regulating political behaviour had broken down and where, to differing degrees, the conditions were favourable for political gangsterism. Violence was a metaphor at the forefront of both Italian fascism and the PRM. Mussolini actually carried out what Vadim constantly threatens to unleash on his opponents. Both denounced democracy as 'mediocracy'—the association of mediocrity with a pragmatic view of politics and a peaceful resolution of conflict is a powerful theme in Vadim's propaganda arsenal.[11] Both men also sought to establish a general interest based to a strong degree on attachment to the fatherland and the realisation of the national revolution. They moved away from defending a class interest, which had been the dominant metaphor in the first stages of their careers when they fought in the socialist movement or else defended in print an avowedly socialist state.

Vadim's task in supplanting the parliamentary right was made easy by the willingness of the CDR parties to abandon much of the 'common interest' terrain by pursuing policies of privatisation when in government. They gave up the state's economic role with even greater alacrity than the mainstream parties have done in Western Europe since the 1970s, and it is not surprising that the backlash—in the form of an upsurge in extremist parties standing for state paternalism and a defence of ethnic purity—has been far stronger in Romania than even in countries like France and Belgium. The large number of Romanians who favour a strong state presence in society are now being wooed both the PDSR and PRM, and it is perhaps not surprising that the two dominant forces in contemporary politics are these parties that have inherited the mantle of authoritarian paternalism from the communist regime.

Polling evidence suggests that Romania remains a left-wing country where egalitarian values are strong, and Vadim is careful not to repudiate this aspect of the pre-1989 heritage. Invited to the 1997 conference of the PDSR at a time when relations with the PRM were briefly cordial, he pleaded for both parties to sink their differences and form 'a national left' to save Romania.[12] He will acknowledge a left-wing orientation as long as it is national not international. At a May Day rally in 1997 he protested when the Socialist Workers Party (PSM) arrived with a portrait of Lenin, and threatened to pull out of an alliance with it.[13] But he was content regularly to publish congratulatory messages from the national communist regime in North Korea.[14]

The PRM and the communist heritage

Vadim may on some occasions lend his backing to enlightened capitalism, but the core of his economic programme is left-wing. He has called for an end to economic sell-offs and for a re-nationalisation of large economic holdings and even land. He has even advocated compulsory labour service 'so that no one can complain that they would like to work and there isn't any'.[15] But in PRM propaganda appeals to organic values based on concepts like ethnicity and common roots feature far more prominently. The constant emphasis on 'blood and soil' helps to explain why Vadim's movement is seen as extreme-right, but there have been recurring moments when these emotions have been tapped by the left. George Sorel, an anti-Semite and proponent of anarcho-syndicalism, has already been mentioned, and Ferdinand Lassalle, the leading nineteenth-century German socialist, was also known for his anti-Semitism. Ethnocentric views were expressed by both Marx and Engels. Those peoples whose nationalist aims were seen as likely to hinder the cause of socialism were dismissed by Engels as 'ethnic trash'.[16] He wrote in the *Neue Rheinische Zeitung* of 10 September 1848: 'By the same right with which France has taken Flanders, by that same right Germany takes Schleswig as well as Alsace-Lorraine: with the right of civilisation against barbarism, progress against stability.' In the *Communist Manifesto* Marx referred to 'barbarian' and 'civilised' nations.[17] Jack London, a widely-read socialist novelist, demanded the triumph of the fittest proletariat on earth, which in his eyes could only be white. 'The lesser breeds cannot endure,' he wrote in 1899 'I cannot but hail as unavoidable the Black and the Brown going down before the White.'[18] In 1902 H. G. Wells's book *Anticipations* called on a socialist utopia to destroy the 'grey confusion' of democracy through a world state governed by a self-appointed white élite who would purify mankind by exterminating the dark races.[19]

Vadim was not required to pioneer a new and radical nationalist discourse because the pre-1989 regime which he served had already done exactly that. Romanian communism had projected itself as a national liberation movement whose audacious efforts to create a self-reliant industrial state would complete the centuries-long freedom struggle. The media, the education system, the party's presence in the workplace and the military barracks were all utilised to socialize (or perhaps more accurately resocialize) Romanians in a nationalist sense. The PRM has never ceased to acknowledge its debt to Nicolae Ceauşescu. Vadim has frequently declared that he was the victim of an international plot in December 1989 which involved the secret services of the Soviet Union and the United States as well as Hungary.[20] At the first congress of the PRM in March 1993 he felt able to praise Ceauşescu for a long list of policy achievements which included the creation of a skilled workforce, the abolition of illiteracy and a vast programme of economic modernisation; for defending Romania's national integrity and winning the respect of 'Soviet imperialism when it was at its most expansionist'; and finally for his success in keeping control over wrongdoers, especially those from the Hungarian and Gypsy minorities who 'no longer dare to terrorise the majority Romanian population'.[21] In October 2000 Florin Preda called on his fellow senators to pass a motion 'reconsidering the activities' of the former dictator, whom he praised as a 'patriot' and a 'good diplomat' who became 'one of the world's greatest statesmen'. He had been executed in 1989 to curtail his efforts to 'consolidate Romanian independence'.[22] It was to Vadim's advantage that the traditional xenophobia of Romanian public life extended beyond the communist regime, enabling him to describe his own activism as the culmination of efforts by poets like Eminescu, philosophers like Eliade, parliamentarians like A. C. Cuza, and military leaders like Antonescu to wage war against Romania's national enemies. His original contribution to Romanian nationalism has perhaps been to make remove any inhibitions from chauvinist discourse to a far greater extent than was ever the case in communist times and before.

The social psychologist Erich Fromm identified various social types who are uncomfortable with freedom, illiberal in their attitudes, and happiest with a strong centrally-directed state which lays down how they should think and behave.[23] The experience of two generations of rigid state paternalism in Romania created large groups of citizens ill-equipped to cope with the opportunities and the demands of an open, competitive society. Such people were attracted to the Greater Romania Party whose weekly newspaper by mid-2000 had a readership of around 400,000.[24] Thirty years of forced industrialisation had produced a social type, sometimes known as the worker-peasant or the neo-urbanite, accustomed to carrying out the state's orders without question. The Romanian version of *homo sovieticus* (Soviet man) also possessed a strong desire for social protection. The journalist Şerban Orescu wrote in 1998 that Romanian public opinion disliked the idea of private property: 'They grew unfamiliar with it... in communist times when there were work places assured by the state and a standard salary, and consequently they could not come to terms with the inevitable inequality created by the market economy.'[25] Thus it is no surprise that the ranks of the PRM have become filled with individuals who feel out of place in the new economic conditions: 'Elderly people nostalgic for the strict hierarchy of the communist regime and for stable and predictable economic benefits; youth confused by the cruel competition of a "heartless" labour market as well as the clash between what the Romanian education system can offer and what the labour market demands...'.[26] A 1999 poll found that no less than 54.2% of respondents believed the state should investigate how the well-off had acquired their wealth.[27] Vadim perhaps did not misjudge the public mood when, in a speech delivered on 16 August 1998 that became known as the Proclamation of Turda, he promised to 'renationalise factories, installations and hotels which passed to foreign ownership by illegal means, to create a strategy to exploit the national wealth for the benefit of the population, organize a national referendum for the introduction of the death penalty... social integration of the Roma or their isolation in colonies, ban the UDMR, impose martial law in Harghita and Covasna, install a dictatorship of laws and declare a state of emergency over the whole Romanian economy'.[28] By promising economic salvation and targeting Romania's presumed ethnic enemies, Vadim appealed to malcontents on both the left and right of politics.

In 1999, according to data released by the World Bank in 2000, 41.2% of Romanians lived on or below its poverty threshold compared with 25.3% in 1995, and those living in extreme poverty comprised 16.6% of the population—double the total for 1995 (8%).[29]

It is no coincidence that the sharp decline in living standards coincided with the equally sharp rise in support for the PRM. Harsh economic privation created a disorientated population, many of whom wished to find out who had caused their misfortune, Vadim and his allies went to great lengths to demonstrate that it had not been the communist state. Frequent articles in *România Mare* praised the communists' nationalisation of property after 1948.[30] Leaders like Dej were hailed as being closer to the people than their post-1989 successors. Articles on communist figures such as Emil Bodnăras were apt to end with the words 'History will judge the good they did as well as the bad.'[31] Not untypical was the claim made by Ion Coja that powerful external interests decided to remove Ceauşescu in the late 1980s because he was on the verge of launching 'a grandiose international bank' along with Iran and Libya, which would have provided an unacceptable level of competition for the existing banking system.[32] In 1999 Vadim was arguing that the fall of Bancorex, Romania's largest state bank, had nothing to do with looting by well-placed former communists; what had actually happened was that 'Bill Clinton and the CIA asked for Bancorex to be destroyed as a matter of urgency': The efficient information system it had built up through its international operations before and after 1989 made it a danger to powerful Western interests.[33]

A world full of anti-Romanian conspiracies

Vadim has argued ever more boldly that it is foreigners who really control Romania.[34] Strangely he has usually neglected conventional facts from which nationalists might argue with some plausibility that foreign interests do indeed enjoy enormous influence at the level of national affairs, such as the deep involvement of the EU and IMF in shaping economic policy, especially after 1996. The intervention of these multilateral agencies has determined the tax levels the state has imposed on small- and medium-sized business and the level of tariff on foreign agricultural goods—decisions with profound implications for the survival of farmers and newly-launched capitalists in harsh economic times. But the PRM rarely offers a critique of Western-influenced economic policy, at least not in any detail.

In his speeches Vadim betray, little or no grasp of economic affairs, and instead falls back on arguing that foreign influence over

Romania is exercised through hidden channels. Thus in 2000 he did not hesitate to argue that Constantinescu's decision to pull out of the presidential race was due to 'the intervention of the very same occult forces which had invented him in the first place.... On Saturday 15 July he got a phone call from the White House in Washington, informing him that the West had now dropped him, and it was suggested that he ought to disappear from the political scene.'[35] But the United States in its turn was not an independent actor: in fact it was nothing less than 'a colony of Israel's'.[36]

It should not be altogether surprising that many Romanians have a large and unhealthy appetite for conspiracy theories—which normally proliferate in parts of the world prone to violent upheavals.[37] The wars, invasions and changes of borders which periodically overwhelmed Romania during the twentieth century make it rather easy to claim that the country was the object of successive conspiracies.[38] The fate of Ceauşescu and the many unresolved aspects of the 1989 revolution have given rise to many fanciful theories. That violent event had no parallel elsewhere in the Warsaw Pact states. Vadim alleges that Soviet and Hungarian agents played a role, while opponents of communism, for their part, do not dismiss the Soviet contribution, but attribute an important role to Middle Eastern terrorists. When the Greater Romania Party (PRM) was launched in June 1991, the following statement occupied pride of place in its programme: 'In our country occult forces exist, extremist and anti-democratic ones, which, sustained and manoeuvred from outside, provoke a state of chaos, of continuous disorganization in the national economy, the education system, and culture.'[39]

Often Vadim's political programme has the appearance of a shopping list of extreme measures that need enactment urgently if the multifarious conspiracies designed to terminate Romania's existence are to be overcome. Şerban Orescu observed: 'CV Tudor's lack of a programme recalls Codreanu in 1937 when, in reply to the question 'What intentions do you have if you come to power? Do you have a programme?' Codreanu replied: 'I don't need a programme. First I'll come to power, then I'll see what I can do.'[40] Vadim has been careful to keep his distance from the Iron Guard, but both pointed the finger at international Jewish financial interests which they insisted were seeking to destroy Romania.[41] In Western Europe, the National

Front argues, 'cabals and occult forces [are] working to repress France.'⁴² In Russia, Vladimir Zhirinovsky's Liberal Democratic Party propagated a similar discourse. Vadim cannot be seen in the company of a Russian demagogue (many claim that he is of Jewish extraction), who once dismissed Romania as a land largely inhabited by 'Italian-speaking gypsies'; but Jean-Marie Le Pen, the leader of the French National Front, was guest-of-honour at the second PRM national conference in November 1997.⁴³ Except for a brief revival in the first round of the 2002 French presidential elections, Le Pen has been in eclipse ever since the 1998 split in his movement, but his assaults on the 'irresponsible power' wielded by transnational bodies like the IMF, the World Bank, and the EU now enjoy vogue among broad sections of the international left as well as the far-right.

Grievances to be exploited

The desire for order and a clean-up of public life are widely-held sentiments that Vadim has been able to exploit for his own ends. It is not just the PRM but a wide section of national opinion which believes that the Roma community is behind much of the crime and disorder which has preoccupied Romania in recent years. As usual it is Vadim who has the most dramatic solution. 'What can we do against bands of gypsy killers and rapists?', he asked on 24 March 2000, and answered himself: 'No problem, they are going to be liquidated.'⁴⁴ The number of recorded crimes per 100,000 of the population had gone up 471% in the decade after 1990. However, Romania still found itself at the bottom of the table for recorded crimes in the former Warsaw Pact states, the incidence being half of the Czech Republic's and less than one-third of Hungary's.⁴⁵ The perception that communist Romania was virtually crime-free is one that the PRM has frequently advanced and it strikes a chord with many Romanians. At the end of 2000 the press published many articles insisting that if crime and corruption were major concerns, then the PRM was part of the problem. *Adevărul* pointed out on 30 November that Valentin Vasilescu, a newly-elected PRM deputy, had been sentenced to a prison term of eight years, reduced on appeal to five, for his role in the Tigareta II scandal. The same issue shone the spotlight on another new PRM deputy, Dumitru Puzdrea, who for years has successfully defied Bucharest city council and even the Supreme Court by constructing a large illegal commercial centre and mobilising armed bands whenever the authorities try to demolish it.[46] General Nicolae Nitu, the PRM candidate for the Bucharest mayoralty in 1998, was accused by the press of having protected the gypsy mafia in the city when he was its chief of police.[47]

In June 2001 *Ziua* ran a series of articles investigating Vadim's financial affairs. It claimed that in 1997 he had suborned a senior official in the Bucharest mayor's office in order to obtain villa, valued today at around $100,000, for a fraction of its market price.[48] It discovered that in 1991 he had bought a sizeable tract of land at Butimanu for a similar knock-down price.[49] Earlier, several newspapers published evidence that he had paid no taxes on the income earned from his press empire. A PD Senator in the 1996–2000 parliament even claimed that during the 1980s Vadim had been a trafficker of pornographic cassettes[50] acquired, according to *Ziua*, on shopping trips while accompanying the Romanian national football team to matches abroad. On his return to Bucharest he sold them for a substantial profit and only got away with it through his close contacts with the regime.[51] Vadim's penchant for easily acquired money and property does not seem to have harmed his credibility in the eyes of Romanians influenced by his populist discourse. It would not be the first time that a demagogue lashing out against ill-gotten wealth had himself practised what he had been so keen to denounce.

By the end of his presidency Constantinescu was complaining that citizens allowed their minds to be controlled by ex-Securitate people and vulgar demagogues prominent in the media.[52] His first prime minister, Victor Ciorbea, became a universal laughing stock, according to Cornel Nistorescu, for leaving the government offices at the end of his time in office in the same old Dacia car in which he had arrived fifteen months earlier.[53] Romanian attitudes to corruption are not clearcut. Strong anti-corruption movements have emerged, but there is plenty of evidence from the royal and communist epochs to suggest that many Romanians are ready to put up with more flagrant abuses of power than are many of their neighbours. Indeed the word most frequently used in connection with corruption, *şmecherie* is 'a term of half-admiration for fraudulent activity performed with a degree of poise or dexterity'.[54]

A totalitarian regime like Ceauşescu's may have instilled a strongly egalitarian outlook, but its ruthless insistence on obedience meant that few people were ready to speak out against abuses of power. Only a few individuals in the democratic era have been prepared to say loudly and clearly that the Romanians have emerged from communist times with a somewhat warped mentality. One such critic is Valeriu Stoica, leader of the Liberals in 2000–2; in 1999 he complained that 'the same dissatisfied Romanians continue to look to the state as a kind of parent, demanding "give it to me". But from where? The state has nothing to give if it is not producing.'[55] Citizens may be ready to forgive the shortcomings of a would-be redeemer like Vadim if he can provide them with economic salvation at little cost. During his election broadcast on the eve of the 10 December presidential election, he promised the tens of thousands of investors in the failed FNI investment fund that he would return them everything they had lost, but did not explain how this would be done.[56] Cornel Nistorescu has frequently criticised what he sees as a Romanian culture of dependence. He wrote in 1997: 'The residents of a block of flats, or some living on the same street, still cannot come together to erect something without an intervention from the state or the mayor. And, as soon as such an initiative is started, the row over who should be the leader starts too. Petty vanities hold back big or small projects and the people fail to team up for causes which don't need…millions but a dozen individuals who agree with one another.'[57]

While desperate reformers and their media supporters sometimes came near to saying that the Romanians needed to re-invent themselves, Vadim by contrast demanded that those who had served Ceauşescu during 'the Era of Light' should be restored to positions of power. In a whole range of ministries Ceauşescu loyalists had never gone away; the Foreign Ministry remained a stronghold of individuals opposed to Euro-Atlantic integration, and similar types in the Interior Ministry were able to block the timid efforts at reform proposed after 1996. Pro-Ceauşescu elements actually flooded back to the Ministry of Culture in 1994–5, a period when the PRM was a junior partner in government.[58] But what appears to have enabled Vadim to survive difficulties that on numerous occasions caused his political obituary to be written was access to highly compromising information on opponents in the PDSR or its coalition successors. In 1998 Cornel Nistorescu rhetorically asked: 'How has a tiny party whose members are generally old and with basic education only, become a real danger?... Through dishonesty, cheek, and base use of personal contacts. Through blackmail... PRM veterans have succeeded in placing informers inside the police, the directorate of Military Information, the SRI, 0215 and other secret services... The danger of the PRM's secret service is that it is capable, in a moment of political instability, of grabbing power...'[59]

Irresolute opponents and ruthless allies

Eleven months later, the PRM came very close to toppling the elected government during the miners' uprising which it helped to organise. By December 2000 some of the desperados around Vadim were in Parliament and the PRM was no longer 'a tiny party'. Andrei Zeno, a former Securitate official who had tried to destroy President Constantinescu's reputation by claiming he had been a foreign agent, was one such figure. (The President filed charges and in 1999 Zeno was given a two-year suspended sentence.)[60] Another was Dumitru Dragomir, a militia officer who had fallen foul of the communist authorities for his involvement in illegal gambling, but who was named in 1987 as president of the militia's national soccer team, Victoria Bucharest. Like Vadim, he profited from his ability to travel abroad and return with items commanding a high price on the black market. In a 1990 police report he even boasted: 'Whenever I arrived at the airport, officers from the ministry of the interior would be waiting for me and I didn't need to bother with customs.' ... I was a rich man under communism as well as in capitalist times.'[61] Dragomir has become one of Romania's *nouveaux riches* by carving out a career in popular (yellow) journalism and football management. He has profited from transferring Romanian players abroad (one of the few lucrative export industries in Romania), and he mixes with the celebrities of the international soccer world. In 1999 the New York-based Anti-Defamation League complained to the International Soccer Federation (FIFA) about the anti-semitic journalism sponsored by Dragomir. Facing charges of incitement, Mihai Antonescu, a former deputy editor of *Atac la persoana*, a scandal-sheet owned by Dragomir, told Romanian prosecutors that he had been instructed to write articles denigrating Jews: 'I wrote my reports in the spirit of orders issued by the owner.' Prosecutors found at least fifty anti-Semitic articles written under at least ten names. Dragomir was one of three vice-presidents of the Romanian Soccer Federation, but FIFA contented itself with issuing a reprimand to someone who was a top figure in one of its national affiliates; interestingly, Mircea Sandu, president of the Romanian Soccer Federation, sprang to Dragomir's defence and said that Romania had no anti-semitic groups.[62]

The PRM's influence in the domain of popular culture extends from football (a national craze in Romania) to private television, where Antena I, the main private TV channel, is an unabashed ally of Vadim. The party's ability to manipulate public opinion by influencing the bodies that offer mass entertainment and recreation may yet prove just as damaging as its links with the shadowy intelligence world. The private security industry is another area where the PRM enjoys valuable contacts. Many of the businesses offering protection were set up by former members of the Securitate and the militia, and have no interest in seeing the industry effectively regulated. The PRM is ready to speak on their behalf. The party also enjoys support among the tenants who obtained property after it was expropriated from private owners in the late 1940s and later. The PRM deputy Eugen Pleşa is President of the Tenants Association. Only the PRM voted against a law on nationalised houses (granting some compensation to former owners) when it was passed by the Chamber of Deputies on 16 January 2001.[63]

The inability of successive democratically-elected governments to enforce the law against Vadim must be regarded as another primary reason for his outstanding success. He first demonstrated that he was above the law in July 1991 when his supporters broke up a court hearing in which he was answering charges of having libelled Gheorghe Robu, the former prosecutor-general of Romania.[64] President Iliescu refused to come out in defence of the man he had previously appointed to a top post in the Romanian justice system, and Vadim emerged from the criminal prosecution unscathed. In 1993 no action was taken against him when, engaged in an altercation with the PD deputy Aristide Dragomir, he summoned a bodyguard who proceeded to beat up Dragomir in the lobby of parliament.[65]

During the night of the CDR's 1996 election victory, Vadim dominated the discussion in the television studios with many politicians reluctant to interrupt him and quite evidently rather frightened of him. A similar scene occurred in the Romanian Parliament on 20 January 1999: Miron Cozma's coal miners were marching on Bucharest, and parliamentarians were clearly afraid for their skins when he turned up with his bodyguards; only the Hungarians were prepared to challenge his menacing invective.[66] A few months later Vadim boasted that he had successfully intervened with two generals to have the (by them) imprisoned Cozma transferred from a cell for 'murderers' to one for 'intellectuals'.[67]

Valeriu Stoica, minister of justice in 1996–2000, was virtually alone in the political world in being prepared to trade verbal blows with Vadim and use the full rigour of the law against him. In a reported interview in 1999 entitled 'Vadim and Cozma want a world in which only they count and in which anything is possible', he said: 'One of the most dangerous agents responsible for the destruction of the Romanian moral code is Corneliu Vadim Tudor. All the time he tries to transform what is bad into something that appears good and what is good into something that looks bad. If the healthy part of the Romanian people do not react quickly against this danger, it might collapse.'[68]

But Stoica's efforts to get parliament to remove Vadim's immunity from prosecution foundered, not least because of the PRM leader's compromising hold over senior members of his own PNL. The assault by Vadim on institutions recalls the way the Iron Guard intimidated the courts and persuaded members of the political elite to look the other way after they had carried out bloody deeds. At the time there were members of the press prepared to investigate the unsavoury side of the Iron Guard, and this was true again after 1989. Newspaper editors like Sorin Rosca Stănescu of *Ziua* and Cornel Nistorescu of *Evenimentul Zilei* are tireless in their efforts to expose the underbelly of Vadim and his party to their readers. Some of the best investigative reporting on the PRM has appeared in *Ziua* under the pen of Razvan Savaliuc. In one of the many editorials he devoted to the rise of Vadim Nistorescu wrote on 12 November 1997: 'If the Romanians don't realise that beyond the pompous speeches the great patriots have no brain, then... our escape looks like a mouse hole. Then all we could do is place a "madhouse" sign at all the border checkpoints and walk on our hands on Calea Victorie Avenue.'[69]

Vadim escapes from his sponsors' control

The threat to Romanian democracy posed by populist extremism is magnified by the Vadim's own range of abilities. Born in 1950, he made his mark, before 1989, thanks to his ability as a writer, denigrating liberal intellectuals who refused to toe the Ceauşescu party line, and writing chauvinistic articles.[70] When the dictator fell, he briefly lost his nerve and tried to reach an accommodation with the forces of democracy who then seemed likely to triumph in Romania. On 21 December 1989 he wrote a letter to the Voice of America radio station, harshly criticising Ceauşescu and describing him as 'mad as a hatter' and 'a bloody tyrant'.[71] Ceauşescu had fled Bucharest that day and Vadim could realistically expect no further sponsorship from that quarter. Soon he tried to become a member of the relaunched Peasants Party (PNTCD).[72] Along with his ally, the novelist and editor Eugen Barbu, he then dropped out of sight for several months, but in April 1990 he resurfaced. By this time someone with Vadim's keen eye could see that the National Salvation Front (FSN) was emerging as Romania's dominant political force, and in addition was prepared to use strong-arm methods—which no doubt Vadim would have approved of—to confirm its ascendancy. The democratic forces in Romania were too inexperienced, as well as being suspect in the eyes of a population which remained largely under the influence of communist-era values.

The willingness of the FSN to sponsor hardline nationalism in order to direct popular resentment towards the Hungarian minority, Hungary itself and even the West in general seemed to provide Vadim with his chance to recover and perhaps move on to greater things. On 2 April 1990, along with Barbu, he wrote to Prime Minister Petre Roman, asking to be given premises from which to publish a magazine that would be 'an instrument to counter-attack the "fascist" circles', among which Radio Free Europe was included.[73] The letter ended: 'We assure you that by Christmas we can quieten things more effectively than the army or the miners.'[74] Roman acceded and signed the necessary papers.[75] Roman's father had been Jewish, the son of a Hungarian-speaking rabbi in Oradea who had been a member of the central committee of the PCR until his death in 1983, and must have been aware of the strongly anti-Semitic nature of some of Vadim's writings in the official press before 1989. Perhaps he and his FSN colleagues, then struggling to retain control of a volatile situation, felt that 'without the support of professionals from Ceauşescu's Securitate' they could not stem the demand for the complete democratisation of Romania.[76] Within three months, the first issue of *România Mare* had appeared, and its print-run of 600,000 copies quickly sold out.[77] Soon Vadim was attacking Roman, accusing him of being unfit to play a role in Romanian politics because of his family and ethnic background. Petre Roman was the first politician to be systematically smeared by Vadim, and was thrown on to the defensive. He even published his own birth certificate in the FSN daily *Azi* on 13 September 1990 to refute some of the more exaggerated anti-Semitic charges *România Mare* was directing against him.

Vadim devised a formula in his newspaper which remained substantially unchanged for the next decade. Most of the space in it was devoted to polemic, and individuals he close to regard as enemies of Romania were systematically vilified. Perhaps most attention was given to the Hungarian UDMR and its perceived attempt to break up the Romanian state, thus furthering the interests of the Budapest government. Here Vadim was handicapped by the fact that the UDMR failed to produce a hate figure whom he could lampoon or vilify.[78] The paper next directed its fire at Romanian politicians across the political spectrum. Few prominent members of the PDSR, PNTCD or PNL escaped denunciation as traitors, thieves or idiots. In the early 1990s special attention was given to denouncing ex-King Mihai at a time when it was felt in some quarters that he might emerge as a strong rival to Iliescu and the FSN.[79]

Vadim also went to particular lengths in his efforts to eliminate Romania's nascent civil society movement as a contender for national influence. In the early 1990s *România Mare* ran a campaign against 'False Dissidents', who it argued had done nothing to merit special consideration. It drew on personal files which could only have been provided by well-connected state officials to reveal that dissidents had made shabby compromises like everyone else to survive the rigours of life before 1989. Lengthy attacks on Romanian liberals appeared under banner headlines such as 'Andrei Plesu, or a Bandit in the Romanian Government' and 'Dossier of Komintern Agent Mihai Sora', these two onslaughts being directed against the minister of culture in 1990–1 and the minister of education in 1990.[80] (Vadim eventually promoted himself as one of the few genuine dissidents before 1989, claiming to have resigned from the PCR in June 1989 in disgust at the decision to knock down a building associated with the national poet Eminescu.[81])

In the early 1990s he went to great lengths to discredit the centre-right opposition and prevent it from being seen as a government-in-waiting. He then turned his attention to the PDSR when its alliance with the ultra-nationalist bloc foundered in 1995–6, but since the 2000 elections his primary target has been the PDSR. Clever and sometimes highly amusing cartoons ridicule the pretensions of those in power, but it is the information passed to Vadim by former and serving members of the intelligence services and ex-informers that he has used to deadliest effect in his publications. In thousands of articles he has mocked politicians, revealing intimate details of their private lives, and because of the slow-moving Romanian justice system there have been very few successful actions against him for defamation. It has been estimated that by 1989 one in thirty of the population worked as informers for the Securitate.[82] Thus Vadim is able to draw upon a huge reserve of helpers—people reluctant to give up their old trade and see the emergence of a strong democracy in which their misdeeds might face public exposure. Vadim has even invited all former Securitate collaborators 'who want to serve the country' to join the PRM. In 1998 he wrote: 'We must put an end to this hysteria related to informers, as nobody is interested anymore in who collaborated with the Securitate.'[83] Colonel Ilie Merce, who had been a leading Securitate officer and who specialised in intimidating journalists and writers who showed any signs of dissent during the 1980s, emerged as no. 2 in the PRM after the 2000 elections. Appearing on television, in October 2001, he calmly related how he had pursued the well-known dissident Dumitru Iugu, unmasked him as 'a class enemy' and had him thrown into jail.[84]

With a constantly refreshed data bank about his opponents, Vadim is never short of cruel taunts. In 1999 one Bucharest daily republished some of the more flagrant attacks Vadim had made against his political rivals: ————, 'a cross-breed between a badger and a tur-key…a shameless dummy'; ————, 'deserves to be in a lunatic asylum'; ————, 'drinks like a pig, and beats his wife and children until blood flows'; ————, 'The biggest bandit known to 20th-century Romania is the Hungarian Jew.…who steals and lies in the way that comes naturally to him…'; ————, 'with the ulcerated brain of a hereditary syphilitic'.[85]

Recurring anti-Semitism

Jews are the hate-figures who seem to draw the most venom from Vadim. The former Chief Rabbi Moses Rosen was a regular target up till his death in 1995. The Soros Foundation has frequently been denounced, not least because the founder of this philanthropic organization which has supported civil society projects right across the former communist bloc, is Jewish.

In *România Mare's* eyes, it is the country's ethnic minorities who were responsible for the worst excesses of communism; times were hardest for the Romanian people when Jews, Hungarians and others who slavishly executed Moscow's orders had disproportionate influence in the communist party's upper echelons. The sufferings of the people were only eased when native Romanians came to the fore within the party from the mid-1950s onwards. Dej and his successor Ceauşescu may have been communists, but they showed their fidelity to national values by doing their utmost to make the country autonomous in relation to the Soviet Union. (Antonescu is also felt to have acted in a patriotic way by allegedly basing his alliance with Nazi Germany on defence of Romanian national interests).

To bathe the Romanian communists responsible for consolidating party control in the purifying light of patriotism, it was necessary to cast the initial years of communism in a lurid light. *România Mare* did not flinch from this task, as an article entitled 'Who has brought Bolshevism, Terror and Crime to Romania?', which appeared in the autumn of 1991, showed.[86] Vadim's unequivocal answer to this question was: the Jews. Several excerpts quotes from the article will serve to show how far his indictment extends:

It was the Jews who arrived on the tanks of the Red Army, who brought bolshevism to Romania, who contributed decisively to the massacre of Romanian patriots, and who smothered any popular resistance. [...] I have heard some excuses such as: the Jews having suffered too much at the hands of European Fascism, embraced the communist ideology and it was a natural reaction. Nonesense! The Jews did not embrace the communist ideology, they created it. The proof lies in the fact that long before fascism and nazism, they led the Bolshevik Revolution in Russia as well as the revolutions in Germany and Hungary. [...] Of course it can be said that it was not only the Jews who ran the party, the Securitate and the jails. Of course there were Romanians, but very few of them. More numerous were the Jews followed by the Hungarians, gypsies and Russians. But even among those Romanians, there were many who had contracted mixed marriages with Jews.

Silviu Brucan, the former leading communist who in his mid-eighties remained an influential media commentator, was attacked almost weekly. He played an important role in the events leading up to the execution of the Ceauşescus, and it suits the PRM that a veteran Jewish figure who was active in the communist movement long before it captured power should have been a prominent voice demanding drastic action against the dictatorial couple. Vadim sees international Jewish interests as engaged in a ceaseless effort to destroy Romania for ever. In an article titled 'Romania under occupation' the Jews were accused of being occupiers. The United States, he argued, was in a similar state, 'the US press [being] dominated and controlled by the Jews'.[87] Characterising the United States in this way has frequently enabled Vadim to brush aside American criticism of Romania's human rights records, on the basis that it is inspired by Romania's ancient enemies. Vadim's anti-Hungarian diatribes are often tame compared to the ire he can summon up against Jewish targets. In the issue of his newspaper marking the tenth anniversary of the founding of the PRM, he published a list under the large headline 'Jews who govern us'.[88] They included parliamentarians as well as an American investor and a Romanian-born academic living in the United States.

Frustrated by the smallness of the Jewish population in Romania, Vadim has frequently dubbed non-Jewish adversaries as Jews if he feels that it will discredit them. A team of allies—journalists and historians by training—regularly joins with him to show that Romania has an honourable record in its treatment of Jews. A two-page article in 1992 entitled 'In Romania anti-Semitism doesn't exist but anti-

Romanianism does' was typical.[89] His contacts with former officials in the propaganda bureau of the communist regime enabled him to obtain a vast archive of rare photographs of twentieth-century Romania, which he regularly uses to reinforce controversial articles on the past. Articles dealing with the monarchy, wartime Romania or relations with the Soviet Union acquire greater authenticity when photographs of leading personalities and even original archival material appear alongside them. All these articles have one thing in common: they depict Romania as the helpless victim of the actions of others. Romanians are only guilty if they betray the homeland by entering the service of a foreign power. Figures like Antonescu or Ceauşescu, who are generally seen outside Romania as being among twentieth-century Europe's most despotic rulers, are seen as heroes because their mission was to preserve the nation in times when difficult decisions needed to be made. Those who served them were excused for similar reasons. But no quarter could be given to someone like General Ion Pacepa, Ceauşescu's intelligence chief till his defection to the United States in 1977. In 1991 *România Mare* was running a series entitled 'A Price on the Head of Pacepa', by 'a Group of Romanian Generals'.[90] Eight years had to elapse a before the authorities dropped charges of treason against him arising from his defection.

România Mare: the formula for success

No other party has a newspaper with the appeal and influence of *România Mare*. The readership of the PDSR's *Dimineaţa* is confined to party stalwarts. The PNTCD's *Dreptatea* is dull and has failed to appear over long periods. Vadim's newspaper seeks to acquire credibility by commemorating events in Romanian history, whether it be the anniversary of giant figures in the nation's cultural life such as Mihai Eminescu or Brancusi, or traumatic events in the national calendar. It regularly publishes pictures of Vadim being received by illustrious personages like the Pope, King Juan Carlos of Spain and President Herzog of Germany (when both heads of state paid official visits to Romania in 1995).[91] They give the impression that his explosive views do not prevent him from being a force in the world.

Vadim also uses his newspaper to appear as a philanthropist. In 1991 an article entitled 'Let the Children Come to me' was published about 146 Bucharest children orphaned in the revolution, accompanied by photographs of Vadim distributing Christmas presents to them at his headquarters.[92] Each year he has awarded prizes for cultural achievement, and it was appropriate that the first such award was made to Edgar Papu, who in the 1970s devised a theory (known as protochronism) which insisted that many of the great advances in the sciences and the arts had been pioneered by little-known Romanians who had failed to obtain just recognition on the world stage.[93]

Each issue of *România Mare* also publishes messages from readers which reflect its editor's view on topical controversies and concerns. Many may be fictitious, but it is clear that some at least of the thousands published since 1990, from named individuals who give their occupation and place of residence are authentic.[94] Quite often readers complain about poverty or injustice and do not make any chauvinistic or politically extreme point. It is a sign of Vadim's ability to act as a magnet for the discontented that these complaints come to him and not to the mainstream parties. The failure of the PRM's rivals to hold surgeries in their constituencies, or encourage voters to write in to their publications with their problems, gives an enormous boost to an anti-system politician like Vadim. It is ironic that the only party which appears to pay similar attention to grassroots concerns is the PRM's deadly enemy: the UDMR.

România Mare never failed to publish verbatim Vadim's parliamentary speeches and the statements he issued at his regular Friday press conferences. They are often dull and repetitive, and there have been times when the circulation of the paper has failed to rise much above 100,000 copies. But the accusations without proof and unfounded insinuations have proved to be a very profitable journalistic formula. It is perhaps necessary to go back to the French rightist movement, Action Française, to find a movement which has used the blunt instrument of journalism to such effect. During the Dreyfus affair in 1890s it pioneered an art and technique of calumny hitherto unknown.[95] It must have had impact in a country such as Romania dominated by French cultural tastes and expressions.

Regularly through the pages of its newspaper Action Française threatened its opponents with violent retribution. *România Mare* does the same, and it is amazing that such rhetorical violence has not yet spilled over into the political arena. No major political figure has been assassinated since 1989, but it may only be a matter of time before PRM supporters, fired up by Vadim's aggressive rhetoric, are driven to lash out at some of the movement's hate-figures. Always high on such a list has been Mircea Dinescu, a dissident poet under Ceauşescu and later the founder of the satirical magazine *Academia Catavencu*, which has frequently lampooned Vadim and other extremists. During the 2000 election campaign he was set upon in Piatra Neamt after speaking on behalf of a local PD candidate and almost lynched by a group of PRM activists led by Dumitru Badea. Badea was the PRM senator for Neamt and a member of the Senate's juridical committee. According to one press spokesman, it was a warning that 'even a person as well known as Dinescu could not escape unscathed from the revenge of the party'.[96]

Vadim's formidable powers of expression have transferred well to the television screen. His access to sympathetic private channels enabled him to damage Emil Constantinescu, perhaps irreparably by claiming that he had been having an affair with an actress. The timing of the smear was significant: it occurred just before the January 1999 miners' revolt, and the story was picked up by global TV networks such as CNN, the BBC and NBC, perhaps seeing a parallel with the Monica Lewinsky affair in Washington.[97] In the television studio Vadim outclasses every other political figure in the country, the words pouring forth unceasingly. To many educated Romanians the spectacle is grotesque. Cornel Nistorescu sums up the disdain felt by the cosmopolitan Romanian towards such appearances by Vadim: 'His sentences split somewhere in the middle, don't make sense, and slide to another truth which they barely touch before veering to something else. It is a discourse no grammar teacher could split into sentences, and…is a perfect example of political delirium.'[98]

It is not clear that most viewers react in the same way to Vadim's performances. At times he can rouse a normally listless audience by using emotive language about past injustices or the historic mission of the Romanians, and this has a mesmerising effect on his listeners, leaving them almost completely in his power. One such exhibition was Vadim's hour-long slot on state television on 6 December 2000, where his denunciation of Iliescu as a betrayer of the Romanian

people had a powerful effect. Nevertheless, Iliescu easily managed
to win the deciding round in the election four days later.

Vadim and Iliescu

Vadim's relations with Iliescu perfectly illustrate how he has been
able to manipulate Romania's post-communist leadership. Silviu
Brucan, a close ally of Iliescu when the National Salvation Front was
first formed at the end of 1989, later wrote: 'Vadim Tudor…is the
creation of President Iliescu who brought him into the limelight,
encouraged him to publish *România Mare*, received him at Cotroceni, launched him on television, and allowed him to escape condemnation in the Robu process'.[99]

In the early 1990s Vadim's skills at defamation came in useful
when Iliescu needed to weaken both the democratic opposition and
Petre Roman's breakaway movement from the FSN as serious contenders for power. In 1993, when Nicolae Vacaroiu's government
was under attack for its willingness to sell a large part of the Romanian merchant fleet to Greek interests for a price widely seen as below the market value of the ships Vadim came to its aid by launching
a diversion in the form of furious attacks on Petre Roman and the
ministers of his 1990–1 government for the radical economic legislation they drew up (but which was never implemented). But Vadim
went too far, describing the Democratic Party as 'the first Jewish
party in contemporary Romania' and its leader Roman as a pawn in
the hands of the chief rabbi, Moses Rosen.[100] This blatant anti-
Semitism brought swift international condemnation and was thus an
inconvenience to those in power. Nevertheless, Iliescu had made it
clear that he was voting for the PRM in the 1992 Bucharest local
elections rather than supporting a candidate from Petre Roman's
wing of the split FSN.[101] He also did not spurn the PRM leader
when he called on his supporters to back Iliescu in that year's second
presidential election round.[102]

Iliescu may have asked himself more than once whether he
should follow the example of Slobodan Milošević neighbouring in
Serbia and promote radical nationalism as a means of staying in
power. If he had, it is likely that there would have been few protests
from the ex-communist party and state officials who had joined the
FSN *en masse* in the early days of 1990. Indeed, a steady flow of FSN

parliamentarians defected to the PRM in 1991–2 when it was clear that Iliescu would not revive Ceauşescu's nationalist discourse in the democratic context. Iliescu was less bold than Milošević: an excursion to the wilder shores of nationalist politics would probably have sounded alarm bells in the West earlier than it did in the case of Serbia because Ceauşescu's excesses were far from forgotten. Indeed they had become a metaphor for the worst aspects of communism in Eastern Europe.

Vadim craves recognition and notoriety, but it is not altogether clear that he hungers for absolute power, the exercise of which involves concentrating on a range of mundane tasks. Perhaps journalism and oratory will always be his chief preoccupations; if so, he probably would have liked nothing better than to serve a nationalist dictator as his propaganda chief in the way that Goebbels assisted Hitler.[103] Romania's wartime leader General Ion Antonescu is perhaps Vadim's ideal model of an authoritarian leader. He is constantly invoked in the PRM press, but as early as 1991 Iliescu showed that he was unwilling to patronise this personality cult, declaring in July that he 'did not share the opinion of those who wished to rehabilitate him, keeping silent on the negative aspects of his activity.' Iliescu did not question Antonescu's military qualities, but he refused to overlook the fact that 'he took power with an Iron Guard government, that he was Hitler's ally, that he pushed the country into war… I can not see the merit Ion Antonescu had as a political man, and that is why I do not agree with those who praise him so much today.'[104]

President Iliescu could not fail to be aware that international opinion would have been scandalised if he had rehabilitated a dictator who had sanctioned and condoned bloody acts against the Jews of Bessarabia, northern Moldavia and Bucovina in the early 1940s.[105] Vadim, as his regular diatribes against the Jews make clear, would have simply relished such provocation. As he built up his own separate power-base, he was increasingly unwilling to be an odd–job-man for Iliescu and the FSN, ready to carry out attacks on the President's domestic foes or on Hungarian interests if it suited Iliescu's electoral calculations. The first overt disagreement between Iliescu and Vadim occurred over the anti–Semitic tone of the ultra-nationalist press. In September 1991, shortly before embarking on a state visit to Israel, Iliescu felt obliged to criticise a lurid example of Vadim's writing: 'I disavow all anti-Semitic positions... The article in *România Mare* terrified me. It had everything short of the attitude that we should go and kill the Jews.'[106]

From then on *România Mare* periodically subjected Iliescu to the abuse which it meted out to all 'anti-national' politicians, but this still did not prevent occasional episodes of reconciliation: during one of these the PRM became a junior partner in the Vacaroiu government. On a visit to the United States in September 1995 Iliescu explained that he had no choice but to count as allies 'emulators of Zhirinovsky's political style' because there was then no other way to obtain a parliamentary majority for laws designed to complete the transition from communism.[107] This rather lame explanation hardly convinced Western critics of his regime, but it enraged Vadim who was soon denouncing the President in the crudest terms. However, one other reconciliation occurred in 1997 when the PDSR, then in opposition, decided to raid the PRM's armoury for nationalistic weapons to use against the centre-right coalition (then pressing ahead with a reconciliation with the Hungarians). Iliescu, then sitting in the Senate, instructed the PDSR to vote against a government motion to strip Vadim of his parliamentary immunity; this was only a year after the PDSR itself had tried to bring Vadim to heel by lifting his immunity. Vadim has profited immeasurably from the failure of the major parties to unite in order that he should answer in a court of law for the numerous charges lodged against him. Vadim was invited to the PDSR conference and received such a warm reception from the delegates when he entered the hall on 21 June 1997 that Iliescu was obliged to invite him on to the platform. There the two leaders embraced.[108]

Vadim needs to detach a sizeable part of the PDSR electorate over to his side if he is to have any hope of winning power. Iliescu obstructs that goal, so that he needs to be a constant target of his criticism. But the unprecedented degree of popularity Iliescu enjoyed in 2000 and well into the following year showed that Vadim had not succeeded in vilifying him. Indeed Ceauşescu's successor is the only senior public figure who appears immune from the poison darts he has directed at numerous opponents. Writing just after the 2000 elections, Cornel Nistorescu eloquently showed how Iliescu manages to bring out all the inconsistencies in Vadim's political personality: 'On Sunday night he announced the most stupendous electoral rigging in our history, and three day later, he went to parliament and shook hands with Ion Iliescu... Today he may pluck out Ion Iliescu's eyes, tomorrow he may kiss his hand in reverence and the day after tomorrow he may say he's never heard of him.'[109]

As his political role has increasingly come to take the place of his journalistic one, Vadim has needed to find different tactics. During the second half of the 1990s, he was giving less attention to the Hungarian question in Parliament than in the pages of *România Mare*, where the true believers cannot be told enough about the 'Hungarian danger'. He never succeeded in making a big issue out of the presence of the UDMR in the coalition. He cannot fail to be aware that Hungarian issues have little resonance beyond Transylvania; a nationwide poll taken in May 1999 revealed that 64% respondents had a good opinion of Hungary (compared with 67% for the United States) and only 24% had a negative opinion (compared with 25% for the United States).[110] To the surprise of many, Vadim threw his support behind the bilateral agreement with Hungary that Iliescu concluded in the final months of his second presidential term.[111] His Transylvanian ally, Gheorghe Funar, was a fierce critic of the accord, just as he was of the proposal that the Pope should come to Transylvania in the course of his visit to Romania in May 1999. By contrast, Vadim insisted that 'the Pope should be totally free to go wherever he wants, even to Transylvania.'[112]

In April 1999 the PRM even abstained in the parliamentary vote taken to decide whether to allow NATO the use of Romanian airspace during its military offensive against Milošević's Serbia. Vadim declared: 'Things are very complicated and it is time we treated them with prudence. A party does not always do what it wants.'[113] After the failed miners' revolt organized by PRM officials, the air was thick with rumours that Vadim's party might be banned. It was also unclear how strong the reaction of public opinion would be against the bombing of Serbia as a neighbouring state usually viewed as an ally of Romania. When the polls revealed a highly negative response, Vadim reflected popular anger and was soon producing furious diatribes against NATO and the West in general.

Vadim's Achilles Heel

Vadim is not the only ambitious Romanian nationalist with the skills to articulate populist sentiments. But he has only been able to work with other able ultra-nationalists when he and they have respected each other's spheres of influence. Relations appear amicable with Iosif Constantin Dragan, the Italian-based businessman long involved in trying to rehabilitate the Iron Guard and build up his commercial interests in Romania.[114] A reconciliation has even been arranged with fellow poet and nationalist firebrand, Adrian Păunescu and with the leading journalist Ion Cristoiu when it became clear that they posed no threat to him and indeed shared part of his outlook.[115]

Rather surprisingly, a political alliance has endured with Gheorghe Funar, the ultra-nationalist mayor of Cluj. Like Vadim, Funar insisted on keeping an iron grip on his own nationalist movement, the PUNR, and he quarrelled with a succession of parliamentarians who resented having to take long-distance orders from the mayor's office in Cluj. When the PUNR split in 1997, Funar took his time before deciding to join the PRM, finally doing so in October 1998.[116] But it is clear that an alliance between men who believe that each is uniquely placed to look into the Romanian national soul can only endure for as long as they keep to their respective spheres of influence. Vadim gives Funar a free hand in Cluj and treats him as a partner rather than as a subordinate.

But ever since he became a public figure in 1990, Vadim has promoted a cult of personality occasionally comparable to Ceauşescu's. *România Mare* is dominated by coverage of his speeches, press conferences and engagements at home and abroad. True believers content to operate in the shadows are occasionally given space to promote the national position already laid down by him. The cult of personality has been seen at its most glaring when the PRM convenes as a national movement: at the first two national conferences, held in 1993 and 1997, the press were struck by the extent to which Vadim grabbed the spotlight throughout the proceedings.

Inevitably, Vadim's leadership style has led to a string of embarrassing quarrels and defections. When Dan Corneliu Hudici, a former investigative reporter on *România Mare*, broke with him in the late 1990s, he made awkward disclosures about how Vadim acquired information and used it to defame his enemies.[117] The defection in 1996 of Dan Ioan Mirescu, a past vice-president of the PRM and for the previous six years one of the most senior members of his entourage, was a much greater loss; in the autumn of 1995 he talked extensively about Vadim's methods to the SRI general, Ion Popescu, at a time when the chief domestic intelligence agency was actively seeking to discredit him.[118] Mirescu's claims, which might be summed up under the headline in *Evenimentul Zilei* of 6 July 1996, 'Dan Ioan Mirescu shows that the rise of Corneliu Vadim Tudor is based on the use of blackmail and the complicity of power factors', received extensive press coverage. When he continued to produce unwelcome revelations in *Ziua*, Vadim delivered a furious outburst in *România Mare* on 14 November 1997, under a ten-line headline: 'Through the capital wander two rabid dogs: Dan Ioan Mirescu and Sorin Rosca Stănescu [editor of *Ziua*]. Under the influence of their hereditary syphilis, these two gypsy terrorists publish, in the filthiest pigsty seen in the history of the Romanian press, the newspaper '*Ziua*', a series full of lies and insults directed at Corneliu Vadim Tudor and the PRM! To these two sewer-dwellers, the President of the PRM will give a stinging lesson on the evening of Monday 10 November 1997 on Antena I television channel. Look out, you lepers, a storm is coming your way!'[119] Ironically, it was Mirescu who had delivered the *coup de grace* to Colonel Radu Theodoru, one of the few political heavyweights in the PRM, who briefly occupied the limelight with Vadim in the early 1990s before quarrelling with him.[120] Theodoru could wield an effective pen in defence of the chauvinist cause, and he had obtained a good result as the PRM's candidate for mayor of Bucharest in 1992. But before the year was finished, he had become a non-person, accused in *România Mare* of being a drunk and a Soviet agent.[121] But Theodoru fought back, denouncing Vadim for his dictatorial style and going on to become the leading light in the campaign to rehabilitate General Antonescu.

Four PRM parliamentarians renounced the party between 1992 and 1996. One of them, Ioan Hristu, accused Vadim of turning 'each party member into his personal lackey'.[122] Such claims were repeated almost word for word by disappointed PRM parliamentarians after the 2000 elections. Ion Radu, one of Bucharest's four deputy mayors, quit the party in December unable to stomach Vadim's overbearing attitude.[123] More serious was the departure in early 2001 of a further five parliamentarians, Mircea Bucur, Dorin Lazar Maior, Valentin Paduroiu, Codrin Ştefanescu and Luca Ştefănoiu. They had belonged to the small Party of Democratic Forces which had agreed to combine with the PRM in return for eligible places on its electoral lists.[124] Maior described the PRM as a citadel of extreme Bolshevik communism with Vadim clearly having the character of a dictator.[125] 'We are going to make sure that the electorate learns the reality about the PRM,' he insisted, but his colleague Mircea Bucur put the blame not so much on Vadim as 'on a group of Securitate people with a mentality frozen in the era of the 1950s who form a shield around Vadim... [who] is fed with all sorts of disinformation... My conviction is that the PRM is not really led by Vadim— instead it is the malign creation of a retrograde group nostalgic for bolshevism.'[126] (Dan Ioan Mirescu believed that such people were important, but argued that Vadim was content to have them around him.)[127] At least one defector found a home in the PDSR while others agreed to join the Socialist Party of National Rebirth formed in February 2001.

România Mare responded in the usual manner to news of the defections. On 23 February 2001 it described one of the defectors, Luca Ştefănoiu, as a thief who had a criminal record and was in the pay of the PDSR. Before announcing that he was taking Vadim to court for such falsehoods, a furious Ştefănoiu hit back in an open letter to Vadim published in the national press:

> 'the respective communication to the press is an outstanding example...of the mechanism of diversion which you learned from your younger days at the magazine *Sâptamina* and which you practised with success after 1989 in *România Mare*. During the ten years I have known you, you have been fascinated by the methods of Goebbels: 'First deform your opponent and then present him to the world as a monster'. The methods are simple: some concrete facts (a name, a place, a date) and then a host of untruths. That's how you have always proceeded, incorrect and dishonest. That's how you've brought misfortune on individuals and entire families....Many of them have gone to their graves dishonoured and wronged. Don't their images disturb your sleep?
>
> Sadly, it has to be observed, Mr Corneliu Vadim Tudor, that you are a sick man. Alas, the sickness which ails you cannot be treated with tranquillizers. Arrogance, disdain for others, generalized suspicion, has made many who sustained you because they believed in you walk away. You are more and more alone, Mr Corneliu

Vadim Tudor. Look around you and you will see a desert bigger than the Sahara…

I have gone, and from me you have escaped. Others have stayed on in the Directing Committee of the PRM. There are more and more, more determined, better organized. They will observe your movements, count up your mistakes, and make an inventory of your weak points. They will strike when you least expect it. They will seek your head and they will get it. Far more quickly than you can ever imagine, you will become a memory. Alas, for many Romanians you were part of a series of hateful and nightmarish memories that nobody ever needed.[128]

The original complaint of Deputy Ştefǎnoiu, who had been a member of the PRM's political bureau, was that Vadim regularly made statements without bothering to consult it.[129] Sever Meşca and Ilie Neacşu, who quit the party in February 2002, also complained that Vadim rarely attended meetings of the political bureau, and when he did so it was to deliver lengthy monologues. They were two senior party figures, with undoubted political abilities, whose departure left the PRM in a weakened state. They wrote a book purporting to be an exposé of Vadim, which neglected to say anything about Neacşu's own extremist past. Meşca talked about Vadim's 'psychological instability, his hormonal reactions, irrational attacks in all directions, his lack of proper conduct (including an inability to keep his word), the destructive influence of the journalist over the politician'.[130] Various embarrassing and revealing accounts of the party's inner life—or, more accurately, lack of it—were provided; ultimately they would be unlikely to harm the PRM in the small communities where its support base increasingly lies.

Still, the PRM could ill-afford the departure of independent-minded figures. If Vadim's long political march was to bring him to Cotroceni palace, he badly needed radical nationalists prepared to think for themselves and not expecting to be treated as eternal subordinates. But all the evidence suggests that Vadim can only interact effectively with subordinates who do not answer back. He has promoted people with criminal records, or facing criminal investigations before entering the refuge of Parliament—people wholly dependent on his goodwill. Elderly officials from the Ceauşescu era who faithfully served the communist regime in its most extremist

phase are also prominent; deputies like Romulas Budaru, Ceauşescu's ambassador to China, owe Vadim everything for plucking
them from obscurity. Proportionately more women sit on the parliamentary benches for the PRM than for any other party. They included his political 'hitwoman' Daniela Buruiană, ready to accept
any political contract,[131] the folksinger Irina Loghin, Mitzura Arghezi,
the daughter of one of Romania's greatest poets; and Leonida Lari, a
poet from Moldova, as well as several close relatives of Vadim's. No
woman has been among the numerous senior defectors from the
PRM, so Vadim may have grounds for feeling that his position is
secure if they are given a prominent role in party affairs.[132]

But it is members of Vadim's immediate family whom he appears
to trust the most. His brother Colonel Marcu Tudor has been a
PRM deputy since 1996 and since 2000 has served as secretary of
the defence commission in the Chamber of Deputies. Now a wealthy
businessman, he worked before 1989 with arms companies controlled by the Securitate, and was one of three people designated by
Ceauşescu to coordinate the sale of arms to Arab countries.[133] Far
more important for the smooth running of the newspaper and the
party is Vadim's elder sister Lidia Samson, who for many years has
been in charge of the movement's finances.[134] The press has paid increasing attention to the wealth accumulated by Vadim and other
family members, who have set up various foundations to manage the
large sums of money coming into the movement.[135] Vadim's movement has some of the hallmarks of a family affair. If he succeeds in
coming to power, it is not unreasonable to suppose that his regime
would soon acquire the nepotistic character that made that of Ceauşescu notorious. One surprising fact is the close connections Vadim
has with American Evangelical Protestants who, it is alleged, have assisted the PRM in transferring funds in and out of Romania.[136] It is
ironic that any body with such affiliation should be prepared to consort with Vadim's movement: under Ceauşescu, Romanian Evangeli-
cals (who are usually described as 'neo-Protestants') faced persecution
because their international outlook challenged the nationalist perceptions of his regime.

The negative personality traits of its leader arguably prevent Romania's premier nationalist movement achieving its full potential.
Vadim's quarrelsome and vindictive nature, his suspicion of collabo-

rators who display too much initiative, and even his alleged mean-
ness with money, have driven talented people from the ranks of the
PRM. His movement has failed to become a big tent encompassing
the main nationalist campaigning groups, and enabling them to focus their energies on capturing power. However, all Romanian parties have experienced debilitating splits at one time or another; it is
difficult for the party concept to accommodate conflicting personalities and ambitions, perhaps because their doctrines are often very
nebulous. The fact that a nationalist movement like the PRM is
supposed to be unifying the Romanians around a national mission
will make periodic infighting disappointing for true nationalist believers. But Vadim has hitherto been able to survive internal blood-
letting, and three elections have seen his political fortunes steadily
rise. The role of redeemer of the nation, able to sound the alarm
about the multiple challenges to Romania's national existence, soon
blocks out the evidence of Vadim's excesses, which anyway rarely
percolate down to small town or village Romania where the bed-
rock of his support increasingly lies. His ordinary supporters soon
forget the accusations of defectors repelled by his style of leadership,
as long as he continues to give performances of rhetorical brilliance
in which he scatters Romania's multiple enemies. Nationalism offers disoriented or alienated social groups a category in which they
can locate themselves and forget about their harsh material existence. While Vadim the showman is able to perform his populist
magic, he can endure reverses which would plunge more conventional political figures into deep trouble.

Post-2000 successes and controversies

Anti-system parties which have been the beneficiaries of a protest
vote against the establishment often fade from view in the aftermath
of elections. This did not happen to the PRM in 2001. Its poll ratings remained high—between 15 and 17% in the first six months of
the year. During the lifetime of the previous coalition the party seldom rose above 10% in the polls despite mounting disillusionment
with the coalition's performance. So the PRM is starting from a
much higher baseline of support and it is the only obvious destina-
tion for voters who become dissatisfied with the PDSR's performance in government.

Several issues have kept the PRM in the limelight. It was able to exploit workers' unrest in the city of Reşita, arising from the takeover of Romania's oldest steel mill by an American company which is accused of reneging on its promise to improve the plant.[137] The government was concerned by the ability of the PRM to take control of the regular demonstrations in Reşita, with the result that slogans against integration with the EU and NATO became ever more commonplace.[138] On 27 June 2001 the privatisation minister, Ovidiu Musatescu, announced that judicial proceedings were being launched to annul the contract because of 'the risk of losing control over the extremely serious Reşita situation which could trigger [nationwide] economic and social destabilisation'.[139]

The release from prison on 5 May 2001 of Ilie Ilascu, a Moldovan politician committed to unification with Romania, benefited the PRM substantially. Ilascu had been arrested in 1992 by the pro-Russian breakaway forces in the self-proclaimed Republic of Tiraspol, and in 1993 he was sentenced to death after a trial in which was found guilty of terrorism.[140] In the 2000 elections Ilascu stood on the PRM list for Bacau and was returned to the Romanian Senate. On his arrival in Romania on 8 May, he said that he owed his liberation 'above all' to President Iliescu, but the PRM appeared to be best placed to exploit his return to freedom and his determination to make Moldova an issue in Romanian politics.[141]

The PRM also benefited from a controversial law passed by the Budapest Parliament on 19 June 2001 and due to come into effect at the start of 2002. The Status Law gives a range of social, educational, transport and health benefits to Hungarians outside Hungary who wish to work in the rapidly growing Hungarian economy. The law is in fact designed to deter the 3.2 million-strong Hungarian diaspora in Eastern Europe from settling in Hungary. It attracted particular attention in Romania where about half of this diaspora is to be found.[142] Not only the PRM but the PDSR and even the Liberals accused Budapest of showing favouritism towards ethnic Hungarians in Romania at the expense of the rest of the population. Critics alleged that there could well be a flood of applications from ethnic Romanians who have some Hungarian ancestry and that it would undermine the Romanian identity of Transylvania where the Hungarian population comprises one-quarter of the population. Sections of the press claimed that as many as 7 million people might apply for the identification certificate being issued in Hungary from 2002 onwards. So the PRM was able to highlight a new Hungarian 'danger' that was not based on extravagant imaginings, and of course its remedy was more extreme than anyone else's. On 22 June Vadim demanded the outlawing of the UDMR, the abrogation of the 1996 friendship treaty with Hungary, the temporary closure of the border with Hungary, and 'preparation of the army for a crisis situation'.[143]

EU and NATO delegations regularly visited Bucharest in 2001 to check on Romania's performance in relation to its bid to join these respective organisations, and the PRM, with a quarter of all parliamentary seats, was now under scrutiny from these bodies more than ever before. Rather than play up to his 'bad boy image', Vadim decided to cultivate moderation. There were no denunciations of Western officials for interfering in Romanian politics, a constant theme in the 1990s, or statements such as the one by Vadim on 23 April 1999 that 'NATO is nothing more than a Satanist organization, a malignant tumour in the brain of humanity'.[144] A rare olive branch was even extended to the Jews: on 21 May Vadim apologised in the Senate for the 'inaccurate and inadmissable' dissemination of a collection of jokes compiled by a PRM councillor in Cluj. Two of the jokes made light of the use of ovens, and one of them compared Jews to pizzas. Vadim said that 'a serious warning' had been issued to the author;[145] but the following month *România Mare* had returned to its anti-Semitic preoccupations, perhaps seeing an opportunity to make electoral capital out of the Israel-Palestine conflict.

In August 2001 Vlad Hogea, a twenty-four-year-old lawyer and PRM deputy from Iasi, published a book entitled *The Nationalist* which attacked the standard enemies of chauvinists like himself in virulent style. It reportedly included the sentence 'Whoever fights the Jews, fights the devil', and it called the Roma 'a black tide that poisons the ocean'. Hogea warned: 'Unless we stand up against this wave of dirt which is gradually covering us, we risk becoming a minority in our own country.'[146] When the state threatened to ban the book, Vadim dissociated himself from it despite much of the material it contained having appeared at different times in the PRM press. Possibly Vadim was irritated at one of his acolytes having stolen from him the limelight he normally craved.[147]

The ruling PDSR has been careful to prevent the PRM building on its 2000 successes. The appearances of the party and its leader on state television are restricted—it is still the state channels which Romanians in the countryside and smaller towns mostly watch, and this is the PDSR's power-base, which it is determined not to cede to the PRM. However, in Parliament relations between the two parties have often been harmonious. Cornel Nistorescu remarked in March 2001: 'Inside the parliamentary commissions, a real PDSR-PRM voting machine works every time they raise their hands.'[148] The PRM managed to obtain far more positions in the two chambers of Parliament than the PD, the PNL or the UDMR. It collaborated with the PDSR to dominate the various Senate commissions where laws are prepared before being sent on for a full debate.[149]

In February 2001 there was consternation in the government when two PDSR parliamentarians accompanied three from the PRM on an unofficial visit to Iraq. It was claimed that the aim of the mission was to 'discuss with Iraqi officials ways for Romania to re-cover $1.7 billion dollars in debt',[150] but the Bucharest press specu-lated that sanctions-busting might also be a motive. Vadim has not been afraid to court some of the Middle East's most anti-Western re-gimes. In April 1997 he went in person to Tripoli to participate in an 'international congress on youth' organised by the Libyan gov-ernment. His press critics have claimed that the true purpose of this visit was actually to participate at a congress of the Mathabei, an anti-American and anti-Jewish body answering directly to the Lib-yan leader, Colonel Moammar Gadaffi.[151] In a television debate in November 2000, irritated by taunts and questions from the press and opponents about where he had obtained the gold Rolex watch he was wearing, Vadim announced to the viewers that he was donating it to a children's orphanage; it emerged later that the watch had been a present from Saddam Hussein and had been inscribed with a per-sonalised dedication to Vadim.[152]

After the terrorist attacks in the United States on 11 September 2001, widely attributed to the al-Qaida network of Osama bin Laden, Vadim caused maximum consternation by publicly accusing the ruling party of having allowed Palestinian Hamas militants to be trained by members of the Romanian security services in 1994.[153] The accusations were detrimental to Romania's image abroad, and the government soon took steps to lift Vadim's parliamentary immunity. President Iliescu severed all contact with him, and Nicolae Vacaroiu, during whose premiership such training was supposed to have occurred, prevented him from going on a parliamentary delegation to the Far East.[154] A month after the September 11 bombings, prosecutors were seeking to lift his parliamentary immunity so that he could face charges of communicating false information.[155]

The PRM's third conference took place in late November 2001 in a subdued atmosphere with Vadim warning PRM colleagues not to be tempted to cooperate with the government. He had already prepared for a trial of strength with the authorities by selling all the companies he and his family owned (including România Mare) to a twenty-seven-year-old Iranian businessman, Reza Kaja.[156] But the wheels of the law turn slowly in Romania, and in the country's justice system Vadim is not short of friends, as well as others prepared to act, sometimes under pressure, on his behalf. One journalist warned that Vadim could yet emerge from the whole process a hero if not a martyr, and be more dangerous than ever to those in the Romanian state who would wish to end his years of provocation.[157] Despite his fishing in troubled waters, it is likely that discreet cooperation between the PRM and the PDSR will continue at the parliamentary level, with or without Vadim. It has not passed unnoticed that the elected officials of both parties have a similar sociological profile. Despite efforts by Adrian Năstase to promote young technocrats rapid into the higher echelons of the PDSR, the parliamentary groups of both the PRM and, to a lesser extent, the PDSR are drawn from 'second-ranking elements in the PCR'. This enables them to share a common outlook on a range of issues.[158]

The 2000 elections demonstrated clearly that the PDSR's electoral support is concentrated among the rural population, inhabitants of small towns, and the elderly. In the first presidential round Iliescu obtained 55% of the votes of those aged sixty and over, and 48% of the rural vote. By contrast, the PRM's electoral support is spread fairly evenly across all age groups, except the elderly: in the first presidential round Vadim got 33% of the 18–29 and also the 30–44 age group; 26% of the 45–59 age group, but only 16% of those aged sixty and over; in terms of location, Vadim performed most strongly in small and medium-sized towns (31% of support respectively), and in terms of education it is individuals who remained in school from thirteen to eighteen who were most attracted to his cause. Vadim's support was distributed fairly evenly across the four main regions of Romania whereas Iliescu got 46 and 48% support in Muntenia and Moldavia but only 22% in Transylvania and 34% in Bucharest.[159] Thus Vadim and the PRM can claim a more balanced electorate than the PDSR and indeed the former CDR parties.

The PRM's electoral success in 2000 was due far more to the abundant mistakes of its opponents than to Vadim or the party's own campaign. The PRM did poorly in the June 2000 local elections, and at the start of the campaign in the autumn its leader had a much lower recognition-factor than Iliescu or Isărescu. Despite media attacks on Vadim, no candidate was prepared to confront him, expose his record and point out what kind of future Romania might expect with him in charge. He is now seen as a 'loose cannon' capable of blowing apart the Romanian political system, but it is not clear if the mainstream parties will be able to control him. All of them remain vulnerable to a challenger with a strong nationalist discourse. The PDSR is pressing ahead with a policy of Euro–Atlantic integration which will involve the closure of factories employing many of its supporters. It has also worked out an informal alliance with the UDMR in return for its parliamentary backing. As for the centre-right parties, they remain in a greatly weakened state; indeed in the summer of 2001 the PNTCD started to break up following the abrupt resignation of its leader, Andrei Marga. Only the PD under its new leader Traian Băsescu appears capable of disputing the nationalist terrain with Vadim, but in June 2001, its poll rating was only 8%. So Vadim has good reason to believe that he can repeat his strong electoral performance in 2004 when Iliescu will be ineligible to stand again for President. It is not at all clear that Adrian Năstase will be able to assume the presidential mantle (or even become the PDSR's presidential candidate), especially if his government fails to improve the economy.

In the past the idea of an editor combining a journalistic career with an active political one appeared bizarre, but it is no longer the case. Perhaps most Romanians now obtain their view of the world from TV: the personalities of that medium enjoy more credibility than politicians, and at times their influence on political matters can be greater. Vadim is the only leading politician who can dominate the medium of television. However, what may prevent him from fulfilling his political ambitions is the enmity he has stirred up among fellow-nationalists. Many who have fallen out with him would agree with Dan Ioan Mirescu that he is 'a windbag who has devalued the ideas of nationalism and patriotism'.[160] His megalomania is not completely out of place in an editor's office or TV studio where people with inflated egos often thrive, but different qualities are needed to weld together a coherent and effective political movement. The lack of moderation and sensitivity Vadim shows in relations with collaborators may prove fatal flaws. One weakness already apparent is the low quality of many of the PRM's parliamentarians; only fifteen of the PRM's seventy-eight deputies intervened in the lower chamber in the first six months of the new parliamentary session.[161] Perhaps Vadim is content that most prefer him to do the talking, but his party will suffer if it fails to produce effective second-ranking figures who enjoy strong national recognition.

The exposure of the Romanian people to socialisation along nationalist lines, the failure of measures of economic liberalism to make a positive difference to their lives after 1996, and the deep failures of the conventional parties in other areas are all indications that a party with a programme stressing indigenous values and policies ought to be flourishing in Romanian politics. Perhaps it is the case that under Vadim a nationalist movement is *incapable* of delivering the killer blow to the mainstream parties because the leader has too many defects. In any future electoral contest it is these defects which may outweigh his undoubted political skills, but a more subtle and balanced leader, prepared to give a wide range of nationalists a chance to exercise their talents in the service of a broad nationalist movement, could take it past the winning line. A party lacking anti-Semitism and giving as much emphasis to economics as to the presence of large numbers of gypsies and Hungarians in the country, surely has a bright future as long as most of the mainstream parties alienate significant groups of voters socialised in the communist era. Perhaps the world of private television will produce a cleancut, eloquent nationalist leader whose personality inspires confidence and trust in the way Ronald Reagan's did in the United States.

So it could well turn out that Vadim's role will be that of a John the Baptist who prepares the way for a more effective nationalist messiah, someone who not only inspires faith but also has the good sense to attract and keep allies, and prepare a coherent programme for power—something Vadim does not have. In ten years of campaigning he has made a radical nationalist perspective increasingly respectable. The national communist era is no longer seen as a dark period of history. Instead, it is those on the political right and in the centre who are struggling to defend their vision of a post-nationalist Romania prepared to abandon some of its sovereign prerogatives in order to be part of a common project of European integration.

In a spectacular U-turn at the start of 2004, Vadim announced that his views on Jewish issues had been 'misunderstood'. He now styled himself a philo-Semite and announced plans to go to Auschwitz to recant past utterances viewed as anti-Semitic. Valentin Vasilescu, a PRM deputy, was expelled in February when he complained that Vadim's anti-Semitic stance had always been his own personal concern and had not been reflected inside the party. Accordingly, he had no right to associate the party with any retraction.

Vadim's renunciation of anti-Semitism (and his appointment of a top Israeli PR expert as his image-maker in the 2004 elections) may stem from a realisation that his most radical positions could be an excuse for the PSD to crack down on him with American approval in the new atmosphere that has emerged since the 2001 Al-Quaida attacks. His anti-Semitism and past links with radical Arab regimes became a big liability after that event. But his U-turn reveals his obsession with Jewish issues and is probably a change of tactics rather than a genuine conversion to philo-Semitism.

10

LOOTERS OF THE STATE BY
APPOINTMENT OF BRUSSELS

RETURN OF THE SOCIAL DEMOCRATS, 2001–2003

The Party of Romanian Social Democracy (PDSR) changed its
name to the Social Democratic Party (PSD) in July 2001. Social democracy has been historically weak in Romania and some optimistic spirits hoped that under West European influence the PSD might
embrace a genuine social democratic vision rather than merely
mimic it. In the spring of 2003 intense lobbying by the PSD on the
malleable president of the Socialist International, António Guterres
of Portugal, had secured entry to the prestigious social democratic
club for the party led by Adrian Năstase. But its left-wing credentials
appeared threadbare. Năstase felt obliged to lecture his party in June
2003 on the need to 'reassert its leftist social democratic ideology'.[1]
It was no coincidence that such an appeal was issued after a new law
(brought in under international pressure) on the declaration of assets
belonging to politicians and other public officials revealed that many
PSD elected representatives had bank accounts, cars and homes that
they could not have acquired from their official salaries alone.[2]

Returned on a negative vote, the PSD was in a stronger position
to shape the direction of Romania than any political force since 1989.
It enjoyed control of Parliament, despite having only 42% of the
seats. Legislation faced few of the delays that blunted the reform efforts of the previous four-party coalition. In November 2001 a major objective of the Năstase government had been secured when the
IMF agreed a fresh stand-by accord with Romania worth $380 mil-
lion, due to expire in 2003.

For the first half of its term, the PSD was well ahead in the polls,
enjoying ratings of between 43 and nearly 60% (it got 37% of the

vote in the 2000 parliamentary elections). By June 2003 its support had slipped as Romanians saw little improvement in their living standards, but it remained 26% ahead of its nearest rival, 47% of the population feeling that no party existed that represented their interests.[3] A string of defections from other parties to the PSD occurred as the prospects of it being in power for an extended period increased; the number of mayors affiliated to the PSD went up from 35.51% in 2001 to 64.4% in 2003.[4]

Adrian Năstase is the first strong head of government Romania has had since the end of communism. In 2001 it was widely held that he had re-invented himself as a confident practitioner of pluralist politics, but it is hard to forget that before 1989 he belonged to the ruling élite. His father-in-law had been ambassador to China and before that minister of agriculture. Năstase, trained in international law, was one of the few relatively young officials whom the hardline communist regime permitted to travel freely. By the end of the Ceauşescu regime he was one of the few junior members of the élite sufficiently trusted to attend receptions held at Western embassies.

He has tried to combine fitful measures of social protection with adherence to the medium-term economic agreement which his predecessor signed with the European Union in 2000 and which commits Romania to firmly move away from a state-led economy. In 2001 and 2002 it was clear that he possessed his own power-base within the PSD, consisting of regional barons whose wealth-creating schemes, often at the expense of the public purse and EU funds, he has been unwilling to interfere with unless they become too flagrant. Planning to secure the leadership of the PSD, he appointed as its general-secretary Cosmin Gusă, a young and aggressive media manager without a firm ideological outlook. The beneficiary of several periods of study in the fields of public relations and management in the United States, Gusa is the most visible representative of a new type of Romanian politician, with no background in communism, and able to interact effectively with Western officials whose technocratic language and mannerisms he effectively mimics.

Năstase's rise was smoothed by an improvement in the economy, which grew at a rate of 4.5% in 2001, ending four years of contraction or minimal growth. Romania's internal debt dropped from 13.1 to 9.3% in 2000, which prompted different economic ratings agencies to upgrade the country's risk for a range of indicators. In July 2001 the Sidex-Galati steel mill, the largest in Southeastern Europe, was sold to LNM/ISPAT, an Anglo-Indian consortium. The ailing plant accounted for 5% of GDP and had been a huge drain on state finances. Under the deal it was be modernised and production increased by 40% over the next five years. Then in September the Prime Minister announced that the loss-making defence industry, employing 27,000 people, would no longer obtain the state subsidies required for it to stay in existence;[5] he declared that it could no longer be viewed as of strategic importance for Romania.

The World Bank was pressing for privatisation to be accelerated if Romania was to benefit from credits of $1 billion in 2002–4; in October 2001 there was agreement with the IMF to privatise some of the larger state enterprises and general utilities as well as the largest state-run commercial bank. But progress was limited partly due to the economic downturn both globally and in most EU states: the EU is the destination of 70% of Romania's exports and the source of most foreign direct investment.

The PSD parliamentary benches were dominated by figures from the early 1990s as well as local businessmen who prospered along with the party. Ion Iliescu (aged seventy-one in 2001) was back in Cotroceni palace, by now the most durable figure among East European political leaders. Nicolae Văcăroiu, an ex-communist transformed into a banker who presided over an anti-reform government from 1992–6, was made president of the Senate, a post he stubbornly clung to as he came under increasing accusations of corruption. In 1970 the political scientist Dankwart Rustow argued: 'We should allow for the possibility that circumstances may force, trick, lure or cajole non-democrats into democratic behaviour, and that their beliefs may adjust in due course by some process of rationalisation or adaptation.'[6]

Ion Iliescu had embarked upon a political journey in 1989 and it is fair to say that he was a somewhat different political animal than he had been during his early years of power when he relied on a praetorian guard of coalminers to keep his enemies at bay. In the first half of his final term, he appeared to have mastered the arts of pluralist politics more effectively than rivals—arguably including Emil Constantinescu—who insisted on their fidelity to democracy. He showed no conspicuous signs of his personal wealth. Nor was he bent on seeking revenge against those who had slighted or opposed him. Adrian Severin, a sharp critic who had bitterly opposed him when the FSN split in 1991–2, was reconciled and given a foreign policy role in 2000. Iliescu's reconciliation with ex-King Mihai in 2001 was unexpected and apparently genuine. These were years when he be strode the international stage, demonstrating his prowess in English and Russian and trying to be the nearest thing in the Balkans to a statesman of European stature. But as his term approached its end, he appeared to revert to type. In June 2003 he berated the West for its 'paternalist, arrogant, stiff-lipped, imperial position' towards his part of Europe, claiming that the West had only thrived because Eastern Europe had been under foreign subjugation.[7] In July he bestowed a top honour on Adrian Păunescu, formerly the court poet of Ceauşescu and now being groomed as a literary magus bridging different eras. Most controversially of all, on 25 July 2003 he declared: 'The Holocaust is not unique to the Jewish people in Europe,' comparing it to the suffering of pre-war communists. He also opposed the restitution of property confiscated from Jewish citizens in Romania. Israel's foreign ministry issued a note of protest, and Mircea Geoana, the Romanian foreign minister, had to meet US Jewish leaders to limit the damage caused by Iliescu's remarks.[8]

He was now planning to reoccupy the leadership of the PSD from 2005 onwards and no doubt felt the need to mouth the nationalist grievances of many lower-income supporters, few of whom had gained much from PSD rule. The PSD remained a personal vehicle for Iliescu: internal debate is non-existent, and until he is replaced, whoever speaks out against him is shown the door, as Cosmin Gusă found to his cost in June 2003.[9]

A power-struggle has smouldered behind the scenes between Iliescu and Năstase and their adherents. It arose because of Năstase's determination to carve out his own personal power-base and Iliescu's determination not to opt for retirement. Both men inserted their protégés into important official positions. Năstase plucked from obscurity Victor Ponta, a political bruiser, who was parachuted in as head of the party youth wing and then appointed to the much more important position of head of the Corps of Control, a watchdog body supposed to oversee the proper spending of government finances. But Iliescu kept the initiative: it is widely assumed that he is grooming for a major role (perhaps even that of his successor as President), Mircea Geoana, the foreign minister, who only joined the PSD in 2000. He has taken the credit for diplomatic successes, and is more popular in the polls than Năstase and easier to manipulate.[10]

Both the PSD camps seek to harm one another by sometimes tipping off law-enforcement agencies about criminal acts or leaking damaging revelations to the media. Sometimes foreigners are the victims. Convicted on a charge of paedophilia on 11 December 2002 and jailed for seven years, the maximum sentence Romanian law allows, the American historian Kurt Treptow was a protégé of Ion Iliescu's chief adviser, Ioan Talpes.[11] He had been best man at the wedding of Treptow who had resided in Romania since 1988. On hearing of the arrest, Talpes protested that Treptow had served the Romanian national cause and expressed his belief that 'the initial accusations against Treptow will be dropped at the end of the investigations'.[12] However, it emerged at the time that Treptow had been ensnaring under-age girls for many years without the authorities intervening, and it was widely assumed that pro- Năstase elements in the security apparatus had decided to take action with the primary aim of discrediting the presidential camp. A similar purpose may also have been behind the arrest in March 2003 of a top NATO official from the Netherlands, Willem Matser, on a charge of false use of documents.[13] He had grown close to advisers of Iliescu, and the tip-off to the Dutch authorities appears to have come from Bucharest.[14] In the pre-trial investigations, it emerged that certain Romanian ministers were eager to discard all pretence of following the law in order to obtain a generous cut from any new investment that came before them.[15]

It was the turn of Năstase's wing to suffer when Octavian Ionescu, a former footballer who lived in Switzerland, made a damaging admission in October 2003. He revealed he had paid 100,000 US dollars out of a 2 million dollar bribe required in order to give him planning permission to develop a tourist complex in the Carpathian mountains. Virgil Teodorescu, a top government official, resigned on 17 October after being accused of receiving a bribe from Ionescu.[16] Teodorescu was a subordinate of Şerban Mihailescu, in charge of co-ordinating government operations. This close ally of Năstase had been in difficulties since another of his subordinates Fanel Pavelache had resigned after being accused of taking bribes. Mihailescu was himself a controversial figure in the media. In March 2001 the then head of the Corps of Control, Ovidiu Greçea, had been quietly moved from this sensitive post to the less exacting one of Romanian consul in Rio de Janeiro after he had criticised the running of the Ministry of the Interior.[17] Mihailescu himself resigned on 21 October 2003, but Năstase showed that he still had confidence in him by taking him to Brazil to the conference of the Socialist International at which the PSD was to be admitted as a full member. Simultaneously, with Mihailescu out of the way, it was now safe to bring Greçea back from exile: in November it was announced that he would be the new Prefect of Bucharest and the PSD candidate for mayor of the city in 2004. Thus, as the pre-election season approached, the PSD donned a virtuous mask in order to remain in the good graces of the electorate.

Evidence which is increasingly difficult to ignore suggests that international interests are prepared to reinforce the current system by turning a blind eye to irregularities and even heaping honours on controversial figures. The PSD's admission to the Socialist International as corruption scandals unfolded on a daily basis in Bucharest is one such example. And it should not be forgotten that France conferred the Légion d'Honneur on Mihailescu in 2002. The European Commission is evidently prepared to live with the appointment of Victor Ponta, one of Năstase's chief enforcers, as head of the Corps of Control; this is a body which it has entrusted specifically with the investigation of the fraudulent use of EU funds, and which the press, in its more restrained comments on its role, has described as toothless. One 2003 article showed how the Leonardo da Vinci programme of the EU, designed to strengthen vocational training, has been systematically looted with little action taken.[18]

A new and disturbing pole of influence emerged in the PSD soon after its return to office. This was a group of powerful local politicians known as 'the barons'. They acquired this name because of accumulating evidence that they exercised almost total control in the areas they ruled. These were among the poorest parts of the country where the party had never been effectively challenged and where it controlled the courts, the police and most economic power as well as dominating elected bodies. The best-known barons were Nicolae

Mischie, Marian Oprisan, Lilion Gogonçea and Constantin Bebe Ivanovici all of whom at different times had been leaders of the council in Gorj, Vrancea, Galaţi and Ilfov provinces; Dumitriu Sechelariu, the mayor of the Moldavian city of Bacau was also a leading regional baron, and 'the pig baron', Culiţa Ţaraţa, counted for much in this part of the country.[19] These men repeatedly made headlines because of the way they acquired and flaunted power and wealth and their often ruthless attitude to those in the media who tried to expose their records. Nevertheless, they were needed by the PSD centrally because of their ability to enforce decisions on the ground. This was shown on the second day of the referendum on the revised constitution held on 18–19 October. With the hours passing and the turnout falling far below the 50% required to validate the result, they, along with the county prefects, sought to boost the turnout. Evidence from NGOs showed that multiple voting was widespread in several PSD fiefdoms.[20] The EU did not complain about this ballot-rigging, perhaps because it appeared to be in a good cause: a Yes vote meant that Romania could sign the EU treaty of accession. Some EU officials in Bucharest have even praised one well-known baron for his ability to spend EU money efficiently on good roads and secure agreement in his region for an infrastructure project regarded as vital by the EU.[21] But the same person has also been at the centre of allegations that he has used pre-accession funds from Brussels to amass a fortune and boost his political influence.[22]

The ability of the barons to run their towns, cities and, in some cases, counties as private fiefdoms shows the extent of the authority they wield in the PSD. Năstase has encouraged this trend and even sometimes defended their behaviour because he sees them as allies in his struggle with Iliescu. For the party as a whole they are an indispensable source of election funds. When the PSD secretary-general Dan Matei Agathon tried to assert central control in November 2003, several of them unceremoniously slapped him down. Agathon declared in Botoşani (a town that is a metaphor for poverty in Romania): 'We need donations and whoever wants to be a candidate for any position, or wants to stay in the current one, must contribute to campaign funds.' Sechelariu responded: 'Who gives a lot is going to have to be a beneficiary.' Oprisan declared Agathon's statement to be a bad joke. Trita Faniţa, the grain baron, said: 'How can he say such things in public?'[23] But he did and not one figure in the PSD (not even Adrian Severin, the party's arch-liberal) upbraided him for saying publicly what was already a well-known fact: that to run on the party ticket for a winnable seat depended on the size of your financial contribution and not on your professional merit. Some barons used to favour different parties when PSD domination seemed less assured and that could happen again. If the PSD's rivals convince the barons that they will not confiscate their assets if they return to power, then it is quite possible that they will obtain sponsorship from that quarter.

Within the EU, only in Italy is economic wealth translated into political power in the way that is rapidly happening in Romania. Năstase has established a close friendship with Silvio Berlusconi, the media mogul who, since becoming Prime Minister of Italy in 2001, has undermined the separation of powers by seeking to curb the independence of the magistrates and making himself immune from prosecution. The PSD has everything to gain from being able to demonstrate that low standards apply in at least one of the key democratic states of Western Europe; this would make their own aberrant behaviour less likely to fall under the critical spotlight.

The willingness of the European Union to allow Romania to join its ranks, if it fulfilled its accession terms, opened up a new vista. In 2002 the European Commission announced that it hoped Romania could join the EU in 2007, and in 2003 it became increasingly clear that this entry date would be adhered to even if it meant that flexible terms would have to be worked out to enable Romania to enter. Romania's eligibility increased thanks to the sponsorship of pro-American heads of government in Britain, Italy and Spain mindful of the country's strategic position as the Middle East was becoming ever more unstable. As for the PSD, the billions of Euros due to be provided by the EU in the first decade of the new century to prepare Romania for entry were a powerful incentive to making a show of discarding old habits and mentalities. Pressed as to why the PSD appeared ready to bury its nationalist and authoritarian tendencies, a senior EU official familiar with Bucharest realities could only reply that for Năstase and his acolytes the EU 'was the only show in town'.[24] He was hardpressed to point to any deep-seated commitment by the PSD to distribute wealth and opportunity across society and give citizens numerous access-points to decision-making.

The EU is appreciated as a vast potential employment exchange into which PSD leaders can place family members, protégés and members of their ever-expanding clientels. It hopes that young people equipped with degrees in the areas of European Studies and management, especially from the unregulated private universities in Romania, will be a lobby (or Trojan horse) in Brussels, exploitable by the oligarchy in years to come. As for NATO, membership is likely to enable the oligarchy to enjoy its wealth in more secure conditions than before 1989 and to expand it with little effort if Romania can be presented as a normal Western country.

It still takes a tremendous leap of faith to envisage the PSD as the party decreed by history to lead Romania into a democratic future. It was clear within its first weeks back in office that the party of Iliescu and Năstase had not lost its desire to dominate the state machinery and use it to reward supporters and isolate opponents. Early signs that it was prepared to build a common reform front with the centrist opposition parties were soon dashed. Instead the PSD has tried to increase its domination over different branches of government and those agencies which check and monitor its activities. In the first quarter of 2001, 1,300 tenured civil servants were dismissed despite the existence of legislation intended to depoliticise the civil service and allow security of tenure.[25] Membership of the party is increasingly seen as necessary for ambitious graduates intent on a public service career. Evidence also began to accumulate that the government was seeking to restrict media independence, with both state and private television coverage of alternative points of view being increasingly restricted. It was only with difficulty that in the first half of 2002 restrictive press laws, specifying heavy jail sentences for defamation of public officials, and requiring a right of reply, were shelved after being passed by Parliament. But pressure on the independent media, especially outside the bigger cities, remained relentless. Newspapers reporting abuses of power could expect repeated visits from the financial police and tax inspectors to make sure that they had complied with every minute regulation in what is a forest of endless red tape: if not, heavy fines were imposed. Pressure was also placed on advertisers to withhold their custom from newspapers seen as anti-PSD. The view of Freedom House, the US-based NGO in its 'Freedom of the Press 2003' report, was unflattering, singling out Romania as the only EU candidate country in which the media are not entirely free.[26]

Personal ties, sometimes extending before 1989, influence important appointments. In January 2001 the first major appointment made by the new Minister of Justice Mrs Rodica Stanoiu was of the former top Securitate official General Marian Ureche as the head of the ministry's intelligence service. It later emerged that the minister's links with Ureche went back to the days when she worked for the Romanian Academy's Institute for Judicial Studies which Ureche supervised for the Securitate.[27] She fought to retain him until the extent of his involvement in controversial intelligence work before and after 1989 led to his being ousted in November 2003.[28] Before 2001 was out Stanoiu, dismissed every procurator involved in anti-corruption trials and trials of state officials accused of acts of repression in the bloodshed accompanying the fall of the communist regime in 1989. In July 2001 the President appointed Stanoiu's husband to the constitutional court, raising fears of nepotism. Justice is one of the least reform-oriented ministries, and has shown little enthusiasm for supporting prosecutors, especially when they have tried to investigate corruption in the ranks of the ruling Social Democratic Party. One of them, Cristian Panait, committed suicide on 10 April 2002 apparently because he refused to turn on a trusted colleague who had got into trouble for arresting the son of the former prefect in Bihor county. Năstase attended his funeral, but within weeks the ministry was insisting that Panait had taken his own life because he was 'a schizophenic' not because of pressure directed at him to bury the case. (The expulsion from the PSD on 12 October 2002 of four parliamentarians who drew attention to allegedly corrupt behaviour by party colleagues, and warnings of a similar fate for other whistle-blowers, probably best summed up Năstase's attitude to corruption.)

The increasing weakness of the democratic opposition in Romania means that there is now little effective scrutiny of government actions. The lynch-pin of the previous coalition, the PNTCD, effectively broke up in 2001; after failing to enter Parliament in 2000 it selected Andrei Marga, rector of the University of Cluj, as leader with a mandate to relaunch the party, but he retained his university rectorship and failed to devote sufficient energy to the task. On 6 July he submitted his resignation by fax, complaining that his efforts to revitalise the party had been blocked by rivals. The party then split over who should succeed him; Victor Ciorbea, prime minister from 1996 to 1998, gained control of the party machine and expelled the deputy chairman Vasile Lupu who was associated with efforts to reverse communist-era nationalisations of land and property. The two men organised rival party congresses in the second half of August 2001.

The split in the PNTCD was less over ideology or future political tactics than over the party's resources as well as the perennial personality disputes without which no Romanian party split would be complete. Christian Democracy has not been a pole around which the PNTCD can align itself since its links with the majority Orthodox Church are tenuous. Its Peasantist traditions increasingly lack meaning since this section of the population is in decline and is loyal mainly to the PSD.

The humiliating end to Marga's effort to relaunch the PNTCD further undermined the credibility of intellectuals who wished to play a progressive role in politics. There are very few impressive thinkers contributing to periodicals and the press who are likely to be widely quoted in the years to come. Not many civil society stalwarts are keen to launch debates on issues such as how to improve the education system and how to protect vulnerable Romanians from the negative side of EU membership. Some journals increasingly seek to promote the merits of Romanians who have achieved academic renown abroad. But if foreign-based academics were to return and play active roles in public life, it is by no means certain that they would strengthen the democratic cause. At least one well-known US-based figure, a former opponent of Iliescu, has his own coterie and is keen to control promotions and indeed publications in his academic domain. This monopolistic approach plays into the hands of the PSD, which is keen to see a reduction in critical coverage of Romania from abroad. An ambitious academic *émigré* could prove as unhelpful for the prospects of Romanian democracy as the return of Andreas Papandreou, the US-based economist, was for Greek democracy in the 1960s. Even more to the point, the self-destruction of the PNTCD, combined with the defeat of the CDR in 2000, effectively destroyed the appeal of moderate right-wing ideas in the eyes of all but a small portion of the electorate. Increasingly it appears that if the Right has a future in Romania, it may well be as a promoter of chauvinist and authoritarian ideas, rather than progressive and self-improving ones. If the centre-right parties which governed between 1996 and 2000 are ever to form a credible opposition, then they will probably have to merge into a single force.

Currently the only continuous scrutiny of government actions is provided by the European Union, and its effectiveness is increasingly in doubt. The EU's annual report for 2001 on Romania's progress towards accession expressed concern about the slow pace of administrative and judicial reform. The new American ambassador Michael Guest publicly warned in December 2001 that corruption could affect the chances of Romania joining NATO.[29] This was an issue he returned to in the spring of 2003, drawing a rebuke from Iliescu: 'No ambassador of any country is entitled to come here and teach us lessons on how to fight against corruption'.[30]

Much government ire also greeted the publication in May 2001 of the critical report by the European Parliament's monitor on Romania, Emma Nicholson, on its progress towards meeting EU accession requirements. Nicholson singled out the poor treatment that some of the 60,000 children in state orphanages were still likely to receive. She expressed concern that child care officials were gaining financially from selling children on an international black market, and warned that if the state did not show greater concern, then the suspension of entry negotiations was a real possibility.[31] The government reacted with indignation to these charges. Romania's chief negotiator for entry, Vasile Puscas, even argued that Nicholson had drafted such a report out of the need to increase her profile in Britain where he claimed (erroneously) that she was a candidate in the June 2001 parliamentary election.[32] Nevertheless, the government soon swung into action and took the steps demanded by Nicholson to end abuses in the Romanian child care system.

A debate exists among international observers about whether the 'rough-house' tactics used by Emma Nicholson pay off in Romania. Some see top Romanian officials as proud and sensitive people who immediately become uncooperative if they are patronised and lectured, but others argue that in too many cases those officials have little to be proud of and only respond effectively when under unstinting public pressure. The EU's hard-nosed insistence on strong

Romanian guarantees before lifting (at the start of 2002) the requirement for visas for Romanian nationals intending to visit EU states, backs up this view. So may the ability of the Eminescu Trust and the Liga Pro-Europa, to prevent the government despoiling the historic Saxon town of Sighisoara by installing a Dracula theme park close to a district designated a Unesco World Heritage Site.

Without EU vigilance, it is difficult to see what would have prevented the ratification of a law passed by both parliamentary chambers on 7 March 2001 on the protection of state secrets, which human rights groups both inside Romania and abroad believed went far beyond what was necessary to protect human rights in a democratic society. The guarding of state secrets was described in the bill as the 'civic duty' of all citizens and an expression of their 'national fidelity'. The SRI was entrusted with overseeing maintenance of the law, and jail sentences of up to ten years could be imposed for securing, publishing, disclosing or destroying classified information. The law was passed just a few days after President Iliescu admitted that corruption in the justice system was a serious problem. Much of the press complained that under such a vaguely written act the temptation to classify documents providing evidence of corruption as secret would be overwhelming. On 11 March 2001 Năstase said the law had been passed to comply with NATO requirements for the protection of military secrets as well as the EU's Schengen Accord.[33] But the EU delegation in Bucharest replied in a statement that it had not called for such a law but instead had argued for one strengthening public access to official information.[34] On 11 April the bill was scrapped when the Constitutional Court declared it unconstitutional.[35]

It is likely that only sustained international vigilance will prevent the revival of a monopolistic approach to government which in Romania has always been associated with widespread misuse of public funds. Between October 2001 and the spring of 2003 the government mapped out, launched and then re-launched its own anti-corruption strategy amid domestic and international scepticism about the seriousness of its intentions. Only grudgingly did it agree in July 2003 to alter the parliamentary rules which currently allow suspected law-breakers to enjoy immunity from prosecution. Instead the government prefers to scapegoat senior officials in the former government whose affairs it has encouraged prosecutors to investigate.

Alin Giurgiu, the former deputy head of the state privatisation agency, was held in custody for three months without charge in the summer of 2001, his release only being secured after international concern over his health. Giurgiu's treatment can be contrasted with that accorded to Sever Muresan, founder of Dacia Felix Bank, the first private bank to open in post-communist Romania, which crashed in 1995 with the savings of many small investors being wiped out in the process. In 2000 Muresan was imprisoned in Switzerland for three-and-a-half years for financial misconduct, but on being extradited to Romania to face graver charges concerning the failure of his bank he was released by a sympathetic judge.[36] The government expressed no alarm when he left Romania shortly afterwards.[37]

A National Anti-Corruption Prosecutor's Office (PNA), set up largely in response to EU pressure in the autumn of 2002, was the government's answer to critics that it had no interest in rooting out corruption. The most prominent victim of the PNA was a judge from Tirgu Mureş, Mrs Andreea Ciuca, who was arrested in that month charged with accepting a bribe. Known previously as one of the minority of judges keen to maintain high standards on the judicial bench, she was subjected to lengthy interrogations and placed in a cell with common criminals, but released through the intervention of the head of the Supreme Court, Paul Florea, who ruled that she had no case to answer owing to the flimsiness of the evidence.[38] However, Ciuca's treatment was a warning to judges and magistrates prepared to act independently of the PSD and interfere in its clients' affairs that they would face political reprisals. Florea himself was subject to the ire of Iliescu, who openly criticised the action of someone appointed by his predecessor;[39] he had revealed himself to be a thorn in the side of the government when he warned in April 2003 of growing political pressure on the judiciary.[40] The humiliation of a judge known for her correct conduct was also a warning to more humble Romanians that challenging a state which trampled on their rights could have deeply unwelcome consequences and was thus a fruitless course of action.

It is incidents like these which ought to generate acute concern in Brussels about Romania's ability to slay the dragon of corruption. The mentality that well-placed individuals are entitled to divert public money and goods for their own private gratification is deeply ingrained. In its 2001 'Corruption Perceptions Index' the respected international body Transparency International' placed Romania sixty-ninth of ninety-one countries. The only European country to earn a lower position was Russia, placed seventy-ninth; Bulgaria, with which Romania is often compared, was far ahead in forty-seventh place.[41]

In 2003 Năstase appointed as national supremo to deal with corruption, Ionel Blanculescu. The pro-government media tried to build a mystique around him as various middle-ranking officials and businessmen were detained on corruption charges. Blanculescu himself declared: 'There are elderly people who, when they see me on television, kiss the TV screen. Believe me![42] His mission was described as one designed to 'put most of the dirt under the mat so that the ruling group will look clean and fit to take part in the elections, but also to impress the foreigners'.[43] It was certainly not part of Blanculescu's job description to expose the primitive accumulation of capital by the close-knit elite in charge of the country for most of the time since 1989.

At the EU's Laeken summit in December 2000, ten out of twelve candidate countries were officially described as being on course to join the EU by around 2004. Romania (along with Bulgaria) was given the target date of 2007. By the end of July 2002 Romania had concluded negotiations for only thirteen of the thirty-one chapters of the *acquis communautaire*, had still to open three, and had made little progress on key issues. Bulgaria, by contrast had closed twenty-one out of the thirty chapters of the accession negotiations, and opened all the rest including those on agriculture, industry and economic and monetary union.[44] In an earlier work the present author argued that Romania's chronic incapacity in many vital areas of governance required concentrated help from outside which would inevitably reduce its sovereignty temporarily while strengthening the ability of the state to serve the needs of its citizens effectively in the longer term.[45]

Năstase did not advance Romania's hopes of entering NATO by trying to appoint a close aide, Ristea Priboi, as head of the parliamentary commission monitoring the foreign intelligence service, SIE. It soon emerged that Priboi had been a dedicated member of the Securitate, particularly its foreign intelligence wing, and that the regime turned to him whenever it encountered difficulties, even ones such as the 1987 Brasov workers, uprising.[46] On 13 February 2001 Senator Radu Alexandru of the opposition PNL described Priboi's appointment as 'a provocation and a lack of responsibility' in relation to Romania's NATO aspirations. It was soon withdrawn, but it was clear that Priboi remained one of Năstase's closest confidants.

Năstase himself took on some of the imperious airs associated with Priboi's pre-1989 boss. While he was holidaying on the Romanian Black Sea coast in 2002 in the same mansion as Ceauşescu, the police toured the local discos ordering the music to be turned down. His hunting pursuits were well-known, as was his art-collecting propensity.[47] Nor did he shrink from putting foreign officials in their place, as when he upbraided the EU ambassador Jonathan Scheele for daring to warn him that EU money designed to modernise Bucharest's infrastructure (and reduce the heating bills of its inhabitants) was in danger of being lost because of Năstase's reluctance to see it falling into the hands of his arch-rival, Mayor Băsescu.[48] The interior ministry became dominated by newly-appointed allies of Năstase, some of whom were linked to acts of repression before 1989.[49] It is widely thought that these officials cracked down on the alleged author and distributor of a report known as Armagedon II, distributed electronically to foreign embassies and news agencies on 16 January 2002, which focussed on the personal wealth of the prime minister and his family, and his connections with controversial businessmen.[50] Most of the claims had already been published by the press or aired in parliamentary debates. Nevertheless, on 17 January 2002 the prosecutor-general's office ordered the detention of the man alleged to have distributed the document and searched the office of Mugur Ciuvica, the former chief of staff of ex-President Constantinescu, whom the authorities initially claimed to be its author. The Penal Code allows the authorities to act in such a way if national security or Romania's international standing are placed at risk; Romania's leading human rights watchdog, Apador, accused the prime minister of confusing the defence of his own reputation with national security and warned that it was only the most serious example of a growing authoritarian trend in state behaviour. This charge was also made by ex-President Constantinescu in a letter to his successor Ion Iliescu.

Năstase soon admitted that the authorities had over-reacted and that the government and public institutions were still learning how to cope with criticism.[51] At least Romania offered unswerving support to NATO during the drive against the Al-Qaida terrorist network following the 11 September bombings in the United States. But there have been persistent claims that Arab-led smuggling, money-laundering and tax-dodging operations have gone on with the compliance of high-ranking figures in the Romanian justice and interior ministries. Communist-era intelligence operatives who are now flourishing businessmen with close links to the government maintained extensive links with radical Middle East regimes. Thus in order not to lessen its chances of acquiring NATO membership the government had to convince its NATO allies that Romania was not a potential weak link in the drive against terrorism, and Năstase has done this by appearing to be a zealous defender of American interests. On 1 August 2002 Romania became the first country in the world to sign a bilateral agreement with the United States giving American soldiers and diplomats immunity from prosecution by the International Criminal Court (ICC), a global war crimes court under the jurisdiction of the United Nations. Romania was condemned for taking its own unilateral course by the European Commission which declared on 9 August: 'We would have expected a future member-state to have at least coordinated with us on such an important issue.'[52]

The unexpected rapprochement between NATO and Russia in 2001, after it became clear that they had a common enemy in Islamic terrorism, has advantages and disadvantages for Romania. It had neglected to improve its relations with a country widely viewed by public opinion and much of the political élite as a historic enemy, but relations improved thanks to the regular meetings between the two foreign ministers, Ivan Ivanov and Mircea Geoana, in 2001, the year Romania held the OSCE Chairmanship in Office. Romania was responsible for coordinating high-profile OSCE initiatives in the Caucasus where Russia had strong security interests, and Geoana carried these out without antagonising Moscow. Negotiations on a bilateral treaty hurriedly got under way in October 2001 and were only concluded in July 2003 when Iliescu travelled to Moscow to put his signature to the document. He is aware that Russian cooperation is needed to improve strained relations with Moldova, on part of whose territory (the breakaway Trans-Dniester), Russian army forces continue to be stationed. But the most immediate effect of normalising relations might be to enable Russian firms to gain a big stake in the Romanian energy sector, which is being privatised in response to IMF pressure. Since 1997 Romania has had a bilateral treaty with Ukraine, which occupies territory that belonged to it before 1940, but relations have languished. Romania considered appealing to the International Court of Justice at The Hague when the Ukraine decided to drill for oil in waters still disputed between the two countries.[53] Relations are worse with Moldova: after the Justice minister of Moldova complained to the same forum in The Hague about 'Romanian expansionism', Năstase cancelled a visit he was due to make to Chisinau in October 2001.[54]

Unless Romania's links with its eastern neighbours can be transformed, it remains difficult to argue that admitting it to NATO can be viewed as enhancing the security of the alliance. But from the early spring of 2002 it began to appear that these impediments were no longer a check to Romania's NATO hopes, at least as far as its most powerful member was concerned. The events of September 11 greatly increased Romania's strategic importance to the United States, which suddenly found itself needing countries in the Black Sea region ready to provide bases, overfly rights and even local troops for terrorist threats further to the east. Romania (along with Bulgaria) proved willing to fulfill such roles when the existing NATO members in South-Eastern Europe, Greece and Turkey were reticent or unwilling. Even before 11 September President George W. Bush had been re-evaluating America's strategic objectives. Growing American interest in the vast oil and gas supplies of the Caspian Sea and on securing pipelines for delivery of these energy sources was raising the profile of South-Eastern Europe in the White House.[55] But Romania has few consistent advocates among its European partners, and leaving aside the preoccupation with oil of a US President from the USA's main oil state it is unclear to what degree the country is vital for NATO security; indeed it could easily be argued that it might be more troublesome inside NATO rather than outside it.

Greece is the only fully Balkan state so far to be admitted to either the EU or NATO, but until a more cooperative spirit emerged in

Athens in the late 1990s not a few leading EU officials said off the record that allowing Greece to join the EU in 1981 had been a foolish oversight; its economy was far from ready and it had been a troublesome member, especially as EU responsibilities in South-Eastern Europe steadily increased. Greece was received into the EU in 1981 not least because the modern state was seen in some West European policy circles as the heir to a great civilisation that had contributed to the making of Europe. Such a claim does not rest on strong foundations, and it is certainly not one that could be made of Romania. The heroic images from Timişoara and Bucharest in December 1989 briefly made Romania appear a European champion of freedom. But with the June 1990 *mineriada* 'Romania became a strange country' in Western eyes and it has never since shaken off that slightly schizophrenic image.[56]

But the EU has been increasingly encouraging towards Romania despite public admonishments about the slowness of the reform process. A powerful consortium of EU states now want Romania inside the EU by 2007, even if the entry terms have to be made more flexible. Romania will increasingly be assessed not according to its capacity to fulfill entry terms or compete effectively with other EU members, but by a different set of criteria. It is no coincidence that Romania's most vocal backers—Britain, Italy and Spain—are also the EU states who have given strongest support to President Bush's military aims in the Middle East. These Atlanticist states, dependent on Middle East oil supplies for their economic viability, have been impressed by Romania's readiness, as a country that finds itself in an increasingly strategic part of the world, to act as a bridgehead for US-led operations there. Secondly, Romania's prospects for entry have brightened because of political disputes within the EU about its future direction. Britain, Italy and Spain wish the nation-state to retain its primacy even as common EU arrangements become the norm in important areas of decision-making. They know that pressures for fully federal arrangements in the EU will grow as an economic union becomes a reality. To postpone federalism, it is in their interests to allow in weak states with major problems like Poland—and Romania. It will take years, probably decades, before the EU can overcome the severe indigestion that will ensue as it absorbs new members with acute difficulties. Only then will it be possible to return to the federalist goals of the EU's founding fathers.

In early 2003 there was a momentary jolt when France, angered by Romania's extravagant backing for the US invasion of Iraq, sounded as if it might be ready to veto Romanian and Bulgarian entry. But in November of that year President Chirac publicly reverted to being a strong sustainer of Romania.[57] Germany's Chancellor Gerhard Schroeder appears equally supportive. In October 2003 he referred to the 'impressive' rate of reforms in Romania.[58] Back in June 2001 Năstase had been told by him that Romania was still a long way from joining the EU.[59] The EU does not stop to think why democracy in Romania has failed to put down sturdy roots ever since its engagement with the country actively began in 1999 when membership talks began. During that period the mainstream centre-right parties have been wiped out or gravely weakened, the ultra-nationalists have emerged as the most popular opposition force, and the PSD's authoritarian tendencies and propensity for corruption have been shown to be as strong as ever.

One success that still encourages Brussels is the reconciliation between the PSD and the Hungarian UDMR which the EU masterminded at the end of 2000. The EU made clear to the PSD that it must abandon its own chauvinist stance on the Hungarian question in Transylvania, and a formal cooperation pact was signed between the two former foes after the 2000 election. The UDMR has sustained what is a minority government with its parliamentary votes. In return the PSD agreed to lift its opposition to the Law on Public Administration which was signed into law in April 2001 after years of delay. It allows ethnic minorities to use their native languages in dealings with local authorities in regions where they account for more than 20% of the population. They can address public administration officials in their mother-tongue, either orally or in writing, and are entitled to receive bilingual replies.

One unforeseen outcome is that the most pragmatic wing of the UDMR has become heavily involved in the politics of patronage. A leading UDMR parliamentarian, Attila Verestoy, had already grown close to the PSD oligarch, Viorel Hrebenciuc, but it still came as a surprise when it was revealed that Verestoy was one of the wealthiest politicians in Romania, much of his fortune being derived from the timber industry which has boomed as the forests have started to be chopped down.[60]

The ability of the UDMR to stay aloof from the money-making side of Romanian politics has always been exaggerated. Probably it would have been tactically more astute if the party had adopted a watchdog role towards the government; then it could have made its parliamentary support conditional on correct behaviour by the PSD in crucial areas of government that affect the lives of ordinary citizens very directly. Such an approach would have boosted the party's status among Romania's citizens and prevented disillusionment eroding its own support base. But this has not happened. In 2002 there was controversy over the declaration of assets of figures in public life. Prominent UDMR figures allied with old guard elements of the PSD who were opposed to having a strong and transparent law. The excuses they gave for not having full disclosure were the kind normally to be expected from cynical PSD figures with plenty to hide.

György Frunda, twice the UDMR's presidential candidate, was most vehement in his opposition to a law requiring politicians to declare their private wealth. He also insisted on a law to penalise the media heavily where a politician could claim to be misrepresented.[61]

Part of the UDMR is becoming absorbed in the deal-making culture of Bucharest politics. If the UDMR decides to adopt what is the model for a conventional Romanian party, it may prove to be an unexpected victory for those forces in Romania which wish fully to assimilate the Hungarian minority and deny it an autonomous existence. Longstanding parliamentarians hope that this is the beginning of a golden era for the UDMR, and that it will be a party for all political seasons, indispensable for creating a viable government when no party has an absolute majority. But this is probably misconceived. The 2002 census figures revealed that the Hungarian population in Romania had fallen by nearly 15% in the previous decade;[62] thus it will be a struggle for the UDMR to reach the 5% threshhold of votes cast necessary for it to remain in Parliament. This might have been less difficult if the party had promoted the interests of Romanian society generally and emphasised Translyvanian concerns which were not just those of the Hungarian minority. It is hardly surprising that there is now disillusionment with the party among former supporters, especially the young.

Adrian Năstase cannot be unaware that a pact which was promoted by the EU in the first instance, is having an increasingly destabilising effect on the Hungarians. If the UDMR splits or it fails to get the 5% minimum required to enter parliament, he can say to Brussels, 'Well, who are the Hungarians? Of course we have Hungarians, but we have other minorities as well. Why should we pay special attention to them if they are out of parliament? Henceforth they will be treated like the Armenians, the Ukrainians, the Italians and other minorities who have one seat each. Our alliance with the UDMR was a phase and that phase is now over.' Most of the seats that would have gone to the UDMR, would be distributed to the largest party, the PSD. If removed from parliament, it would be even more difficult for the mainstream opposition to form a viable government if its vote goes up. Moreover, in the absence of the UDMR, it would be easier for the PSD to reach out to nationalist voters. The PSD has not stopped doing so even while this alliance has lasted. The strength of nationalist feeling was shown by a poll published on the website of the UN Development Programme in Romania at the end of 2001. It asked the following questions to which it received strident answers:

	Agree (%)	*Disagree (%)*
Romania is a country both rich and beautiful but its proper development is prevented by its enemies.	59.0	17.6
Only people who speak the official language should vote.	38.6	35.3
No international organisation such as the EU or the IMF should tell Romanians how to run their own country.	53.3	17.4
There are ethnic groups within Romania which act regularly against our national interest.	44.4	21.0
There are parts of the country which really belong to us and we should fight to get them back.[63]	56.7	21.3

If the EU thinks that it has displaced such attitudes by sponsoring an alliance between two former foes, it is likely to have been mistaken. A hard-headed appraisal of the PSD since 2001 shows that most of its leading figures see the alliance with the UDMR as a temporary phase. The only way the UDMR can sustain it in the long-term is if it merges with the PSD and becomes its Transylvanian Hungarian wing. With the possibility of having no deputies in Parliament, there is a danger that many Hungarians who choose to remain in Romania will become radicalised. If this occurs, it will make the decision of the EU to broker a marriage between the PSD and UDMR somewhat questionable. It would have been better if the UDMR had been advised to offer critical support to the PSD, which would have made it easier to keep its line of communications with the centre-right parties open. Relations with them are now poor. In 2001 the PNL proposed a parliamentary motion that the government had lost control over mainly Hungarian counties and was not embarrassed to receive the backing of the ultra-nationalists (as well as the PD).[64] In 2004 and indeed in years to come many parties will have an incentive for investing heavily in the currency of nationalism. Only the prospect of sustained economic recovery and improving living standards is likely to dislodge nationalist explanations for problems large and mundane.

11

CONCLUSION
THE CRUCIAL ROLE OF THE E.U.

The main argument of this book is that a number of long-term factors have undermined the prospects of a substantive democracy emerging in Romania. Exploitative relations between a privileged group at the apex of society and most of the rest of the population have been the norm for centuries. Not long before Romania started to experiment with representative institutions in the 1860s, most of the rural population had been serfs, and the gypsies had only recently been freed from slavery. In the 1990s a fresh experiment with democracy began with a more urbanised population who had endured two generations of outright totalitarian rule, with their political masters treating them as subjects and not as citizens. Against such a background, it is hardly surprising that there is a strong disposition on the part of much of the population to be dependent on the state. This sense of dependence has *grown*, rather than decreased, in the course of modern Romanian history. There is also frustration with the inadequate performance of a state which is simultaneously too big and too weak. But the coercive power of an under-performing state has usually prevented popular dissatisfaction from reaching dangerous proportions.

This sense of frustration has not resulted in autonomous groups becoming strong enough to promote a civic culture which might limit the absolute power of the state and encourage it to acquire a sense of social responsibility. Rarely have such groups been successful, at least for extended periods. Nor have commercial groups committed to social progress and the rule of law been able to impose their values on the state and nurture institutions which could assist in the country's modernisation. A social formation which has enjoyed recurrent influence in Romania is the intellectual élite, particularly those members who promote a nationalist outlook, often in order to extract resources from the state. Much of the intellectual élite has exalted nationalism and the exponents of Romanian specificity in order to divert the people's attention from the state's policy failures. The best current example of this species of intellectual is the PRM's George Pruteanu, who in October 2002 united the PSD and PRM deputies by getting them to pass a law imposing heavy fines on anyone using non-Romanian words on public hoardings.[1]

Contemporary democrats are hampered by the absence of examples of reformist movements which have succeeded in prevailing against an unjust or corrupt state. There are also few examples of successful resistance to tyranny and injustice which can offer inspiration; hardly a murmur of protest was heard when a royal dictatorship was imposed in 1938; anti-communist resistance was more widespread and sustained than is often believed, but it ultimately failed; the 1989 revolution failed to break the power of the communists and was largely taken over by second-ranking ones. Acquiescence towards those in power usually appears the most prudent course. A communist like Cornel Burtică, fully involved in the communist modernization process between the 1960s and the 1980s, still believed that 'the philosophy of life of the Romanians' in Ceauşescu's time was shaped by ancient proverbs such as 'The bowed head will not be cut by the sword' or 'Be friends with the devil until you cross the bridge'.[2]

Fifty years of Communism reinforced authoritarian elements in political culture. Behind a façade of egalitarianism, deeply unequal relations were encouraged within a rigidly hierarchical system of political control. The years since 1989 have seen Romanian citizens acquire more political freedoms than they have ever previously known. But it is possible that this period will go down in history not as the start of a democratic era but as one in which rampant economic and social inequality quickly became entrenched (or, more accurately, was re-imposed). There have been wholesale illicit transfers of public money and resources to private hands, and the period is likely to be remembered for its successive scandals, involving the embezzlement of huge sums, than for any advances in building democracy.

In states with steep economic inequality the struggle of daily existence saps energy. In 1989 Romanians were weighed down by shortages, but household costs such a rent and heating usually did not exceed 10% of an average monthly income. Today, by contrast, these costs *exceed* the average salary or pension on which most citizens try to subsist.[3] In Romania's case institutions such as the Orthodox Church also discourage the population from critically examining how they are treated by the state. But social frustrations are never far below the surface, ready to be harnessed by populists if voting for conventional parties fails to bring about a reduction in deprivation and injustice.

In 1996, when the PDSR lost the parliamentary and presidential elections, it was the historic parties of the centre-right which benefited from popular dissatisfaction with its record in office. Ion Iliescu's defeat by Emil Constantinescu created optimism about the future. However, within months coalition infighting was dwarfing the previous left-right confrontations. Problems which had plagued Romanian politics during earlier democratic interludes returned to prominence: lack of coordination among forces committed to reform, the ability of factionalism and personal ambition to sabotage specific reform initiatives, and the willingness of rhetorical reformers to satisfy their appetites at the state's expense, albeit in a far less flagrant way than under their immediate predecessors.

In 1998 President Constantinescu saw Romania's problems as being caused by 'élites in permanent disagreement'. This was an interesting retreat from the view, which he and most of those then in office had previously adhered to, that Romania's chief problem was the determination of ex-communists to perpetuate their influence. This view would be further undermined after June 2000 by the willingness of numerous politicians originally elected for anti-communist parties to join the supposedly 'neo-communist' PDSR (it became the Social Democratic Party: PSD in 2001) when their parties fell into decline. By then much less was heard about Iliescu's party's pre-1989 origins.

The comprehensive failure of most reform initiatives contemplated or begun in the 1996–2000 period undermined the credibility of those who, only a short time before, were arguing that Romania's deepening problems were due to the communist origins of their predecessors in office. The shortcomings of the CDR-led governments were hard to avoid: the lack of a clear vision and the inability to communicate effectively with the population; the refusal to create a single reform party; the absence of leadership from the President, who failed to become an effective rallying force for change; the failure to start building a public service-oriented bureaucracy capable of implementing a range of reforms. Of course, the influence of a totalitarian system which trampled initiative and promoted the exploitation of the many by the few should not be denied. What became clear after 1996 was that many of those located in the so-called camp of reform were unable to break free from its deeply inhibiting influences.

The stimuli for fundamental change nearly all came from the international institutions seeking to assist Romania in the gargantuan task of preparing for Euro-Atlantic integration. The corrupt and disorderly state which historically has served a narrow group of élite interests is unable to meet the challenge of integrating Romania with mainstream Western institutions without such concentrated assistance. In 1999 the EU and its partners, the IMF and the World Bank, were relieved when the PDSR agreed to allow external institutions to influence the reform process if it was returned to office in 2000. But these international officials might have been less sanguine if they had understood the long Romanian tradition of acquiescence to foreign recommendations and demands while in practice seeking to ignore them or frustrate their implementation. After all, Romanians had shown outward conformity to a state whose demands have usually been unwelcome, but actually sought to sidestep its unwelcome interference in their lives, so why should Romanian politicians behave any differently towards international institutions?

International bodies and national governments with aid programmes in Romania sometimes make it all too easy for recipients to sidestep or ignore their advice. International officials reluctant to experience realities outside the ministries they liase with are prone to trust officials if they approximate in a superficial way to their perception of how a modern-minded manager should sound and act—this in a country where the word 'chameleonism' is an integral part of Romanian vocabulary. Different foreign programmes often duplicate one another; several EU governments in successive years have tried to implement schemes to create a public-service-oriented bureaucracy, without even being aware of the duplication: the

Romanian government never bothered to enlighten them, and there is no compelling evidence that it has seriously tried to implement the particular structural reforms recommended by West European donor states.

The EU plans to donate in the period 2000–6 pre-accessional aid worth billions of euros to assist with restructuring the economy and the infrastructure.[4] Yet a poll carried out early in 2002 found that 69% of respondents felt that Western countries did not support Romania at all (only 3.7% expressed a contrary opinion).[5] Perhaps this dispiriting result arose from the fact that few Romanians outside the élite have directly benefited from pre-accession funds. Not surprisingly, strong backing for European integration has failed to emerge among key groups like educated youth; instead the EU relies on the ruling party as its main contact-point with Romania. Perhaps as a result the perception was strong by 2003 that the PSD and its retinue was a part of Romania already inside the EU. The storm about the ability of firms belonging to the husband and son of Hildegard Puwak, the minister of European Integration, to obtain funds to the value of € 150,000 from the EU's 'Leonardo da Vinci' programme designed to promote professional skills strengthened that perception.[6]

What are likely to be the future trends in the distribution of political and economic power, and relations between state and society, as a result of the first dozen years of democracy?

The growth in inequality is likely to be seen as one of the key trends of the 1990s and beyond. In 2003 it emerged that thirty-three people had accumulated enormous wealth (between 736 and 797 million US dollars) in the poorest region of the country, Moldavia, where 30% of the population are poor and 25% extremely poor.[7] Many of these millionaires acquired privatised state assets for nominal sums, without proper validation or competitive bidding; some were state officials themselves who plundered the state's assets. This grand theft was easier to accomplish in poor regions where exploitative relations had long been the norm.

In 2002 an international car dealer expressed his astonishment about the constant demand in Romania for expensive and prestigious motor vehicles such as *Mercedes,* BMW and jeeps like Cherokee and Land Rover. He noted that in Slovenia, an ex-communist state whose average income was 7–8 times higher than Romania's, the demand was always for the cheaper model of foreign cars.[8] Such conspicuous expenditure by a small élite keen to flaunt their wealth exists in a country where over 40% of the population is reckoned to live in poverty.

Valerian Stan, head of the government's anti-corruption unit in 1996–7, claimed in 2001 that some 70% of elected representatives had their own businesses to which they devoted more attention than to their parliamentary duties.[9] In January 2002 more attention was focussed on high-level corruption than at any time in the previous five years when a report on the personal wealth of Prime Minister Adrian Năstase and his family, and his connections with controversial businessmen, was distributed electronically under the title Armageddon II.[10] After a clumsy attempt to crack down on the authors, Năstase came on television on 22 January and appealed for 'national solidarity', promising to take steps to avoid 'the super-polarisation of society'. Similarly in May 2003 he appealed to the PSD to rediscover its left-wing orientation after the wealth of its national and local representatives, and their allies in the public service, became public knowledge.

Such gestures are only likely to be short-term palliatives. The mounting evidence that money buys positions fills newspapers almost daily. Concessions are awarded by politicians to themselves or to their allies in the world of business and finance. In May 2003 a housing bill came before parliament obliging public institutions, ministries and state-owned companies to build holiday cottages on public land. Officials who had not already enriched themselves were to be provided with these perks from the state budget.[11] What is different from the early 1990s is that when it comes to distributing the spoils of office the PSD is prepared to make room for business figures from other parties. It is not surprising that in 2003 they were to the fore in opposing calls to form a single centre party to confront the PSD in the next elections, which was widely seen as the only way of preventing the PSD obtaining a second term. Thus the PSD uses its control of state funds to manipulate the opposition and prevent a strong recovery threatening its hold on power.

In an address to Parliament in December 2002 President Iliescu complained of the alacrity with which the parties exploited 'the advantages emanating from being in power in order to…enrich themselves rapidly'. He launched the idea of 'shock therapy' against corruption and warned that 'if we don't make visible progress in fighting corruption there is a real danger for Romania to be seen as an unsuitable candidate for joining the EU and NATO…we will be marginalised.' But it was soon clear that the house-cleaning was not meant to affect those protégés who had benefited from their association with him, but was a warning to Năstase to treat him more respectfully. Iliescu's bold anti-corruption rhetoric soon died down when he and his Prime Minister managed to stitch up an accommodation early in 2003.[12]

At a time when Eniko Landaburu, the EU's Number Two in the enlargement process, was talking about the need to make more flexible terms to enable Romanian bureaucracy to absorb EU funds, the independent press was full of claims that only interest groups promoted by the PSD stood a real chance of obtaining the lion's share of this money.[13] It went on to claim that franchises for TV stations and contracts for the privatisation of utilities and state firms were not awarded on a neutral basis. An indication that top political jobs might be available to the highest bidder came from no less a figure than Corneliu Rusu-Banu, the Prefect of one of Romania's most important *judets*, Iasi, who issued a statement on 16 January 2002 in which he said that it had come to his attention that an unnamed person was ready to pay $150,000 to replace him in his position.[14] He provided some interesting details about how this might occur, saying that the cash would change hands at the Ministry of Administration in Bucharest. Rusu-Banu declared: 'I cannot believe that at the top levels of the party such decisions will be made for monetary considerations.'

The Prefect is supposed to coordinate relations between the central state and the different organs of local administration. Properly conducted, the job is a demanding one, especially in a time of painful economic and social transition, but it is reasonable to assume that anyone wishing to pay a large sum to secure the post for himself has his eyes on the opportunities for personal enrichment offered by a position where the holder has to oversee numerous contracts and comes into regular contact with many businessmen. If Rusu-Banu's warning is correct and the post of prefect is coveted for its wealth-creating opportunities, then the continuity with the Phanariot era in

eighteenth-century Romania is truly striking. Then the governorship of Moldavia was sold to the highest bidder in Istanbul, and the
new incumbent concentrated on making good his investment by
fleecing the population through heavy taxes in as short a time as
possible before he was recalled.

With none of its opponents in a position to challenge the PSD for
supremacy, it is quite possible that quarrels within the party over the
spoils of office could emerge as a new fault-line in politics. The PSD
lacks a clearcut ideology, and it is clear that many of its adherents,
some at very high level, have joined in order to benefit from being in
power. The PSD is unlikely to find a stable formula for governance if
the chief motivating force of its leading players is to occupy the state
and benefit accordingly. The party possesses an amorphous identity,
and the reserves of loyalty it can draw upon are probably shallow in
the absence of its founder, Iliescu. It is a left-wing party supported by
the wealthiest businessmen. Its leader talks of social protection, but
has the means to send his children to an exclusive school and build
up an expensive art collection. His predecessor as Prime Minister
from 1992 to 1996—Nicolae Văcăroiu, an expert in centralized planning under Ceauşescu—is now head of a well-known private bank.
They belong to different factions of the PSD; unavoidable turf wars
over the allocation of resources could mean that the predictions
commonly heard after 2000 that the party was destined to remain in
office for a long time will prove to have been unfounded. President
Iliescu remains a key stabilising element. When his last term in office
expires in 2004, all the signs are that he plans to return to active politics and he may set up a philanthropic foundation bearing his name
which business allies would be expected to sponsor. An Iliescu
Foundation would promote the welfare of the citizen, something he
was instrumental in ensuring that the state failed to do. Iliescu clings
to a reputation for economic probity. Without such a figure in
charge of the leading party, it would have been far less easy for those
who plundered the state to get away with it so easily. If Romania is
compared to a jewellery shop, for twelve years Iliescu has been a *bona
fide* customer who has successfully distracted the attention of the
sales staff while his accomplices have repeatedly made off with the
best gems.

It is difficult to see which opposition forces can hold the PSD to
account and provide a stable alternative if its grasp on power falters.

The fragmented centre-right is likely to be in a state of redefinition for a long time to come. It is difficult to know whether the National Liberal Party (PNL) can still be described as a force of the moderate right after it formally merged with the Alliance For Romania (ApR) in January 2002. In many parts of Romania the ApR is dominated by left-wingers and people with Securitate connections, and there is every chance that Liberalism will become an empty term for a party like the PNL that has made perhaps too many compromises in a bid to remain a leading political contender with an original message.

For the PNTCD the prospects are much more gloomy. Once the alliance with civil society carefully constructed by Coposu in the early 1990s ceased to function later in the decade, the party lost its way. The split in 2001 seemed to be less about political strategy and ideology and more about the settling of personal scores and the acquisition of the party's assets. Other small parties on the right also disdain civil society, and are looking for wealthy backers to fuel their growth—thus patron-client relations are very much alive in Romanian society.

Emil Constantinescu is also attempting a comeback by inaugurating 'Popular Action' in July 2003. It places emphasis on civil society, but one can scarcely imagine the forces of liberal civil society in Romania playing a strong role in driving a dishonest and incompetent government from office, as happened in 1996 in Bulgaria. It is also hard to imagine them being able to mount resistance during the early stages of an illegitimate seizure of power in Romania because of the low standing non-party associations promoting democracy enjoy in the public consciousness. Instead, it is populists, offering personal solutions for national problems, who appear best placed to challenge a ruling party with monopolistic traits like the PSD. Romania appears ripe for populism. The prevalence of relationships of dependence and the weakness of independent autonomous organisations with an impersonal character provide ample scope for charismatic leaders ready to appeal to the masses along traditional lines. The existence of unassimilated groups of former rural dwellers in the cities and urban returnees to the land—both are doing conspicuously badly in their environments—can provide a launching-pad for political entrepreneurs with simple answers for complex problems. This again is not encouraging for Romanian democracy.

Nationalism is the political currency in which nearly all political contenders are likely to deal in order to exploit a theme of perennial relevance in Romanian political culture. The main nationalist formation has been the Greater Romania Party (PRM), which entered the big league of politics in 2000 by mobilising a large protest vote, denoting the electorate's alienation from the political system. Its links with the pre-1989 regime are simply seen as unimportant: memories of the hard times experienced during the 1980s have faded. The young, many of whom face bleak economic prospects unless they can emigrate, have few recollections of the communist era.

It is difficult to undermine the PRM by referring to its leader's communist antecedents or the similarity of his discourse to that of neo-fascist leaders. Most Romanians do not categorise parties according to their position in a right-left spectrum (political awareness was blunted by totalitarianism, but this is not necessarily a sign of naivety), but in any case the behaviour of parties in the early twenty-first century often makes discerning their position in that spectrum difficult. Romanian parties lack social bases and to say that they consist primarily of networks of individuals drawn together by economic incentives and past associations is not a great exaggeration. There are no true right-wing parties. Vadim's PRM is seen in the international context as a far-right phenomenon, but in Romania it derives much of its appeal from identifying with aspects of the national communist regime for which many people feel nostalgia. Romania lacks the class structure which can provide a strong base of support for successful social democratic, liberal or conservative parties. A tiny middle class is squeezed between an oligarchy which claims an ever-larger share of national wealth and millions of poor urban and rural dwellers. Except for the degree of urbanisation that has occurred subsequently, this class structure increasingly resembles that of the pre-1945 era. Romania is becoming a polarised society, which makes it a highly favourable arena for populist politics. The growth of a dispossessed peasantry and a working class facing mounting economic in security make Romania's ability to sustain a viable democratic system highly questionable. Membership of the EU and NATO draw closer, but these may offer no tangible economic benefits for most of the population for a long time to come. Indeed, it should not be hard for an anti-system party like the PRM to depict

Euro-Atlantic integration as a form of modernisation imposed from outside which is alien to Romania's true needs, a discourse which enjoyed powerful appeal before 1945 when parliamentary democracy was described in these terms by the radical right.[15]

Voters often judge politicians on their ability to speak their language and reflect their hopes and frustrations. Vadim, by building up an image as an inveterate foe of corruption, manages to be perceived as a genuine man of the people, despite his wealth and links with dubious figures in politics and business both before and after 1989. Future trends in Romanian politics are likely to assist national populists, whether or not Vadim is their standard-bearer. The legacy of authoritarian collectivism allows the army and the church to remain the most prestigious institutions in the eyes of the electorate. Successive polling surveys place them at the top, despite the lack of evidence that they have played any conspicuous role in assisting Romania to climb out of the crisis in which it has been in for several decades past. By contrast, Parliament and the political parties, the sinews of formal democracy in Romania, are usually the most despised institutions irrespective of who is in power.

Worryingly, the education system in Romania mirrors some of the worst authoritarian aspects of politics. Education is an area on which the EU and domestic civil society should have focussed their energies in order to create a strong body of support among the best educated of the younger generation for Romania's engagement, both with mainstream Europe and with the democratisation process. Instead, many students in the universities (especially those in the private sector) are demoralised and find no outlet for their energies. Old-fashioned teaching methods remain the norm in many faculties where a more diverse approach to education could ensure much better results. Not a few professors rely on authoritarian means of control to impose their will on students, and abuses of their position which would create an outcry in most EU countries are usually accepted rather than denounced. Student associations fail to defend the human rights of students perhaps because these minor office-holders are grooming themselves for membership of hierarchical professions such as law, public administration and education where they in turn will be able to impose their will on subalterns.

If international bodies and domestic NGOs with a democratisation agenda were to direct a greater amount of energy at education,

more talented and socially responsible young people could be encouraged to engage in public activism rather than shun such involvement. For many years Romania's education budget has been one of
the smallest in Europe. Targeted assistance for institutions willing to
be innovative in learning methods, and allow students greater influence over the conditions they experience at university, could begin
to create a more participatory political culture. Education is perhaps
the key institution which could enable large numbers of Romanians
to internalise values which have enabled countries like Finland (with
far less natural resources) to promote sustainable economic development. But the EU pre-accession roadmap contains few provisions
for education. Indeed Brussels has stood aside as the government has
taken funds away from the meagre education budget to comply
with NATO and EU requirements in other administrative areas. It
also appears nonchalant in the face of mounting evidence that the
Leonardo da Vinci fund for vocational training has, in a growing
number of instances, been looted by a consortium of Western and
Romanian academics and NGOs.[16]

By their tendency to abstain, or vote in large numbers for the
PRM, in December 2000 Romanian youth fully displayed their unwillingness to get involved in a political system from which they feel
alienated. Such alienation is not confined solely to them, but its dangerous effects have been held in check by the power of television to
tranquillise society. The main private channels are owned by entrepreneurs dependent on the goodwill of the PSD, not least because of
the debts which in some cases they owe to the state. Increasingly
television schedules are dominated by game shows, violent crime
series imported from abroad, and programmes with a nationalist
slant often fronted by leading personalities. Such programme matter
diverts viewers from critically assessing the behaviour of the powerful and how it affects their lives. In different countries with high levels of inequality and injustice, the domination of such forms of
television encourages political passivity and serves as a handy tool for
a selfish ruling élite.

The rural–urban divide is also a worrying social trend; factory closures have resulted in a steady flow of people returning to the land
who can benefit from the restitution of land that occurred in the
1990s. Already before the land redistribution of the 1990s 35% of all

jobs were in the agricultural sector, but a precarious living at subsistence level is probably what awaits most returnees.[17] All Romanian governments since 1990 have continued the longstanding neglect of agriculture which was a feature of the communist and pre-communist era. Early indications suggest that the beneficiaries of agricultural assistance from the EU worth €300 million (between 2001 and 2003) are going to be large-scale owners and those who have turned former state farms into lucrative private enterprises, not small farmers.[18]

The communist regime turned the Romanian peasantry into an agricultural proletariat, thereby creating a new form of wholesale dependence on the state.[19] But it does not appear that the successor state is prepared to carry out its obligations to a vulnerable section of the population facing rising illiteracy, declining health standards, and a collapse in its ability to generate income (because of the smallness of most rural holdings). Social assistance programmes introduced in 2002 by a nervous government to ward off possible unrest arising from a projected large rise in fuel bills are targeted at the urban poor. A long time will elapse before many rural dwellers benefit from the EU-sponsored Sapard development programme designed to promote sustainable agriculture. The ministry of agriculture only devised an implementation strategy in mid-2002 when there was a real concern that Romanian inefficiency would cause the EU to cancel the aid. This was a damaging oversight: in 2000 no less than 40% of the Romanian labour force were employed in agriculture but the sector only contributed 12% of GDP (compared with Bulgaria where 26% were found in that sector which contributed 17% of GDP in 1999). Bulgaria's rural development plan for 2000–6 was one of the first from a candidate state to be approved by the EU.[20]

It will be fascinating to observe if the EU preference for concentrating rural holdings in the interests of efficiency has the unintended result of reviving the boier class of landowners (this time drawn from ex-communist oligarchs). There could be a political price to be paid for neglecting the rural world. Polling evidence in the summer of 2002 suggested that the PRM was making striking gains among rural communities, especially in Moldavia.[21] Previously inhabitants of rural communes and small towns which had experienced forced collectivisation and industrialisation had been a solid support group for the PSD (except in Transylvania). But that might be changing, especially given the tendency for not a few PSD mayors in these places to distribute social welfare among their own family, friends and political supporters.[22] With the mainstream opposition discredited, Vadim's party appears to be the only force capable of channelling rural despair to its own advantage.

So far it is EU pressure that has resulted in such heavily contested laws as those concerning the removal of the ban on adult homosexual relations, and the restitution of property to former owners (however imperfect the final version), being passed in Romania. Now the EU has concluded that Romania is becoming a normal place politically. It even allows the government to distribute Brussels money set aside for Romanian NGOs, assuming that this will be done in an even-handed manner. Foreign donors are now withdrawing their funds from NGOs with a proven record of effectiveness, because they trust the EU assessment of the situation.

Iliescu in the 1990s hankered after a kind of 'third way' in which a dominant party in charge of a mainly state-led economy tolerated pluralist mechanisms but made sure that its grip on power would never be in danger. Alina Mungiu-Pippidi has referred to 'a sort of political corporatism' being his preferred option.[23] Ironically, Romania may be much closer in the early 2000s to a politically corporatist model than it was in 1990, notwithstanding pressure from international institutions to deepen and widen political pluralism. Politicians active from the ruling party who are in business and commerce share power with large entrepreneurs and speculators, many with *nomenklatura* backgrounds. The formal opposition is depleted but the danger of resentment among competitors has been reduced by dangling money-making opportunities in front of many businessmen active in the PNL and previously the PD. Much of this funding originates from the EU, which has promoted consensus among previously warring elements in Romanian politics at the expense of the material well-being of ordinary citizens.

Voters are uncomfortable with freewheeling political competition. It makes an uneasy contrast to the authoritarian arrangements which they have become used to in politics, education and other aspects of social life. Few can remember a time when regular political competition proved beneficial for Romania. Certainly the 1996–2000 administrations did not inspire confidence in controlled competition.

Polls in the late 1990s showed nostalgia for one-party rule or out-right dictatorship to an unsettling degree. It is hard to argue that Romania has witnessed a steady strengthening of the fragile democracy ushered in under controversial and confused circumstances in 1989–90. On the positive side, free and fair elections have resulted in the substitution in office of the governing parties (and two Presidents) in two successive elections. Freedom of expression exists within limits as does associational autonomy and civilian control of the armed forces. These are some of the minimal procedural conditions for democracy formulated by the American political scientist Robert Dahl. In adapting them to post-communist Eastern Europe Mary Kaldor and Ivan Vejvoda also emphasised the rule of law, the separation of powers and inclusive citizenship, each of which is incomplete or retarded in Romania.[24]

Moving away from procedures to political behaviour, the situation is hardly more reassuring. The PSD, the lineal successor of the FSN and PDSR, seems reconciled to democracy at procedural level, but it displays monopolistic tendencies and is only willing to strengthen pluralist arrangements under external pressure. *The low level of public pressure for reform and renewal is a matter for real concern.*[25] It could at least be said of the Phanariots and the Moscow-groomed communists that they were largely outsiders in the land they set about reducing. But that cannot be said of the several thousand individuals elected to the Romanian Parliament since 1990 in increasingly free and fair elections. However much Romanians may be tempted to view them as a separate caste, these elected representatives come from their own ranks.

Romania still lacks a political culture in which there is widespread support for democratic institutions and practices. Until 1989 it did have a culture of dependence in which most citizens were willing to endure colossal mistreatment from the state, and it remains to be seen to what extent this has been eroded by the liberalisation of the 1990s. But popular resignation as successive bank failures, investment fund scams and pyramid saving dodges have robbed millions of their savings suggests that the sense of dependence may actually be getting stronger. Most of the time resignation rather than outrage greets the latest disclosures about the misdeeds of an economic élite consisting of between 3,000 and 5,000 businessmen who have grown rich, in

some cases fabulously so, by obtaining preferential contracts and unsecured credits from the state. In an editorial written on the first anniversary of the PSD's return to power, entitled 'A golden future is
what our country doesn't have', Cornel Nistorescu argued despairingly that the any hope of material improvements lay in those who
had plundered the state, growing 'richer and richer until they have
more than they need *and only then will they raise wages.*'[26] Meanwhile,
a virtuous official rhetoric based around sham patriotism conceals
the 'grab-what-you-can' ethos which enables the new oligarchy to
flourish. Well-placed officials contemplate the ruination of historic
towns like Sighisoara by creating a money-making 'Dracula Park' or
collude in bids to despoil parts of the Apuseni mountains whose
Romanian villages epitomise venerable traditions. International pressure (and the campaign of one effective domestic NGO, the Liga
Pro-Europa) killed the first scheme, which had clearly shown that
the desire for architectural vandalism had not been confined to
Ceauşescu. But the bid to create a huge open-cast gold mine in historic Ţara Moţilor seems to be well on course and in late 2002 its
main sponsor even financed a NATO-sponsored meeting in Romania. With such political and business ethics prevalent, international sustainers of reform in Romania who think that a transparent
market economy will soon emerge are deluding themselves.

In the early 1960s Gabriel Almond and Sydney Verba explored
the link between political culture and democratic systems,[27] developing the theory of a civic culture in which there is a high level of
trust among the public and basic support for democratic arrangements despite dissatisfaction with particular office-holders.[28] Polls
show that in Romania such trust is significantly absent. It has also
declined in long-established Western democracies since the 1960s
but not to the degree seen in Romania (and these countries usually
have stabilising factors, absent in Romania, which prevents a collapse
in support for free institutions, such as a viable economy and a dense
web of associational activity). De-democratisation is an option for
states experimenting with pluralist arrangements, and in Romania it
cannot be ruled out. Currently the most optimistic scenario would
suggest a lengthy period of transition in which democratic arrangements face regular stiff tests, before eventually sinking durable roots.
As long as firm and focused external support for Romania's experiment

continues, the chances of it slowly consolidating its democratic system may be moderately good. But if the EU project suffers important setbacks, then the health of Romanian democracy would soon suffer too.

It can also not be assumed that the democratic process will automatically be deepened once Romania finds itself under the NATO umbrella. Concern over an increasingly monopolistic attitude to power by the ruling party steadily increased in 2002, but without endangering the invitation to open accession talks with NATO made in November. It is reasonable to assume that these residual authoritarian forces will remain strong once the country's internal affairs cease to be routinely monitored by NATO officials. If rulers see democracy as an inconvenience to be tolerated in order to satisfy external patrons rather than as a key component of a value system Romania needs to install in order to make a complete break with a totalitarian past, entry to neither NATO nor the EU will place decisive checks on authoritarian behaviour of a serious kind.

Post-1859 Romania has yet to see the birth of a political party capable of turning the values and aspirations with which it may have been launched as a capable opposition force into a viable strategy for government. All too often, party leaders, their lieutenants, district officials and youth members are driven by the need to obtain material well-being through political activity. Ideology and programmes count for very little. The stampede of the most opportunistic defectors towards the PSD after 2000 shows how the need to divert public or European money into private hands is an all-consuming preoccupation. Indeed, it is hardly an exaggeration to claim that capturing the state and diverting part of its resources towards an individual and his retinue, or a faction, are the sinews of Romanian politics. As a result, contemporary parties have a weak identity and a low standing in the eyes of the electorate. It is difficult to create free institutions capable of enduring when the gratification of individual appetites preoccupies the Romanian political élite to the extent that prevails well over a decade after the events of 1989.

In the mid-nineteenth century Alexis de Tocqueville warned that democracy can degenerate into despotism when elected officials seek office for gain at the public expence.[29] In Romania low standards in high places have produced widespread disillusionment with democracy and elevated authoritarian forces which would gladly extinguish it completely. The mainstream opposition is inert, and it appears quite possible that the country might be absorbed into NATO and the EU with authoritarian structures left substantially intact.

The tenor of the statements emanating from Brussels and EU member-states in 2003 suggested that Romania's chances of joining the EU in 2007 had risen dramatically. This is due to the patronage of powerful EU members enjoyed by the Năstase government rather than any capacity or willingness to comply with EU entry terms. Romania has difficulties in absorbing EU funds due to poor administrative capacity. One of the main EU instruments for transformation relies on a curious process known as twinning whereby several thousand officials are sent to do advanced degrees in Western universities, or be interns in Western ministries and institutes. The hope is that they will return to their posts ready to implement Western management processes and a public-service-orientated bureaucracy will emerge. It is unclear to what extent the acquisition of new skills will strengthen the capacity of the Romanian state. Under the PSD, the chances are that if officials adopted a public service (rather than a pro-PSD approach) to their job, they would be punished. The way the EU's pre-accession instruments—Phare, Ispa and Sapard—have sometimes been implemented does not provide convincing proof that they are adequate for overcoming massive problems inherited from communism and a decade of non-reform. It is alarming to think that the EU's hopes of transforming the Romanian state rest on such a flimsy basis.

In 2000–1 the PSD endured critical evaluations by the EU, which continued to highlight problems in the justice system and the fight against corruption. The ruling party was then true to the old Romanian proverb 'Be nice to the devil until you have crossed the bridge', but when the EU ambassador, Jonathan Scheele, was told by Năstase in December 2002 to mind his own business because he had expressed concern at the government's refusal to carry out EU-funded infrastructural improvements in Bucharest (because the money would be used by the opposition mayor), it was clear that Romania had 'crossed the bridge' and that the PSD no longer needed to be polite to the EU's most senior representative in Romania. The powerful support for Romanian entry to the EU from Britain, Italy and Spain appeared to nullify the Commission's concerns, particularly over whether Romania still adhered to the political criteria for EU entry. It is no coincidence that Italy is Romania's most vocal champion. It is already benefiting enormously from the way the Romanian market of over 20 million people has been opened up to its goods and services. It is hard to see how Romania will become a functioning market economy if one of the main results of EU entry is a flood of cheaper and better—produced goods (not only from Italy) which Romanian producers will be powerless to match.

In 2003 the PSD want through the motions of reform, displaying the old Romanian approach to governance: 'form without content'. The only prominent victim of the anti-corruption watchdog, formed after much EU prodding in 2002, has been a judge widely felt to be among the more honest in her profession. Local journalists are assaulted openly in the street in areas of the country where there is no check on PSD power.[30] The day before one such incident, Jonathan Scheele admitted in a press interview the limited influence the EU was able to exert over Romania.[31] No longer fearing that Brussels would suspend negotiations or make entry conditions more onerous, top officials are increasingly brazen in their approach to EU funds.[32] Directing these funds, amounting to € 4.6 billion, to a country governed by an oligarchy to which the concept of public service is alien might be seen in some quarters as a major stimulus for corruption. The EU doesn't seem keen to ask itself why office-holders in Bucharest agree to its roadmap: they would be marginalized if Romania were to adopt reforms of the kind Eastern Germany has seen since German re-unification. However, they are confident that they can get around the roadmap and make sure that its tough features are simply never implemented. If Jonathan Scheele (one of the better international officials active in Romania since 1989) can say 'The chances of Romania entering the EU in 2007 have grown … because the process of reform has continued and, in some cases, accelerated', then it is obvious why the PSD feels confident.[33]

It is possible that even under party bosses formed in the communist era and business sharks, Romania will be transformed inside the EU because of the attraction exercised by the quite well-governed larger states that dominate the Union. Parties with a Western approach and firms practising good business ethics could, in tandem with foreign companies interested in more than the quick extraction of profits, groom an alternative élite who within a few decades could attain dominance. This is the hope of the mainstream opposition and civil society which continue to back entry even if the PSD should be in the driving-seat. Only a few questioning voices recall that in the 1970s there was optimism that closer ties with the West would liberalise the communist system. Instead Western endorsement was used by Ceauşescu as a cover to tighten repression. In 2002 the EU did virtually nothing when at the G-8 summit in the Italian city of Genoa the local police carried out orders to beat up a large number of peaceful protesters while they were sleeping in their beds. This is what Romanians would call a *mineriada* after the miners' rampages of the 1990s against anti-communist opponents, usually with the blessing of the state. If the Italian state can get away with such tactics, then it is likely that few eyebrows would be raised in Brussels if the government in Bucharest were to carry out similar actions against its opponents.

Brussels remained tight-lipped when the Romanian government used irregular methods in October 2003 to make sure of the 50% turnout required in a referendum on the revised constitution. Năstase correctly assumed that the European Commission would overlook multiple voting in some PSD strongholds, mobile voting booths in supermarkets and railway stations, and tombolas outside voting stations, since these dubious methods were in a good cause: the ratification of a constitution enabling Romania to sign the EU accession treaties. It remains to be seen if the EU has given birth to a monster, with the PSD assuming that it will overlook electoral fraud in forthcoming national elections.

The PSD appeared to suffer a stinging rebuke at the hands of Brussels on 11 March 2004 when the European Parliament endorsed a report strongly criticising the government's record in fighting corruption and ensuring the independence of the media and the judiciary. It warned that EU accession in 2007 would be imperilled unless Năstase and his ministers took seriously their reform obligations. The EU declared that it was re-orientating its strategy, concentrating its attention on the above critical areas. But by the summer candid EU officials were admitting that 're-orientation' was simply a device to pacify the redoubtable Baroness Nicholson who had authored the critical report on discovering that the government was flouting its promises not to send abroad children who were in state care.

Mischie, the PSD baron from Gorj was sacrificed in order to appease Brussels. But other far more important figures, who had been the subject of criminal enquiries for years over large-scale financial fraud, continued to be left unscathed. The PSD appeared confident that the June local elections would confirm its invincibility prior to November's major elections. To be absolutely on the safe side, it stepped up pressure on public officials and private businessmen to identify with the party and shun the opposition. It tightened its grip on television and it also backed spoiling parties designed to fragment opposition to the PSD in the cities. But the PSD was outvoted by the Alliance for Truth and Justice, a coalition of the PNL and PD formed the previous autumn. 65.4% of mayors had belonged to the PSD due to defections from other parties, but after two rounds of voting this had fallen to 28%, (with 36% for its chief opponent).

A road disaster at Mihaileşti on 24 May had brought much adverse publicity to the PSD when ministers came on the scene and ordered that the remains of 19 victims be asphalted over in order to allow traffic to resume on a busy road link. The gesture encapsulated the arrogance of the ruling party towards the population and the best-known opposition figure, Traian Băsescu took full advantage of it. He crushed Geoana, the foreign minister who had been unwisely pushed into the Bucharest mayoral race. The capital fell to the Alliance which also ejected Funar in Cluj, the victor being the PD's Emil Boc. In its Moldavian fiefdom, the PSD lost ground, the mayor of Bacau, Dumitru Sechelariu (who epitomised the vulgarity of the PSD *arriviste*) needing a police escort to avoid the voters wrath.

A month of infighting and recriminations within the PSD followed. Cosmetic changes involving a cabinet reshuffle and a shake-up of the party's top echelons could not disguise the feeling of panic; electoral defeat appeared an imminent prospect with shadow companies already being constructed to divert the unprecedented amount of EU funds due to pour into the country in 2005. On 5 July Iliescu completely disregarded the constitutional rule that a President does not interfere in domestic party politics and heavily criticised Năstase in front of his senior colleagues. A tense five days followed when it appeared that the Prime Minister was on the verge of resigning and preparing to go to war with Iliescu for control of the party. Difficulties were patched up with the advantage resting with Năstase who secured a freer hand to prepare for difficult elections.

Three months earlier, Iliescu's prestige had been at its zenith. Romania had joined NATO and the USA appeared poised to announce the creation of military bases near Constanta. He was also the subject of a praiseworthy biography which appeared to mark the submission of much of formerly critical intellectual opinion before him. Vladimir Tismăneanu who wrote it in collaboration with the President, was a leading historian based at the University of Maryland who commanded great influence over publications, grant awards, and appointments both in Romania and the USA. He had previously been a champion of democratic civil society who had once described the structure of power under Iliescu as 'a populist, corporatist and semi-fascist type'.[34] But in his 2004 work he saluted Iliescu as 'a symbol of...the pluralist left' in Romania who had a major responsibility for consolidating democracy.[35]

Iliescu appeared poised to entice a wide range of former opponents into his camp with deft use of patronage, and even groom a new generation of intellectuals ready to accommodate themselves to the PSD. But Tismăneanu's audacious bid to revise history's verdict on Iliescu, stoked furious controversy, culminating in the denunciation of both men by Şerban Papacostea, the eminent historian and survivor of 1950s labour camps.[36] Withering criticism of Iliescu also came from the independent media, especially when his role in ousting Paul Florea, the only independent-minded senior judge left on the bench, emerged.[37] The PD and PNL leaders boycotted their regular consultations with the President on 16 July 2004 because of his perceived misuse of his office. But it was non-political figures that citizens eager to be free of the PSD, turned to for inspiration: the outgoing US ambassador, Michael Guest, the fearless press editor Cornel Nistorescu, and Archbihop Pimen, of Suceava and Radauti in Moldavia who accused Iliescu and his fellow PSD leaders of being 'strangers to...religious and patriotic sentiments. They are the leftovers of the communist party'.[38]

What appeared likely to save the PSD, or at least limit its losses, was the failure of the opposition to carry out an internal transformation that made it an attractive alternative. The Alliance (above all the

PNL) was ready to recycle discredited figures from the last government rather than bring forward untarnished and capable young people. The inner life of the PNL seemed similar to the PSD in some
respects with a few chiefs dominating an obedient membership and
nearly all alive to the spoils of office. The PD offered more hope of
renewal but it was the junior partner in the Alliance. If the PNL's
Theodor Stolojan won the presidential elections, the PSD might
still be able to form a government with the support of smaller parties
(including Vadim's PRM). And, in the event of the Alliance forming the government with smaller parties, such as the UDMR (itself
now an oligarchic force), the prospects for deep-seated reform looked
meagre. Writing four months before the November 2004 contest,
new faces may well emerge and the threat of a PSD 'silent dictatorship' seems to have receded. The leaders of the PSD devoted too
much time to acquiring personal fortunes than to creating a party of
domination. It is more an improvised party of power, its lust for
money distorting its outlook and blunting its ruthlessness. But Romania appears to be far away from witnessing the break up of the
ruling structures which interests from the communist era painstak-
ingly created in the 1990s and further refined with the help of EU
money and turncoat figures after 2000. Millions of voters are impa-
tient for change and go into the 2004 elections with less illusions
about the PSD and far more anger about its conduct than was the
case in 1996. But its domination of the state machine is stronger
than ever and the opposition against it inspires less confidence than
in 1996. Indeed much of the opposition is infiltrated by forces ultimately loyal to the PSD, or amenable to its overtures. New parties
are planned which will be its satellites. The football mogul Gigi
Becali has established a cult of personality reminiscent of communist
times, his New Generation Party being launched with the help of
Dan Pavel, a leading social scientist and press columnist.[39] Despite
the readiness of intellectuals circling in the PSD orbit to describe
Romania as a consolidated democracy, it is far from being that and
the uninspired engagement of the EU appears to have made it less
pluralist since 2000. Romanian voters have shown maturity and
courage, in some cases, in confronting the PSD but they have very
little to thank the EU for. Its attempts to absorb Romania on flexible terms in 2007 or soon after only strengthens the authoritarian

features of Romania politics and gives a powerful boost to the corruption which has been completely impervious to its token controls.

The EU is writing a vital page in Romanian history. In 2002 and 2003 it received incontrovertible evidence that the PSD and its satellites prefer to loot EU funds and ignore key aspects of its road map for EU entry. If Romania's rulers will only pay lip-service to much of its reform package and then discard it after entry, the EU is doing a great disservice to Romanians and placing the well-being of its own ambitious strategy for Europe in some jeopardy. The EU is contributing to the growth of inequality at a very harmful rate by the often careless way it allows its pre-accession funds to be used. Its roadmap for Romania includes little provision to assist the elderly and will leave groups like peasants and unskilled urban workers worse off. This increases the risk of a nationalist backlash *after* Romania enters the EU, a period when it is supposed to become a normal country politically.

It is ironic that an outside power, the EU, is repeating some of the same mistakes made by a much less welcome overlord, the Soviet Union, by insisting on the implementation of a blueprint for change, crucial elements of which may be unsuitable for Romania's needs. Unlike the Russians, the EU is giving as well as taking and there is far more genuine goodwill towards Romania. This goodwill can surely be harnessed to seek a modification of the accession terms where it is clear that they harm rather than benefit Romanian society. When Brussels says 'We have a plan that will solve all problems if implemented in the way we recommend', the managerial mindset associated with Comecom and other ill-starred Soviet projects comes forcibly to mind.

Marxism-Leninism as practised by the Ceauşescus, and the pursuit of wealth by their post-communist successors, has left a moral void in Romania. It has become a political and economic jungle where only the fittest survive. An array of techniques has been devised subtly to subvert democracy and leave the nation's wealth in few hands. A sense of social obligation to the weakest in society is rapidly disappearing. Unscrupulous demagogues are left to sketch a national vision and the weakest and most vulnerable are drawn to them. Very few from the mainstream opposition and even civil society are able to articulate a vision that depicts a sustainable economic future embracing the whole of society. Instead they wait like stranded passengers on a slowly sinking ship for salvation courtesy of the EU rescue service which is blind to the harmful implications of some of its key prescriptions for Romania.

The mishandling of Romania's difficult exit from communism poses real problems for European stability and is no longer a domestic or even a Balkan concern. It will be ironic if the principal outcome of the EU's engagement with Romania is decisively to consolidate the influence of a ruling élite that regrouped upon the fall of communism in 1989. If this happens, the EU will be reinforcing the historical traditions and methods that have made Romania synonymous with bad governance throughout much of its history.

Epilogue

To the surprise of the EU and probably most resident Western diplomats in Bucharest, the PSD failed to consolidate its hold on power in the elections at the end of 2004. In the parliamentary elections of 28 November the PSD was the largest party, but far short of an overall majority. Moreover, ballot-rigging had occurred, as was shown by an investigation by Mircea Kivu of the IMAS polling institute. It involved special lists for people voting outside their place of residence and spoiled ballots. At polling stations where a large proportion of the vote was cast on special lists, or where an unusually large proportion of the votes were invalid, the PSD won by a margin of some 20%. However, where there was a low proportion of special-list votes or spoiled ballots, victory went to the Alliance by a margin of some 3%.

International pressure, particularly from the United States, resulted in a clean second presidential round on 14 December. The narrow winner was Traian Băsescu who had replaced Stolojan when he dropped out of the presidential race in October on grounds of ill-health. Băsescu had fought a populist campaign, promising real reforms and the break-up of a corrupt system of patronage that only benefited narrow interests. He established his mastery of events by insisting that the Alliance was the real winner and that he would dissolve parliament and call fresh elections if an Alliance-led government was not formed. On 27 December 2004 Calin Popescu-Tariceanu, the interim leader of the Liberals (PNL), formed a government which included, as well as Băsescu's PD, two small parties which had sided with the PSD in the elections: Voiculescu's PUR and the UDMR.

It included as justice minister, the well-known human rights lawyer Monica Macovei, signalling the intention to take justice reform seriously. Indeed the EU, under a new enlargement commissioner, Olli Rehn of Finland, believed that progress in this area would determine whether Romania could join the EU in 2007. When negotiations were formally concluded in mid-December he obtained the agreement of the European parliament for the imposition of a safeguard clause which required broad and demonstrable progress in reform of the judiciary and also the strengthening of competition policy in order for entry not to be delayed till 2008.

The accession treaty between Romania and the EU was formally signed in Luxemburg on 25 April 2005, but growing resistance to further enlargement left open the possibility that membership would be postponed beyond 2008 probably through the national parliament of a country like France refusing to give its binding approval. Judicial reform was blocked in the first half of 2005. With the support of the PSD and its new leader Mircea Geoana, the Constitutional Court (stuffed with personalities who had served Iliescu in differing capacities) rejected government proposals for judicial reform that had the explicit support of the EU. The government was not in control of its own legislative programme since the heads of both houses of parliament were the two previous PSD Prime Ministers, Năstase and Văcaroiu. They had been kept in place by the junior partners in the government, thus demonstrating how disunited it was. Pressure for a government of national unity—which would be dominated by the PSD because of its continuing control over much of the local state, the economy and the central bureaucracy—was strong in the summer of 2005. Alliance parliamentarians, particularly in the PNL, showed a lack of combativeness towards the PSD which resumed the political offensive after a period of internal troubles. An unpopular and irresolute government under Tariceanu has not disturbed the PSD's still intact networks of local power. Unless early elections are able to give the Alliance, or an alternative reformist bloc, a clear-cut governing majority, the real danger exists that the PSD will return to power after a brief interregnum in opposition. By its seventh month in office, rising prices, disastrous floods in the spring and summer of 2005, and the unimpressive performance of a string of government ministers had weakened the Tariceanu government's credibility. Reformist hopes increasingly rested on President Băsescu, but it was unclear whether he had the control over key levers of state necessary to stem the corruption and trafficking of influence which blighted Romania's hopes of breaking free from its communist-era legacy.

July–August 2005

[pages 1–16]

NOTES

Introduction

1. Petr Kopecky and Cas Mudde, 'What has Eastern Europe taught us about the democratisation literature (and vice versa)?', *European Journal of Political Research*, vol. 37, pp. 518–19.
2. Leszek Balcerowicz, 'Understanding post-communist transitions' in Wojciech Kostecki *et al.*, *Transformations of Post-Communist States*, Basingstoke: Macmillan, 2000, p. 237.
3. The growth in political awareness is well-described in Aurelian Craiutu, 'Light at the end of the tunnel: Romania, 1989–1998' in T. Gallagher, and G. Pridham (eds), *Experimenting With Democracy: Regime Change in the Balkans*, London: Routledge, 2000, p. 184.
4. Romania: Annual Plan and Performance Review, London: Department of International Development (DFID) April 2001, p. 5.
5. J. Linz and A. Stepan, *Problems of Democratic Transition and Consolidation: South Europe, South America and Post-Communist Europe*, Baltimore: Johns Hopkins University Press, 1996, p. 6.
6. Jean Grugel, *Democratization: a Critical Introduction*, Houndmills: Palgrave, 2001, p. 243.
7. Tom Gallagher, 'The Balkans' in Stephen White *et al.*, *Developments in Central and East European Politics*, Basingstoke. Macmillan, 1998, pp. 44–5.
8. P. Nikiforos Diamandouros and F. Stephen Larrabee, 'Democratization in South-Eastern Europe: Theoretical considerations and evolving trends' in T. Gallagher and G. Pridham (eds), *Experimenting With Democracy: Regime Change in the Balkans*, London, Routledge, 2000, p. 29.
9. Tom Gallagher, *Romania after Ceauşescu: the Politics of Intolerance*, Edinburgh University Press, 1995, p. 32.
10. Grugel, *Democratization*, p. 30.
11. *Expres*, 18 October 1994.
12. 'Romania: Annual Plan and Performance Review, p. 3.
13. Institute for Democracy and Electoral Assistance, *Democracy in Romania: Assessment Mission Report*, Stockholm: International Idea, 1997, p. xiv.
14. Alison Mutler, 'Ill wishes for mayor who partied like lord', *The Independent*, 17 July 2002.
15. *The Economist*, in its issue of 2 March 2002, published two separate stories about flagrant economic inequality in one-party states which are still, or have been recently, Marxist-Leninist in composition. One described an Angola where

359

one-third of state revenues could not be accounted for while mass poverty abounded in one of the most mineral rich countries on earth; the other, about Laos, in which the Communist Party still enjoyed monopoly control, showed that 30.6% of the national wealth was in the hands of 10% of the population.

16. Declan Walsh, 'Angolan elite accused of 'squandering oil billions', *The Independent*, 23 August 2002.
17. United Nations, *Uncommon Opportunities: An Agenda For Peace and Equitable Development*, London: Zed Books, 1994.
18. *Romania, Country Report, 4th Quarter of 2000*, London: Economist Intelligence Unit, 2000.
19. Romania: Annual Plan and Performance Review, p. 6.
20. Robert Putnam, *Making Democracy Work: Civic Traditions in Modern Italy,* Princeton University Press 1993.
21. Putnam, *Making Democracy Work*, p. 181.
22. For the argument that the Saxons provided Romania with considerable social capital as well as a model for decentralized government, see Tom Gallagher, 'O critică a centralismului eşuat şi egotismului regional în România' in Gabriel Andreescu and Gusztáv Molnár (eds), *Problema transilvană*, Iasi: editura Polirom, 1999, pp. 112–3.
23. This is a point which the Romanian commentator Dan Pavel has occasionally made.
24. Putnam, *Making Democracy Work*, p. 145.

Chapter 1   Democracy Constrained by Backwardness

1. Keith Hitchins, *Rumania, 1866–1947*, Oxford University Press, 1994, p. 2.
2. Barbara Jelavich, *History of the Balkans: Eighteenth and Nineteenth Centuries,* Cambridge University Press 1983, p. 103.
3. See Viorel Achim, *Ţiganii în istoria României*, Bucharest: Editura Enciclopedica, 1998.
4. Hitchins, *Rumania…*, p. 4.
5. Hitchins, *Rumania…*, p. 295.
6. Henry L. Roberts, *Rumania: Political Problems of an Agrarian State*, New Haven: Yale University Press, 1951, p. 9.
7. Daniel Chirot, *Social Change in a Peripheral Society: the Creation of a Balkan Colony,* New York: Academic Press, 1976, p. 106.
8. Vlad Georgescu, *Istoria românilor. De la origini pînă in zilele noastre*, Bucharest: Humanitas, 1992, pp. 154–7.
9. Chirot, *Social Change…*, p. 111.
10. John Campbell, *French Influence and the Rise of Roumanian Nationalism*, New York: Arno Press, 1970, pp. 22–3 (Ph.D originally submitted to History Department, Harvard University, in 1940).
11. M. S. Anderson, *The Eastern Question, 1774–1923: a Study in International Relations,* London: Macmillan, 1966, pp. 150–1.
12. Jelavich, *History of the Balkans: Eighteenth and Nineteenth Centuries*, p. 293.
13. Hitchins, *Rumania…*, p. 13.

14. Hitchins, *Rumania...*, p. 13.
15. Frederick Kellogg, *The Road to Romanian Independence*, West Lafayette, IN: Purdue University Press, 1995, p. 175.
16. Hitchins, *Rumania*, pp. 25–6; Catherine Durandin, *Histoire des Roumains*, Paris: Fayard, 1995, pp. 183–4.
17. Hitchins, *Rumania*, p. 31.
18. Eugen Weber, 'Romania' in H. Rogger and E. Weber, *The European Right: a Historical Profile*, Berkeley: University of California Press, 1974, p. 538.
19. Hitchins, *Rumania*, p. 164.
20. Joseph L. Love, *Crafting the Third World: Theorising Underdevelopment in Rumania and Brazil*, Stanford University Press, 1996, p. 29.
21. Jelavich, *History of the Balkans: Eighteenth and Nineteenth Centuries*, p. 294.
22. Chirot, *Social Change*, p. 135.
23. Hitchins, *Rumania*, p. 169.
24. Ibid., p. 162.
25. Love, *Crafting the Third World*, p. 10.
26. Lucien Boia, *Istorie şi mit in constiinţa româneasca*, Bucharest: Humanitas 1997, pp. 92, 181.
27. L. S. Stavrianos, *The Balkans Since 1453*, London: Hurst, 2000 (1st publ. 1958), p. 484.
28. George Castellan, *History of the Balkans: from Mohammed the Conqueror to Stalin*, New York: Columbia University Press, 1992, pp. 139–40.
29. Catherine Durandin, *Histoire des Roumains*, Paris: Fayard, 1995, p. 181.
30. Love, *Crafting the Third World*, p. 28.
31. Hitchins, *Rumania*, pp. 171–2.
32. Constantin Iordachi, '"La California des Roumains", l'intégration de la Dobrudja du Nord à la Roumanie, 1878–1913', *Balkanologie*, Vol. 6, Nos 1 & 2, December 2002, p. 189.
33. Hitchins, *Rumania*, p. 109.
34. Florin Constantiniu, *O Istorie Sincera a Poporului Român*, Bucharest: Univers Enciclopedic, 1997, p. 239.
35. Hitchins, *Rumania*, p. 63.
36. Durandin, *Histoire des Roumains*, p. 199.
37. Chirot, *Social Change*, p. 125.
38. Ibid., p. 150.
39. Ibid., p. 103.
40. Hitchins, *Rumania*, pp. 177–8.
41. Chirot, *Social Change...*, pp. 150–5.
42. Roberts, *Rumania*, p. 4.
43. Hitchins, *Rumaniam*, p. 136.
44. Ibid., p. 126.
45. Robert Bideleux and Ian Jeffries, *Eastern Europe: Crisis and Change*, London: Routledge, 1998, p. 40.
46. Alina Mungiu-Pippidi, *Politica Dupa Communism*, Bucharest: Humanitas, 2002, p. 158.

47. Ioan Scurtu and Gheorghe Buzatu, *Istoria Românilor In Secolul XX*, Bucharest: Paideia, 1996, p. 22.
48. Durandin, *Histoire des Roumains*, p. 276.
49. Paul Lendvai, *Eagles in Cobwebs: Nationalism and Communism in the Balkans*, London: Macdonald, 1969, p. 24.
50. Irina Livezeanu, *Cultural Politics in Greater Romania*, Ithaca, NY: Cornell University Press, 1995, p. 297.
51. Scurtu and Buzatu, *Istoria Românilorm*, p. 36.
52. Hitchins, *Rumaniam*, p. 219.
53. Tom Gallagher, *Outcast Europe: the Balkans from the Ottomans to Milosevic, 1789–1989*, London: Routledge, 2001, pp. 92–3.
54. Hitchins, *Rumania*, p. 410.
55. Gallagher, *Romania After Ceauşescu*, p. 26.
56. Roberts, *Rumania*, p. 39.
57. A. L. Cartwright, *The Return of the Peasant: Land reform in post-communist Romania*, Aldershot (UK): Ashgate, 2001, pp. 34–5.
58. Roberts, *Rumania*, p. 124.
59. H. Hessell Tiltman, *Peasant Europe*, London: Jarrolds, 1936, pp. 112–13.
60. Scurtu and Buzatu, *Istoria Românilor*, p. 147.
61. Livezeanu, *Cultural Politics*, p. 21.
62. Hitchins, *Rumania*, p. 414.
63. Ibid., p. 382.
64. Sorin Alexandrescu, *Paradoxul Român*, Bucharest: Univers, 1998, p. 280.
65. Fischer-Galati, *20th Century Rumania*, p. 45.
66. Alexandrescu, *Paradoxul Român*, p. 113.
67. Nagy-Talavera, *N. Iorga*, p. 283.
68. Scurtu and Buzatu, *Istoria Românilor*, p. 49.
69. Love, *Crafting the Third World*, p. 78.
70. Ibid., p. 94.
71. Michel Sturdza, *The Silence of Europe*, Boston, MA: Watchtower Books, 1968.
72. Nagy-Talavera, *N. Iorga* p. 362.
73. Hitchins, *Rumania*, p. 306.
74. Scurtu and Buzatu, *Istoria Românilor*, p. 31.
75. Lucjan Blit, *The Eastern Pretender: the Story of Boleslaw Piasecki*, London: Hutchinson, 1965.
76. Matei Calinescu, 'Ionesco and Rhinoceros: Personal and Political Backgrounds', *East European Politics and Societies*, vol. 9, no. 3, fall 1995, pp. 410–1.
77. Eugen Weber, 'The Men of the Archangel', in George Mosse (ed), *International Fascism*, London: Sage, 1979, p. 319.
78. Hitchins, *Rumania…*, p. 404.
79. Roberts, *Rumania*, p. 345.
80. Weber, 'The Men of the Archangel', p. 323.
81. Ibid., p. 322.
82. Fischer-Galati, *20th Century Rumania*, New York: Columbia University Press, 1991 edn, p. 57.
83. Ioan Scurtu, *Istoria Partidului Natiojnal Taranesc*, Bucharest: Ed. Enciclopedica, 1994, p. 313.

84. Zvi Yavetz, 'An Eyewitness Note: Reflections on the Rumanian Iron Guard' in J. Reinharz and G. Mosse (eds), *The Impact of Western Nationalisms*, London: Sage, 1992, p. 251.
85. Scurtu and Buzatu, *Istoria Românilor*, p. 333.
86. R. G. Waldeck, *Athene Palace Bucharest: Hitler's 'New Order' comes to Rumania*, London: Constable, 1943, p. 79.
87. Radu Ioanid, *The Holocaust in Romania: the Destruction of Jews and Gypsies under the Antonescu Regime, 1940–1944*, Chicago: Ivan R. Dee, 2000, p. 18.
88. Joseph Rothschild, *East-Central Europe between the Two World Wars*, Seattle: University of Washington Press, 1974, p. 311.
89. Hitchins, *Rumania*, p. 422.
90. Alexandrescu, *Paradoxul Român*, p. 105.
91. Ibid., p. 135.
92. See Mihail Sebastian, *Journal 1935–1944: the Fascist Years*, Chicago: Ivan R. Dee, 2000, pp. 139–299.
93. Hitchins, *Rumania*, p. 453.
94. Fischer-Galati, *20th Century Rumania*, p. 63.
95. *Monitorul*, 13 January 2001.
96. Ibid.
97. Ioanid, *The Holocaust in Romania*, pp. 70–7.
98. Ibid., pp. 178–9.
99. Michael Burleigh, *The Third Reich: a New History*, London: Pan, 2001, p. 657.
100. Burleigh, *The Third Reich*, p. 658.
101. Ioanid, *The Holocaust in Romania*, pp. 291–2.
102. Durandin, *Histoire des Roumains*, p. 331.
103. Hitchins, *Rumania*, p. 499.
104. Ivor Porter, *Operatiunea "Autonomous"*, Bucharest: Humanitas, 1990, p. 296.
105. *Enciclopedica Romaniei*, Bucharest, 1940, vol. 3, p. 651, quoted in a letter to *22* (Bucharest weekly), 26 June–2 July 2001, from Prof. Dan Stanescu.
106. See Tom Gallagher, *Outcast Europe*, pp. 168–9, for the argument that a different approach to Romania by the Western Allies, or a realisation by King Mihai that he and his country had been abandoned by them, could have saved Romania from some of the worst effects of the communist system.

Chapter 2   Return to Underdevelopment: The Imposition and Consequences of Communist Rule

1. R. V. Burks, *The Dynamics of Communism In Eastern Europe*, Princeton University Press, 1961, pp. 164–5.
2. Şerban Papacostea, 'Captive Clio: Romanian Historiography Under Communist Rule', *European History Quarterly*, vol. 26, 1996, p. 181.
3. Dennis Deletant, *Communist Terror in Romania: Gheorghiu Dej and the Police State, 1948–1965*, London: Hurst 1999, p. 5.
4. Robert Levy, *Ana Pauker: The Rise and Fall of a Jewish Communist*, Berkeley: University of California Press, 2001, p. 5.
5. Pavel Câmpeanu, 'Aspects of Romanian Stalinism's History: Ana Pauker, A Victim of Anti-Semitism', *East European Politics and Societies*, vol. 14, no 2, 2000, p. 176.

6. Levy, *Ana Pauker*, p. 235.
7. Robert Levy, 'Did Ana Pauker Prevent a "Rajk Trial" in Romania', *East European Politics and Societies*, Vol. 9, no 2, 1995, p. 144.
8. Deletant, *Communist Terror in Romania* 157.
9. Deletant, *Communist Terror in Romania*, p. 171.
10. Levy, 'Did Ana Pauker...' p. 150.
11. Gheorghe Buzatu, 'Romania dupa lovitura de stat' in Ioan Scurtu and Gheorghe Buzatu (eds), *Istoria Românilor In Secolul XX (1918–1948)*, Bucharest: Paideia, 1999, pp. 499–500.
12. Sergo Beria, *Beria my Father: Inside Stalin's Kremlin*, London: Duckworth, 2001, p. 316, n. 6.
13. Reuben Markham, *Romania under the Soviet Yoke*, Boston, MA: Meador, 1949, pp. 214–17.
14. J. F. Brown, *Nationalism, Democracy and Security in the Balkans*, Aldershot, England: Dartmouth Publishing, 1992, pp. 101–2.
15. Robert Lee Wolff, *The Balkans in our Time*, Cambridge, MA: Harvard University Press, 1974 edn, p. 45.
16. V. Tarau, 'Campania electorala şi rezultatul real al alegorilor din 19 noiembrie 1946 in judetele Cluj, Somes şi Turda', in Sorin Mitu and Florin Gogaltan (eds), *Studii de Istorie a transilvâniei*, Cluj: Asosociatia Istoricol din Transilvânia şi Banat, 1994, pp. 204–12.
17. Lavinia Betea, *Alexandru Bîrlădeanu despre Dej, Ceauşescu si Iliescu*, Bucharest: Evenimentul Romanesc, 1998, p. 85.
18. Dennis Deletant, *Ceauşescu and the Securitate*, London: Hurst 1995, p. 24.
19. A. L. Cartwright, *The Return of the Peasant: Land Reform in Post-Communist Romania*, Aldershot: Ashgate, 2001, p. 68.
20. Deletant, *Communist Terror in Romania*, pp. 225–34.
21. Michael Shafir, 'Political Culture, Intellectual Dissent, and Intellectual Consent: the Case of Romania', *Orbis*, 1983 pp. 404–6.
22. Shafir, 'Political Culture', *Orbis*, p. 407.
23. Durandin, *Histoire des Roumains*, p. 374.
24. For Nicodim's recalcitrance, see Alexandre Safran, *Un Taciune Smuls Flacarilor*, Bucharest: Hasefer, 1996, pp. 49–50; also published in English as *Resisting the Storm: Memoirs*, Jerusalem: Yad Vashem, 1987.
25. Dan Ciachir, 'Patriarhul Justinian', *Cuvintul*, January 1997.
26. In 1949 Justinian declared: 'The Vatican is the centre of the oldest imperialist traditions and it does not hesitate to use all the means of the capitalist system to commercialise holy things.' See Durandin, *Histoire*, p. 376.
27. These words appeared in the Orthodox newspaper, *Telegraful Roman*, in 1945 and are quoted in Vasile Marchis, *Drama Bisericii Române Unite cu Roma (Greco-Catolica), documente şi marturii*, Bucharest: Crater, 1997, p. 83. Metropolitan Balan had been close to the Iron Guard in the 1930s and in 1937 had organized the funeral service of two Guardists killed in the Spanish Civil War. See Marchis, *Drama*, p. 83; Livezeanu, *Cultural Politics*, p. 262.
28. Deletant, *Ceauşescu and the Securitate*, p. 170.
29. Shafir, 'Political Culture, Intellectual Dissent' p. 402.
30. Câmpeanu, 'Aspects of Romanian Stalinism's History', p. 161.

31. Lucien Boia, *Istorie şi mit in conştiinta româneaşca*, Bucharest: Humanitas, 1997, pp. 71–2.
32. For Nikolski's crimes see Deletant, *Communist Terror in Romania*, chapters 6 and 9.
33. Pavel Câmpeanu', 'Din nou despre anti-Semitism, Contributii evreisti la instaurarea dictaturii staliniste in România', *22*, 27 February-5 March 2001.
34. Deletant, *Communist Terror in Romania*, pp. 61–2.
35. Ibid., p. 16.
36. Ibid.
37. Betea, *Alexandru Bîrlădeanu*, pp. 46–7.
38. Deletant, *Communist Terror in Romania*, p. 217.
39. Mircea Suciu and Cristian Troncota, 'Doua "romane de iubire" din anii lui Gheorghiu-Dej', *Dosarele Istorie*, 7 (12), 1997, pp. 30–43.
40. Deletant, *Communist Terror in Romania*, p. 147.
41. Câmpeanu, 'Aspects of Romanian Stalinism's History', p. 147.
42. Deletant, *Communist Terror in Romania*, p. 250.
43. Levy, 'Did Ana Pauker', pp. 172–3.
44. Deletant, *Communist Terror in Romania*, p. 255.
45. Ion Mihai Pacepa, *Cartea Neagra a Securitatii*, vol. II, Bucharest: Editura Omega, 1999, pp. 41, 99.
46. Deletant, *Communist Terror in Romania*, pp. 273–5; Silviu Brucan, *The Wasted Generation: Memoirs of the Romanian Journey from Capitalism to Socialism and Back*, Boulder, CO: Westview Press, 1993, pp. 55–6.
47. Betea, *Alexandru Bîrlădeanu*, p. 133.
48. Dennis Deletant, *Romania sub regimul communist*, Bucharest: Fundaţia Academia Civica, 1997, p. 115.
49. Gallagher, *Romania after Ceauşescu*, pp. 55–6.
50. François Fejtö, *A History of the People's Democracies*, Harmondsworth: Penguin 1974, pp. 158–9.
51. Lendvai, *Eagles In Cobwebs*, p. 2.
52. Fejtö, *A History of the Peoples Democracies*, p. 162.
53. R. J. Crampton, *Eastern Europe in the Twentieth Century*, London: Routledge, 1994, p. 313.
54. Pacepa, *Cartea Neagra*, vol. 2, p. 91.
55. Betea, *Alexandru Bîrlădeanu...*, p. 249.
56. Pacepa, *Cartea Neagra*, vol. 2, p. 77.
57. Shafir, 'Political Culture, Intellectual Dissent', p. 408.
58. Deletant, *Communist Terror in Romania*, p. 27.
59. Annele Ute Gabanyi, *The Ceauşescu Cult*, Bucharest: Romanian Cultural Foundation, 2000, p. 36.
60. Gheorghe Apostol, a rival for the succession in 1965, used this term as a barely-disguised reference to Ceauşescu in a letter he wrote to the party daily *Scânteia* on 30 April 1968 complaining about the direction of events in the party and state; it was never published. See Deletant, *Communist Terror in Romania*, pp. 292–5.
61. Pacepa, *Cartea Neagra*, vol. 2, pp. 108–14.
62. Deletant, *Communist Terror in Romania*, p. 285.

63. Betea, *Alexandru Bîrlădeanu*, p. 180.
64. Maurer later said to a political colleague: 'I could not have become First Secretary for two reasons: one, I have a German name; two, I just don't get along with the Russians.' See Rodica Chelaru, *Culpe care nu se uita. Convorbiri cu Cornel Burtică*, Bucharest: Curtea Veche, 2001, p. 89.
65. Betea, *Alexandru Bîrlădeanu*, p. 183.
66. R. V. Burks, 'The Rumanian National Deviation: an Accounting' in Kurt London (ed), *Eastern Europe In Transition*, Baltimore: John Hopkins Press, 1967, p. 103.
67. Fejtö, *A History of the Peoples Democracies*, pp. 317–8.
68. Dumitru Dumitru, 'August 1968—marea pacaleala', *Adevârul*, Bucharest: 21 August 1998.
69. Tony Benn, *Office Without Power: Diaries 1968–72*, London: Hutchinson, 1988, p. 79.
70. Nicholas Bethell, *Spies and Other Secrets: Memoirs from the Second Cold War*, London: Penguin, 1995, p. 283.
71. Livea Betea (in dialog cu Corneliu Mănescu), *Convorbiri neterminate*, Iasi: Polirom, 2001, p. 323.
72. Ronald Linden, 'After the Revolution: A Foreign Policy of Unbounded Change' in Daniel Nelson (ed.), *Romania After Tyranny*, San Francisco: Westview Press, 1992, pp. 203–4. Ronald Linden.
73. Edward Behr, *'Kiss The Hand You Cannot Bite': the Rise and Fall of the Ceauşescus*, London: Hamish Hamilton, 1991, p. 185.
74. David B. Funderburk, *Un Ambassador American: Între Departmentul de Stat şi Dictatura Comunista din România*, Constanta, Romania: Editura Dacon, 1994, p. 45.
75. Funderburk, *Un Ambassador American*, p. 74.
76. Mark Almond, *Decline without Fall: Romania under Ceauşescu*, London: Institute for European Defence and Strategic Studies, 1988, p. 25.
77. Ibid.
78. Benn, *Office Without Power*, p. 74.
79. For evidence see chapters 4 and 5 of Gallagher, *Outcast Europe*.
80. Behr, *'Kiss The Hand'…*, p. 147.
81. Annele Ute Gabanyi, *The Ceauşescu Cult*, Bucharest: The Romanian Cultural Foundation, 2000, p. 45.
82. Bodnăras disagreed with Ceauşescu when he broke with precedent and refused to delegate his powers to the permanent praesidium of the central committee while he was on visits abroad. See Chelaru, *Culpe…*, pp. 139–40.
83. For Bodnăras, the need to preserve his party and state positions took precedence over any desire to preserve socialist legality. Only one leading communist office-holder appears to have been bold enough to defy Ceauşescu outright. This was Cornel Burtica, minister of external trade who resigned at a meeting of the Politburo in 1981 after disagreeing with Ceauşescu's proposals for Romanian investment in Iraq. See Chelaru, *Culpe…*, pp. 140–1, 206–7.
84. Betea, *Alexandru Bîrlădeanu…*, p. 153; Gabanyi, *The Ceauşescu Cult*, pp. 47, 49, 50.
85. Gabanyi, *The Ceauşescu Cult*, pp. 110–11.

86. Behr, *'Kiss The Hand*, p. 159.
87. Betea, *Alexandru Bîrlădeanu*, p. 200.
88. *Sâptamina*, 25 January 1980, quoted in Gabanyi, *The Ceauşescu Cult*, p. 42.
89. Papacostea, 'Captive Clio…', p. 197.
90. Deletant, *Ceauşescu and the Securitate*, pp. 188, 191.
91. Andrei Pippidi, 'Nation, Nationalisme et Democracie en Roumanie', *L'Autre Europe*, 1993, part 26–27, pp. 136–7.
92. Laszlo Kurti, 'Transylvania, Land beyond Reason: Toward an Anthropological Analysis of a Contested Terrain', *Dialectical Anthropology*, vol. 14, 1989, p. 41.
93. Shafir, *Romania*, p. 174.
94. Brucan, *The Wasted Generation*, pp. 126–7.
95. Deletant, *Romania sub regimul communist*, p. 150.
96. Gabanyi, *The Ceauşescu Cult*, pp. 49–50.
97. Deletant, *Romania sub regimul communist…*, p. 151.
98. Deletant, *Romania sub regimul communist…*, p. 151.
99. Mihnea Berindei, 'Romania lui Ceauşescu—un naufragiu planifiat II', 22, vol. 9, no 47, November 1998.
100. Deletant, *Romania sub regimul communist…*, p. 176.
101. Betea, *Alexandru Bîrlădeanu*, p. 95.
102. David Kideckel, *The Solitude of Collectivism: Romanian Villagers to the Revolution and Beyond*, Ithaca, NY: Cornell University Press, 1993, p. 178.
103. Behr, *'Kiss The Hand'*, pp. 220–7; Deletant, *Ceauşescu and the Securitate*, pp. 343–4.
104. Ion Mihai Pacepa, *Cartea Neagra a Securitatii*, vol. III, Bucharest: Editura Omega, 1999, p. 131.
105. See Helena Drysdale, *Looking for Gheorghe*, London: Sinclair-Stevenson, 1995.
106. Deletant, *Ceauşescu and the Securitate*, p. 200.
107. Richard Hopwood, 'Nationalism and Church-State Relations in Ceauşescu's Romania', MA thesis, University of Bradford, England 1995, p. 26; information derived from Fr Constantin Galeriu whom Hopwood interviewed in Bucharest on 21 July 1995.
108. Cornel Nistorescu, editorial in *Evenimentul Zile* (English language edition), 9 December 1998.
109. Deletant, *Ceauşescu and the Securitate*, p. 212.
110. For the growth of denominations known in Romania as 'neo-Protestants' see Deletant, *Ceauşescu and the Securitate*, pp. 224–9; Hopwood, 'Nationalism and Church-State Relations', pp. 58–61.
111. See Deletant, *Ceauşescu and the Securitate*, pp. 294–319; also Dinu C. Giurescu, *The Razing of Romania's Past*, London: Phaidon Press, 1990.
112. For the damaging effects of collectivisation on the peasant world and Romanian national identity, see Horia Patapievici, 'Anatomia unei catastrofe' in Iordan Chimet, *Momentul Adevârului*, Cluj: Dacia, 1996, pp. 169–83.
113. See Horatiu Peppine, 'Armata si Biserica', *22*, no. 44, 1–7 November 1995.
114. Steven Runciman, *The Orthodox Churches and the Secular State*, Oxford University Press, 1971, p. 96.

115. See the interview with Cicerone Ionitoiu, an Orthodox Church member and author of *Persecuţia Bisericii din Romania* (Persecution of the Romanian Churches) in the Bucharest daily *România libera*, 10 May 1997.
116. Deletant, *Ceauşescu and the Securitate*, p. 257.
117. Deletant, *Romania sub regimul communist*, pp. 171–2.
118. Betea, *Convorbiri neterminate*, p. 344.
119. Betea, *Convorbiri neterminate*, p. 345.
120. Norman Manea, 'Blasphemy and Carnival', *World Policy Journal*, vol. 13, no. 1, spring 1996, p. 76.

Chapter 3   Comrades Discard the Ideology but Conserve the Power: 1990–2

1. See Şerban Papacostea, 'Captive Clio: Romanian Historiography under Communist Rule', *European History Quarterly*, vol. 26, no 4, 1996, p. 202.
2. See Alin Bogan and Violeta Fotache, 'Presidentele Constantinescu n-a gasit nici in 98 adevârul despre Revolutie', *Adevârul*, 16 December 1998.
3. For the duplicity at the heart of the 1989 events see see Radu Portocale, *Autopsie du coup d'etat Roumain: Au pays du mensoge triumphant*, Paris: Calmann-Levy, 1990.
4. Deletant, *Ceauşescu and the Securitate*, p. 339.
5. Nestor Ratesh, *Romania: the Entangled Revolution*, New York: Praegar, 1991, pp. 121–2.
6. Doina Alexandrescu, *Coposu: confesiuni*, Bucharest: Editura Anastasia, 1996, p. 209.
7. Ratesh, op. cit., pp. 59–60.
8. Ibid., p. 62.
9. Behr, *Kiss the hand you cannot bite*, p. 16.
10. *22*, 12–18 June 2001.
11. Gabanyi, *The Ceauşescu Cult*, p. 13.
12. This view is advanced in the thoughtful survey of the post-Ceauşescu political landscape produced by Mary Ellen Fischer. See her 'The New Leaders and the Opposition' in Daniel Nelson (ed.), *Romania after Tyranny*, Boulder, CO: Westview Press, 1992.
13. Peter Siani-Davis, 'Political Legitimisation and the Romanian Revolution', paper presented at a conference on Romania at the School of Slavonic and East European Studies, University of London, May 1994.
14. Siani-Davis, 'Political Legitimisation'.
15. For biographical details of Iliescu see Vladimir Tismaneanu, *Re-Inventing Politics: Eastern Europe from Stalin to Havel*, New York: The Free Press, 1992, p. 225; Bogdan Szajkowski, *New Political Parties of Eastern Europe and the Soviet Union*, London: Longman, 1991, p. 221; and Vladimir Socor, 'The New President', *Report on Eastern Europe*, vol. 1, no. 23, 8 June 1990.
16. Vladimir Tismaneanu, 'The Quasi-Revolution and Its Discontents: Emerging Political Pluralism in Post-Ceauseşcu Romania', *East European Politics and Societies*, vol. 7, no. 2, summer 1993.

17. Szajkowski, New Political Parties, p. 220.
18. Rompres, 6 January 1990, BBC World Service, Survey of World Broadcasts (hereafter SWB) EE/0657 B/11, 9 January 1990.
19. *Ibid.*
20. Rompres, 11 January 1990, SWB EE/066 B/13 19 January 1990.
21. Martin Rady, *Romania In Turmoil*, London: I. B. Tauris 1992, p. 149, SWB, 23 February 1990. p. 18.
22. Judith Patacki, 'Free Hungarians in a Free Romania: Dream or Reality', Report on Eastern Europe, vol. 1, no. 8, 23 February 1990, p. 22.
23. Rady, *Romania*, p. 149; Doina Cornea, *Fata Nevazuta A lucracilor (1990–1999). Dialoguri cu Rodica Palade,* Cluj: Dacia 1999, p.
24. See Tom Gallagher, 'Vatra Româneasca and resurgent nationalism in Romania', *Ethnic and Racial Studies,* vol. 15, no. 4, 1992.
25. Szajkowski, 'New Political Parties', p. 222; R. R. King, 'Romania' in R. Staar (ed.), *1991 Yearbook of International Communist Affairs,* Stanford, CA: Hoover Institution Press, 1991, p. 333.
26. Szajkowski, *New Political Parties,* p. 222.
27. Michael Shafir, 'The Provisional Council of National Unity: is History Repeating Itself?', *Report on Eastern Europe,* vol. 1, no. 9, 2 March 1990, p. 21.
28. H. R. Patapievici, *22,* 2–8 February 1999.
29. Emil Hurezeanu, *22,* 26 January-2 February 1999.
30. Patapievici, *Politice,* p. 22.
31. Dan Ionescu, 'Countdown For Romania's Germans', vol. 2, no. 36, *Report on Eastern Europe,* 13 September 1991, p. 32.
32. Richard Bassett, *The Times,* 1 March 1990.
33. Rompres, 27 January 1990, SWB EE/0676 B/11 (31 January 1990).
34. Rompres, 6 February 1990, SWB EE/0683 B/9 (8 February 1990).
35. Budapest home service, 19 February 1990, SWB EE/0695 B/5, 22 February 1990.
36. Budapest home service, 20 March 1990, SWB EE/0720 B/3, 23 March 1990.
37. Vladimir Socor, 'Forces of old Resurface in Romania: the Ethnic Clashes in Tirgu Mureş', *Report on Eastern Europe,* vol. 1, no. 15, 13 April 1990, p. 42, n. 6.
38. Rompres, 23 March 1990, SWB EE/0722 B/7 (26 March 1990).
39. E. Illyes, *National Minorities in Romania: Change in Transylvania,* New York: Columbia University Press, 1982, p. 65.
40. Illyes, *National Minorities,* pp. 56–7.
41. Between May 1990 and 1993 I interviewed a range of people in Tirgu Mureş and Cluj to obtain a cross-section of views about the state of inter-ethnic relations before and after March 1990 and was able to view conditions for myself on fieldwork trips starting in May 1990.
42. These events are summarised by Cornel Ivanciuc, 'Evenimentele de la Tirgu-Mureş din martie 1990, sau impus recunoasterea oficiala a SRI', *22,* 5–11 July 1999.
43. Rompres, 23 January 1991, SWB EE/0980 B/6, 26 January 1991.
44. Socor, *Report on Eastern Europe,* 13 April 1990, p. 39; Andras Süto interviewed on Hungarian television, 30 March 1990, SWB EE/0731 B/9, 5 April 1990.

45. Cornea, *Faţa Nevazuta A lucracilor,* p. 209.
46. Socor, *Report on Eastern Europe,* 13 April 1990, p. 39.
47. Bucharest home service 21 March 1990, SWB EE/0720 A2/3 (23 March 1990).
48. Ibid.
49. Rompres, 21 March 1990, SWB EE/A20 A2/2, 23 March 1990.
50. Rompres, 23 January 1991, SWB EE/0980 B/6, 26 January 1991.
51. Rompres, 23 March 1990, SWB EE/0722 B/7, 26 March 1990.
52. *Human Rights in Romania,* New York: Helsinki Watch, 1991, p. 16.
53. Ibid., pp. 15–16.
54. SWB EE/07190, 22 March 1990.
55. Rompres, 24 March 1990, SWB EE/0722 B/9, 26 March 1990.
56. Rompres, 2 April 1990, SWB EE/0731 B/8, 5 April 1990.
57. Larry L. Watts, 'The Romanian Army in the December Revolution and Beyond' in Daniel Nelson (ed.), *Romania after Tyranny,* Boulder, CO: Westview Press, 1992, p. 98.
58. Bucharest home service, 25 March 1990, SWB EE/0724 B/3, 28 March 1990.
59. Bucharest home service, 22 March 1990, SWB EE/0722 B/5, 26 March 1990.
60. Ivançiuc, 'Evenimentele'.
61. Doina Cornea, *Faţa Nevazuta,* p. 207.
62. SWB EE/0720 A2/1, 23 March 1990.
63. Crisula Stefanescu, '"Free Romanian Television" Loses Its Credibility', *Report on Eastern Europe,* vol. 1, no. 8, 23 March 1990, p. 26.
64. The full text of the Timişoara Proclamation was carried in *Report on Eastern Europe,* vol. 1, no. 14, 6 April 1990.
65. Walter Bacon, 'Security as seen from Bucharest' in Nelson (ed.), *Romania after Tyranny,* p. 199.
66. *România Líbera* (Bucharest), 11 April 1990.
67. Vladimir Socor, 'Foreign Policy in 1990', *Report on Eastern Europe,* vol 1, no. 50, 28 December 1990, p. 29.
68. Tom Gallagher, 'Nationalism and democracy in South-East Europe' in T. Gallagher and G. Pridham (eds), *Experimenting with Democracy: Regime Change in the Balkans,* London: Routledge, 2000, pp. 93–4.
69. See *Monitorul,* 12 November 1997.
70. For Coposu's life see V. Arachelian, *Corneliu Coposu. Dialoguri,* Bucharest: Ed. Anastasia, 1992.
71. Ioan Mihailescu, 'Mental Stereotypes in Post-Totaliarian Romania', *Government and Opposition,* Vol. 28, no. 3, (1993), p. 318.; details of the second poll were in the Romanian daily, *Adevarul de Cluj,* (14 February 1992).
72. Neagu Djuvaru, *Amintiri Din Pribegie, 1948–1990,* Bucharest: Albatros, 2002, p. 445.
73. Arachelian, *Corneliu Coposu,* p. 134.
74. Information about Timişoara democracy movement and the government response from Nicolas and Doina Harsanyi-Pascu whom I interviewed in July 1991.
75. Nicolas Harsanyi-Pascu.

76. *Human Rights in Romania since the Revolution*, pp. 26–30 Only one trial resulted from the June 1990 events. Three officials attached to the ministry of the interior were accused of wrecking the house of the opposition leader, Ion Raţiu. *ARPRESS*, no. 688, 14 June 1993.

77. Constanta Corpade, 'Ion Iliescu a salutat "spiritul civic" al minerilor care au capasit civili in Bucuresti', *Adevărul*, 2 March 1998.

78. Andrei Badin, 'Magŭreanu si legionarii', *Ziua*, 21 August 2000.

79. *The Independent* (London), 21 June 1990.

80. R. R. King, 'Romania', p. 341.

81. Mihai Sturdza, 'The President and the Miners: the End of a Privileged Relationship', *Report on Eastern Europe*, vol. 1, no. 37, 28 September 1990, p. 35.

82. Adrian Cioflanca, 'Ziua desiluziei', *Monitorul*, 14 June 2000.

83. Mihai Sturdza, 'The Politics of Ambiguity: Romania's Foreign Relations', *Report on Eastern Europe*, vol. 2, no. 13, 5 April 1991, p. 16.

84. Dan Ionescu, 'Government Moves to Recentralize Local Administration', *Report on Eastern Europe*, vol. 1, no. 33, 7 September 1990, p. 23, n. 21; *Cuvintul* (Bucharest), 9 March 1993.

85. *Human Rights in Romania since the Revolution*, p. 54.

86. *Monitorul*, 18 May 2000.

87. Adrian Severin, *Lacrimile Diminetii. Slabiciunile Guvernalui Roman*, Bucharest: Editura Scripta, 1995.

88. Ibid., p. 27.

89. Ibid., p. 28.

90. Ibid., p. 205.

91. Michael Shafir, '"War of the Roses" in Romania's National Salvation Front', *RFE-RL Research Report*, vol. 1, no. 3, 24 January 1992, p. 19.

92. *Report on Eastern Europe*, Digest of Weekly Events, 20 October 1991.

93. Michael Shafir, *RFE-RL Research Report*, vol. 1, no. 3, 24 January 1992.

94. Hungarian radio, 4 October 1991, SWB EE/1197 B/17, 8 October 1991.

95. The Report of the Parliamentary Commission which interviewed people who, after 22 December 1989, had to leave their places of work and homes in the counties of Harghita and Covasna, Bucharest: Ed. Scripta, 1991.

96. *NU*, 28 October 1991; *Baricada*, 12 November 1991.

97. Hungarian radio, 4 October 1991, SWB EE/1197 B/17, 8 October 1991.

98. Cornel Nistorescu, 'Mahalaua lui Iorgovan', *Evenimentul Zilei*, 10 December 2001. Iorgovan went on to be known for his collection of cars and his readiness to defend wealthy members of the economic oligarchy careless enough to find themselves indicted on corruption charges. See *Monitorul*, 16 April 2002.

99. Michael Shafir, 'Romania: Constitution Approved in Referendum', *RFE-RL Research Report*, vol. 1, no. 2, 10 January 1992, pp. 53, 55.

100. Michael Shafir, *RFE-RL Research Report*, vol. 1, no. 3, 24 January 1992.

101. *NU*, 2 December 1991.

102. *Adevărul de Cluj*, 3 December 1991.

103. Tom Gallagher, 'Ultra-Nationalists Take Charge of Transylvania's Capital', *RFE-RL Research Report*, vol. 1, no. 13, 27 March 1992, p. 28.

104. Tom Gallagher, 'Ethnic Tension in Cluj', *RFE-RL Research Report*, vol. 2, no. 9, 26 February 1993, p. 28.
105. *Baricada*, 13 July 1992. Favourable assesments of Ceauşescu by Funar were also given in interviews carried by *22*, 24 April 1992 and *NU*, 22 July 1992.
106. Michael Shafir, 'Romania: Main Candidates in the Presidential Elections', *RFE-RL Research Report*, vol. 1, no. 35, 4 September 1992, p. 16.
107. *22*, 18 March 1993.
108. Andrei Cornea, *22*, 7 January 1993.
109. *RFE-RL Research Report*, 11 September 1992.
110. *Dimineaţa*, 23 September 1992.
111. Michael Shafir, *RFE-RL-Research Report*, 30 October 1992, p. 5, n. 20.
112. *Pro-Minoritate* (journal of the Hungarian political party Fidesz), Oct.–Nov. 1992, p. 25.
113. Such is the recollection of Stefan Niculescu-Maier, pre-1989 dissident and publisher of *Telegrama*, the daily Romanian news service based in the United States. See *Telegrama*, no. 365, 18 November 1996.
114. Private information; accusation aired by Andrei Cornea, 22, 5 August 1993.

Chapter 4   1992–1996: Romania Adrift

1. Andreea Pora, *22*, 23–29 January 2001.
2. Iosif Boda, *Cinci Ani La Cotroceni*, Bucharest, Evenimentul Romanesc: 1999, p. 195.
3. Calin Hera, *Evenienmtul Zilei*, 16 May 2000.
4. Boda, p. 180.
5. Ibid., pp. 369–409.
6. Ibid., p. 63.
7. Andrei Cornea, *22*, 4–10 February 1997.
8. Andrei Cornea, *22*, 18–24 September 1996.
9. Liviu Vălenaş, *Eşecul unei Reforme, 1996–2000: Convorbire cu Serban Orescu*, Iasi: Editura Ars Longa, 2000, pp. 70–1.
10. Dennis Deletant, 'The Post-Communist Security Services in Romania' in Rebecca Haynes (ed.), *Occasional Papers in Romanian Studies*, no. 2, London: School of Slavonic and East European Studies, University of London, 1998, p. 177.
11. The 1991 National Security Law did not establish what were the functions of the secret services. As well as the SRI, there was Protection and Guard Service (SPP), and the External Information Service (SIE). Attached to the Defence Ministry were, the Directory of Military Information (DIM) and the Directory of Military Counter-Espionage (DCSM) The Information Service of the Interior Ministry (DIMI), better known as UM 0215, and the Directory for Supervising Operations and Investigations (DSOI) belonged to the Interior Ministry. The Ministry of Justice has an information service linked to the Directorate Generals of Prisons (UM 04300). The Government has its own information agency known as the Service of Special Telecommunications. See *Monitorul*, 5 June 1998.
12. Deletant, 'The Post-Communist Security services', p. 178.
13. *Evenimentul Zilei*, 1 May 1997.

14. Dennis Deletant, 'Ghosts From The Past: Successors to the Securitate in Post-Communist Romania' in Duncan Light and David Phinnemore (eds), *Post-Communist Romania: Coming to Terms with Transition*, London: Palgrave, 2001, p. 46.
15. Cornel Nistorescu, *Evenimentul Zilei* (English Online edn), 22 May 1998. See also *Monitorul*, 10 April 2000.
16. Ilie Stoian, 'Un miliard pentru vila lui Măgureanu', *Evenimentul Zilei*, 3 November 1997.
17. Economist Intelligence Unit, *Romania*, Country Report, 3rd quarter 1993, London 1993, p. 17.
18. *Telegrama* Press Review, 30 March 1996.
19. *LUPTA*, no. 249, 7 July 1996.
20. *Adevărul*, 2 June 1998.
21. Cornel Nistorescu, *Evenimentul Zilei*, 6 July 1998.
22. Ibid.
23. Ilie Serbanescu, *22*, 16–22 June 1998.
24. Christian Tudor Popescu, *Adevărul*, 13 May 1998.
25. Ibid.
26. Boda, p. 381.
27. Ibid., p. 382.
28. Voiculescu has sued newspapers which claimed that he belonged to the Securitate. At a press conference on 2 September 2004, he insisted that it was due to his smartness alone that he was able to work in the export trade in the 1980s without having any Securitate links. His Securitate file appeared to have gone missing. *See Evenimentul Zilei*, 3 September 2004.
29. Ilie Serbanescu, 'Bancorex—istoria emblematică a României postdecembriste', 22, 16–22 February 1999.
30. Joe Cook, Emergency loan to Romania bank', *Financial Times*, 23 February 1999.
31. *Adevărul*, 23 February 1999.
32. Ilie Serbanescu, 'Bancorex', 22, 16–22 February 1999.
33. Elena Christian and Raluca Bărbuneau, 'Statul roman plătit peste 4,1 miliarde dolari pentru acoperirea gaurilor din 12 bănci', *Adevărul*, 19–20 June 2004.
34. *Ziarul Finanţiar*, 24 June 2004.
35. A description of Romania's new economic elite is provided by veteran political insider Silviu Brucan. See his *Stalpii Noii Puteri in Romania*, Bucharest: Editura Nemira, 1996. Brucan held top diplomatic assignments in the United States for six years before the Ceauşescu era which may have enabled him to see that in a country like Romania aspects of the economic and political systems of the free West could be adopted without fundamentally altering the communist power structure.
36. *Evenimentul Zilei*, 9 July 1996.
37. *Evenimentul Zilei*, 9 July 1996.
38. Cornel Nistorescu, *Evenimentul Zilei* (English Online edn), 3 July 1997.
39. Ondine Ghergut, '500.000.000 de marci pentru Măgureanu & Co.', *Evenimentul Zilei*, 4 August 2000.
40. Boda, p. 129.

41. Boda, p. 169.
42. Mihai Dim. Sturdza, 'Prin coridoarele d-lui Silviu Brucan'. 22, 23 October 1996.
43. LUPTA, nr 265, 22 April 1996.
44. *Cuvantul*, 15 September 1992.
45. *22*, 18–25 October 1996.
46. ARPRESS, no. 627, 29 March 1993.
47. ARPRESS, no. 631, 2 April 1993.
48. Boda, p. 298.
49. Gelu Ionescu, 'PUNR in Guvern', 22, 31 August–6 September 1994.
50. Rompres, 20 January 1995.
51. RFE/RL Newsline-Southeastern Europe, 10 March 1998.
52. RFE/RL Newsline-Southeastern Europe, 14 September 2000.
53. Full coverage of Pitulescu's press conference and the charges he made against Măgureanu are contained in the article by Ondine Ghergut entitled '500.000.000 de marci pentru Măgureanu & Co.', *Evenimentul Zilei*, 4 August 2000.
54. Romanian radio, 5 April 1994, in BBC World Service, Survey of World Broadcasts, Eastern Europe/1965 B/3 (7 April 1994).
55. See Sorin Mircea Botez, 'An Alternative Romanian Foreign Policy' in Nelson, op. cit., pp. 267–8.
56. 22, 9–15 November 1994.
57. *Romania libera*, 7 January 1995.
58. Aurel Zidaru-Barbulescu, 'Romania Seeks Admission to the Council of Europe', RFE-RL Research Report, vol. 2, no. 2, 8 January 1993, p. 14.
59. Details come from Dennis Deletant, 'The Post-Communist Security Services in Romania', pp. 186–7.
60. *Romania Country Report on Human Rights Practices for 1996*, Washington: US Department of State, 1997.
61. Adrian Campbell, 'Local Government in Romania' in Andrew Coulson (ed.), *Local Government In Eastern Europe: Establishing Democracy at the Grassroots*, Aldershot: Edward Elgar, 1995, p. 85.
62. *Democracy in Romania*, Stockholm: Institute for Democratic and Electoral Assistance, 1997, p. 109.
63. Elaine Eddison, *The Protection of Minorities at the Conference on Security and Co-operation in Europe*, Human Rights Centre, University of Essex, 1993, p. 19.
64. Edith Oltay, 'Minorities as Stumbling Block in Relations with Neighbours', RFE-RL Research Report, vol. 1, no. 19, 8 May 1992, p. 33.
65. See the Romania Country Report on Human Rights Practices for 1996, Washington, DC: US Department of State, 1997.
66. For the impact of democracy assistance both state-sponsored and private, see Thomas Carothers, *Assessing Democracy Assistance: the Case of Romania*, New York: Carnegie Foundation, 1996.
67. *22*, 1–7 March 1995.
68. Deletant, 'Ghosts from the Past', pp. 47–8.
69. Ted Anton, *Eros, magic și asasinarea profesorului Culianu*, Bucharest: Nemira, 1997.
70. Deletant, 'Ghosts', p. 48.

71. Around 300 senior officers in the armed forces, some in active service, others retired, published a memorandum in the 20 June 1995 edition of *Romania Mâre* in which they accused President Iliescu of destroying the army and selling it out to 'traitors, spies and speculators'.

72. *Adevârul*, 26 February 1996.

73. Ionescu, 'Government Moves to Recentralize Local Administration', p. 24.

74. Edith Oltay, 'Minorities as Stumbling Block', p. 28.

75. Edith Oltay, 'Minority Rights Still an Issue in Hungarian-Romanian Relations', *RFE-RL Research Report*, vol. 1, no. 12, 20 March 1992, pp. 16–17.

76. Vladimir Socor, *Report on Eastern Europe*, 28 December 1990.

77. Oltay, 'Minority Rights….'

78. *Monitorul*, 18 July 1996.

79. Telegrama, News Bulletin, 15 August 1996.

80. Rompres, 17 August 1996.

81. Telegrama Press Review, 3 September 1996.

82. Antoine Roger, 'Les Partis Anti-Systeme dans la Roumaine Post-Communiste', *Revue d'Études Comparatives Est-Ouest*, vol. 31, no. 2, 2000, p. 120.

83. Dennis Deletant, 'The Successors to the *Securitate*: Old Habits Die Hard' in Kieran Williams and Dennis Deletant, *Security Inteligence Services in New Democracies*, London: Macmillan 2000, pp. 233, 234, and 241 for the information contained in this and the previous sentence.

84. Roger, 'Les Partis', p. 121.

85. Telegrama News Bulletin, 18 October 1996.

86. See Petru Mihai Bacanu, *România líbera*, 14 March 1996.

87. Boda, p. 383.

88. *Nine O'Clock*, 17 May 2000.

89. *Evenimentul Zilei*, 9 July 1996.

90. Telegrama Press Review, 29 March 1996.

91. Boda, p. 381.

92. Boda, p. 144.

93. Telegrama Press Review, 3 May 1996.

94. *România libera*, international edn, 11 May 1996.

95. Ibid., 22 and 28 August 1996.

96. Cornel Nistorescu, *Evenimentul Zilei* (English Online edn), 6 November 1997.

97. Telegrama Press Review, 8 June 1996.

98. For the telephone affair, see *Evenimentul Zilei*, 3 October 1996; a summary of the charges levelled against the PDSR. concerning its conduct of the elections, is provided by Marian Chiriac, *22*, 30 November 1996.

99. Liviu Vălenaş, *Eşecul unei Reforme*, p. 51.

100. Cornel Nistorescu, *Evenimentul Zilei*, 9 October 1997.

101. Telegrama News Bulletin, 22 August 1996.

102. Telegrama Press Review, 4 July 1996.

103. Telegrama Press Review, 1 August 1996, quoting Academia Catâvencu.

104. See the editorial by Ion Cristoiu in *Evenimentul Zilei* of 2 September 1996.

105. *Evenimentul Zilei*, 10 October 1996.

106. Ibid., 28 October 1996.
107. *Evenimentul Zilei*, 7 November 1996.
108. The Braila and Arges anomalies are examined in *Evenimentul Zilei*, 7 November 1996.
109. Details of the IRSOP survey are contained in *Evenimentul Zilei*, 7 November 1996.
110. *Monitorul*, 5 November 1996.
111. *Evenimentul Zilei*, 13 November 1996.
112. Ibid., 7 November 1996.

Chapter 5 'In Office but Not in Power': Constantinescu's Honeymoon, 1996–8

1. Nicolae Constantinescu, *22*, 24–30 December 1996.
2. Nicolae Constantinescu insisted that 'qualifications' not a person's 'dossier' were to be the criteria upon which staff were hired to assist the President. See *22*, 24–30 December 1996.
3. Petre Mihai Bacanu, *Cuvintul*, June 1998.
4. The CDR obtained 30.17% of the parliamentary vote compared with 23.08% for the PDSR. Iliescu's vote in the presidential election fell more steeply than his party's did in the presidential poll, down from 47% in the first round in 1992 to 32.35% in 1996. In the second round held on 17 November, Constantinescu's vote increased from 28.21 to 54.43%.
5. For details, see Gabriel Andreescu, *Ziua*, 8 March 2000; also Valerian Stan, *Cotidianul*, 27 September 1999. Zoe Petre, the President's chief-of-staff, has denied that a donation from Gheorghe Păunescu was ever solicited or received. Undated memorandum presented to Tom Gallagher by Professor Petre in June 2001.
6. Not all PD notables fall into this category. Victor Babiuc, Defense minister after 1996, had never been a party member. Other rising figures in the PD may have been too young to have been actively involved with the former regime.
7. Adrian Severin (in dialog cu Gabriel Andreescu), *Locurile unde se construieste Europa*, Bucharest: Polirom, 2000, see chapter 2.
8. The PD was formerly represented in the coalition by the Union of the Democratic Left (USD), an electoral alliance formed with the much smaller Social Democratic Party of Romania (PSDR). One of its members, Alexandru Athanasiu, was minister of social welfare for most of the coalition's period in office.
9. *Monitorul*, 31 March 1998.
10. Biographical information about Ciorbea (including this point) was mainly obtained from *Monitorul*, 31 March 1998.
11. Interview with Victor Ciorbea, 28 September 1999.
12. Interview with Victor Ciorbea, 28 September 1999.
13. *Monitorul*, 18 January 2000; interview with Victor Ciorbea, 28 September 1999.
14. Lucien Boia, *Romania: Tara de Frontieră A Europei*, Bucharest: Humanitas, 2001, p. 143.

15. Emil Constantinescu, *Timpul dărâmării, timpul zidirii*, (Vol. 1), Bucharest: Universalia, 2002, pp. 122–4.
16. Radu Vasile, Constantinescu's later rival, expressed his outrage that 'a woman' had the effrontery to give advice to venerable leaders like Coposu. See his *Cursă Pe Contrasens: Amintirile unui prime-ministru*, Bucharest: Humanitas, 2002, p. 86.
17. He was criticised for not doing more to transform the university he had been rector of. See Andrei Cornea, *22*, 16–23 January 2001. Zoe Petre argues that Constantinescu made his mark in university life by defending academic freedom successfully along with the financial autonomy of universities. She said that, unlike Cornea, she did not believe that it was the rector's duty to 'mop floors'. Undated memorandum presented to Tom Gallagher by Professor Petre in June 2001.
18. Vlad Nistor, *22*, 21–27 January 1997.
19. *Monitorul*, 19 November 1998.
20. Constantinescu, *Timpul dărâmării*, (vol. 1), pp. 341–3.
21. Vălenaş, *Eşecul unei Reforme*, p. 151. See Constantinescu, *Timpul dărâmării*, (vol. 1), pp. 579–610, for his relations with ex-King Mihai during his presidential term.
22. Cornel Nistorescu, *Evenimentul Zilei*, 21 March 1997 (English Online edition).
23. Cornel Nistorescu, *Evenimentul Zilei*, 17 November 1997 (English Online edition).
24. Vălenaş, *Eşecul unei Reforme*, p. 131.
25. *Ziua*, 15 January 2001.
26. *Le Monde* (Paris), 22 February 1997.
27. Andrei Cornea, *22*, 14–21 January 1997.
28. Monitorul, 15 March 1997.
29. *22*, 21–27 January 1997.
30. For his campaign contributions, see *Catavencu*, 22 September 1999, quoted in *Ziua*, 8 March 2000.
31. *Nine O'Clock*, 22 February 1999.
32. *Evenimentul Zilei*, 14 June 1997 (English Online edition).
33. *Monitorul*, 1 February 1997.
34. Anatol Lieven and Kevin Done, 'Rocky road ahead for the reformers', *Financial Times*, 25 June 1997.
35. Ibid.
36. Radu Busneag, *Radio Free Europe*, 22 April 1997.
37. *Evenimentul Zilei*, 30 March 1998 (English Online edition).
38. 'Romania Starts to Rebuild', *The Economist*, 3 May 1997.
39. Zoe Petre, *Ziua*, 26 January 2001.
40. *Monitorul*, 12 March 1997.
41. *România líbera*, 28 May 1997.
42. *Monitorul*, 14 March 1997.
43. Rompres, Romanian state news agency, 21 August 1992.
44. *Monitorul*, 12 March 1997.
45. *Monitorul*, 13 and 14 March 1997.

46. *Evenimentul Zilei*, 22 October 1997. Babes-Bolyai University was now described by Ciorbea as 'a multi-national university' whose status could not be altered.
47. Cornel Nistorescu, *Evenimentul Zilei*, 4–5 March 2000 (English Online edition).
48. Telegrama, 15 April 1997.
49. Telegrama, 15 March 1997.
50. *Evenimentul Zilei*, 23 June 2000 (English Online edition).
51. *Dilema*, 12–18 September 1997.
52. Cornel Nistorescu, *Evenimentul Zilei*, 23 March 1998 (English Online edition).
53. Letter from Ana Blandiana, 10 August 2005.
54. Undated memorandum presented to Tom Gallagher by Professor Petre in June 2001; Ana Blandiana, 10 August 2005.
55. *22*, 24–30 November 1998.
56. Victor Ciorbea, 'PNTCD la rascruce', *22*, 9–15 June 1998.
57. Undated memorandum presented to Tom Gallagher by Professor Petre in June 2001. But Emil Hurezeanu, the well-connected head of Deutsche Welle in Romania, has continued to insist that 'in the first half of 1997, the former government was advised by the former President to slow down economic reform…in order to reduce the likelihood of social unrest…and create a false but peaceful image of post-socialist reality'. See 22, 5–11 March 2002.
58. *22*, 21–27 January 1997.
59. Cornel Nistorescu, *Evenimentul Zilei*, 12 May 1997 (English Online edition).
60. Jonathan Eyal, *22*, 13–19 January 1998.
61. Deletant, 'The Post-Communist Security Services…', p. 191.
62. *Evenimentul Zilei*, 2 May 1997 (English Online edition). Only the extremist *România Mare* had previously made such an accusation.
63. *România líbera*, 3 May 1997.
64. Vălenaş, *Eşecul unei Reforme*, p. 575.
65. 'Romania Brings Spy Agency Under Parliamentary Control', Central Europe Online, 22 October 1997.
66. Neagu Djuvara, 'Sintem ori nu in balcani', *Dilema*, 18–24 April 1997.
67. *The European*, 19 June 1997.
68. *Evenimentul Zilei*, 14 June 1997.
69. *Evenimentul Zilei*, 14 June 1997.
70. *Monitorul*, 12 July 1997.
71. *Monitorul*, 23 June 1997.
72. Cornel Nistorescu, *Evenimentul Zilei*, 7 June 1997 (English Online edition).
73. Cornel Nistorescu, *Evenimentul Zilei*, 24 October 1997 (English Online edition).
74. Kevin Done, 'Investing in Central and Eastern Europe', *Financial Times*, 8 May 1998.
75. Victor Ciorbea, 'PNTCD la rascruce', *22*, 9–15 June 1998.
76. Elena Stefoi, 'Romania—organizing legislative impotence', *East European Constitutional Review*, vol. 4, No. 2, spring 1995, pp. 78–9.
77. *Evenimentul Zilei*, 20 January 1998.
78. Central Europe Online, 28 November 1997.

79. *Evenimentul Zilei*, 27 February 1998.

80. Mircea Dutu, *Nine o'Clock*, 29 December 2000.

81. Cornel Nistorescu, *Evenimentul Zilei*, 2 June 1997 (English Online edition).

82. Cornel Nistorescu, *Evenimentul Zilei*, 11 August 1997 (English Online edition).

83. Victor Ciorbea, 'PNTCD la rascruce', *22*, 9–15 June 1998.

84. Telegrama, 15 September 1997; 'Romania To Lift Privileges of 1989 Revolt', Central Europe Online, 22 September 1997.

85. *Evenimentul Zilei*, 29 September 1997 (English Online edition).

86. Constaniescu's chief of staff thought the President's gesture was a mistake. Undated memorandum presented to Tom Gallagher by Professor Petre in June 2001.

87. *Evenimentul Zilei*, 15 and 16 October 1997 (English Online edition).

88. *22*, 30 September–6 October 1997.

89. H. R. Patapievici, *22*, 10–16 November 1998.

90. *22*, 3–9 November 1998.

91. He had served with the Horea, Closca and Crisan Division set up by the communists in the wartime Soviet Union from captured Romanian soldiers. After briefly attending the party school, he was governor of Sighet prison from 1950 to 1954. Perhaps because he had harmed figures who had contributed to Romanian independence, he received no promotion during the era of national communism, but in 1990 and 1995 he was promoted to captain and major respectively in decrees signed by President Iliescu. See *22*, 3–9 November 1998.

92. *22*, 3–9 November 1998.

93. In the defence of her colleague, Zoe Petre argues that only a small number of the eighty staff at Cotroceni were able to deal with military matters. The President had, by law, to confer distinctions periodically on more than 25,000 veterans. The list was drawn up by the Ministry of Defence, and Cotroceni had little choice but to assume that the Ministry would only nominate individuals worthy of the honour. Undated memorandum presented to Tom Gallagher by Professor Petre in June 2001.

94. *22*, 22–28 July 1997.

95. One of the names published in *22* was Constantin Constantin, patron of the 'Sexy Club' in Bucharest, who received land grants in four areas around Bucharest. See *22*, 22–28 July 1997.

96. *România libera*, 2 September 1997.

97. Rodica Palade, *22*, 8–14 July 1997.

98. *România libera*, 8 June 1998.

99. Alina Mungiu-Pippidi, 'Breaking Free At Last. Tales of Corruption From the Post-Communist Balkans', *East European Constitutional Review*, vol. 6, no. 4, fall 1997.

100. Constantinescu, *Timpul dărâmării*, vol. 1, p. 559.

101. Mungiu-Pippidi, 'Breaking Free At Last'.

102. Cornel Nistorescu, *Evenimentul Zilei*, 30 March 1998 (English Online edition).

103. Cornel Nistorescu, *Evenimentul Zilei*, 4 July 1997 (English Online edition). Constantinescu, for his part, praised Ciorbea's dedication to reform and his capacity for hard work, but faulted him for avoiding tough decisions. See Constantinescu, *Timpul dărâmării*, vol. 1, p. 415.

104. *Adevărul*, 17 December 1997.

105. Telegrama, 16 January 1998.

106. Central Europe Online, 3 February 1998.

107. Sorin Rosca Stănescu, *Ziua*, 24 May 1999.

108. *Nine o'Clock*, 20 April 1999.

109. *Monitorul*, 2 April 1998.

110. For Vasile's view of his own role in the party before 1996, see his memoir *Cursă Pe Contrasens. Amintirile unui prim-ministru*, Bucharest: Humanitas, 2002, especially, pp. 73–134.

111. Rodica Ciobanu, *Adevarul*, 9 April 1998.

112. Ibid.

113. *Evenimentul Zilei*, 2 August 1999.

114. Vasile, *Cursă Pe Contrasens*, pp. 75, 114.

115. *România líbera*, 1 December 1997.

116. Emil Hurezeanu, 'La vremuri noi, omul nou', *22*, 7–13 April 1998.

117. Cornel Nistorescu, *Evenimentul Zilei*, 21 December 2000 (English Online edition).

118. For Vasile's disparaging views of the President, see his memoir *Cursă Pe Contrasens*, p. 87.

119. Cornel Nistorescu, *Evenimentul Zilei*, 27 December 1998 (English Online edition).

120. *Monitorul*, 5 and 7 March 1998.

121. Cornel Nistorescu, *Evenimentul Zilei*, 6 June 1997 (English Online edition).

122. Cornel Nistorescu, *Evenimentul Zilei*, 14 February 1998 (English Online edition).

123. *Evenimentul Zilei*, 11 December 1997, 28 January 1998.

124. *Evenimentul Zilei*, (English language ed.), 7 November 2002.

125. *Monitorul*, 27 February 1998.

126. Cornel Nistorescu, *Evenimentul Zilei*, 28 September 1998 (English Online edition).

127. *Evenimentul Zilei*, 6 July 1998.

128. *Monitorul*, 7 July 1998.

129. *Evenimentul Zilei*, 13 April 1998. Bogdan's name was hastily withdrawn when this information about his background emerged.

130. Central Europe Online, 30 April 1998.

131. Ten months later Suciu and Trutulescu were sentenced to 14 and 7 years in prison respectively. *Evenimentul Zilei*, 19 February 1999.

132. *22*, 12–18 May 1998. See also Filip Florian and Marius Oprea, 'Mostenitorii Securitatii—in primii ani de democratie', *Sfera Politicii*, No 52, 1997.

133. This is according to a report about the intelligence services of member states published by the Council of Europe on 26 March 1998. See *Monitorul*, 27 March 1998.

On 13 November 1998 Szabo Karoly, a UDMR senator and member of the defence commission, named a front company which he claimed enabled certain intelligence services to dispose of money by bypassing the law. See *Monitoril*, 10 April 2000.

134. *Adevărul*, 21 May 1998; *Evenimentul Zilei*, 22 May 1998.
135. Deletant, 'The Post-Communist Security Services', p. 189.
136. *Adevarul*, 30 April 1998.
137. Emil Hurezeanu, *22*, 5–11 May 1998.
138. *National* (Bucharest), 27 May 1998.
139. Emil Hurezeanu, *22*, 5–11 May 1998. This PRM claim was made by Ilie Neacsu. See 'Romania', *East European Constitutional Review*, vol. 7, no. 2, Spring 1998.

Colonel Ilie Merce was removed from the SRI for passing information to Vadim Tudor. See *Ziua*, 8 December 2000. Another SRI officer, Captain Constantin Bucur, was given a 2-year suspended sentence for handing over to the PRM transcripts of phone conversations by politicians which he claimed had been carried out by the SRI in contravention of the law. See *Monitorul*, 10 April, 5 December 2000.

140. *Monitorul*, 4 February 1998.
141. *Monitorul*, 22 January 1998.
142. *Monitorul*, 23 May 1998.
143. Interview with Valerian Stan in *Evenimentul Zilei*, 20 May 1998. Stan was portrayed by the President as a troublemaker, intent on stirring up coalition unrest. See Constantinescu, *Timpul dărâmării*, vol. 1, p. 415.
144. Serban Orescu, *Ziua*, 20 November 2000.
145. Interview with Şerban Radulescu-Zoner, Bucharest 21 January 2002. A PNL deputy from 1992 to 2000, he mentioned that the Alianţa Civica got little support when it urged the CDR parties to operate as a bloc.
146. Interview with Şerban Radulescu-Zoner, Bucharest 21 January 2002.

Chapter 6   A Broken-backed Coalition

1. *Lupta*, 288, 7 June 1997.
2. This admission was made in July 1999 by Radu Sârbu, then the head of the privatisation agency. *Nine o'clock*, 23–25 July 1999.
3. *Evenimentul Zilei*, 17 July 1997 (English Online edition).
4. Economist Intelligence Unit, Romania, Country Report, 3rd Quarter 1998, London 1998, p. 18.
5. The data on the privatisation process sent by the State Ownership Fund was found to be at variance with that from the Ministry of Privatization, both agencies then being run by Sorin Dimitriu. *Telegrama*, 2 September 1998.
6. Adevârul, 13 March 1998.
7. Economist Intelligence Unit, *Romania: Country Report*, 3rd quarter 1998, London 1998, p. 19.
8. *Monitorul*, 30 October 1999.

9. Ilie Şerbanescu, 'IMF: team changes so do tactics', *Nine o'Clock*, 20 October 1998.
10. *Evenimentul Zilei*, 17 June 1998.
11. Economist Intelligence Unit, *Romania: Country Report*, 2nd quarter 1998, London 1998, p. 11.
12. See Tom Gallagher, *Democratie si Nationalisme in Romania, 1989–1998*, Bucharest: Editura All, 1999, p. 370.
13. Şerban Orescu, *22*, 21–27 June 1998.
14. Cristian Tudor Popescu, *Adevârul*, 14 November 1998.
15. 'Romania', *East European Constitutional Review*, vol. 9, no. 3, summer 2000, p. 33.
16. *Nine o'Clock*, 10 April 2000.
17. 'Romania', *East European Constitutional Review*, vol. 9, no. 3, summer 2000, p. 33.
18. *Nine o'Clock*, 10 April 2000.
19. Marius Tinu, *Adevârul*, 2 June 1998.
20. Cristian Tudor Popescu, *Adevârul*, 13 May 1998.
21. Cristian Tudor Popescu, *Adevârul*, 13 May 1998.
22. Cornel Nistorescu, *Evenimentul Zilei*, 20 January 1998 (English Online edition).
23. Cornel Nistorescu, *Evenimentul Zilei*, 25 August 1998 (English Online edition).
24. Cornel Nistorescu, *Evenimentul Zilei*, 16 November 2000 (English Online edition). In this article allegations are made that some negotiators on the Romanian side benefited handsomely from the process.
25. Daniel Oantă, *Adevârul*, 20 October 1998.
26. Cornel Nistorescu, *Evenimentul Zilei*, 7 May 1998 (English Online edition).
27. Tudorel Urian, *Cuvintul*, December 2000.
28. Interview with Mariuca Vasile in *Cronica Romana*, cited in *Evenimentul Zilei*, 6 September 1999 (English Online edition).
29. Cornel Nistorescu, *Evenimentul Zilei*, 7 October 1999 (English Online edition).
30. See the editorial by Cornel Nistorescu, *Evenimentul Zilei*, 24 January 2001.
31. *Ziua*, 19 April 2001.
32. *Evenimentul Zilei*, 3 August 1998 (English Online edition).
33. *Evenimentul Zilei*, 4–5 July 1998 (English Online edition).
34. Silviu Brucan, 'Underground economy and Politics', *Nine o'clock*, 20 March 2000.
35. Vălenaş, *Eşecul unei Reforme*, p. 100.
36. *Central Europe Online*, 28 September 1998.
37. The PD lobbied hard in 1997 for one of its allies to be appointed head of Bancorex, the main state bank. See *Business Central Europe*, February 1998.
38. *Central Europe Online*, 28 September 1998.
39. Stefan Wagstyl and Virginia Marsh, 'Time to Deliver the Promised Land', *Financial Times* (supplement on Romania), 28 September 1998.
40. I am grateful to Dennis Deletant for this information.
41. Monica Macovei, 'The Post-Communist Procuracy: Romania', *East European Constitutional Review*, vol. 8, nos 1 & 2, winter–spring 1999, p. 95.
42. Macovei, 'The Post-Communist Procuracy: Romania', p. 97.

43. Monica Macovei, 'Legal Culture in Romania', *East European Constitutional Review,* vol. 7, no. 1, winter 1998.
44. Cornel Nistorescu, *Evenimentul Zilei,* 4–5 March 2000 (English Online edition).
45. Ibid.
46. Adrian Ursu, *Adevârul,* 25 February 1999.
47. 'Opening of Securitate Files may be Limited', Central Europe Online, 7 November 1997.
48. *Evenimentul Zilei,* 17 November 1997 (English Online edition), Şerban Orescu, *22,* 16–22 September 1997.
49. Vălenaş, *Eşecul unei Reforme,* pp. 230–1.
50. *Evenimentul Zilei,* 10 June 1999 (English Online edition).
51. 'Romania', *East European Constitutional Review,* vol. 7, no. 2, spring 1998.
52. Filip Florian and Marius Oprea, 'Mostenitorii Securitatii—in primii ani de democratie', *Sfera Politicii,* no. 52, 1997.
53. Vălenaş, *Eşecul unei Reforme,* pp. 230–1.
54. 'Opening of Securitate Files may be Limited', Central Europe Online, 7 November 1997.
55. 'Romania', *East European Constitutional Review,* vol. 9, nos 1/2, winter/spring 2000.
56. Gabriel Andreescu, *Ziua,* 8 March 2000, Vălenaş, *Eşecul unei Reforme,* p. 469.
57. *22,* 23–29 March 1998.
58. *Nine O'Clock,* 2 September 1999.
59. *Nine O'Clock,* 23 February 2000.
60. Alin Bogdan, *Adevârul,* 16 December 1998.
61. Ibid.
62. *Evenimentul Zilei,* 20 July 1999 (English Online edition).
63. *Nine o'Clock,* 22 July 1999.
64. *Nine o'Clock,* 21 July 1999.
65. *Evenimentul Zilei,* 20 July 1999 (English Online edition).
66. *Evenimentul Zilei,* 12 April 1998.
67. *Evenimentul Zilei,* 17 June 1998. SRI Captain Constantin Alexa testified in public in November 1998 that the file on Vilau had been leaked on the instruction of the PD leadership. See Adrian Severin, *Ziua,* 3 December 1998.
68. *Monitorul,* 22 June 1998.
69. Catherine Lovatt, 'Securitate Shuffle', *Central Europe Online,* vol. 2, no. 15, 17 April 2000. Alexe belonged to the branch of SRI called 'the Division for the Defence of the Territorial Integrity and Unity of the Romanian State', a concept to which he believed Baranyi posed a threat. See *Monitorul,* 10 April 2000.
70. *Evenimentul Zilei,* 12 November 1998, 3 June 1999.
71. *Evenimentul Zilei,* 19 June 1998.
72. Dennis Deletant, 'The Successors to the *Securitate*: Old Habits Die Hard' in Kieran Williams and Dennis Deletant (eds), *Security Inteligence Services in New Democracies,* London: Macmillan 2000, p. 241.
73. *Evenimentul Zilei,* 11 June 1998.
74. Elena Stefoi, *Drept Minoritar, Spaime Nationale,* Editura Kriterion, Bucharest 1997, p. 19.

75. *Evenimentul Zilei*, 3 April 1998 (English Online edition).

76. *Monitorul*, 21 March 1998.

77. Alina Mungiu Pippidi, *Transilvania Subiectivă*, Bucharest: Humanitas, 1999, p. 156.

78. *Monitorul*, 14 March 1997.

79. Zsolt-Istvan Mato, 'Romanian Coalition Conflict Continues', Radio Free Europe, *Newsline*, 13 October 1998.

80. Radio Free Europe, RFE/RL *Newsline, Southeastern Europe*, 4 September 1998.

81. Radio Free Europe, RFE/RL *Newsline, Southeastern Europe*, 4 March 1998.

82. Mungiu-Pippidi, *Transilvania Subiectivă*, p. 206.

83. *Nine O'Clock*, 17 January 2000.

84. *Monitorul*, 20 June 1998.

85. Ibid.

86. *Evenimentul Zilei*, 23 September 1997.

87. Cornel Nistorescu, *Evenimentul Zilei*, 24 November 1998 (with English Online edition). Severin later gave detailed interviews criticising Roman's leadership style and claiming that he constantly interfered in the running of the Foreign Ministry when Severin was in charge. See *Nine o'Clock*, 6 October 1999. He stood by his spying allegations in an interview with *Monitorul* on 12 January 1998.

88. Cornel Nistorescu, *Evenimentul Zilei*, 19–20 September 1998 (English Online edition).

89. *România libera*, 6 November 1998.

90. Sorin Rosca Stănescu, *Ziua*, 11 November 1998.

91. *Telegrama*, 7 September 1998.

92. Cristian Tudor Popescu, *Adevărul*, 10 March 1998.

93. *Nine o'Clock*, 27 July 1999. PNL deputy, Şerban Radulescu-Zoner who quit the party in 2000 because of its search for allies on the post-communist left agreed with the claim that perhaps most in the PNTCD had no higher vision than to capture the state. He said that like the PDSR, the PNTCD was greatly preoccupied, during its period in office, with trying to satisfy its clientele. Interview with Şerban Radulescu-Zoner, Bucharest 21 January 2002.

94. *Adevărul*, 28 March 1998. The other signatories were Andrei Pleşu, Foreign Minister and Ilie Şerbănescu, Reform minister.

95. *Adevărul*, 24 September 1998.

96. *Monitorul*, 9 June 1997.

97. Radu Buşneag, 'Romania: Ciorbea Faces Problems From Worried Workers', Radio Free Europe, 11 June 1997.

98. Ioan Scurtu, *Nine O'Clock*, 30 August 2000.

99. According to a poll by the Quality of Life research institute, the PDSR was on 29% and the CDR 26%. See Central Europe Online, 19 October 1998.

100. *Monitorul*, 10 February 1999. It reported Alin Teodorescu, director of the IMAS polling company, as saying that in December 'the numbers backing the PRM were so great that I didn't dare publish the figures'.

101. Interview with Şerban Radulescu-Zoner, Bucharest, 21 January 2002. This PNL deputy, a veteran of prison camps in the Gheorghiu-Dej era, held a regular weekly surgery in Tirgoviste, capital of Dimbovita county which he represented for the PNL. Other than requests to intercede in land disputes which were a judicial matter, he was most frequently asked to take up abuses by mayors and local councillors which he brought to the attention of the anti-corruption unit in the Prime Minister's office as well as the Ministry of the Interior.

    He fought to link a commune in his electoral district to the piped water system. Its mayor was from the PDSR which would have dissuaded a majority of his CDR colleagues interceding, even though it was not strictly a political issue.

102. Cornel Nistorescu, *Evenimentul Zilei*, 16 December 1998.

103. *Adevărul*, 28 November 1997.

104. Cornel Nistorescu, *Evenimentul Zilei*, 27 December 1998 (with English Online edition).

105. Poll of Metro Media Institute, *Adevărul*, 28 November 1998.

106. *22*, 24–30 November 1998.

107. Vălenaş, *Eşecul unei Reforme*, p. 505.

108. H. R. Patapievici, *22*, 2–8 February 1999.

109. Cozma was facing four court cases at the end of 1998, two of which involved accusations of violent assaults. *Nine o'Clock*, 5–7 February 1999.

110. Romania', *East European Constitutional Review*, vol. 6, no. 4, fall 1997.

111. Magda Brighidau, *Romania libera*, 12 February 1999.

112. *Evenimentul Zilei*, 29 June 1998.

113. Robert Lyle, 'Romanian Mining Pact Makes IMF Loan More Difficult', Radio Free Europe, Endnote, 26 January 1999.

114. Pavel Lucescu, *Monitorul*, 30 August 1997.

115. *Romanian Economic Daily*, 8 January 1999.

116. *Adevărul*, 2 February 1999.

117. Cozma's own nationalist outlook was in evidence during the 1991 *mineriada* when, after his rival Premier Roman had been toppled, President Iliescu persuaded him to withdraw his forces back to the Jiu Valley, claiming there might be a risk that the Hungarians would occupy Transylvania. See Emil Hurezeanu, *22*, 26 January–1 February 1999.

118. The proclamation was published in *România Mare*, 21 August 1998.

119. *Ziua*, 23 November 1998.

120. *Nine O'Clock*, 13 January 1999.

121. Laurentiu Stefan Scalat, 'Partidul România Mare: un profil doctrinar', *Sfera Politicii*, no. 67, 1999, p. 16.

122. Radio Free Europe, South-East-Europe News Briefing, 20 January 1999.

123. Mircea Dutu, *Nine o'Clock*, 25 January 1999.

124. See for instance *Monitorul*, 25 January 1999. The well-known commentator Octavian Paler was in no doubt that Romania was 'on its way back to the Middle Ages', the title of an article by him in *Romania libera* of 22 January.

125. *Evenimentul Zilei*, 25 January 1999 (English Online edition).

126. *Adevarul*, 25 January 1999, for the jobless figure. Many other journalists confirmed Dumitrascu's claim. See *Ziua*, 25 January 1999.
127. *Ziua*, 25 January 1999; Oancea was interviewed in *22*, 26 January–1 February 1999. The claim that local management played a role in inciting the miners and providing them with transport was made by the moderate miners' leader, Marin Condescu, on 2 February. See *Evenimentul Zilei*, 3 February 1999 (with English Online edition).
128. *Monitorul*, 3 February 1999.
129. *Nine o'Clock*, 25 January 1999; *Ziua*, 24 February 1999. Zoe Petre, the President's chief counsellor, recalls that on the day of the parliamentary debate PRM leaders 'called for an annulment of the Constitution...and the creation of a revolutionary committee'. *Monitorul*, 25 January 2000.
130. *Adevârul*, 21 January 1999.
131. In the course of a conversation in London on 3 March 2001, Tokay expressed his belief that generals attached to the Interior Ministry might have been preparing for such an eventuality. So strong were his fears that he destroyed sensitive documents in the Ministry of Minority Affairs which he represented in government in case they fell into extremist hands. See also *Nine o'Clock*, 25 January 1999. Constantin Duda Ionescu, the new interior minister, was reported on 9 March 1999 as confirming the existence of a detailed plan for a coup to enable the PRM to assume power. See *Nine o'Clock*, 10 March 1999.
132. See *Ziua*, 25 January 1999 and *22*, 2–8 February 1999.
133. All the Bucharest morning papers provided exhaustive coverage of Costeşti on 25 January 1999.
134. See *Evenimentul Zilei* (with English Online edition), 28 January 1999.
135. *Adevârul*, 5 February 1999.
136. *Evenimentul Zilei*, 27 January 1999.
137. *Evenimentul Zilei* (English Online edition), 26 January 1999. These smuggling operations burst to the surface in 1997–8, tarnishing the reputation of various branches of the security forces and the effectiveness of government control over law enforcement agencies.
138. *Monitorul*, 30 January 1999.
139. *Evenimentul Zilei* (with English Online edition), 25 January 1999.
140. *Monitorul*, 15 March 1997.
141. *Nine o'Clock*, 29 January 1999.
142. *Monitorul*, 30 January 1999. The extent to which local villagers had swelled the miners ranks prompted *Ziua* on 25 January 1999 to headline its report of the Costeşti battle, 'The uprising of peasants from Costeşti'.
143. Vălenaş, *Eşecul unei Reforme*, p. 385.
144. 'Bulgarisation' referred to the financial meltdown that occurred in Bulgaria in 1996 while Albanisation referred to the collapse of law and order and the looting of army depots which took place in 1997 after the collapse of a pyramid savings scheme.
145. *Monitorul*, 20 January 1999.
146. *Evenimentul Zilei* (English Online edition), 25 January 1999.
147. *Nine o'Clock*, 22 January 1999.

148. Adrian Ciocolea in *Monitorul*, 25 January 1999 wrote: 'Miron Cozma must be arrested.' Cornel Nistorescu in *Evenimentul Zilei* (English Online edition), 15 January 1999 asked: 'What is the way to break the evil influence that a paranoic delinquent has on the Jiu Valley miners?'

149. *Evenimentul Zilei* (English Online edition), 30–31 January 1999. This was an indictment of the record of those appointed by the President to head the SRI. Radu Vasile has commented that his appointees had no control over the SRI or the SIE. See Vasile, *Cursă pe Contrasens*, p. 31.

150. See Sorin Rosca Stănescu's editorial in *Ziua*, 15 December 1998.

151. *Evenimentul Zilei* (English Online edition), 21 January 1999.

152. PDSR statements, strongly critical of the government, were carried by *Nine o'Clock*, on 17 and 18 February 1999 after the main danger to state institutions had passed.

153. On 25 January the PDSR's action won the praise of *România libera*'s chief political writer, Bogdan Figeac, normally one of its unflinching critics. See *Ziua*, 27 January 1999.

154. *Evenimentul Zilei* (English Online edition), 25 January 1999.

155. *Nine o'Clock*, 16 February 1999. The poll was carried out by IMAS.

156. *Ziua*, 19 February 1999.

157. Cristian Tudor Popescu contrasted 'civilised citizens' with 'a barbarian' state. See *Adevărul*, 18 January 1999.

158. *România libera*, 5 February 1999.

159. The views of Mircea Dutu in *Nine o'Clock*, 28 January 1999 were not untypical: 'To ask for the outlawing of a formation which, in keeping with the latest opinion polls, would rally about 15–20% of the electorate...even if it asked for the toppling of the government, becomes in itself a deeply undemocratic act'.

160. *Adevărul*, 3 February 1999.

161. *Adevărul* of 15 February covered the story with the sub-heading, 'Romanian justice has washed away the shame'.

162. Mediafax, (Bucharest), 15 February 1999. Most of the Bucharest press rejected the opposition's claim and praised the way the justice system had performed.

163. *Nine O'Clock*, 11 February 1999.

164. *Nine o'Clock*, 26 April 1999. The Interior Minister justified his action by saying that Oancea's 'businessman status is incompatible with his position in the ministry'.

165. *22*, 9–15 February 1999.

166. *Monitorul*, 24 February 1999.

167. *România líbera*, 18 January 1999.

168. *Nine o'Clock*, 26 January 1999.

169. A SRI report carried by *Evenimentul Zilei* (English Online edition), 9 March 1999, drew attention to Russian embassy vehicles seen at Costeşti and Rimnicu Valcea, recording on videotape the movements of Romanian security forces (the supposition being that the information may then have been relayed to the rebels). The government never made any comment on this report. See *Monitorul*, 22 March 2001.

170. *Nine o'Clock*, 29 January 1999.
171. This appeared in *22*, 26 January–1 February 1999, the most serious of Romania's political weeklies which Ms Adameșteanu edited for most of the 1990s.
172. *22*, 2–8 February 1999.
173. Martin Malia, *International Herald Tribune*, 5–6 September 1998.
174. The first editorial I have found expressing this anxiety was by Cornel Nistorescu in *Evenimentul Zilei* of 4 August 1998.
175. *Evenimentul Zilei* (English Online edition), 4 February 1999, reported him as saying: 'I won't let some good-for-nothing people like those in Bucharest mock the ideal I've cherished all my life of defending people.'
176. *Adevârul*, 5 February 1999.
177. *Adevârul*, 13 October 1998.

Chapter 7   Staggering to the Finishing-Line

1. In some quarters fears had been expressed in 1994–5 that with his support in the military and the security services, Vadim was strong enough to mount a coup against the Iliescu regime. In *Evenimentul Zilei*, 22 November 2000, it was pointed out that the PRM had published a statement of protest in the edition of *România Mare* of 20 June 1995, signed by 300 generals and other senior officers on active service or in the reserve, protesting at Iliescu's plans to introduce western-style reforms to the military.
2. See Larry L. Watts, 'The Crisis in Romanian Civil-Military Relations', *Problems of Post-Communism*, vol. 48, no. 4, July–August 2001, p. 19.
3. *Nine O'clock*, 23 November 1998; earlier, when the government was in a much stronger position, Cornel Nistorescu underlined the influence Vadim enjoyed in the State Prosecutor's Office. See *Evenimentul Zilei*, 2 July 1997 (English Online edition).
4. See *Evenimentul Zilei*, (English Online edition) 21 January 1999.
5. *Nine O'Clock*, 25 March 1999.
6. Radio Free Europe, *South-East-Europe Newsline*, 13 September 1999.
7. *Monitorul*, 12 February 1999.
8. *Monitorul*, 5 December 2000.
9. *Nine O'Clock*, 30 April–2 May 1999.
10. *Monitorul*, 29 April 1999.
11. *Nine O'Clock*, 9 November 1998.
12. Nine o'Clock, 18 April 1999.
13. Cristian Vasile, 'Fata nevazuta a relatiilor romano-serb', *22*, 27 April–3 May 1999.
14. See *Adevârul*, 29 March 1999.
15. Peter Finn, 'Anger Growing in Eastern Europe over Nato-Blocked Danube', *International Herald Tribune*, 7 February 2000.
    Romania claimed it had lost $245 million between 24 March and 21 June 1999 from the conflict between NATO and Yugoslavia according to the Foreign Ministry. See 'Romania Accuses the west of Unfair Treatment', Central Europe Online, 14 July 1999.

16. This claim had been made in *The White Book on Romania and NATO, 1997*, Ministry of Foreign Affairs, Bucharest 1997, chapter 7, p. 6.

17. *Nine o'Clock*, 23–25 April 1999. An IMAS poll conducted between 17 and 20 April 1999 showed that 57% of Romanians agreed with Romania joining NATO compared with 89% in February 1997. See *Monitorul*, 28 April 1999.

18. This was particularly true of the daily *Cotidianul*, then being edited by Ion Cristoiu.

19. *Adevârul*, 17 April 1999.

20. *Ziua*, 5 May 1999.

21. South-East Europe Newsline, Radio Free Europe, 27 April 1999.

22. *Adevârul*, 17 April 1999.

23. *Ziua*, 5 May 1999. On returning home Blair told MPs: 'It is essential that we begin work as soon as possible on a regeneration programme for the Balkans, because many of the front-line states—such as Bulgaria, Romania, Macedonia and Albania—have given us support in circumstances of intense internal difficulty.' *Hansard* (record of the proceedings of the House of Commons), 8 June 1999, p. 468.

24. *Monitorul*, 24 April 1999.

25. Christopher Bennett, 'Emergency Aid For Neighbours', IWPR's Balkan Crisis Report, no. 331, 14 May 1999, http://www.iwpr.net

26. Javier Solana, NATO's Secretary-General declared on 17 April that 'Romania and Bulgaria will eventually become members of NATO'. *Nine o'Clock*, 19 April 2000.

27. See the critique of the American law company Herzfeld and Rubin of IMF policy towards Romania in their regular 'Romanian Digest', vol. 4, no. 10, October 1999, http://www.hr.ro/digest10_4htm.

28. 1999 Regular Report From the Commission on Romania's Progress Towards Accession, European Commission, Brussels 1999, p. 28.

29. Colin Woodward, 'Interview with Emil Constantinescu', Transition, vol. 3, no. 6, 4 April 1997.

30. *Evenimentul Zilei*, 29 May 1998.

31. *Adevârul*, 14 July 1999.

32. Tom Gallagher, 'Romania: is the West Watching', *International Herald Tribune*, 23 July 1977.

33. *Nine o'Clock*, 14 June 1999.

34. *Nine o'Clock*, 9–11 June 1999.

35. Ziua, 5 May 1999.

36. Radio Free Europe, *South-East Europe Newsline*, 1 April 1999. Later, in an article published in the *Washington Post*, Iliescu expressed anxiety that the outcome of the Kosovo conflict might result in a massive Russian troop presence in the Balkans which may have been a bid to dent the image he had of being a covert champion of Russian interests in the region. See *Nine o'Clock*, 27 May 1999.

37. *Ziua* on 29 July 1999 published correspondence between local leaders of the respective parties showing how close relations were.

38. The best account of the Bancorex affair and its political ramifications is Ilie Serbanescu's, 'Bancorex-istoria emblematica a Romaniei postdecembrist', *22*, 16–22 February.

39. For the amount lost, see Radio Free Europe, *South-East-Europe Newsline*, 30 July 1999.
40. *Nine o'Clock*, 4 March 1999.
41. *Nine o'Clock*, 4 March 1999.
42. Cornel Nistorescu, *Evenimentul Zilei*, 12 June 1997 (English Online edition).
43. Cornel Nistorescu, *Evenimentul Zilei*, 16 March 1999 (English Online edition).
44. *Nine o'Clock*, 20 October 1998.
45. *România libera*, 3 August 1999.
46. *Adevârul*, 15 July 1999.
47. *Adevârul*, 15 July 1999.
48. *Cotidianul*, 17 July 1999.
49. Cornel Nistorescu, *Evenimentul Zilei*, 17 August 1998 (English Online edition).
50. *Nine o'Clock*, 27 May 1999.
51. The memoirs left by both men reveal the sheer absence of personal chemistry between them and their failure to maintain regular contact over political matters. See Constantinescu, *Timpul dărâmării*, vol. 1, pp. 517–8; and Vasile, *Cursă Pe Contrasens*, p. 259.
52. *Nine o'Clock*, 27 May 1999.
53. Radio Free Europe, *South-East-Europe Newsline*, 11 March 1999.
54. *Monitorul*, 1 March 1999.
55. *Adevârul*, 4 March 1999, *Monitorul*, 3 March 1999.
56. Radio Free Europe, *South-East-Europe Newsline*, 27 April 1999.
57. Daniel Dăianu and Georges de Menil, 'Romania Deserves More From the IMF', *Inside Romania News*, 4 May 2000.
58. Radio Free Europe, *South-East-Europe Newsline*, 30 July 1999.
59. *Nine o'Clock*, 15 July 1999.
60. Herzfeld and Rubin, 'Romanian Digest', vol. 4, no. 12, December 1999.
61. For sceptical accounts of the Western approach to reconstructing the Balkans, see Janusz Bugajski, 'Stability Pact or Status Quo', Bosnia Report, 24 May 2000, http://www.bosnia.org.uk/binews/240500%5Fl.htm. Also Vladimir Gligorov, 'Strategies and Instruments', *Balkan Eye*, vol. 1, no. 1, June 2000.
62. 'Romania', *East European Constitutional Review*, vol. 8, no. 4, fall 1999.
63. Ibid.
64. *Nine o'Clock*, 23 December 1999.
65. Another notable breakdown in communications occurred between Vasile and Sârbu's predecessor Sorin Dimitriu, who in August 1998 announced that he planned to sell Romania's 'large industrial mastodons' for the nominal sum of $1, which was a complete surprise to the Prime Minister who vetoed the idea. See *România libera*, 27 August 1998.
66. Interview with Alin Giurgiu, director-general of the FPS, 24 September 1999.
67. *Nine o'Clock*, 4 March 1999.
68. *Nine o'Clock*, 22 October 1999.
69. Ilie Serbanescu, 'Esecul privatizarii: de ce?', *22*, 14–20 November 2000.
70. See Ion Iliescu, as reported by Reuters on 14 November 2000, *Inside Romania News*, 15 November 2000.
71. Cornel Nistorescu, *Evenimentul Zilei*, 17 August 1998 (English Online edition).

72. Roxana Iordache, *România liberă*, 4 September 1999.
73. 'Romania', *East European Constitutional Review*, vol. 9, nos 1 & 2, winter/spring 2000.
74. Vălenaş, *Eşecul unei Reforme*, p. 529.
75. The president, who negotiated the terms of his departure, also recalls that he insisted his wife keep her well-paid post with the AVAB. See Constantinescu, *Timpul dărâmării*, vol. 1, p. 526.
76. Ciorbea believed Vasile's removal was carried out 'in a profoundly unconstitutional way and constituted an extremely dangerous precedent'. *Monitorul*, 18 January 2000. In his memoirs Constantinescu makes no mention of the constitutional dimension and he claims the initiative for unseating Vasile came from political colleagues who had been lobbying for his replacement for a year or more. See Constantinescu, *Timpul dărâmării...* (vol. 1), p. 518.
77. *Nine o'Clock*, 14 January 2000.
78. *Monitorul*, 14 January 2000.
79. *Monitorul*, 1 November 1999.
80. Radio Free Europe, *South-East Europe Newsline*, 22 March 2000.
81. *The 1999 Report of the European Commission on Romania's Progress towards Accession*, Brussels: European Commission, October 1999, pp. 15–16.
82. *East European Constitutional Review*, vol. 9, nos 1 and 2, winter/spring 2000.
83. *Monitorul*, 20 November 1999.
84. Central Europe Online, 27 August 1999.
85. *Nine o'Clock*, 26 August 1999.
86. Central Europe Online, 27 August 1999.
87. *Monitorul*, 26 August 1999.
88. *Nine o'Clock*, 6 September 1999.
89. *Monitorul*, 30 August 1999.
90. *Monitorul*, 27 August 1999.
91. *East European Constitutional Review*, vol. 9, no. 14, fall 2000.
92. For its shortcomings see Eugen Tomiuc, 'Romania: New Property Law Falls Short of Full Restitution', Radio Free Europe, *Features*, 15 February 2001.
93. Ron Synovitz, 'OECD: Agricultural Review has Praise for Bulgaria, Misgivings about Romania', Radio Free Europe, *Features*, 16 January 2001.
94. *Business Central Europe*, July–August 1997.
95. Radio Free Europe, *South-East Europe Newsline*, 21 June 1999.
96. *East European Constitutional Review*, vol. 9, nos 1 and 2, winter/spring 2000. For doubts about the ability of private farming to recover in Romania, see Andrew Cartwright, *The Return of the Peasant: Land reform in post-Communist Romania*, Aldershot: Ashgate, 2001, especially Chapter 10.
97. *Inside Romania News*, 20 March 2000.
98. 'Romania', *East European Constitutional Review*, vol. 9, nos 1 and 2, winter/spring 2000.
99. Cornel Nistorescu, *Evenimentul Zilei*, 12 April 2000 (English Online edition).
100. Radio Free Europe, *South-East Europe Newsline*, 7 April 2000.
101. 'Romania', *East European Constitutional Review*, vol. 9, no. 3, summer 2000, p. 33.

102. Radio Free Europe, *South-East Europe Newsline,* 7 June 2000.
103. *Nine o'Clock,* 30 May 2000.
104. 'Romania', *East European Constitutional Review,* vol. 9, no. 4, fall 2000.
105. *Evenimentul Zilei,* 31 May (English Online edition).
106. *Nine o'Clock,* 30 May 2000.
107. *Nine o'Clock,* 31 May 2000.
108. *Nine o'Clock,* 18 May 2000.
109. Catherine Lovatt, 'New From Romania', *Central Europe Review,* vol. 2, no. 20, 22 May 2000.
110. Calin Hera, *Evenimentul Zilei,* 16 May 2000.
111. *Nine o'Clock,* 15 May 2000.
112. Cornel Nistorescu, *Evenimentul Zilei,* 15 May 2000 (English Online edition).
113. *Evenimentul Zilei,* 16 May 2000.
114. *Evenimentul Zilei,* 16 May 2000.
115. *Nine o'Clock,* 1 February 2000.
116. *Nine o'Clock,* 27 August 1998.
117. In September 2000 Iliescu was summoned before the High Court in Paris regarding the lawsuit issued by Costea about the alleged non-payment for election materials. See *Evenimentul Zilei,* 3 September 2000 (English Online edition). On 8 November 2001 the Paris court threw out the lawsuit, ruling that the plaintiff had failed to submit any documentation attesting to a contract between the company and either Iliescu personally or the PDSR. See Radio Free Europe, *South-East Europe Newsline,* 9 November 2001.

Chapter 8   Taking Things to Extremes: The 2000 Elections and Their Outcome

1. Cornel Nistorescu, *Evenimentul Zilei,* 26–27 February 2000 (English Online edition). He wrote that it was the first time in ten years that any party had responded in this way to a leading member facing serious corruption allegations.
2. *România libera,* 15 June 2000.
3. For full details of the June 2000 local election results, see the website entitled 'Alegerile locale—iunie 2000,' http://domino.kappa.ro/election/locale2000.nsf/All/Home
4. Radio Free Europe, *South-East-Europe Newsline,* 3 July 2000.
5. For a short explanation of why he withdrew his candidacy, see Constantinescu, *Timpul dărâmării,* vol. 1, pp. 102–3.
6. *Evenimentul Zilei,* 18 July 2000.
7. See the editorials by Cornel Nistorescu, *Evenimentul Zilei,* 19 July 2000, and Dan Pavel in *Ziua,* 19 July 2000.
8. *Evenimentul Zilei,* 18 July 2000 (English Online edition).
9. Radio Free Europe, *South-East-Europe Newsline,* 3 July 2000.
10. *Nine o'Clock,* 19 July 2000.
11. See Cornel Nistorescu, *Evenimentul Zilei,* 18 October 2000 (English Online edition), in an editorial entitled 'Romania, without a president'.
12. Nine o'Clock, 2 August 2000.

13. Nine o'Clock, 28–30 July 2000.
14. *Nine o'Clock*, 11–13 August 2000.
15. *Nine o'Clock*, 24 August 2000. For the revelations about Lazarescu see *Adevârul*, 26 April 2001.
16. *Nine o'Clock*, 11–13 August 2000.
17. *Nine o'Clock*, 8 August 2000.
18. *Evenimentul Zilei*, 9 August 2000.
19. Radio Free Europe, *South-East-Europe Newsline*, 17 October 2000.
20. Tudorel Urian, *Cuvîntul*, December 2000.
21. 'A Battle of Generations at the Romanian Polls', Inside Romania News, 22 September 2000.
22. Cornel Nistorescu, *Evenimentul Zilei*, 12 October 2000 (English edition).
23. *Evenimentul Zilei*, 23 November 1999 (English edition).
24. *22*, 28 March–3 April 2000.
25. 'A Bitter Romania Seeks Election-Time Revenge', Inside Romania News, 10 November 2000, quoting Reuters, 10 November 2000.
26. *Nine o'Clock*, 14–16 April 2000.
27. This is the recollection of a PNL deputy, Şerban Radulescu-Zoner, who in 1999 declared a parliamentary strike, refusing to leave the chamber in protest at the way many of his colleagues were neglecting their duties and abusing their positions. Interview with Şerban Radulescu-Zoner, Bucharest, 21 January 2002.
28. *Adevârul*, 26 February 1998.
29. *Nine o'Clock*, 4 May 2000.
30. *Adevârul*, 28 November 1999.
31. *Nine o'Clock*, 2 March 1999.
32. Rodica Ciobanu, *Adevârul*, 8 May 2001. Her article was entitled 'Rich Parliamentarians in a Poor Country'.
33. *Evenimentul Zilei*, 28 June 2001 (English edition).
34. *Adevârul*, 15 August 2000.
35. *România libera*, 25 June 2001.
36. *Ziua*, 26 February 2000.
37. *22*, 9–15 February 1999; Radio Free Europe, *South-East-Europe Newsline*, 8 December 2000.
38. *Adevârul*, 30 September 1999.
39. Ana Blandiana, 10 August 2005.
40. *Nine o'Clock*, 8 May 2000.
41. Ana Blandiana, 10 August 2005.
42. Cotidianul, 2 April 2001.
43. *Nine o'Clock*, 21 March 2000. Cristian Tudor Popescu wrote about the affair in *Adevârul* of 20 March 2000 under the headline, 'Analyst Dan Pavel, an Old Member of the GDS, expelled from the GDS Journal as if it were in the Kremlin'.
44. Sorin Rosca Stănescu was warning over a month before the elections of November 2000 that many students had moved over to Vadim's camp. See the editorial in *Ziua* of 18 October 2000.
45. *Monitorul*, 17 February 2000.

46. *Nine o'Clock*, 2 February 1999.

47. *Monitorul*, 17 February 2000.

48. Radio Free Europe, *South-East-Europe Newsline*, 21 June 1999.

49. Commentators disagreed over whether this was a politically smart move on Iliescu's part or not. Dan Pavel expressed some doubts in *Ziua* on 25 October 1999 but Cornel Nistorescu, writing in *Evenimentul Zilei* the next day was in no doubt about the sagacity of the move.

50. *România libera*, 12 December 2000.

51. *Monitorul*, 26 August 2000.

52. *Ziua*, 19 September 2000.

53. Dan Pavel, 'The Danger of the Left's return to Power', *Ziua*, 10 August 1999.

54. *Ziua*, 12 September 2000.

55. *Ziua*, 14 September 1999.

56. *Monitorul*, 6 September 1997.

57. *Nine o'Clock*, 10 May 1999.

58. *Nine o'Clock*, 3 August 1999.

59. See Rodica Ciobanu's article in *Adevârul* of 8 May 2001 entitled 'Rich Parliamentarians in a Poor Country'; also Cornel Nistorescu's editorial in *Evenimentul Zilei* (English edition) of 12 October 2000.

60. See *Ziua*, 6 February 2000 for an investigation of Voiculescu's pre-1989 business activities.

61. See Evenimentul Zilei (English edition), 23 June 2001.

62. This view was expressed to me by a friend who mixed in student circles in Sibiu and Cluj and was also advanced in editorials in *Adevârul* by Cristian Tudor Popescu after the first electoral round on 26 November.

63. These pledges were taken from the PRM manifesto and were quoted by *Nine o'Clock*, 8 December 2000.

64. Radio Free Europe, *South-East-Europe Newsline*, 21 November 2000.

65. Sorin Rosca Stănescu, *Ziua*, 13 December 2000.

66. *Adevârul*, 22 November 2000.

67. Evenimentul Zilei, 22 November 2000, typified the coverage.

68. Prime Minister Isărescu was sufficiently worried that he wrote to 'Reporters sans Frontières'. 'I cannot remain indifferent that in Romania 2000, a political leader threatens a journalist just like in the blackest period of our history.' *Evenimentul Zilei*, 6 December 2000.

69. *Nine o'Clock*, 30 November 2000.

70. See press reports in the Bucharest dailies for 22 November 2000.

71. Cornel Nistorescu, *Evenimentul Zilei*, 23 November 2000 (English edition).

72. Cornel Nistorescu, *Evenimentul Zilei*, 18–19 November 2000 (English edition).

73. *22*, 28 March–3 April 2000.

74. *Nine o'Clock*, interview with Vadim, 29 November 2000.

75. Reuters, 5 December 2000.

76. Radio Free Europe, *South-East-Europe Newsline*, 16 October 2000.

77. *Nine o'Clock*, 30 November 2000.

78. In the first presidential round Vadim emerged ahead of his rivals in 13 out of 41 Romanian counties, all but two of which were in Transylvania.

79. Evidence suggests that the PRM vote went up in Transylvania not so much because of mass defections from previous CDR voters but because of strong support from first-time young voters or those under 30 who had not regularly turned out to vote before. The PRM also benefited from the collapse of the more moderate ultra-nationalist party, the Party of Romanian National Unity.

80. In elections held on 6 June for county and local councils on a 44.5% turnout the PRM won just over 6% of the vote. It failed to capture any large city in Romania with the exception of Cluj whose mayor, Gheorghe Funar, had joined the PRM in 1998. See the website with details of local election result in 2000 at http://domino.kappa.ro/election/locale/2000.nsf/All/Home

81. Except for Brasov and mainly ethnic Hungarian counties, Vadim won the first round in all Transylvanian counties, but he was second last in Mureş (on 27.57%) and only managed 30.44% in Cluj compared with 38.04% in Alba and 41.98% in Bistrita, counties not known for inter-ethnic tensions. The only seat won by a non-Hungarian party in the counties of Harghita and Covasna went to the PDSR.

82. Metro Media Transylvania poll, *Evenimentul Zilei*, 6 December 2000.

83. *Nine o'Clock*, 30 November 2000.

84. *Nine o'Clock*, 30 November 2000.

85. See the letter from Mihai Nicolae in *România libera* of 6 December and the reply from one of its leading journalists Bogdan Figeac.

86. *Nine o'Clock*, 30 November 2000.

87. *Nine o'Clock*, 6 December 2000.

88. *Nine o'Clock*, 8 December 2000.

89. *Adevârul*, 29 November 2000.

90. Radio Free Europe, *South-East-Europe Newsline*, 5 December 2000.

91. *Nine o'Clock*, 30 November 2000.

92. *Nine o'Clock*, 4 December 2000.

93. Cornel Nistorescu wrote: 'Whereas other companies in Romania have been under the terror of constant fraud squad checks, "România Mare" has remained a protected island.... If it can't enforce financial and tax legislation on Vadim, then the Romanian state is on its way to dissolution.' See *Evenimentul Zilei* (English edition), 9–10 December 2000.

94. *Sâptamina*, 10 January 1986, quoted in *Evenimentul Zilei* (English edition), 9–10 December 2000.

95. *România libera*, 9 December 2000.

96. *România libera*, 7 December 2000.

97. *Adevârul*, 4 December 2000.

98. *România Mare*, 15 December 2000.

99. The editor of *22*, Gabriela Adameşteanu, was one of Constantinescu's most loyal defenders in the media during almost the whole of his presidency. A year after he quit the presidential race, she was blaming him not only for the electoral debacle of the PNTCD but for contributing, in no small way, through his abdication, to the impending disintegration of the party in 2001. See Gabriela Adameşteanu, 'PNTCD si rectorii săi', *22*, 17–23 July 2001.

100. *Monitorul*, 18 November 2000.

101. *Nine o'Clock*, 8 December 2000.
102. *Adevârul*, 11 December 2000.
103. See *Adevârul*, 4 November 2000, and two editorials in *Ziua* on 1 and 6 November 2000.

Chapter 9   A Messiah for Romania?: Corneliu Vadim Tudor and the Greater Romania Party

1. *România Mare*, 22 June 2001.
2. For a discussion of the features which the PRM shares with 'post-modern fascism, see Iris Urban, *Le Parti de la Grande Roumanie, doctrine et rapport au passé. Le nationalisme dans la' transition post-communiste*, Cahiers d'études, no. 1/2001, Bucharest: Institut Roumain d'Histoire Récente, pp. 68–9.
3. Vadim has made room in the PRM for an apologist for the Iron Guard, Gheorghe Buzatu, a PRM Senator for Iasi who is a historian and the mentor of the organization called 'the Crusade to Relaunch the Homeland'. He was made a Vice-President of the Romanian Senate in 2000. See *Monitorul*, 2 December 2000.
4. François Furet, *The Passing of An Illusion: the Idea of Communism in the Twentieth Century*, University of Chicago Press 1999, pp. 191–2.
5. Petre Mihai Bacanu, 'Pericolul fascisto-communist', *Romania líbera*, 12 January 1999.
6. Zeev Sternhell, *Neither Right nor Left: Fascist Ideology in France*, Princeton University Press 1986, p. 118.
7. Furet, p. 138.
8. Zeev Sternhell, 'Fascist Ideology' in Walter Laqueur, *Fàscism: a Reader's Guide*, Harmondsworth: Penguin 1979.
9. Norberto Bobbio, *Left and Right: the Significance of a Political Distinction*, London: Polity Press, 1996, p. 19.
10. Sternhell, *Neither Right nor Left*, p. 14.
11. See Bobbio, p. 25.
12. *Evenimentul Zilei*, 26 June 1997.
13. *Monitorul*, 3 May 1997.
14. See *România Mare*, 21 June 2002.
15. *Evenimentul Zilei*, 20 October 2000.
16. Ian Cummins, *Marx, Engels and National Movements*, London: Croom Helm, 1980, p. 177.
17. *Ibid*.
18. For the examples of Engels and Marx, see George Watson, *The Lost Literature of Socialism*, Cambridge: Lutterworth Press, 1998, p. 78.
19. Watson, *The Lost Literature of Socialism*, p. 9.
20. See Iris Urban, *Le Parti de la Grande Roumanie*, pp. 52–3.
21. 'Speech on the state of the nation presented at the 1st Congress of the Greater Romania Party', *Politica*, 13 March 1993, p. 3.
22. Radio Free Europe, *South-East-Europe Newsline*, 3 October 2000.
23. See Erich Fromm, *Fear of Freedom*, London: Routledge, 1960 ed.

24. George Voicu, *Zeii Cei Rai. Cultura conspiratie in Romania postcomunista*, Bucharest: Polirom 2000, p. 212.
25. Vălenaş, *Eşecul unei Reforme*, p. 261.
26. Nine o'Clock, 22 November 2000. It is not clear how Romanians who voted for the PRM in 2000 will react to press stories about the wealth of newly-elected PRM deputies. In an elaborate hoax, a newspaper persuaded the PRM deputy and folksinger, Irina Loghin, to agree to perform dressed in 'a vampire's costume' at a wedding for a fee of $3,000. See *Evenimentul Zilei*, 21 July 2001.
27. Nine o'Clock, 2 March 1999.
28. *Monitorul*, 17 August 1998.
29. *Adevărul*, 19 January 2001.
30. See for instance an article entitled 'The Nationalization of 1948 was necessary' by Simona Izemenescu, published in *România Mare*, 20 September 1999.
31. *România Mare*, 12 January 2001, p. 7.
32. Ion Coja, *Marele manipulator si asasinarea lui Culiasnu, Ceauşescu, Iorga*, Bucharest: Ed. Miracol, 1999, p. 149.
33. Voicu, *Zeii Cei Rai*, p. 71, quoting *România Mare*, 24 September 1999.
34. See for instance the editorial in *România Mare*, 6 November 1998.
35. *Politica*, 22 July 2000, quoted by Voicu, *Zeii Cei Rai*, p. 142.
36. *România Mare*, no. 181, 1994, quoted by Voicu, *Zeii Cei Rai*, p. 159.
37. An account of conspiracies which offers many parallels with Romania is Daniel Pipes, *Hidden Hand: Middle East Fear of Conspiracy*, Basingstoke: Macmillan, 1996.
38. One of the longest-running series in *România Mare* during 1991 was one entitled 'Romania, a pawn in the interests of the Great Powers (1940–1947)'.
39. Greater Romania Party: Draft Programme, *România Mare*, 21 June 1991.
40. Liviu Vălenaş, *Eşecul unei Reforme*, p. 361.
41. For the Iron Guard's anti-Semitism, see Eugen Weber, 'Romania' in Hans Rogger and Eugen Weber (eds), *The European Right*, Berkeley: University of California Press, 1966, pp. 530–1.
42. John Vincour, 'Even as French Far-Right Implodes, its Ideas Remain', *International Herald Tribune*, 16 December 1998.
43. *Adevărul*, 16 December 1998.
44. *Evenimentul Zilei*, 22 November 2000.
45. Ana Nicholls, 'Out of Control', *Business Central Europe*, May 2001, p. 16.
46. See also *Monitorul*, 5 December 2000.
47. *Monitorul*, 5 December 2000.
48. Petre Niteanu, 'Averea Mascariciuliu', *Ziua*, 29 June 2000.
49. Petre Niteanu, 'Coicoiul de Butimanu', *Ziua*, 30 June 2000.
50. *Ziua*, 24 November 2000.
51. Razvan Savaliuc, 'Dictator Vadim', *Ziua*, 20 November 2000.
52. *Nine o'Clock*, 15 November 2000.
53. Cornel Nistorescu, *Evenimentul Zilei*, 13 October 2000 (English edition).
54. Roberts, *Rumania*, p. 377, n. 2.
55. *România libera*, 5 February 1999.
56. *Nine o'Clock*, 8 December 2000.

57. Cornel Nistorescu, *Evenimentul Zilei*, 23 December 1997 (English edition).
58. Alina Mungiu-Pippidi, 'The Return of Populism—the 2000 Romanian Elections', *Government and Opposition*, vol. 36, no. 2, spring 2000.
59. Cornel Nistorescu, *Evenimentul Zilei*, 8 May 1998 (English edition).
60. *Monitorul*, 21 December 2000.
61. *Monitorul*, 5 December 2000.
62. 'Romanian Editor Accuses Soccer Boss of Anti-Semitism', Central Europe Online, 31 August 1999, quoting Reuters, 31 August 1999.
63. *Monitorul*, 17 March 2001.
64. Gallagher, *Democratie si Nationalisme in Romania*, p. 6.
65. ARPRESS, Selected Daily Bulletin, no. 674, 28 May 1993.
66. *Adevărul*, 21 January 1999.
67. *Nine o'Clock*, 10 May 1999.
68. *România líbera*, 5 February 1999.
69. Cornel Nistorescu, *Evenimentul Zilei*, 12 November 1997 (English edition).
70. See Michael Shafir, 'The Men of the Archangel Revisted: Anti-Semitic Formations among Communist Romania's Intellectuals', *Studies in Comparative Communism*, vol. 41, no 3, autumn 1983, pp. 233–4.
71. *Evenimentul Zilei*, 9–10 December 2000 (English edition).
72. Alexandru, *Coposu: confesiune*, p. 177.
73. Emil Hurezeanu, 'Feţele nopţii', *22*, 5–11 December 2000.
74. Ana Blandiana, quoted in *22*, 5–11 December 2000.
75. Cornel Nistorescu, *Evenimentul Zilei*, 7 December 2000 (English edition).
76. Emil Hurezeanu, 'Feţele nopţii', *22*, 5–11 December 2000.
77. *Monitorul*, 25 November 2000.
78. Laszlo Tökes, well-known for his role in the 1989 revolution and for asserting Hungarian demands in a militant way, never became a leader of the UDMR despite being its honorary president for several years.
79. In early 1991 *România Mare* ran a series entitled 'Your Majesty Isn't wanted'. It regularly published photographs showing the ex-King with Marshall Antonescu, whom he was accused of betraying.
80. *România Mare*, 22 March 1991, 2 September 1991.
81. *Politica*, 26 February 1993.
82. Deletant, 'The Securitate Legacy in Romania', p. 199. This figure excludes others who informed for the militia.
83. *Evenimentul Zilei*, 20–21 June 1998 (English edition).
84. Christian Levant, *Evenimentul Zilei*, 4 October 2001.
85. *România líbera*, 13 January 1998. The newspaper named the politicians thus attacked but their names have been removed here.
86. *România Mare*, 25 October 1991.
87. *România Mare*, 2 September 1991.
88. *România Mare*, 22 June 2001.
89. *România Mare*, 10 April 1992.
90. *România Mare*, 26 July 1991.
91. *România Mare*, 5 May 1995, 2 June 1995.
92. *România Mare*, 13 December 1991.

93. Katherine Verdery, *National Ideology under Socialism: Identity and Cultural Politics in Ceaușescu's Romania*, Berkeley: California University Press, 1991, pp. 174–6.

94. Dan Ioan Mirescu, writing in *Evenimentul Zilei* on 2 July 1996, claimed that up till then the majority of such letters had been fabricated in '*România Mare*'s laboratory'.

95. Sternhell, *Neither Right nor Left*, p. 101.

96. Cristian Teodorescu, 'Atacul la Dinescu', *România Literara*, 15 November 2000.

97. *Nine o'Clock*, 13 January 1999.

98. Cornel Nistorescu, *Evenimentul Zilei*, 2 July 1997 (English edition).

99. *22*, 18–24 October 1995.

100. ARPRESS, *Selected Daily Bulletin*, 2 August 1993.

101. *East European Newsletter*, vol. 6, no. 4, 17 February 1992.

102. *România Mare*, 4 September 1992. Before the second round of the 1996 presidential election, Vadim and Funar urged their supporters to back Emil Constantinescu, nobody from the latter's team repudiating such support either.

103. One newspaper argued that the newspaper had predominance over the party in an article entitled 'The party of the review'. See Adrian Ursu, *Adevărul*, 26 June 2001.

104. Rompres, 7 June 1991, SWB EE/1095 B/12 (11 June 1991).

105. For the record of Antonescu and his regime towards the Jews, see Ioannid, *The Holocaust in Romania*, 2000, *passim*.

106. Rompres, 15 August 1991, SWB EE/1158 B/12 (23 August 1991).

107. Andrei Cornea, *22*, 4 October 1995.

108. Gallagher, *Democratie si Nationalisme in Romania*, p. 353.

109. Cornel Nistorescu, *Evenimentul Zilei*, 14 December 2000 (English edition).

110. *Monitorul*, 9 June 1999.

111. *Evenimentul Zilei*, 20 August 1996.

112. *Nine o'Clock*, 26 April 1999. In the end the papal visit was confined to Bucharest.

113. *Ibid.*

114. In its 5 March 1993 edition *România Mare* published a 3-page article entitled 'In defence of the Great Romanian Patriot Iosif Constantin Dragan'.

115. Paunescu was allowed to deliver a lengthy speech at the 1997 congress of the PRM which was published in full by *Politica* on 22 November 1997; on 13 December 1997 *Politica* argued that Cristoiu was now a journalist worthy of the name because he realised the error of his ways for attacking Vadim in the past.

116. The standing bureau of the PUNR unanimously voted to expel Funar in November 1997. He then made an abortive attempt to form a successor party, the Alliance for the Unity of Romanians in the spring of 1998 before accepting Vadim's patient courtship and becoming secretary-general of the PRM in October of that year.

117. *Ziua*, 24 November 2000.

118. *Ziua*, 4 September 2000.

119. *România Mare*, 14 November 1997.

120. See *România Mare*, 4 December 1992.
121. *România Mare*, 4 December 1992.
122. ARPRESS, *Selected Daily Bulletin*, 6 February 1993.
123. *Adevărul*, 22 December 2000.
124. *Adevărul*, 18 May 2001.
125. *Adevărul*, 17 May 2000.
126. *Adevărul*, 18 May 2001.
127. *Evenimentul Zilei*, 3 July 1996.
128. *Evenimentul Zilei*, 23 February 2001.
129. *Monitorul*, 15 February 2001.
130. Sever Meșca, Ilie Neacșu, *Vadim. Intre Preșidenție și Ospiciu*, Bucharest: Editura Universal, 2002, p. 180.
131. Meșca and Neacșu, *Vadim*, p. 207.
132. But in 2000 Vadim did less well among women voters than Iliescu. On 26 November 2000, he got 24% of the women's vote compared to 38% of the male vote. By contrast, 32% of men voted for Vadim, Iliescu being only 3 percentage points ahead in this category.
133. Razvan Savaliuc, *Ziua*, 23 November 2000.
134. Petre Niteanu, 'Averea Mascariciuliu', *Ziua*, 29 June 2001.
135. *Ziua* ran a series on the finances of Vadim's movement from 29 June to 2 July 2001.
136. Petre Niteanu, 'Averea Mascariciuliu', *Ziua*, 29 June 2001.
137. Ilie Șerbanescu, 'Reșita: o privitizare cu cantec', *22*, 10–16 July 2001, describes the complexity of the dispute.
138. Radu Sârbu, *România líbera*, 7 July 2001.
139. Radio Free Europe, *South-East-Europe Newsline*, 28 June 2001.
140. *Monitorul*, 7 May 2001.
141. Radio Free Europe, *South-East-Europe Newsline*, 9 May 2001.
142. Adrian Cioflanca, *Monitorul*, 9 May 2001.
143. Radio Free Europe, *South-East-Europe Newsline*, 25 June 2001.
144. *Evenimentul Zilei*, 22 November 2000.
145. Radio Free Europe, *South-East-Europe Newsline*, 22 May 2001.
146. Eugen Tomiuc, 'Romanian Authorities Launch Probe into Controversial Book', 'End Note', Radio Free Europe, *South-East-Europe Newsline*, 28 August 2001.
147. *Evenimentul Zilei*, 25 August 2001 (English edition).
148. Cornel Nistorescu, *Evenimentul Zilei*, 20 March 2001 (English edition).
149. *Monitorul*, 21 December 2000.
150. PRM Senator Mihai Lupoi gave this explanation. See *Evenimentul Zilei*, 15 February 2001.
151. *Ziua*, 2 July 2001.
152. Christian Levant, 'Arsenalul lui Saddam, la mina lui Vadim', *Evenimentul Zilei*, 19 November 2001.
153. *Evenimentul Zilei*, 13 October 2001 (English edition).
154. *Evenimentul Zilei*, 11 October 2001; *Evenimentul Zilei*, 27 September 2001 (English edition).

155. *Evenimentul Zilei*, 13 October 2001 (English edition).
156. Razvan Savaliuc, 'Vadim sterge urmele', *Ziua*, 28 August 2001.
157. Sorin Rosca Stănescu, 'Puterea cade in cursa Vadim', *Ziua*, 17 October 2001.
158. Adrian Cioflanca, 'Cosmetica Politica', *Monitorul*, 14 February 2001.
159. On 26 November 2000, Vadim obtained 27% of the vote in Transylvania, 28% in Muntenia, 29% in Moldavia, and 26% in Bucharest. These statistics were compiled from an exit poll carried out by CURS/CSOP on 26 November 2000 and carried on PRO TV on 27 November. See http://www.protv.ro/stiri/center.html
160. *Evenimentul Zilei*, 2 July 1996.
161. *Cotidiânul*, 16 July 2001.

Chapter 10   Looters of the State by Appointment of Brussels: Return of the Social Democrats, 2001–3

1. Radio Free Europe, *South-East-Europe Newsline*, 6 June 2003.
2. Radio Free Europe, *South-East-Europe Newsline*, 22 May 2003.
3. *Ziarul de Iaşi*, 27 June 2003, www.monitorul.ro
4. Cristian Ghinea, 'Povestea primarului ratacitor', *Dilema*, 31 October 2003.
5. *Adevârul*, 15 September 2001.
6. Dankwart Rustow, 'Transitions to democracy: toward a dynamic model', *Comparative Politics*, April 1970, pp. 344–5.
7. Radio Free Europe, *South-East-Europe Newsline*, 3 June 2003.
8. Radio Free Europe, *South-East-Europe Newsline*, 28 July 2003.
9. Cristian Ghinea, 'Severin, Năstase, Gusă and Patriciu', *Dilema*, 25–31 July 2003.
10. Dan Tapalaga, 'The Arrogant or the American', *Evenimentul Zilei* (English language edn.), 18 November 2003.
11. For a detailed account of the background to the case see Bogdan Comaroni, 'Adevârul despre Treptow', *Ziua*, 3 October 2002.
12. Laurentiu Ciocazanu, 'The American lesson', *Evenimentul Zilei* (English language edn.), 11 December 2002; Cornel Nistorescu, 'Presidential adviser's blunder', *Evenimentul Zilei* (English language edn.), 30 September 2002.
13. *Independent on Sunday*, 29 June 2003.
14. Cornel Nistorescu, 'The Network in the Cellar', *Evenimentul Zilei* (English language edn), 9 November 2003.
15. M. B. and O. P., 'Willem Matser, fostul ofiter NATO dezvaluie mecanismul coruperii ministrilor', *Evenimentul Zilei*, 23 October 2003.
16. Radio Free Europe, *South-East-Europe Newsline*, 16 October 2003.
17. *Evenimentul Zilei* (English language edn), 13 November 2003.
18. Adrian Bidilici and Marius Ghilezan, 'Vila cu bani UE', *Evenimentul Zilei*, 19 November 2003.
19. The Bucharest daily *Adevârul* has provided much useful information on the source of the barons wealth and political power. See 'Harta baronilor şi mafiilor locale din PSD' in its 18 July 2002 edition; 'Baronii PSD continua balul', 21 January 2003; and 'Baron Mischie, in competitie cu sir Gogonçea', 28 January 2003.

20. Mirel Bran, *Le Monde*, 22 October 2003.
21. In conversation with the author.
22. Barons run several of the regional development agencies in Romania through which EU funding is channelled. For the use they allegedly try to make of it, see 'Clientela PSD se infrupta din fondurile PHARE', *Monitorul*, 1 November 2002.
23. Rodica Ciobanu, 'PSD scos la liçitaţie', *Adevârul*, 18 November 2003.
24. Private information.
25. 'Romania', *East European Constitutional Review*, vol. 10, 2/3, spring/summer 2001.
26. Radio Free Europe, *South-East-Europe Newsline*, 5 May 2003.
27. Radio Free Europe, *South-East-Europe Newsline*, 6 November 2003.
28. Iulian Anghel, *Ziarul Finançiar*, 5 November 2003.
29. *Monitorul*, 7 December 2001.
30. *Evenimentul Zilei*, 5 May 2003.
31. Bogdan Chirieac, 'Suspendarea negocierilor—poarta spre cosmare', *Adevârul*, 1 June 2001; Eugen Tomiuc, 'Romania: EU Report Assails Nation Over Treatment of Orphans', Radio Free Europe, *Newsline*, 4 June 2001.
32. *Evenimentul Zilei*, 4 June 2001.
33. Radio Free Europe, *South-East-Europe Newsline*, 8 March 2001.
34. *Nine o'Clock*, 12 March 2001.
35. Radio Free Europe, *South-East-Europe Newsline*, 12 April 2001.
36. *Adevârul*, 9 July 2001.
37. *România líbera*, 18 July 2001.
38. *Ziarul de Iaşi*, 20 June 2003.
39. *Ziarul de Iaşi*, 28 June 2003.
40. Radio Free Europe, *South-East-Europe Newsline*, 24 April 2003.
41. Transparency International, '2001 Corruption Perceptions Index', *Global Corruption Report 2001*, pp. 234–6. In December 2002, the Open Society Institute published a report on corruption in Romania which described it as 'endemic if not systematic' in most areas of public life.
42. Dan Cristian Turturica, *Evenimentul Zilei*, 16 November 2003.
43. Dan Cristian Turturica, *Evenimentul Zilei*, 16 November 2003.
44. 'Romania Country Report', Economist Intelligence Unit, October 2001, p. 18.
45. See Gallagher, *Democratie Si Nationalism in Romania*, pp. 369–76.
46. See *Ziua*, 19 November 2002.
47. In August 2002 surprise greeted the news that a parliamentary bill on the declaration of dignitaries' wealth being tabled by the government would not cover paintings and sculptures. See *Evenimentul Zilei*, 18 October 2002 (English-language edition).
48. *Ziua*, 5 December 2002.
49. *Evenimentul Zilei*, 23 January 2002.
50. *Evenimentul Zilei*, 21 January 2002.
51. *Evenimentul Zilei*, 22 January 2002.
52. Reuters, 9 August 2002.

53. Monitorul, 13 July 2001; Radio Free Europe, *South-East-Europe Newsline*, 12 April, 1 August 2001.
54. Radio Free Europe, *South-East-Europe Newsline*, 4 October 2001.
55. George Jahn, 'U.S. eyes Romania, Bulgaria for Help', Associated Press, 9 April 2002.
56. Adrian Cioflanca, 'Ziua desiluziei', *Monitorul*, 14 June 2000.
57. *Ziua*, 22 November 2003.
58. Radio Free Europe, *South-East-Europe Newsline*, 3 November 2003.
59. Eugen Tomiuc, 'Romania: German Chancellor Says Nation Still Long Way From Joining EU'. Radio Free Europe, *Newsline*, 5 July 2001.
60. *Evenimentul* Zilei, 12 November 2003.
61. Rodica Ciobanu, 'UDMR, la fel ca PSD', *Adevârul*, 20 June 2002.
62. Radio Free Europe, *South-East-Europe Newsline*, 17 December 2002.
63. UNDP, Early Warning Report—Romania 6/2001, in association with the Romanian Academic Society, p. 16.
64. Radio Free Europe, *South-East-Europe Newsline*, 18 December 2001.

Chapter 11   Conclusion

1. In December 2002 the law was shelved after the intervention of the President.
2. Chelaru, *Culpe care nu se uita*, p. 224.
3. Liviu Ioan Stoica, *Cotidianul*, 5 August 2002.
4. It will rise from €600 million euro per annum from 2001–3 to (approximately) 800 million in 2004, 900 million in 2005 and €1 billion in 2006. See Antonia Oprita, 'Romania must shape up laws to get into EU—analysts', Reuters, 17 December 2002.
5. *Evenimentul Zilei*, 24 January 2002.
6. *Ziarul de Iasi*, 28 August 2003.
7. *Evenimentul Zilei*, 14 November 2003.
8. Alexandru Lăzescu, 'Lecţia argentiniană', 22, 8–14 January 2002.
9. Valerian Stan, *A few Remarks about the Transparency and Integrity of Public Administration in Romania*, This text was sent to international bodies and institutions on 1 June 2001.
10. *Evenimentul Zilei*, 21 January 2002.
11. *Evenimentul Zilei* (English edition), 4 June 2003.
12. *Ziarul de Iasi*, 20 December 2002.
13. *Evenimentul Zilei* (English language edition), 19 and 20 January 2003.
14. *Evenimentul Zilei*, 17 January 2002.
15. See Z. Ornea, *Anii Treizeci. Extrema dreaptă românească*, Bucharest: Editura Fundaţiei Culturale Române, 1995, p. 87.
16. Adrian Bidilici and Marius Ghilezan, 'Vila cu bani UE', *Evenimentul Zilei*, 19 November 2003.
17. Ron Synovitz, 'OECD: Agricultural Review has Praise for Bulgaria, Misgivings about Romania', Radio Free Europe, *Features*, 16 January 2001.
18. *Evenimentul Zilei*, 15 February 2002.

19. Horia Patapievici, 'Anatomia unei catastrofe', in Iordan Chimet, *Momentul Adevărului*, Cluj: Dacia, 1996, p. 169–83.
20. *Review of Agricultural Policy: Bulgaria*, Paris: OECD, 2000, p. 154.
21. See M. Chiper, 'Alarm pentru democratie: Vadim Tudor cucereste satele', *Ziarul de Iasi*, 31 July 2002.
22. M. Chiper, 'PRM tace si face', *Ziarul de Iasi*, 2 August 2002.
23. Alina Mungiu-Pippidi, 'Romania' in Mary Kaldor and Ivan Vejvoda (eds), *Democratization in Central and Eastern Europe*, London and Pinter, 1999, p. 141.
24. Mary Kaldor and Ivan Vejvoda (eds), *Democratization in Central and Eastern Europe*, London: Pinter, 1999, p. 4.
25. In 2001 the main public campaign with civil society origins was mounted against the effort of Bucharest's mayor to reduce the estimated 500,000 stray dog population in the city.
26. *Evenimentul Zilei*, 30 December 2001 (English language edition).
27. Gabriel Almond and Sydney Verba, *The Civic Culture: Political Attitudes and Democracy in Five Nations*, Princeton University Press, 1963.
28. Geoffrey Pridham, *The Dynamics of Democratization: A Comparative Approach*, London and New York: Continuum 2000, p. 6.
29. Stjepan Meštrović, *The Balkanization of the West: the Confluence of Postmodernism and Postcommunism*, London: Routledge, 1994, p. 24.
30. *Evenimentul Zilei*, 26 July 2003. Nine months after his disappearance in June 2002, the body was discovered of Iosif Constinas, a journalist from Timişoara who was preparing a book on the role of the Securitate in suppressing demonstrators there in 1989. See Eugen Tomiuc, 'Romania: Journalist's Suspicious death Raises New Doubts About Media Freedom', Radio Free Europe/Radio Liberty, 12 June 2003.
31. *Evenimentul Zilei*, 25 July 2003.
32. Dan Cristian Turturică, 'Why the Silence of the European Union', *Evenimentul Zilei*, 3 August 2003.
33. *Evenimentul Zilei*, 25 July 2003.
34. Dan Pavel, 'Filerele mafiote contra intereselor nationale', *Ziua*, 29 February 2000.
35. See Ion Iliescu în dialog cu Vladimir Tismăneanu, *Marele Şoc: Din Finanului Unui Secol Scurt*, Bucharest: editura Enciclopedica, 2004, p. 269.
36. Şerban Papacostea, '"Marele Soc" Al Mistificarii', *22*, No 749, 13–20 July 2004.
37. *Evenimentul Zilei*, 17 June 2004.
38. *Evenimentul Zilei*, 12 July 2004.
39. Laurenþiu Cocazanu, 'The intellectuals in the Becali Republic', *Evenimentul Zilei*, (English Online ed.) 20 July 2004.

BIBLIOGRAPHY

News agencies

ARPRESS (Bucharest)
Associated Press
BBC World Service, Survey of World Broadcasts for Eastern Europe
Monitorul (Iasi)
Radio Free Europe/Radio Liberty, Newline, http://www.rferl.org
Rompres
Telegrama (Chico, California)

Newspapers, periodicals and journals consulted

Adevârul, http://adevârul.kappa.ro (from 2002: http://www.adevarul-online.ro) (Bucharest)
Adevârul de Cluj (Cluj)
Balkan Forum (Skiopje)
Balkanologie (Paris)
Baricada (Bucharest)
Bosnia Report http://www.bosnia.org.uk (London)
Commentary (New York)
Cotidiânul (Bucharest)
Cuvîntul (Bucharest)
Cuvîntul Liber (Tirgu Mureş)
Desteapte-Te Române (Brasov)
Dilema (Bucharest)
Dimineaţa (Bucharest)
Dreptâtea (Bucharest)
East European Constitutional Review (New York)
East European Politics and Societies
East European Reporter (Budapest)
The Economist (London)
Economist Intelligence Unit, *Romania Country Reports* (1993–2001)
Evenimentul Zilei, http://www.expres.ro
Expres Magasin (Bucharest)

Financial Times (London)
Government and Opposition (London)
In faţa alegatorilor (Cluj)
International Herald Tribune (Paris)
Lupta (Paris)
Mesagerul Transilvân (Cluj)
Monitorul, http://www.monitorul.ro (Iasi)
New Statesman and Society (London)
NU (Cluj)
The Observer (London)
Politica (Bucharest)
Pro-Minoritate (Budapest)
Report on Eastern Europe
Revue d'études comparatives Est-Ouest
RFE-RL Research Report
România Líbera (Bucharest)
România Mare (Bucharest)
Sfera Politicii (Bucharest)
Studies (Dublin)
The Times (London)
Transition (Prague)
Tribuna Ardealului (Cluj)
22 (Bucharest)
Viaţa Crestina (Cluj)
World Policy Journal
Ziarul de Iasi, http://www.monitorul.ro (Iasi)
Ziua, http://www.ziua.ro (Bucharest)

Reports

Herzfeld and Rubin, *Romanian Digest*, 1997–2001 http://www.hr.ro
Human Rights in Romania, New York: Helsinki Watch, 1991
Institute for Democracy and Electoral Assistance, *Democracy in Romania: Assessment Mission Report*, Stockholm: International Idea, 1997.
IWPR's Balkan Crisis Report, http://www.iwpr.net.

Review of Agricultural Policy: Bulgaria, Paris: OECD, 2000.

'Romania Country Report', Economist Intelligence Unit (1993–2002) 1999 Regular Report From the Commission on Romania's Progress Towards Accession, European Commission, Brussels 1999.
RFE/RL Newsline, http://www.rferl.org.

Romania Country Report on Human Rights Practices for 1996, Washington, DC: US Department of State, 1997.

Transparency International, '2001 Corruption Perceptions Index', *Global Corruption Report 2001.*

United Nations, *Uncommon Opportunities: an Agenda for Peace and Equitable Development*, London: Zed Books, 1994.

UNDP, Early Warning Report—Romania 6/2001, http://earlywarning. undp.sk.

The White Book on Romania and NATO, 1997, Ministry of Foreign Affairs, Bucharest 1997.

Books and articles

Achim, Viorel, *Ţiganii în istoria României*, Bucharest: Editura Enciclopedica, 1998.

Alexandrescu, Doina, *Coposu: confesiuni*, Editura Anastasia, Bucuresti 1996.

Alexandrescu, Sorin, *Paradoxul Român*, Bucharest: Univers, 1998.

Almond, Mark, *Decline Without Fall: Romania under Ceauşescu*, London: Institute for European Defence and Strategic Studies, 1988.

Anderson, M. S., *The Eastern Question, 1774–1923: a Study in International Relations*, London: Macmillan, 1966.

Andreescu, Gabriel, *Ruleta: Români şi maghiari, 1990–2000*, Bucharest: Polirom, 2001.

Arachelian, V., *Corneliu Coposu, Dialoguri*, Bucharest: Ed. Anastasia, 1992.

Bacon, Walter, 'Security As Seen From Bucharest' in Daniel Nelson (ed.), *Romania after Tyranny*, Boulder, CO: Westview Press, 1992.

Balcerowicz, Leszek, 'Understanding post-communist transitions' in Wojciech Kostecki *et al., Transformations of Post-Communist States*, Basingstoke: Macmillan, 2000.

Behr, Edward, *'Kiss the Hand you Cannot Bite': the Rise and Fall of the Ceauseşcus*, London: Hamish Hamilton, 1991.

Benn, Tony, *Office Without Power: Diaries 1968–72*, London: Hutchinson, 1988.

Beria, Sergo, *Beria my Father: Inside Stalin's Kremlin*, London: Duckworth, 2001.

Berindei, Mihnea, 'Romania lui Ceauşescu—un naufragiu planifiat II', *22*, vol. 9, no. 47, November 1998.

Betea, Lavinia, *Alexandru Bîrlâdeanu despre Dej, Ceauseşcu şi Iliescu*, Bucharest: Evenimentul Romanesc, 1998.

Betea, Livea (in dialog cu Corneliu Manescu), *Convorbiri neterminate*, Iasi: Polirom, 2001.

Bethell, Nicholas, *Spies and Other Secrets: Memoirs from the Second Cold War,* London: Penguin, 1995.

Bideleux, Robert, and Ian Jeffries, *Eastern Europe: Crisis and Change,* London: Routledge, 1998.

Blit, Lucjan, *The Eastern Pretender: the Story of Boleslaw Piasecki,* London: Hutchinson, 1965.

Bobbio, Norberto, *Left and Right: the Significance of a Political Distinction,* London: Polity Press, n.d.

Boda, Iosif, *Cinci Ani La Cotroceni,* Bucharest: Evenimentul Romanesc, 1999.

Boia, Lucien, *Istorie şi mit in constiinţa româneaşca,* Bucharest: Humanitas, 1997.

———, *Romania: Tara de Frontieră A Europei,* Bucharest: Humanitas, 2001.

Botez, Sorin Mircea, 'An Alternative Romanian Foreign Policy' in Daniel Nelson (ed.), *Romania after Tyranny,* London & San Francisco: Westview Press, 1992.

Brown, J. F., *Nationalism, Democracy and Security in the Balkans,* Aldershot, England: Dartmouth, 1992.

Brucan, Silviu, *The Wasted Generation: Memoirs of the Romanian Journey from Capitalism to Socialism and Back,* Boulder, CO: Westview Press, 1993.

———, *Stalpii Noii Puteri in Romania,* Editura Nemira, Bucuresti 1996.

Burks, R. V., *The Dynamics of Communism In Eastern Europe,* Princeton University Press, 1961.

———, 'The Rumanian National Deviation: an Accounting' in Kurt London (ed.), *Eastern Europe in Transition,* Baltimore: Johns Hopkins University Press, 1967.

Burleigh, Michael, *The Third Reich: a New History,* London: Pan, 2001.

Buşneag, Radu, 'Romania: Ciorbea Faces Problems from Worried Workers', Radio Free Europe, 11 June 1997.

Buzatu, Gheorghe, 'Romania dupa lovitura de stat' in Ioan Scurtu and Gheorghe Buzatu (ed.), *Istoria Românilor In Secolul XX (1918–1948),* Bucharest: Paideia, 1999.

Calinescu, Matei, 'Ionesco and Rhinoceros: Personal and Political Backgrounds', *East European Politics and Societies,* vol. 9, no. 3, fall 1995.

Campbell, Adrian, 'Local Government in Romania' in Andrew Coulson (ed.), *Local Government in Eastern Europe: Establishing Democracy at the Grassroots,* Aldershot: Edward Elgar, 1995.

Campbell, John, *French Influence and the Rise of Roumanian Nationalism,* New York: Arno Press, 1970 (originally submitted as Ph.D. thesis to History Department, Harvard University, 1940).

Câmpeanu, Pavel, 'Aspects of Romanian Stalinism's History: Ana Pauker, a Victim of Anti-Semitism', *East European Politics and Societies,* vol. 14, no. 2, 2000.

Carothers, Thomas, *Assessing Democracy Assistance: the Case of Romania*, New York: Carnegie Foundation, 1996.

Cartwright, A. L., *The Return of the Peasant: Land Reform in Post-Communist Romania*, Burlington, VT: Ashgate, 2001.

Castellan, George, *History of the Balkans: from Mohammed the Conqueror to Stalin*, New York: Columbia University Press, 1992.

Chelaru, Rodica, *Culpe care nu se uita. Convorbiri cu Cornel Burtica*, Bucharest: Curtea Veche, 2001.

Chirot, Daniel, *Social Change in a Peripheral Society: the Creation of a Balkan Colony*, New York: Academic Press, 1976.

Ciachir, Dan, 'Patriarhul Justinian', *Cuvintul*, January 1997.

Cioflanca, Adrian, 'Ziua desiluziei', *Monitorul*, 14 June 2000.

Coja, Ion, *Marele manipulator si asasinarea lui Culiasnu, Ceausescu, Iorga*, Bucharest: Ed. Miracol, 1999.

Constantinescu, Emil, *Timpul dărâmării, timpul zidirii* (vol. 1), Bucharest: Universalia, 2002.

Constantiniu, Florin, *O Istorie Sincera A Poporului Român*, Bucharest: Univers Enciclopedic, 1997.

Cornea, Doina, *Faţa Nevazuta A lucracilor (1990–1999). Dialoguri cu Rodica Palade*, Cluj: Dacia 1999.

Corpade, Constanta, 'Ion Iliescu a salutat "spiritul civic" al minerilor care au capasit civili in Bucuresti', *Adevarul*.

Craiutu, Aurelian, 'Light at the end of the tunnel: Romania, 1989–1998' in T. Gallagher and G. Pridham (eds), *Experimenting with Democracy: Regime Change in the Balkans*, London, Routledge, 2000.

Crampton, R. J., *Eastern Europe in the Twentieth Century*, London: Routledge, 1994.

Crişan, Gheorghe, *Piramida puterii. Oameni politici şi de stat din Romania (23 august 1944–22 decembrie 1989)*, Bucharest: Pro Historia, 2001.

Cummins, Ian, *Marx, Engels and National Movements*, London: Croom Helm, 1980.

Deletant, Dennis, *Ceauşescu and the Securitate*, London: Hurst 1995.

———, *Romania sub regimul communist*, Bucharest: Fundatia Academia Civica, 1997.

———, 'The Post-Communist Security Services in Romania' in Rebecca Haynes (ed.), *Occasional Papers in Romanian Studies*, no. 2, London: School of Slavonic and East European Studies, University of London, 1998.

———, *Communist Terror in Romania: Gheorghiu Dej and the Police State, 1948–1965*, London: Hurst 1999.

———, 'The Successors to the *Securitate*: Old Habits Die Hard' in Kieran Williams and Dennis, Deletant, *Security Inteligence Services in New Democracies*, London: Macmillan, 2000.

————, 'Ghosts from the Past: Successors to the Securitate in Post-Communist Romania' in Duncan Light and David Phinnemore (eds), *Post-Communist Romania: Coming to Terms with Transition*, London: Palgrave, 2001.

Democracy in Romania, Stockholm: Institute for Democratic and Electoral Assistance, 1997.

Djuvaru, Neagu, *Amintiri Din Pribegie, 1948–1990*, Bucharest: Albatros, 2002.

Drysdale, Helena, *Looking for Gheorghe*, London: Sinclair-Stevenson, 1995.

Durandin, Catherine, *Histoire des Roumains*, Paris: Fayard, 1995.

Eddison, Elaine, *The Protection of Minorities at the Conference on Security and Co-operation in Europe*, Colchestor: Human Rights Centre, University of Essex.

Fejtö, François, *A History of the People's Democracies*, Harmondsworth: Penguin 1974.

Fischer, Mary Ellen, 'The New Leaders and the Opposition' in Daniel Nelson (ed.), *Romania after Tyranny*, Boulder, CO: Westview Press, 1992.

Fischer-Galati, Stephen, *20th Century Rumania*, New York: Columbia University Press, 1991 (edn).

Florian, Filip, and Marius Oprea, 'Mostenitorii Securitatii—in primii ani de democratie', *Sfera Politicii*, no. 52, 1997.

Fromm, Erich, *Fear of Freedom*, London: Routledge, 1960 ed.

Funderburk, David B., *Un Ambassador American. Între Departmentul de Stat şi Dictatura Comunista din România*, Constanţa: Editura Dacon, 1994.

Furet, François, *The Passing of an Illusion: the Idea of Communism in the Twentieth Century*, University of Chicago Press, 1999.

Gabanyi, Annele Ute, *The Ceauşescu Cult*, Bucharest: Romanian Cultural Foundation, 2000.

Gallagher, Tom, 'Ultra-Nationalists Take Charge of Transylvania's Capital', *RFE-RL Research Report*, vol. 1, no. 13, 27 March 1992.

————, 'Time to Build Bridges in Romania', *Studies*, autumn 1992.

————, 'Vatra Romaneasca and resurgent nationalism in Romania', *Ethnic and Racial Studies*, vol. 15, no. 4, 1992.

————, 'Ethnic Tension in Cluj', *RFE-RL Research Report*, vol. 2, no. 9, 26 February 1993.

————, *Romania after Ceauşescu: the Politics of Intolerance*, Edinburgh: Edinburgh University Press, 1995.

————, 'The Balkans' in Stephen White *et al.*, *Developments in Central and East European Politics*, Basingstoke: Macmillan, 1998.

————, *Democratie si Nationalisme in Romania, 1989–1998*, Bucharest: Editura All, 1999.

————, 'O critică a centralismului eşuat şi egotismului regional în România' in Gabriel Andreescu and Gusztáv Molnár (eds), *Problema transilvană*, Iasi: Editura Polirom, 1999.

————, 'Nationalism and democracy in South-East Europe' in T. Gallagher and G. Pridham (eds), *Experimenting with Democracy: Regime Change in the Balkans*, London: Routledge, 2000.

————, *Outcast Europe: the Balkans from the Ottomans to Milosevic, 1789–1989*, London: Routledge, 2001.

Georgescu, Vlad, *Istoria românilor. De la origini pînă in zilele noastre*, Bucharest: Humanitas, 1992.

Geron Pilon, Juliana, *The Bloody Flag: Post-Communist Nationalism in Eastern Europe*, New York: Transaction Publishers, 1992.

Giurescu, Dinu C., *The Razing of Romania's Past*, London: The Bath Press, 1990.

Hessell Tiltman, H., *Peasant Europe*, London: Jarrolds, 1936.

Hitchins, Keith, *Rumania 1866–1947*, Oxford University Press, 1994.

Hopwood, Richard, 'Nationalism and Church-State Relations in Ceauseşcu's Romania', MA thesis, University of Bradford, 1995.

Illyes, E., *National Minorities in Romania: Change in Transylvania*, New York: Columbia University Press, 1982.

Ioanid, Radu, *The Holocaust in Romania: the Destruction of Jews and Gypsies under the Antonescu Regime, 1940–1944*, Chicago: Ivan R. Dee, 2000.

Ionescu, Dan, 'Crisis in the Romanian Orthodox Church', *RFE-RL Research Report*, 9 March 1990.

————, 'Government Moves to Recentralize Local Administration', *Report on Eastern Europe*, vol. 1, no. 33, 7 September 1990.

————, 'Countdown for Romania's Germans', *Report on Eastern Europe*, vol. 2, no. 36, 13 September 1991.

Iordachi, Constantin, '"La California des Roumains". L'integration de la Dobrudja du Nord à la Roumanie, 1878–1913', *Balkanologie*, vol. 6, nos 1 & 2, December 2002.

Ivanciuc, Cornel, 'Evenimentele de la Tirgu-Mures din martie 1990, sau impus recunoasterea oficiala a SRI', *22*, 5–11 July 1999.

Jelavich, Barbara, *History of the Balkans: Eighteenth and Nineteenth Centuries*, Cambridge University Press 1983.

Kellogg, Frederick, *The Road to Romanian Independence*, West Lafayette, IN: Purdue University Press, 1995.

Kideckel, David, *The Solitude of Collectivism: Romanian Villagers to the Revolution and Beyond*, Ithaca, NY: Cornell University Press, 1993.

King, R. R., 'Romania' in R. Staar (ed.), *1991 Yearbook of International Communist Affairs*, Stanford, CA: Hoover Institution Press, 1991.

Kopecky, Petr, and Cas Mudde, 'What has Eastern Europe taught us about the democratisation literature (and vice versa)?', *European Journal of Political Research*, vol. 37.

Kosteci, Wojciech, *Prevention of Ethnic Conflict: Lessons from Romania*, Berlin: Berghof Research Center For Constructive Conflict Management, 2002.

Kurti, Laszlo, 'Transylvania, Land Beyond Reason: Toward an Anthropological Analysis of a Contested Terrain', *Dialectical Anthropology*, vol. 14, 1989.

Lendvai, Paul, *Eagles in Cobwebs: Nationalism and Communism in the Balkans*, London: Macdonald, 1969.

Levy, Robert, 'Did Ana Pauker Prevent a "Rajk Trial" in Romania', *East European Politics and Societies*, vol. 9, no. 2, 1995.

————, *Ana Pauker: The Rise and Fall of a Jewish Communist*, Berkeley: University of California Press, 2001.

Linden, Ronald, 'After the Revolution: a foreign Policy of Unbounded Change' in Daniel Nelson (ed.), *Romania after Tyranny*, Boulder, CO: Westview Press, 1992.

Linz, J., and A. Stepan, *Problems of Democratic Transition and Consolidation: South Europe, South America and Post-Communist Europe*, Baltimore: Johns Hopkins University Press, 1996.

Livezeanu, Irina, *Cultural Politics in Greater Romania*, Ithaca, NT: Cornell University Press, 1995.

Love, Joseph L., *Crafting the Third World: Theorising Underdevelopment in Rumania and Brazil*, Stanford University Press, 1996.

Lyle, Robert, 'Romanian Mining Pact Makes IMF Loan More Difficult', Radio Free Europe, Endnote, 26 January 1999.

Macovei, Monica, 'The Post-Communist Procuracy: Romania', *East European Constitutional Review*, vol. 8, nos 1 & 2, winter–spring 1999.

Macovei, Monica, 'Legal Culture in Romania', *East European Constitutional Review*, vol. 7, no. 1, winter 1998.

Manea, Norman, 'Blasphemy and Carnival', *World Policy Journal*, vol. 13, no. 1, spring 1996.

Marchis, Vasile, *Drama Bisericii Romane Unite cu Roma (Greco-Catolica), documente si marturii*, Bucharest: Crater, 1997.

Markham, Reuben, *Romania under the Soviet Yoke*, Boston, MA: Meador, 1949.

Mato, Zsolt-Istvan, 'Romanian Coalition Conflict Continues', Radio Free Europe, *Newsline*, 13 October 1998.

Meşca, Sever, and Neacşu, Ilie, *Vadim. Intre Preşidenţie şi Ospiciu*, Bucharest: Editura Universal, 2002.

Meštrović, Stjepan, *The Balkanization of the West: the Confluence of Post-modernism and Postcommunism*, London: Routledge, 1994.

Mihailescu, Ioan, 'Mental Stereotypes in Post-Totalitarian Romania', *Government and Opposition*, vol. 28, no. 3, 1993.

Mungiu-Pippidi, Alina, 'Breaking Free at Last: Tales of Corruption from the Post-Communist Balkans', *East European Constitutional Review*, vol. 6, no. 4, fall 1997.

———, *Transilvânia Subiectivă*, Bucharest: Humanitas, 1999.

———, 'The Return of Populism—the 2000 Romanian Elections', *Government and Opposition*, vol. 36, no. 2, spring 2000.

———, *Politica După Communism*, Bucharest: Humanitas, 2002.

Nagy-Talavera, Nicholas, *N. Iorga—O Biografie*, Iasi: Institutul European, 1999.

Oltay, Edith, 'Minority Rights still an Issue in Hungarian-Romanian Relations', *RFE-RL Research Report*, vol. 1, no. 12, 20 March 1992.

———, 'Minorities as Stumbling Block in Relations with Neighbours', *RFE-RL Research Report*, vol. 1, no. 19, 8 May 1992.

Ornea, Z., *Anii Treizeci. Extrema dreaptă românească*, Bucharest: Editura Fundaţiei Culturale Române, 1995.

Papacostea, Şerban, 'Captive Clio: Romanian Historiography under Communist Rule', *European History Quarterly*, vol. 26, 1996.

Pacepa, Ion Mihai, *Cartea Neagra a Securitatii*, Vols. II and III, Bucharest: Editura Omega, 1999.

Patacki, Judith, 'Free Hungarians in a Free Romania: Dream or Reality', *Report on Eastern Europe*, vol. 1, no. 8, 23 February 1990.

Patapievici, Horia, 'Anatomia unei catastrofe' in Iordan Chimet, *Momentul Adevarului*, Cluj: Dacia, 1996.

Peppine, Horatiu, 'Armata si Biserica', *22*, no. 44, 1–7 November 1995.

Pipes, Daniel, *Hidden Hand: Middle East Fear of Conspiracy*, Basingstoke: Macmillan, 1996.

Pippidi, Andrei, 'Nation, Nationalisme et Democracie en Roumanie', *L'Autre Europe*, 1993.

Porter, Ivor, *Operatiunea "Autonomous"*, Bucharest: Humanitas, 1990.

Portocale, Radu, *Autopsie du coup d'état Roumain. Au pays du mensoge triomphant*, Paris: Calmann-Levy, 1990.

Putnam, Robert, *Making Democracy Work: Civic Traditions in Modern Italy*, Princeton University Press 1993.

Rady, Martin, *Romania in Turmoil*, London: I.B. Tauris, 1992.

Ratesh, Nestor, *Romania: The Entangled Revolution*, New York: Praeger, 1991.

Roberts, Henry L., *Rumania: Political Problems of an Agrarian State*, Yale University Press, 1951.

Roger, Antoine, 'Les Partis Anti-Systeme dans la Roumaine Post-Communiste', *Revue d'études comparatives Est-Ouest*, vol. 31, no. 2, 2000.

'Romania', *East European Constitutional Review*, vol. 8, nos 1 & 2, winter/spring 1999.

'Romania', *East European Constitutional Review*, vol. 8, no. 4, fall 1999.

'Romania', *East European Constitutional Review*, vol. 9, nos 1/2, winter/spring 2000.

'Romania', *East European Constitutional Review*, vol. 9, no. 3, summer 2000.

'Romania', *East European Constitutional Review*, vol. 9, no. 4, fall 2000.

'Romania', *East European Constitutional Review*, vol. 10, nos 2/3, spring/summer 2001.

Rothschild, Joseph, *East-Central Europe Between the two World Wars*, Seattle: University of Washington Press, 1974.

Runciman, Steven, *The Orthodox Churches and the Secular State*, Oxford University Press, 1971.

Safran, Alexandre, *Un Taciune Smuls Flacarilor*, Bucharest: Hasefer, 1996.

Scurtu, Ioan, *Istoria Partidului Naţional Taranesc*, Bucharest: Ed. Enciclopedica, 1994.

———, and Gheorghe Buzatu, *Istoria Românilor in Secolul XX*, Bucharest: Paideia, 1996.

Sebastian, Mihail, *Journal 1935–1944: the Fascist Years*, Chicago: Ivan R. Dee, 2000.

Seton-Watson, Hugh, *Eastern Europe, 1918–41*, Cambridge University Press, 1945.

Severin, Adrian, *Lacrimile Diminetii: Slabiciunile Guvernalui Roman*, Bucharest: Editura Scripta, 1995.

———, (in dialog cu Andreescu, Gabriel), *Locurile unde se construieste Europa*, Bucharest: Polirom, 2000.

Shafir, Michael, 'Political Culture, Intellectual Dissent and Intellectual Consent: the Case of Romania', *Orbis*, 1983.

Shafir, Michael, 'The Men of the Archangel Revisted: Anti-Semitic Formations Among Communist Romania's Intellectuals', *Studies in Comparative Communism*, vol. 41, no. 3, autumn 1983.

———, *Romania: Politics, Economics, Society*, London: Pinter, 1985.

———, 'The Provisional Council of National Unity: is History Repeating Itself?', *Report on Eastern Europe*, vol. 1, no. 9, 2 March 1990.

———, 'Romania's New Institutions: the Draft Constitution', *Report on Eastern Europe*, vol. 2, no. 37, 20 September 1991.

———, 'Romania: Constitution Approved in Referendum', *RFE-RL Research Report*, vol. 1, no. 2, 10 January 1992.

———, '"War of the Roses" in Romania's National Salvation Front', *RFE-RL Research Report*, vol. 1, no. 3, 24 January 1992.

————, 'Romania: Main Candidates in the Presidential Elections', *RFE-RL Research Report*, vol. 1, no. 35, 4 September 1992.

————, 'Peace or Truce in Romanian Government's Conflict with Miners', Radio Free Europe, *Newsline*, 26 January 1999.

Siani Davis, Peter, 'Political Legitimisation and the Romanian Revolution', paper presented at the University of London School of Slavonic and East European Studies conference on Romania, May 1994.

Socor, Vladimir, 'Forces of old Resurface in Romania: the Ethnic Clashes in Tirgu Mures', *Report on Eastern Europe*, vol. 1, no. 15, 13 April 1990.

————, 'The New President', *Report on Eastern Europe*, vol. 1, no. 23, 8 June 1990.

————, 'Foreign Policy in 1990', *Report on Eastern Europe*, vol. 1, no. 50, 28 December 1990.

Stavrianos, L.S., *The Balkans since 1453*, London: Hurst, 2000 (first published 1958).

Ştefanescu, Crisula, '"Free Romanian Television" Loses its Credibility', *Report on Eastern Europe*, vol. 1, no. 8, 23 March 1990.

Sternhell, Zeev, 'Fascist Ideology' in Walter Laqueur, *Fascism: a readers Guide*, Harmondsworth: Penguin, 1979.

Sternhell, Zeev, *Neither Right nor Left: Fascist Ideology in France*, Princeton University Press, 1986.

Ştefoi, Elena, 'Romania—organizing legislative impotence', *East European Constitutional Review*, vol. 4, no. 2, spring 1995.

————, *Drept Minoritar, Spaime Naţionale*, Bucharest: Editura Kriterion, 1997.

Sturdza, Michel, *The Silence of Europe*, Boston, MA: Watchtower Books, 1968.

Sturdza, Mihai, 'Worldwide Indignation at the Miners' Rampage in Bucharest', *Report on Eastern Europe*, vol. 1, no. 25, 6 July 1990.

————, 'The Politics of Ambiguity: Romania's Foreign Relations', *Report on Eastern Europe*, vol. 2, no. 13, 5 April 1991.

Suciu, Mircea, and Cristian Troncota, 'Doua "romane de iubire" din anii lui Gheorghiu-Dej', *Dosarele Istorie*, 7 (12), 1997.

Synovitz, Ron, 'OECD: Agricultural Review has Praise for Bulgaria, Misgivings about Romania', Radio Free Europe, *Features*, 16 January 2001.

Szajkowski, Bogdan, *New Political Parties of Eastern Europe and the Soviet Union*, London: Longman, 1991.

Ţarau, V., 'Campania electorala şi rezultatul real al alegorilor din 19 noiembrie 1946 in judetele Cluj, Somes si Turda' in Sorin Mitu and Florin Gogaltan (eds), *Studii de Istorie a transilvaniei*, Cluj: Asosociatia Istoricol din Transilvania şi Banat, 1994.

Tismâneanu, Vladimir, *Re-Inventing Politics: Eastern Europe from Stalin to Havel*, New York: The Free Press, 1992.

——, 'The Quasi-Revolution and its Discontents: Emerging Political Pluralism in Post-Ceauşeşcu Romania', *East European Politics and Societies*, vol. 7, no. 2, summer 1993.

Tomiuc, Eugen, 'Romania: New Property Law Falls Short of Full Restitution', Radio Free Europe, *Features*, 15 February 2001.

——, 'Romania: EU Report Assails Nation over Treatment of Orphans', Radio Free Europe, *Newsline*, 4 June 2001.

——, 'Romania: German Chancellor Says Nation Still Long Way from Joining EU', Radio Free Europe, *Newsline*, 5 July 2001.

——, 'Romanian Authorities Launch Probe into Controversial Book', End Note, Radio Free Europe, *South-East-Europe Newsline*, 28 August 2001.

——, 'Romania Lagging Behind Bulgaria in EU Accession Efforts', Radio Free Europe, *Newsline*, 20 December 2001.

Urban, Iris, 'Le Parti de la Grand Roumanie, doctrine et rapport au passé. *Le nationalisme dans la transition post-communiste*', *Cahiers d'études*, no. 1/2001, Bucharest: Institut roumain d'histoire récente.

Vălenaş, Liviu, *Eşecul unei Reforme, 1996–2000. Convorbire cu Şerban Orescu*, Iasi: Editura Ars Longa, 2000.

Vasile, Radu, *Cursă Pe Contrasens. Amintirile unui prime-ministru*, Bucharest: Humanitas, 2002.

Verdery, Katherine, *National Ideology under Socialism: Identity and Cultural Politics in Ceauşeşcu's Romania*, Berkeley: University of California Press, 1991.

Voicu, George, *Zeii Cei Rai. Cultura conspiratie in Romania postcomunista*, Bucharest: Polirom, 2000.

Waldeck, R.G., *Athene Palace Bucharest: Hitler's "New Order" Comes to Rumania*, London: Constable, 1943.

Watson, George, *The Lost Literature of Socialism*, Cambridge: Lutterworth Press, 1998.

Watts, Larry L., 'The Romanian Army in the December Revolution and Beyond', in Daniel Nelson (ed.), *Romania after Tyranny*, Boulder, CO: Westview Press, 1992.

Watts, Larry L., 'The Crisis in Romanian Civil-Military Relations', *Problems of Post-Communism*, vol. 48, no. 4, July–August 2001.

Weber, Eugen, 'Romania' in H. Rogger and E. Weber, *The European Right: a Historical Profile*, Berkeley: University of California Press, 1974.

Weber Eugen, 'The Men of the Archangel' in George Mosse (ed.), *International Fascism*, London: Sage, 1979.

Wolff, Robert Lee, *The Balkans in our Time*, Cambridge, MA: Harvard University Press, 1974 edn.

Zidaru-Barbulescu, Aurel, 'Romania Seeks Admission to the Council of Europe', RFE-RL Research Report, vol. 2, no. 2, 8 January 1993.

INDEX

430 *Index*

287, 290, television skills 254–5, 260, 290–1, 305–6, urges vote for CDR 392 n. 102, vocal on corruption 174, 253, 260–1, vulnerability 299–300, 306, wealth of 278, whitewashes Securitate 285
  Cf inter-war fascists 269–71
Van Velzen, Wim 169
Vasile, Radu: cabinet atmosphere 228, complains about IMF 223, Constantinescu and 171, 222, family jobs 183, 384 n. 75, fears unions 181–2, flexible outlook 170–1, 222, governing style 224–5, 228, Iliescu and 170, miners rebellion and 201, 204–5, ousted 226–7, 238, 264, 384 n. 76, populist instincts 180–1, 222, secret police and 191–2, stark warning (1999) 204–5, West and 180–1
Vasilescu, Valentin 277, 307
Vatra Românească 78, 83, 84–5, 91, 94–5, 221

Vejvoda, Ivan 346
Verba, Sydney 346
Verheugen, Günther 228–9, 238
Verestoy, Attila 327
Vilau, Adrian 190, 195
Vintu, Sorin Ovidiu 235
Voican Voiculescu, Gelu 87
Voiculescu, Dan 116
Voinea, Dan 190
Vyshinsky, Andrei 46, 185

Wallachia 18–21, 26–7
Wells, H.G., 272
World Bank 11, 184, 194–5, 200, 228, 231–2, 277, 334
Wurmbrand, Richard 48–9

Yugoslavia 55, 122, 213–9, 221

Zeno, Andrei 280
Zhirinovsky, Vladimir 277, 293